UNFINISHED
TRANSITIONS

UNFINISHED
TRANSITIONS

WOMEN AND THE GENDERED DEVELOPMENT
OF DEMOCRACY IN VENEZUELA, 1936–1996

ELISABETH J. FRIEDMAN

The Pennsylvania State University Press
University Park, Pennsylvania

Library of Congress Cataloging-in-Publication Data

Friedman, Elisabeth J., 1966–
    Unfinished transitions : women and the
    gendered development of democracy in Venezuela,
    1936–1996 / Elisabeth J. Friedman.
            p.   cm.
    Includes bibliographical references and index.
    ISBN 0-271-02023-7 (cloth : alk. paper)—
    ISBN 0-271-02024-5 (pbk. : alk. paper)
        1. Women in politics—Venezuela—History—
    20th century. 2. Feminism—Venezuela—
    History—20th century. I. Title.
    HQ1235.5 V4. F74 2000
    305.42'0987—dc21   99-047238

It is the policy of The Pennsylvania State University
Press to use acid-free paper for the first printing of
all clothbound books. Publications on uncoated
stock satisfy the minimum requirements of American
National Standard for Information Sciences—
Permanence of Paper for Printed Library Materials,
ANSI Z39.48–1992.

To the memory of my mothers,
Adele Friedman (*Maman*) and
Maxine Auerbach (*Madrina*),
and of a mother of the movement,
Argelia Laya.

CONTENTS

TABLES AND FIGURES

Tables

Figures

PREFACE AND ACKNOWLEDGMENTS

"Why women, and why Venezuela?" So have begun by now innumerable casual or not-so-casual conversations about my work. The intellectual rationale will be made clear in the Introduction, but here I want to tell the story, just briefly, of how I became drawn into this project.

The seeds were planted in my second year as a graduate student at Stanford University. Having decided to write a research paper on a relatively understudied Latin American country, I decided to see if I could link it in any way to my major thematic interest, women's organizing in the process of democratization. However, most of the work I came across either treated Venezuelan politics with little or no mention of the role of women or women's movements, or it addressed women's organizing primarily in the context of democratization in the Southern Cone or Central America. Then one afternoon I came across a description of the 1982 reform of the Venezuelan Civil Code (formerly one of the three most discriminatory such codes in Latin America), which seemed to indicate a large role for women's rights advocates. I seized upon the case as the subject of my research paper and wound up spending the summer of 1992 in Caracas trying to corroborate the story I came up with in the United States.

As it turned out, interviews and archival research proved that I had it over half wrong. But I was far from dismayed, for in the process of getting the story right, I started to hear more and more tantalizing pieces of a history of women's organizing that extended much before, and substantially after, the Civil Code reform. Moreover, because it took place within one of the few democratic success stories in the region, it seemed to be a history that could give valuable perspectives on the findings emerging throughout Latin America—if not elsewhere in the post–Cold War world—that women were facing particular barriers in their attempts to participate in the new democracies and were developing particular strategies for their inclusion. But it was a history that had yet to be told.

That history was revealed to me during fieldwork primarily undertaken during the summer of 1992 and in 1994–95. Because the history of Venezuelan women's organizing is nearly absent from published scholarship, the research was highly dependent on firsthand accounts from interviews. I held sixty-four interviews as well as numerous informal conversations with key activists, analysts, and politicians. I also consulted interview transcripts published by Fania Petzoldt and Jacinta Bevilaqua (1979) and gathered in several unpublished works. These interviews, obtained anywhere from one to sixty years after the incidents occurred, necessarily contain contemporary reflections on past events. Beyond oral testimony, I made extensive use of the archives of the Venezuelan Central University's Women's Studies Center (UCV-CEM) and the Coordinadora de Organizaciones No-Gubernamentales de Mujeres (Coordinating Committee of Women's Nongovernmental Organizations, or CONG), and the private collections of Professors Ofelia Alvarez and Gioconda Espina. I also reviewed the archives of the newspapers *Ahora, El Nacional,* and *El Universal;* the biweekly newsletter *Veneconomy;* and the *Diario de Debates* (Congressional Record). The Central Office for Statistics, the National Library, and the National Newspaper Library provided additional sources of information.

More recent material was obtained through participant observation of contemporary organizing efforts among nongovernmental groups, including CONG, the national conference of the Popular Women's Circles (CFP, Círculos Femeninos Populares, the national organization for low-income women), and various women's groups within and outside of Caracas. I also attended meetings at the National Women's Council (CONAMU, Consejo Nacional de la Mujer, the national women's agency) and the Bicameral (Congressional) Commission on Women's Rights (Comisión Bicameral de Derechos de la Mujer) and studied the operation of state women's offices, municipal women's centers, and the women's bureaus of various political parties.

Despite the formal existence of women's organizations, it is quite difficult to do research on them at both the party and state level. The marginal position of women's bureaus within party life has resulted in a lack of written histories, bylaws, or statistics on membership. The national women's agency also has somewhat haphazard records, at least in part because it has been repeatedly reconstructed at the whim of each new administration.

Because both nongovernmental and governmental preparations for the UN's Fourth World Conference on Women (FWCW) were ongoing during 1994–95, I was able to observe both processes, as well as their results, at both the Latin American and Caribbean NGO (Nongovernmental organizations) Forum in Mar de Plata, Argentina (September 1994) and the NGO Forum and the official conference in Beijing (September 1995). A short return trip in 1997 allowed me to observe changes since the FWCW.

This book would not have been possible without the considerable intellectual, infrastructural, and emotional support of mentors, Venezuelan activists and scholars, institutions, colleagues, friends, and family. For their many contributions to this work, I am deeply grateful. Any errors or omissions that remain are, of course, my own.

I completed the dissertation on which this book is based under the guidance of a superb committee. Terry Karl, my principal advisor, originally suggested that I look at the Venezuelan case. Through years of cogent criticism, practical advice, and always unstinting encouragement, she helped to transform my initial ideas into a completed thesis. Her dedication to mentoring and to academic excellence knows no bounds. Susan Okin's work and teaching served as a fine example of how to focus lucid and committed scholarship on the questions of what, and who, defines politics. In many ways she helped me to find my own answers. Sonia Alvarez wrote the book that most inspired my own research, and she continues to blaze trails where I want to walk. Quite above and beyond any call of duty, she gave advice that only someone as deeply involved with the subject matter as she is could offer. Philippe Schmitter's constant challenge of "What's gender got to do with it?" kept me responsive to a broad set of issues—as did his vast knowledge of democratization theory and practice.

In the field, many *Venezolanas y Venezolanos chéveres* generously shared their histories, analyses, and *chisme* with me in formal interviews and informal conversations. The members of the Coordinating Committee of Women's NGOs (CONG) welcomed me as a participant, not merely an observer, and tolerated my many questions, as did the staff and advisors of the National Council on Women and the Bicameral Commission on Women's Rights. On beaches, in buses, and at *areperas,* Gioconda Espina, Magally Huggins Castañeda, and Argelia Laya patiently tutored me in the distinct modes of Venezuelan feminism. Other conversations with activists, analysts, and politicians about democracy and gender *a la criolla* illuminated many issues, or at least brought the puzzles into sharp relief. For sharing their insights, I would particularly like to thank Fernando Aranguren, Laly Armengol, Nora Castañeda, Adecia Castillo, Marco Cupolo, Vicki Ferrara, Benita Finol, Miriam Kornblith, Carlota Pérez, Marelys Pérez Marcano, Luis Salamanca, Isolda Salvatierra, and Morella Sanabria.

Many institutions provided me with crucial resources. My fieldwork was supported by a Fulbright Fellowship as well as by grants administered through the Stanford Center for Latin American Studies—from the Fundación Ayacucho and the Knowles Fund—and from the Stanford Institute for International Studies and Center for Conflict and Negotiation. The Shaler Adams Foundation, and especially its director, Margaret Schink, made possible my attendance at regional and international meetings on women's rights. At various stages of writing, I was supported by a Woodrow Wilson Dissertation Grant in Women's Studies; by a Stanford University Fellowship, lectureships, and a research assistantship; by a Dissertation Fellowship from the Stanford Institute for Research on Women and Gender; and by my home departments at both Western Michigan University and Barnard College.

In Venezuela the faculty and staff of the Women's Studies Center of the Central University gave me an institutional home away from home in 1994–95; the Institute of Higher Studies of Administration (IESA) also provided a space in the summer of 1992. Ofelia Alvarez, Fernando Aranguren, and Gioconda Espina graciously allowed me to plunder their personal collections; Toby Bottome at *Veneconomy* and Jesús Hurtado at *El Nacional* guided me through their archives. Miriam Kornblith offered me a comfortable place from which to test the waters of fieldwork in the summer of 1992; the Trinkunas family and Gail Kenna provided oases of calm within Caracas and pleasant distractions outside of it during my more lengthy immersion in 1994–95.

At various points in the domestic development of this book, several people made strategic interventions. The book would not have come into being but for the enthusiastic shepherding of Sandy Thatcher at the Pennsylvania State University Press. Reviewing for Penn State Press, Jane S. Jaquette offered detailed and constructive criticism and suggestions on the manuscript; Jennifer McCoy also provided useful commentary. I owe special thanks to Brooke Ackerly and Karen Booth for reading and extensively critiquing earlier drafts. Kathryn Hochstetler, Cathy Rakowski, members of the MacArthur Consortium's Gender Network, and colleagues at Western Michigan University offered key insights into various aspects of the subjects at hand.

They say no man is an island, and this woman is quite contiguous. Over the course of the research and writing of this book, my family and friends formed an *imprescindible* support network. It was woven together by walks, endless talks, wonderful meals, mail, email, and phone calls, through all of which they reminded me that there was more to life than this project—while assuring me that it was the appropriate focus of my entire being. For their loyalty, encouragement, and open ears and arms, I especially want to thank Brooke Ackerly, Erika Bliss, Karen Booth, Katrina Burgess, Ann Marie Clark, Sushi Datta-Sandhu, Edith Friedman, Julian Bryn Hawiger Friedman, Max Friedman, Amy Gordon, Marcel Hawiger, Kathryn Hochstetler, Kathryn Johnson, Temma Kaplan, Terry Karl, Leah Karliner, Jennifer Kern, Derek Scissors, Elena Servi, Karen Brown Thompson, Antje Wiener, and Simone Wojtowicz. In particular, my father, Martin Friedman, was incomparably generous. Throughout the entire process, he helped me to keep my perspective and my balance, no matter the distance or the expense. He also had the foresight to become a professor emeritus just in time to meticulously edit a final draft of the manuscript.

Lastly, Adele Friedman, Maxine Auerbach, and Argelia Laya taught me much of what I know and gave me the desire to find out yet more about women, gender, and transitions—from the first to the last. The following work, and my ability to undertake it, is in great part due to their devotion and inspiration.

ACRONYMS

ACF (Agrupación Cultural Femenina): Women's Cultural Association

ACPS (Academia de Ciencias Políticas y Sociales): Academy of Political and Social Sciences

AD (Acción Democrática): Democratic Action—the Social Democratic Party

AMNLAE (Asociación de Mujeres Nicaragüenses Luisa Amanda Espinosa): Luisa Amanda Espinosa Nicaraguan Women's Association

AVESA (Asociación Venezolana de Educación Sexual Alternativa): Venezuelan Association for Alternative Sexual Education

AV (Asociaciones de Vecinos): Neighborhood Associations

AVM (Asociación Venezolana de Mujeres): Venezuelan Association of Women

CEDAW Convention for the Elimination of All Forms of Discrimination Against Women

CEN (Comité Ejecutivo Nacional): National Executive Committee

CESAP (Centro al Servicio de Acción Popular): Popular Action Service Center

CFP (Círculos Femeninos Populares): Popular Women's Circles

CIDA Canadian International Development Agency

CISFEM (Centro de Investigación Social, Formación y Estudios de la Mujer): Center for Social Research, Training, and Women's Studies

COFEAPRE (Comisión Femenina Asesora de la Presidencia): Presidential Women's Advisory Commission

CONAMU (Consejo Nacional de la Mujer): National Women's Council

CONG (Coordinadora de Organizaciones No-Gubernamentales de Mujeres): Coordinating Committee of Women's Nongovernmental Organizations

COPEI (Comité Independiente Electoral): Independent Electoral Committee—the Christian Democratic Party

CNMD (Concertación Nacional de Mujeres por la Democracia): National Coalition of Women for Democracy—Chile

CTV (Confederación de Trabajadores de Venezuela): Venezuelan Confederation of Workers

EV (Escuela de Vecinos): Neighbors' School

FACUR (Federación de Asocíaciones de Comunidades Urbanas): Federation of Urban Community Associations

FEDECAMARAS (Federación Venezolana de Cameras y Asociaciones de Comercio y Producción): Venezuelan Federation of Chambers of Commerce and Production

FEV (Federación de Estudiantes de Venezuela): Student Federation of Venezuela

FEVA (Federación Venezolana de Abogadas): Venezuelan Federation of Female Lawyers

FMLN (Frente Farabundo Martí Para la Liberación Nacional): Farabundo Martí National Liberation Front— El Salvador

FSLN (Frente Sandinista de Liberación Nacional): Sandinista National Liberation Front—Nicaragua

FVM (Federación Venezolana de Maestros): Venezuelan Teachers' Federation

HCD (Hogares de Cuidado Diario): Daily Care Homes

IACW Inter-American Commission of Women

INAMU (Instituto Nacional de la Mujer): National Women's Institute

IWY International Women's Year

JUVECABE (Comité "Juntas por Venezuela Camino a Beijing"): "United for Venezuela en Route to Beijing" Committee

MAS (Movimiento Al Socialismo): Movement Toward Socialism—the Socialist Party

MEMCH (Movimiento pro Emancipación de Mujeres de Chile): Movement for the Emancipation of Chilean Women

MEP (Movimiento Electoral del Pueblo): People's Electoral Movement

MIR (Movimiento de Izquierda Revolucionaria): Movement of the Revolutionary Left

NGO Nongovernmental organization

ONM (Oficina Nacional de la Mujer): National Women's Office

OPAM (Oficina Parlamentaria de Asuntos de la Mujer): Parliamentary Office on Women's Issues

ORVE (Organización Venezolana): Venezuelan Organization—the forerunner of AD

PCV (Partido Comunista de Venezuela): Venezuelan Communist Party

PDN (Partido Democrático Nacional): National Democratic Party

PRP (Partido Republicano Progresista): Republican Progressive Party

SERNAM (Servicio Nacional de la Mujer): National Women's Service— Chile

SN (Seguridad Nacional): National Security Force

UMA (Unión de Mujeres Americanas): Union of American Women

UNE (Unión Nacional de Estudiantes): National Student Union

UNICEF United Nations Children's Fund

UNESCO United Nations Educational, Scientific and Cultural Organization

UNIFEM United Nations Development Fund for Women

URD (Unión Republicana Democrática): Democratic Republican Union

USAID United States Agency for International Development

INTRODUCTION

One evening in early 1995, I participated in an off-season election in Caracas. The national Coordinating Committee of Women's Nongovernmental Organizations (Coordinadora de Organizaciones No-Gubernamentales de Mujeres, or CONG) was holding its biannual elections for the *trio*, the three people who would act as its governing council for the next six months. Worlds away from the heated pageantry and fierce competition of typical Venezuelan races, this one took place in a modest middle-class apartment, around the central table in the living room. Altogether we were thirteen: twelve women and one man. After we had sipped our strong, sweet *cafecitos* out of small plastic cups and eaten a few *galletas,* it was time for the main event.

The outgoing *trio,* whose members included a Socialist party activist, a leader of a black women's group, and a civil servant, asked for names of candidates. The assembled group offered six. Then one by one, each of us had a chance to express our preferences for the new council members. Discussion ran throughout the process. As we offered our choices, we tried to figure out what the fairest results would be, both in terms of representing the CONG member groups and making sure those who were most interested came out on top.

At the end of the "voting," it was clear who had won: the coordinator of a young women's organization; a long-time women's rights activist and union representative; and the only man present, the CONG's unofficial historian. The winners gave short acceptance speeches, and congratulations were extended all around. Two members of the new *trio* had been nominated but passed over in the previous elections, so we were all pleased that they could now take part.

By the time I saw the CONG's elections take place, I was well aware of what they represented: the ongoing struggle of Venezuelan women's organizations to democratize political practice in general and to represent women's interests in particular. Although varying in intensity and extent, such efforts have, over the past sixty-odd years, provided one of the few significant, if largely unchronicled, alternatives to "politics as usual" in Venezuela. Moreover, they also present an excellent comparative case for furthering the study of women's experience of democratization in Latin America and provide insight into crucial questions about the nature of democratic representation.

Venezuelan Democratization in Context

Venezuela occupies a unique position in the trajectory of modern Latin American democratizations. Because its democratization process began in 1958, it does not form part of the so-called third wave of global democratization that dates from 1974 with the end of Portugal's dictatorship. As such, Venezuela's experience with transition politics offers a useful perspective on possible future developments in the more recent transitions in the region, primarily in the Southern Cone and Central America.[1] Of particular interest is how Venezuela has confronted the issues involved in consolidating, as opposed to installing, democracy—even as there is concern that, with the 1999 constitutional changes under president and former coup leader Hugo Chávez Frías, its hard-won consolidation, first challenged by the political impacts of economic crisis in the last decade, may be further eroding.

In the 1960s and 1970s, "bureaucratic authoritarian" regimes came to power through military coups in several countries in the Southern Cone. These regimes were ruled by the military in conjunction with a technocratic elite in an effort to stabilize economies and promote stagnating industrial development. Political repression, from the outlawing of parties to the torture and disappearance of suspected regime opponents, was directed at the poor and working classes, as well as at students, intellectuals, political activists, and other supporters of human rights and freedom of expression. The degree of repression varied by regime, with the greatest number of killed and disappeared reported in Argentina (30,000).

In Central America, the 1960s found labor-repressive states dominated by entrenched oligarchies of traditional agrarian elite families backed by the military. After parties representing the middle and working classes failed in their attempts to promote political and agrarian reform, guerrilla-based

---

1. For comparative work on Latin American democratization, see O'Donnell and Schmitter 1986; Diamond, Linz, and Lipset 1989; R. Munck 1989; Higley and Gunther 1992; Mainwaring, O'Donnell, and Valenzuela 1992; Domínguez and Lowenthal 1996.

armies rose up against the state in Nicaragua, El Salvador, and Guatemala. In Nicaragua the Sandinista National Liberation Front (FSLN) waged a successful revolution in 1979; in El Salvador and Guatemala civil wars during the 1980s and early 90s claimed 75,000 and 200,000 lives, with government forces held responsible for the vast majority of those killed and disappeared.

Although transitions to democracy in these Latin American subregions during the 1980s and 1990s were accomplished in various ways, one strategy moved to the fore: the use of a negotiated settlement, or "pact." Such settlements usually included the dominant political actors involved in the former regime as well as those positioned to take power in the new one, and they established political and economic frameworks within which all those included could agree to participate. In assessing the process and evolution of negotiated transitions, the early example of Venezuela's "pacted democracy" becomes quite salient.[2]

Venezuela has undergone two transitions to democracy in the twentieth century. The first attempt at democratization came in 1945 with a military coup against the liberalized authoritarian regime that had been established after the death of the former dictator General Juan Vincente Gómez, who had ruled from 1908 to 1935. However, the following three-year experiment with democracy led by the Social Democratic Party, Democratic Action (AD), did not succeed because the party's policies alienated elites, the church hierarchy, the political opposition, and finally the military itself. In 1948 the military took over again, and under the rule of Major Marcos Pérez Jiménez, they eventually repressed most political activity, including the banning of both AD and the Communist party (PCV).

The Pérez Jiménez dictatorship differed in significant ways from the later authoritarian regimes in the region. Although he too sought to reorient the economy and repress labor organizing, Pérez Jiménez relied less on technocratic advisors, and he eventually transformed his rule into a personalistic dictatorship supported by a national security police force rather than the "institutionalized military rule" characteristic of bureaucratic authoritarianism. His regime was responsible for the imprisonment, torture, and assassination of opposition members, but with victims numbering in the low thousands as opposed to the tens of thousands of later regimes.

The opposition also differed from those in other countries: it was heavily based in partisan organizations, in contrast to the combination of social movements and broad civilian alliances in the Southern Cone; and it never re-

---

2. For more on Venezuela's transition to democracy, see Karl 1987; Levine 1989; López Maya, Gómez Calcaño, and Maingón 1989.

lied on force as did the guerrilla movements in Central America. Between 1948 and 1952, the Venezuelan opposition was coordinated by the PCV and AD organized in clandestine "cell" structures within the country in consultation with exiled leaders. After a period of severe repression, in 1957 a unified and mass opposition emerged under the coordination of a council whose leaders represented all the opposition parties—AD, PCV, the Christian Democratic party COPEI, and the small Democratic Republican Union (URD).

Pérez Jiménez fled the country in January 1958 in the face of a united opposition, including the military forces who had been alienated by his personalist rule. Having learned their lesson from the unsuccessful democratization of the mid-1940s, elites guiding the second and successful transition to democracy in Venezuela made use of a "pacted" negotiation process. The three noncommunist parties signed a series of accords that mollified the sectors most threatened by the new regime (military, church, and business) and rewarded potential party supporters (labor, peasantry, and the middle classes). The accords were premised on channeling resources primarily generated from petroleum revenues through the parties and the dominant executive branch. The noncommunist parties agreed to immediate power-sharing measures, which were further formalized in the 1961 constitution.

These agreements formed the foundation of one of the longest lasting contemporary democracies in the region, and Venezuela has often been held up as a model of successful democratization. However, from its inception, it was an exclusionary regime. Not only the communists but also other interests that were not included in the original pact found it quite difficult to gain a foothold in democratic politics. Highly centralized and hierarchical political parties gained center stage and became the principal channel for class-based representation to a strongly centralized state. Groups that did not fit into the representational scheme were marginalized and further weakened by partisan allegiances.

Venezuelan women's organizing began long before the 1958 transition to political democracy. Starting with the predominantly elite civil rights and suffrage campaigns of the 1930s and 40s, Venezuelan women (and some men) sought to challenge the status quo by experimenting with nontraditional structures and processes such as decentralized organizations, petition campaigns, and coalitions. Suffrage was granted in 1947, and such experimentation continued within the clandestine opposition to the dictatorship of the 1950s. But in what has become a disturbingly familiar story across Latin America, with the transition to democracy women found themselves, along with other opposition participants, largely excluded from effective participation. It was only after a significant experience with political demobilization in the 1960s that women began to reorganize and find new strategies for advancing their interests.

Latin American Women in Transition

Charting the more than sixty-year history of women's organizing in Venezuela helps to explain some of the "unfinished business" of Latin American democratization as a whole: why women have had difficulty participating in the very regimes they fought to restore, and how they continue to seek inclusion.

During the past two decades, Latin American women have played an important role in the opposition to repressive authoritarian regimes throughout the region. But hopes that women's organizing would continue to thrive when regimes changed have been dashed. Paradoxically, women's organizational strength and influence, expanded under authoritarianism, declined once democratic institutions were reestablished. Even now, as democracy becomes consolidated in the region, women's gains in economic, social, and political advancement remain very uneven.

Region-wide evidence attests to the depth and persistence of discrimination against women in Latin American democracies. Currently comprising 30 percent of the labor force, women are primarily located in the lower-paying service sector and earn only 26 percent of all income. As a result, female-headed households, now 22 percent of all urban households, are likely to be poor. Rural illiteracy, sex-stereotyped textbooks, and sex-stratified subject areas impede women's access to education. Women's exercise of their reproductive rights is limited by the unavailability of family planning. Abortion, illegal in most countries, is a leading cause of maternal mortality. Penal codes are still aimed at preserving family honor through women's sexual fidelity, an intent that results in discrimination against women in cases of adultery and rape. Domestic workers, a quarter of all women in the labor force, have few workplace rights. Women constitute less than 25 percent of party and union leadership, only 15 percent of the region's parliaments, and 11 percent of government ministers (Valdéz and Gomáriz 1995; UNDP 1996;[3] IPU 1998).

3. UNDP statistics on women's participation in national government and percentage of earned income also include the Caribbean region.

What accounts for the unfinished business of democratic transitions—that is, for the marginalization of women in democratizing societies? This book focuses on the problems women have encountered in achieving effective political incorporation, a foundation for other efforts at their advancement, arguing that women's incomplete incorporation is due in part to the dynamics of social mobilization during the democratization process itself. As is true for social movements in general, the visible mobilization of women rose as authoritarian regimes began to falter, peaked when the regimes fell, and declined as democratic institutions took hold (O'Donnell and Schmitter 1986; Jaquette 1994a).

But general theories of social movements are insufficient to account for the problems of women's participation because they do not take into account how political action and political institutions are influenced by the gender relations of power. Thus this book uses a modified version of the "political opportunity structure" approach to social movement analysis, which focuses on how the macropolitical environment (or the ensemble of political institutions, actors, and discourses) conditions the emergence and strategies of movements (Tarrow 1991b). It is modified by a focus on how the opportunities of each phase of democratic transition are *gendered*, that is, how they reflect the social meanings attributed to sexual difference and, despite women's roles during the transition, reinforce gender bias within the political institutions of democracy.

In response to their continued marginalization, women have challenged these gendered constructions in order to advance their interests and assert their leadership. But this challenge has been neither universal nor uniform. Because women share a sex but differ in other significant ways—both social and ideological—they have not always acted in concert. Women's organizing reflects their varied experience of gendered opportunities as well as their diverse interests. Such differences have often led to difficulties in promoting a shared agenda among women.

Venezuelan women's experience cannot be mapped directly onto the experiences of women throughout the region, but certain parallels are visible. As in other Latin American countries, the early women's movement in Venezuela was made up of predominantly middle-class women focused on "social motherhood"; a demand for rights from the civil to the economic sphere that upheld women's unique role in society.[4] However, the second, more lasting transition to democracy in Venezuela and its impact on women's organizing differed from those in other countries. The Pérez Jiménez dictatorship was less repressive than the authoritarian regimes in the Southern

4. See Miller 1991, chap. 4.

Cone or in Central America. Opposition organizing was carried out principally through clandestine parties rather than by sporadically united elites or by grassroots organizations often supported by the Catholic Church or by armed guerrilla movements. As a result of these factors, Venezuelan women were not as highly mobilized as those who organized in other countries, although they formed an integral part of both the early clandestine, and later mass, opposition actions.

During the 1958 transition, Venezuelan women confronted a much more entrenched set of gender-biased institutions than that faced by women in countries with less organized party systems and less centralized states. The structurally biased, centrally organized political parties that proved key to the development of democracy also proved to be a major obstacle to the promotion of women's leadership and the representation of their interests. The combination of a smaller initial mobilization against dictatorship and the dominance of gender-biased institutions in the transition resulted in a profound weakening of the women's movement during democratization.

That crucial time for Venezuelan women's rights activists also occurred too early to benefit from the international "second wave" of women's movements, the growing regional networks of feminist activists, or the organizing around the UN world conferences, events that were to have an important impact on women's movements in the Southern Cone and Central America. However, when these developments did emerge, from the mid-1970s to the 1990s, they inspired a new phase in Venezuelan women's organizing.

Building on the lessons of the past, activists "regendered" political institutions—that is, changed the ways in which such institutions reflected gender relations—and developed new organizational strategies that resulted in several successful campaigns to change Venezuelan law and popular perceptions of gender roles. Similar efforts at constructing women-friendly institutions were occurring throughout the region, particularly the establishment of women's offices and ministries at the national level. As the Venezuelan movement evolved, however, it was less mass-based and more focused on legal reform than the movements in countries such as Brazil and El Salvador. Crucially, the institutional church had much less of an impact on Venezuelan women's organizing than it had in those Latin American countries where it often had provided protection and support for human rights groups and other groups that coalesced in opposition to dictatorship.

Nonetheless, the Venezuelan women's movement continued to reflect broader regional dynamics. As in the rest of the region, parties on the left were fairly unreliable allies. The gender bias against women reflected in mainstream political institutions (both state- and party-based) conditioned

[handwritten margin note:] because women couldn't unite + they could without including their interest, it could have been any unified group

women's participation and forced them to seek alternative forms of representation. Their efforts, both historically and in the more contemporary period, were complicated by struggles over structural (or "social") differences, particularly that of class, and by debates over feminist ideology and political autonomy.

The Venezuelan Case

Venezuela is a particularly appropriate country in which to study women and democratization. Its two transitions to democracy and corresponding waves of women's mobilization allow for a broad range of comparisons. Political opportunity structure analysis can be used to compare the effects of regime phase—authoritarian, transition, or consolidation—on women's organizing within and across the two democratization periods.[5]

Venezuela also serves as a "crucial" case for the region (Eckstein 1975). Its experiences bring into question two dominant hypotheses concerning successful democratization and women's movement organizing. The active participation of its highly institutionalized, societally penetrative parties in the lasting transition process at first seems to uphold the general argument that strong parties are the most effective mechanism for consolidating democracies (Agüero, Gillespie, and Scully 1986; Diamond, Linz, and Lipset 1989; Pridham 1991; Diamond 1994; Mainwaring and Scully 1995), an argument that has also been extended to the promotion of women's interests (Schmitter 1998).

Traditional analyses of Venezuelan democracy have focused on the accomplishments of the Venezuelan party system as well as its effective state structure (Martz 1966; Levine 1973, 1978, 1989; Martz and Myers 1986; McDonald and Ruhl 1989). But the traumatic events of the last decade show that this forty-two-year-old democracy, formerly considered a model of political development for Latin American countries, has serious structural flaws.[6] More recent or innovative work shows how political parties and the domi-

5. Given the importance of understanding the specific ways in which a particular sequence of political opportunities is gendered in order to assess its impact on women's mobilization under democratization, this book uses a diachronic comparison of Venezuelan political regimes (Lijphart 1971). Because the explanatory variable is regime phase (as specified by political opportunity structure), a comparison of successive phases of political development in a country that has undergone a full democratization process allows for a focus on this variable while keeping other elements relatively constant. This endeavor would be considerably more difficult using cross-country comparisons because of the variations in a host of relevant factors.

6. Since 1989 Venezuela has undergone a series of political, social, and economic crises,

nant executive branch have contributed to the current crises (Karl 1987; Brewer-Carías 1988; López Maya, Gómez Calcaño, and Maingón 1989; García 1992; Ellner 1993–94; Coppedge 1994; Kornblith and Levine 1995; Goodman et al. 1995; McCoy et al. 1995). These studies point in particular to the political parties' longstanding political manipulation of independent, civil society–based organizing and to the nondemocratic character of the channels of access to the state. Women's experiences vividly illustrate the operation of these mechanisms.

A second theory that is challenged by the Venezuelan case is that women's movements are most likely to arise as the result of secular changes in sociodemographic trends affecting women, such as declining fertility rates, higher educational levels, and rising labor force participation (Klein 1984; Miller 1991). The relative stagnation in Venezuelan women's organizing on their own behalf from 1960 to 1980—a period in which their fertility rates dropped from 6.5 to 3.9 children per woman, their enrollment in higher education rose from 31 to near 50 percent of all students, and their labor force participation increased from 18 to 28 percent of all workers (Huggins Castañeda and Dominguez Nelson 1993)—points to the need for a different approach. This book draws on innovative ways in which analysts of women's movements in developed democracies have used the political opportunity approach to explain how women's movements develop and strategize in order to better understand women's movements in a democratizing country (Katzenstein and Mueller 1987; Costain 1992).

Finally, an analysis centered on women reveals the hitherto hidden history of their political participation, supplying a missing piece of the scholarship on Venezuelan democracy. Those analysts who have considered the role of women in Venezuelan politics have focused on their lack of leadership positions. Not that much seems to have been added between John Martz's 1966 observation about the largest and historically most powerful Venezuelan party, that "the fact remains that only a few women have been influential as party leaders" (202) and Michael Coppedge's 1994 statement that "the leadership of AD was overwhelmingly male" (13).[7] A few studies exist that include or focus on women's civil society-based organizing (García Guadilla

---

including a major urban riot resulting in over three hundred deaths, two coup attempts, the impeachment of a president for corruption, the partial collapse of the banking system, continual public protests, and the election of a former coup leader as president.

7. Unusually, Martz does briefly discuss women's role in politics, primarily in the development of AD. However, his focus on the role of AD in Venezuelan politics obscures the female activism that took place through the Communist party, which was considerable during the struggle against the dictatorship of General Pérez Jiménez (1952–58). This is described in some detail in Chapter 3.

1993; Espina 1994; Salamanca 1995). But none of these works show how women's lack of leadership positions or their efforts in organizing depend on the way in which women as a specific sector fit into the general dynamics of Venezuelan politics.

This study shows that Venezuelan democracy is gendered. Institutions of interest representation, such as political parties and state structures, have developed over the course of the country's two democratic transitions to allow for the incorporation of certain sectors, such as labor and peasants, on the basis of their class interests. But these same institutions have marginalized women, who do not form as coherent an interest group and who have not always been welcomed as a potential source of support by political elites. This book also reveals, however, that their very marginalization has led women to develop unique strategies for political organization and collective action, despite ongoing debates among women about how to define their interests and goals.

Democratization Concerns

Examination of the construction and development of discriminatory institutions and discourses, while important in itself, has the added advantage of shedding light on longstanding inegalitarian practices in established democracies. As far as their female citizens are concerned, these polities are still undergoing democratization. As Wendy Sarvasy and Birte Siim argue, "[Women] have never had a democratic practice because [they] have never achieved anything close to equal power in the family, civil society, or the state. From a feminist perspective then, even the nations recognized as democratic are in transition" (1994, 294). Looking at the experience of women as a marginalized group also reveals much about the workings of political power and how it may be used by the less powerful. Chapter 7 briefly examines the Venezuelan neighborhood movement as an illustration of how a different nontraditional political actor operated within a similar system but without gender-based constraints.

In offering an analysis of women's experience, this study speaks to the broad concerns of scholars and practitioners of democratization. As the current wave of democratic transitions crests in Latin America and elsewhere, citizens stand in the shallows wondering where the tide will pull them. It seems unlikely that democratizing countries will revert to authoritarian rule, and many institutions in the region that seemed fragile in the last decade now seem stable. Instead, the consolidation process raises new issues about the quality of the democracy that is being practiced in these new regimes. Analysts are currently asking whether executives and legislatures can be balanced to avoid emerging patterns of rule by presidential decree, whether independent judiciaries can be developed to make possible the rule of law, and whether the press can become more independent in order to support a truly democratic public sphere. Most urgently, what mechanisms—formal or informal—will allow all citizens to pursue full citizenship and adequate representation of their interests?

Many have seen a strong party system as the answer. But this book argues that party dominance during transitions can short-circuit the development of other forms of representation in civil society and the state. Highly centralized parties, while effective at channeling participation and making policy, determine which actors can gain access to decision-making power. Parties that exercise a monopoly over representation through sector-based organizing, as has been often the case in Latin America where corporatist forms of interest representation persist, are likely to ignore or sideline those groups that do not have readily defined class-based interests or who are not in the core coalition. This exclusion can be exacerbated when state-based forms of representation, such as executive advisory committees, are also constructed to represent the same sectors.

The impact of the gendered political opportunities of transition politics on women's organizing is addressed in the chapters that follow. Chapter 1 presents the theoretical framework of the study in four sections. The first links the actions of political parties, social movements, and women's organizing in the process of Latin American democratization. The second explains how the political opportunity structure approach can be used in the analysis of social movement activity during democratization. The third focuses on women's organizing in particular by applying gender analysis to different elements of the political opportunity structure, specifically discourse and institutions. The fourth discusses women's response to their political opportunities in the light of their different gender interests and forms of organizing in Latin America.

Chapters 2 through 6 use the findings of Chapter 1 to analyze the development of women's organizing in Venezuela. They follow a common format, examining the relevant socioeconomic and political changes in women's status during the period under study, the general and gender-based political opportunities of the period, the development of women's organizing and interests, and women's principal moments of mobilization.

Chapter 2 focuses on the experience of the first women's groups during liberalized authoritarianism (1936–45) and the first transition to democracy (1945–48). It examines these groups' makeup, their organizing around issues such as suffrage and legal reform, their struggles with class differences, and their decline in the transition to democracy as parties became dominant. It shows how the political parties have institutionalized and legitimated gender bias. Chapter 3 examines how women's participation against dictatorship (1948–58) led to their increasing mobilization at its fall. It also traces how their demobilization in the next transition (1958–74) was due to the more general effects of the "pact" and the gender-specific impact of party-driven democratization.

Chapter 4 shows how women's organizing advanced in the consolidation of democracy (1974–84). Women experimented with the structure of their organizations to "regender" their opportunities in the three arenas of democratic political interaction: the state, political society, and civil society.[8] In doing so, they took advantage of the international opportunity provided by the UN Decade for Women (1975–85). These innovations had differing degrees of success, but the lessons learned brought a significant result: a coalition that was able to bring about the revision of the Civil Code in 1982.

Chapter 5 charts women's most successful period of mobilization (1984–90), during which they were able to implement the lessons drawn from their long history of organizing. It focuses on the development of an ongoing relationship between the state and civil society-based organizations that succeeded in increasing public concern about single motherhood, reforming labor legislation, and promoting female political candidates.

Chapter 6 shows the effects of intertwined economic and political crises on women's organizing efforts (1989–95). The shift to a neoliberal economic model further impoverished poor women, exacerbating the longstanding class divisions among women. Poor women principally organized among themselves, and the emergence of more hierarchical and traditional political practices within women's organizations proved a general liability to coalition building.

Chapter 7 provides the conclusions of the study. It first briefly compares the experience of women to one other nontraditional interest group in Venezuela, the neighborhood associations, to reveal what lessons can be learned about social movements and civil society in the democratizing state. It then summarizes the findings concerning gender and democratization in Venezuela relative to other Latin American countries. In particular, it exam-

---

8. For the distinction between political and civil society, see Chapter 1, note 3.

ines the impact of gendered political opportunities on women's ability to organize on their own behalf under democratization and assesses their most successful and least successful strategies. The book concludes with a reflection on the potential for women's transformation from antiauthoritarian activists to full-fledged players in the interest-group politics of consolidated democracies.[9]

9. Parts of chapters appear in the following articles: "The Effects of 'Transnationalism Reversed' in Venezuela: Assessing the Impact of UN Global Conferences on the Women's Movement," *International Feminist Journal of Politics* 1:3 (Autumn 1999): 357–81; "State-based Advocacy for Gender Equality in the Developing World: Assessing the Venezuelan National Women's Agency," *Women and Politics* 21:2 (April 2000); "The Paradoxes of Gendered Political Opportunity in the Venezuelan Transition to Democracy," *Latin American Research Review* 33:3 (1998); and "La mujer latinoamericana en la política: ¿Como entrar y retar instituciones masculinas?" *Debates IESA* 3:2 (1997): 50–53.

UNFINISHED TRANSITIONS

The problems faced by women, if they wish to act politically, are qualitatively different from those of other groups. . . . To assume that there is no structured difference among groups is to misread social reality.

—Morris Blachman, "Selective Omission and Theoretical Distortion in Studying the Political Activity of Women in Brazil"

Few guidelines are available to help analyze the gendered dynamics of women's organizing during democratization.[1] Work has been done on social mobilization in the transition process and on women's participation in both democratizing and democratic politics. But there is almost no theorizing about how gender is embedded in the process of the transition to democracy and how this embeddedness affects women's participation. Current approaches remain incomplete and their insights invisible to one another. Democratic transition theory neglects social movements as a whole and women in particular. Social movement theory does not incorporate gender as a category of analysis, instead subsuming women's actions in non–gender-specific discussions of mobilization. Feminist theorists of democracy point to the gendered nature of theoretical discourse but not to that of democratic institutions. While studies of Latin American women describe their experience of democratization, they largely ignore how gender relations influence the political environment in which women are active. The "gender and politics" literature focuses on women's interaction with formal institutions (primarily in consolidated democracies) but neglects gender analysis as well as the role of women's movements in promoting women's access to institutions.

To rectify the lack of theory about the gendered impact of democratization on women's organizing, this chapter lays out four interrelated theo-

1. Sonia E. Alvarez (1986, 1990) presents the most developed framework in this regard; see also Georgina Waylen (1994). These works are discussed in more detail in note 29.

retical propositions. (1) The rise of party politics in the transition to democracy contributes to the demobilization of social movements and has an especially detrimental impact on women's organizing. Moreover, party dominance during the transition may impede the subsequent development of civil society, particularly women's groups, as democracy becomes consolidated. (2) During democratization the *political opportunities* of all social movements vary according to regime type or phase. The opportunities provided by political institutions, actors, and discourses change under authoritarianism, the transition to democracy, and democratic consolidation. (3) Women's organizing is conditioned not only by the general political opportunities of a specific regime type or phase but also by how these opportunities are *gendered*, that is, how they incorporate the social meanings attributed to sexual difference. (4) Women's response to both the general and gendered political opportunities of democratization depends on women's different *gender interests*—those interests women have that vary by their social positioning—and forms of organization. Taken together, these propositions explain why democratic transitions remain unfinished when citizens of both genders are taken into account.

Political Parties, Social Movements, and Women's Organizing in Democratization

Democratization literature has described the overall pattern of social movement activity in the process of regime change—its rise as an authoritarian regime falters, its peak at the regime's demise, and its decline with the inception of political democracy—without explaining the dynamic as a whole or examining the specific role of women.[2] Because of their predominant focus on elite interactions, analysts have mentioned the contributions of social movements to the demise of authoritarian regimes but have not accurately assessed movement length or composition. This has masked the significant contribution of women, whose participation occurs primarily through social movements. Analysts have noted that social mobilization of-

---

2. By "democratization literature" I refer to those general works that seek to map out and theorize the process of political democratization, such as O'Donnell and Schmitter 1986; Diamond, Linz, and Lipset 1989; R. Munck 1989; Higley and Gunther 1992; Mainwaring, O'Donnell and Valenzuela 1992; Huntington 1993. As will be discussed later, works exist that specifically address social movement activity in democratization, but these have yet to be systematically incorporated into the broader discussion. See S. Alvarez 1990; Rochon 1990; Jaquette 1991, 1994a, 1994b; G. Munck 1991; Canel 1992; Foweraker 1995; Hipsher 1996.

ten falls off during the transition to democracy. But most do not examine one of the principal reasons: the rise of party politics. They assume that the establishment of strongly institutionalized parties is the key to achieving political stability and see no conflict between the development of political and civil society.[3] While in consolidated democracies there is often no such conflict, during the transition process the dominance of strong parties may impede the development of civil society, and in particular women's organizing within it.

Democratization theory has noted that the breakdown of authoritarian regimes often encourages widespread political mobilization, yet it misspecifies the dynamics of that mobilization—when it appears and who makes it up. In its focus on the crucial moments of regime change, it argues that some signs of political liberalization, or opening, have to come from within the authoritarian regime before opposition swells, led by particular elites (O'Donnell and Schmitter 1986; Mainwaring, O'Donnell, and Valenzuela 1992). The resulting neglect of social movements in the literature has led to the counterclaim that these movements in fact initiate the process of regime change (Petras 1990). While this overstates the case, the focus on moments of regime change has resulted in some confusion over early social movement activity. Guillermo O'Donnell and Philippe C. Schmitter (1986) initially argue that the first protesters are artists and intellectuals, former elite supporters of the regime, and professionals.[4] But they later state that "human rights advocates," including human rights associations; relatives of the disappeared, tortured, and killed; and churches are "the first to speak out against the more repulsive facets of the authoritarian regime. They do so in the midst of severe repression, when most other actors acquiesce to the regime or choose to ignore its atrocities" (1986, 51). Further study supports the second statement, revealing that both human rights advocates and those protesting on the basis of subsistence issues (such as affordable food and clean water) often do not

---

3. For the sake of analytic clarity, I am following Larry Diamond's separation of civil and political society. Civil society is the "realm of organized social life that is voluntary, self-generating, largely self-supporting, autonomous from the state and bound by a legal order or set of shared rules. It is distinct from 'society' in general in that it involves citizens acting collectively in a public sphere to express their interests, passions and ideas, exchange information, achieve mutual goals, make demands on the state, and hold state officials accountable" (1994, 5). Primary examples of "citizens acting collectively" are social movements and interest associations. Political society is, to put it most simply, the party system.

4. Little work has been done on the specific role of clandestine parties in the opposition, despite case studies that draw particular attention to their importance in organizing other sectors (see García Ponce and Camacho Barrios 1982; Schneider 1995). This oversight is puzzling, considering the emphasis that is placed on the role of parties in constructing the new democracies (as shown below).

wait for schism among the ruling elite.[5] They begin to protest long before splits are apparent and may contribute to the disequilibrium of the regime (Waylen 1994).

The contradiction in specifying movement participants may be due to theorists' focus on elite negotiation. Yet a still more profound problem impedes their assessment of movement activity. Many of the early protesters are invisible *because they do not fall into expected categories of opposition participants.* Those analysts who claim a central role for social movements assert that "the key point about the growth of social movements is that they represent a variety of *social classes*" (Petras 1990, 89, emphasis added). However, not only class but also *gender* determines the makeup of movements. Women are the majority of the participants in many opposition movements, particularly those mobilized around the earliest emerging issues such as human rights and subsistence demands (Jelin 1990; Feijoó and Nari 1994; Jaquette 1994a; Waylen 1994). Thus the contribution of social movements to the demise of authoritarianism is more extensive and differently gendered than has been previously understood.

Democratization theory has been upheld in its overall assessment of a decline in general mobilization during the transition stage, in which authoritarian leaders have ceded (or been compelled to cede) political power and negotiations over democratic politics have begun (O'Donnell and Schmitter 1986; Mainwaring 1987; Canel 1992; Jaquette 1994a). However, social movements may fare better in countries that go through long transition stages. Unlike movements that face a sudden shift in political winds, they have more time to reorient their strategies and goals to the new situation (S. Alvarez 1990; Waylen 1994). Moreover, it may be that social movement activity does not cease completely but is redirected to less visible and less unified ends (Fitzsimmons 1995).

The general decline in visible protest arises partly from necessary changes in the opposition's tactics. As its goal shifts from building a movement against a common authoritarian enemy to constructing the complex alliances within a democratic regime, mobilizational activity wanes. But demobilization can also be a strategy chosen deliberately by political parties. During the transition, "parties . . . show themselves to be not only, or not so much, agents of mobilization as instruments of social and political control" (O'Donnell and Schmitter 1986, 58). As they (re)emerge to play a central part

---

5. For example, the Argentinean Mothers of the Plaza de Mayo, a group of mothers and grandmothers who publicly protested the torture and disappearance of their family members during the "Dirty War," came together in 1977, before the process of liberalization began (Feijoó and Nari 1994, 112).

in political life, parties strive to reduce the uncertainty caused by the shifting political framework of the transition phase by co-opting or repressing independent organizing (Karl 1987).

Despite the uncertainty that characterizes transition politics, initial party dominance may be lasting—and detrimental to the further development of democracy. In some cases transition negotiations have resulted in a "freezing" of democracy under conditions of demobilization, governed by the initial actors (Karl 1990).[6] The most common way in which this takes place is through "pacting," constructing a series of agreements that guarantee certain elite interests—whether political, economic, or social—in exchange for promises to abide by democratic political procedures. Pacting has been promoted as the most effective transition mechanism (Higley and Gunther 1992), but it also has been shown to hinder further democratization.[7] As Terry Lynn Karl argues, pacts can "circumscrib[e] the extent to which all actors can participate or wield power in the future. In the long run, pacts may hinder the prospects for the future" (1987, 88). Therefore, if parties dominate pact making in the transition, they may impede the development of new self-constituted organizations and movements as democracy is consolidated.

Because of their focus on the establishment of stable political regimes that can prevent a return to authoritarian rule, most scholars of democratization ignore the demobilizing potential of parties and the likelihood of "freezing" this demobilization following the transition.[8] Analysts acknowledge that both civil and political society play crucial roles in assuring the conditions of consolidation (Linz and Stepan 1996), that is, when the rules of poli-

6. This has been shown clearly in the case of Venezuela, which has been praised for the inclusion of a strong party system in its successful transition. See Karl 1987; Brewer-Carías 1988; López Maya, Gómez Calcaño, and Maingón 1989; Salamanca 1995. Frances Hagopian argues in a similar vein about Brazil: "Patterns of politics established in periods of transition have a very real and strong potential to become semipermanent features of the political landscape. In moments of transition and convulsion there arise unique opportunities to discard the constraints and the organizational forms inherited from previous regimes, but missed opportunities are seldom regained. Political institutions are molded to suit the regime that they uphold, and state elites and societal organizations build bridges to one another appropriate for the immediate political environment. Individuals rise who are adept at the political game as it is played, and they use their positions to perpetuate modes of political interaction that favor them" (1990, 148).

7. John Higley and Richard Gunther note that pactmaking involves demobilization, but see it as a positive outcome. Pactmaking "usually involves demobilizing mass organizations and social movements so as to discourage the outbreak of polarizing incidents and mass violence" (as cited in Hipsher 1996, 279).

8. Patricia Hipsher (1996) offers one of the few analyses focusing on the interactions between party elites and social movements that result in demobilization during the transition. But her perspective stresses the accommodation of party politics by social movement actors more than the losses they, and democracy as a whole, may sustain in the long term.

tics gain general acceptance and no serious challengers exist outside the system. But analysts also agree that the key to achieving consolidation is the institutionalization of a party system (Agüero, Gillespie, and Scully 1986; Diamond, Linz, and Lipset 1989; Pridham 1991; Mainwaring and Scully 1995).

The problems that can arise if civil society is not separated from political society have been recognized. As Larry Diamond explains, "Organizations and networks in civil society may form alliances with parties, but if they become captured by parties, or hegemonic within them, they thereby move their primary locus of activity to political society and lose much of their ability to perform certain unique mediating and democracy-building functions" (1994, 7). But concern with building strong parties during transitions seems to have prevented analysts from considering how or whether civil society can remain sufficiently independent from political society during this construction. Although the social movements active under the previous regime appear the most obvious basis for reviving civil society, the Uruguayan democratic consolidation phase provides an illustration of the actual fate of these movements as parties develop. As Eduardo Canel notes, "The logic of the consolidation of democratic institutions—which required the active participation of political parties—made party-building a central priority, contributing further to the tendency toward the assimilation or displacement of nontraditional collective actors" (1992, 284–85).

Those who study Latin American social movement activity in democratizing and democratic politics echo this sentiment, finding new social movements to be the "casualties" of the transition, "whose role in defining the issues and setting the terms of public debate has again been taken over by political parties" (Jaquette 1994b, 337). This "takeover" is often hostile. Research indicates that infiltration by party politics has created schisms that are frequently responsible for the demise of movements (S. Alvarez 1990; Chuchryk 1994; Foweraker 1995; Oxhorn 1995).

However, party politics and social movements should not be seen as inevitably at odds. Not all parties have these divisive effects; at times parties on the left have helped social movements expand (S. Alvarez 1990; Schneider 1992; Starn 1992). Evidence from consolidated democracies reveals the potential for coexistence and fruitful interaction between active social movements and political parties (Dalton and Kuechler 1990). A comparison of the different experiences of social movements during regime change indicates that highly institutionalized party systems that rely on parties established prior to the authoritarian period tend to have the most demobilizing effects (Canel 1992; Chuchryk 1994; Oxhorn 1995; Salamanca 1995). These long-established parties possess the organizational ability to co-opt social movements when politics is in ferment and new political actors are uncertain about effective strategies. Thus, "the impact of democratic politics on movement strategies and dynamics . . . in countries with historically strong states and effective party systems . . . has propelled parties onto center stage, displacing movements and diminishing their vital role in forging a more autonomous and vibrant civil society" (Escobar and Alvarez 1992, 328).

The emphasis on the benefits of building party systems during the transition phase—which ignores their potential to exclude actors mobilized in the opposition to authoritarian rule and to impede the later growth of civil society—reveals a flaw in democratization theorizing. Analysts seem to have forgotten the past and thus have begun to repeat it.[9] Samuel Huntington's early study of political transitions (1968) stressed the achievement of "governability," that is, stable political interactions, over all other aspects of governmental action, making differentiation between regime types (such as authoritarian and democratic) immaterial. A key element of his analysis was the importance of constructing strong political parties as the principal method for channeling and stabilizing political participation, to the exclusion of all other mechanisms.[10] One of the central contributions of regime-centered literature was to restore consideration of political quality as well as stability (or governability) by taking issues such as respect for human rights into account in the differentiation between regime types (Linz 1992; G. Munck 1995).

Some analysts have continued to nuance this discussion by making clear that the dynamics that lead to a successful democratic transition are not the same as those that lead to consolidation (Karl 1990; Schmitter 1992). The initial restoration or installation of democratic politics depends on the ability of certain elites to keep the political situation stable enough to counter the threat of authoritarian relapse. However, consolidating the gains of the transition into lasting patterns of interaction calls for multiplying the issues placed on the table and allowing other actors to bring a chair. This may imply the restructuring of transition agreements to permit the expression of new demands through new channels (Karl 1990).

Because democratization theory in general has not focused on the displacement of social movements by political parties, it has not taken into account the disproportionate drop-off of women's participation in transition

---

9. The following discussion was inspired by Gerardo Munck's (1995) comments on the difference between regime "form and function."

10. Huntington (1968, 409–12) defines strong parties as highly institutionalized, mass-based, and organizationally complex, with a high member identification with party ideology.

politics and the resulting difficulties of women in democratic consolidation.[11] As shown in the fight against authoritarianism, social movements "draw women's loyalties and energies more successfully than more conventional forms of participation" (Jaquette 1991, 194). Thus the decline of social movements and the simultaneous rise of party politics have a severe impact on women's ability to organize politically.

The link between women's demobilization and party ascendancy during regime change is a global phenomenon, as described by Barbara J. Nelson and Najma Chowdhury in their introduction to a comparative volume on women's political participation:

> Moments of system change, when the distribution and forms of power are in flux, underscore the importance of parties in structuring women's opportunities to participate in formal politics. There has been growing recognition that even though social disjunctures like war, revolution, or economic distress may temporarily increase the range or intensity of women's political activism, these changes do not endure after political consolidation. The role of parties in returning politics to the gender status quo is demonstrated in . . . the transitions from authoritarian or state socialist regimes to democracies. (1994, 16)

Analysis of women's mobilization in democratizing or democratic politics in Latin America supports these conclusions. Clandestine parties have taken advantage of women's ability to organize aboveground during authoritarianism, and legal parties often pay at least lip service to the importance of women's incorporation during the transition. But as democratization proceeds, party politics tends to be carried out to the detriment of women's organizing (Jelin 1990; Jaquette 1994a; Waylen 1996b). A common finding is that partisan rifts are introduced into women's organizations. As women are recruited into parties, they begin to carry political rivalries into formerly unified groups, often resulting in their dismantling (Barrig 1994; Chuchryk 1994). At times, segments of women's movement organizations are completely absorbed into different parties, thus subordinating women's demands to party priorities. Parties may set up

---

11. In his mention of women's interaction with political parties, Diamond (1994, 10) notes, "Because of the traditional dominance by men of the corridors of power, civil society is a particularly important base for the training and recruitment of women . . . into positions of formal political power." However, like other theorists of transition politics, he does not explore the extent to which the "traditional dominance by men of the corridors of power" presents obstacles to women's "training and recruitment."

their own women's bureaus with a similar result (S. Alvarez 1986; Kirkwood 1986).

As with other social sectors, the problems women's organizations encounter with parties should not be taken to indicate that they are fundamentally at odds. In fact, comparisons of women's experiences of party politics in consolidated democracies reveal that strong (highly organized/rule-based) parties are the most successful at promoting women's leadership and issues because of their ability to implement policy within party structures and impose it on local branches (Lovenduski and Norris 1993). But the sine qua non of gender equality in parties is the existence, both inside and outside of party structure, of women's organized pressure campaigns. It is precisely such organizational strength that is often impeded by the dominance of strong parties during the transition.

Because the democratization literature misspecifies the general dynamics of social mobilization and ignores the gendered nature of transition politics, it has been argued that social movements and women's participation cannot be productively discussed within the framework of the literature (Waylen 1994, 335). But democratization theory remains useful. The cycle of social mobilization during democratization is a pattern confirmed from early studies onward. To fully understand the role of social movements in transition politics, however, we must turn to other forms of analysis.

The Political Opportunities of Democratization

To capture the effects of regime change on social mobilization, the most useful type of analysis is one that focuses on the impact of *macropolitical* context on the development of movements. Much of the social movement literature has focused on the internal dynamics of movements, an approach that has resulted in detailed assessments of *micropolitical* interactions within specific mobilizations. However, such an approach does not take into account the crucial influence of external circumstances on social movements. This omission precludes an explanation of why social movements emerge at particular times, such as during political transitions, and why they develop in some of the forms they do. With some modification, the *political opportunity structure approach* and its related "cycles of protest" concept can be used to highlight the role of social movements in the transition to democracy, acknowledged only between the lines of democratization theory's emphasis on stabilizing elite politics.

By focusing on movement interaction with external institutions, actors, and discourses as they change throughout the transition to democracy, the political opportunity approach explains why the visible activity of social movements begins, rises, and falls. While charting this cycle of mobilization, however, it is important to avoid two problems in the approach: (1) faulting internal dynamics for the decline of social movements, when the impact of political context must be taken into account, and (2) assuming that all social movement activity rises and falls cyclically, when much of it is channeled through ongoing, if less visible, networks.

The two dominant schools of social movement analysis that focus on intermovement dynamics are the *resource mobilization school,* which emphasizes the internal development of the movement, and the *new social movements* or *"identity" school,* which looks at actors' predisposition for mobilization.[12] The former, developed by U.S.-based and -focused scholars, emphasizes the importance of available resources—such as elite support, leadership, membership, and communication networks—in the successful construction of social movement organizations (McAdam, McCarthy, and Zald 1988). Although it takes into account the resources that allow for the construction of a movement, resource mobilization neglects the formation of the collective group identity that underlies all social mobilization. In contrast, the new social movements paradigm, developed by observers of Western European movements, emphasizes the identity formation preceding collective action (Laclau 1985; Melucci 1985; Slater 1985). Focusing on movements that have emerged in postindustrial societies, this model "turns to the fields of alterable but nonetheless structured social relations rather than development, the state, or the market" (Cohen 1985, 699) to explain the emergence of a common consciousness.[13]

The resource mobilization and new social movement schools contribute to the understanding of the resources and identity base of social movements. However, they cannot explain why these identities are galvanized and resources are put to use at any particular time. Moreover, the focus on the micropolitical, especially in the new social movement school, has often resulted in an overly optimistic assessment of the potential for social movement–based activism, including its promotion of "pure" democratic politics (Slater 1985).[14] To account for the cycling of social movement activ-

---

12. For an in-depth comparison of the two approaches, see Cohen 1985; Foweraker 1995.

13. For examples of work that attempts to bring the insights of new social movement research to bear on resource mobilization, see Morris and Mueller 1992.

14. The approach's neglect of "development, the state, or the market" also makes it problematic for application to the developing world, where such issues clearly have an impact on

ity and its failure to radically change the way politics is done, the political opportunities that inspire (or inhibit) collective action must be considered.

The *political opportunity structure approach* frames the development of the micropolitical in its macropolitical environment.[15] Sidney Tarrow and others have described the elements of the political opportunity structure as follows: (1) the openness of political institutions, (2) the availability of allies for the movement, (3) the conflict between elites, and (4) the impact of political alignments (Tarrow 1991b). These elements have been defined differently in the various analyses that make use of the approach. "The openness of political institutions" has been taken to mean formal representation and the responsiveness of government to citizen demands (Eisinger 1973). "Allies" range from religious workers to revolutionary guerrillas to political parties (Brockett 1991). The "shift in political alignments" has generally referred to political parties' competition for the votes of certain sectors (Tarrow 1994); and "elite conflict" can take place among government bureaucrats fighting for territory or political parties in electoral battles (Costain 1992). Although generally taken to refer to the domestic political environment, Tarrow (1991a) has recently expanded the concept of political opportunity structure to include international influences as well (see also V. Randall 1998, 196).

Taken as a whole, the various aspects of political opportunity structure have two common denominators—first, formal political institutions, and second, political actors (in various situations of cooperation and conflict)—which together condition the emergence and development of social movements. In addition to institutions and actors, another neglected yet key external factor is the "universe of political discourse" in which a social movement develops (Jenson 1987).[16] Political discourse specifies the acceptable actors, actions, and subjects of politics, which are determined through ideological interpretation of basic social arrangements (65–66).[17] In the context of Latin American regime change, the nature of political discourses and actors varies widely, while the institutions that most determine the political

---

social movement development. See Foweraker (1995) for a detailed critique of the application of Western social movement theory to Latin American movements.

15. For more detailed accounts of the political opportunity structure, see McAdam 1982; Tarrow 1991b, 1994; G. Munck 1991; Foweraker 1995.

16. Vicky Randall (1998, 194) also emphasizes the need to focus on discourse within political opportunity structure analysis.

17. This concept is similar to that of "political culture" as defined by Sonia Alvarez, Evelina Dagnino, and Arturo Escobar: "The particular social construction in every society of what counts as political; . . . the domain of practices and institutions, carved out of the totality of social reality, that historically comes to be considered as properly political" (1998, 8).

opportunities for social movements are political parties, as discussed above, and the state.

Many have claimed that social movements strive to remain independent from the state, but Joe Foweraker (1995) insists that Latin American social mobilization cannot be understood without investigating its interaction with the state—the bureaucracies, institutionalized legal order, and formal and informal norms that govern formal politics.[18] The work of both Foweraker (1995) and Arturo Escobar and Sonia E. Alvarez (1992) discusses how the rise and crisis of the "developmentalist" state was one of the key factors of social movement emergence in the 1970s and 1980s in Latin America.[19] Moreover, social movement dynamics during democratization cannot be understood in isolation from the state because it is the principal arena for social movement activity, from opposition to incorporation (S. Alvarez 1990; Rochon 1990; Cardoso 1992; Hellman 1992; Foweraker 1995). In these interactions the state is far from a unitary object. Those who incorporate consideration of the state into their analyses differentiate it by type (dependent, developmentalist, neoliberal), branch (judicial, legislative, executive), and level (local and national, as well as regional and international governing structures).

The political contextualization of movement activity is receiving increasing attention (Katzenstein and Mueller 1987; Foweraker and Craig 1990;

18. This Weberian definition of the state is taken from Karl (1997, 14). Early work on Latin American social movements assumed their autonomy (e.g., Slater 1985). This scholarship drew on the new social movement approach, which is based on the experience of Western European social movements. Because these movements were generally more focused on cultural change than on material demands, they largely ignored the state. However, given the importance of the state in Latin American politics, and the basis in material demands of the majority of the region's social movements, no study of Latin American social movements can afford to neglect the larger political environment. Although more recent work on Latin American social movements has taken pains to locate social movement analysis within the appropriate political context, many writers still struggle with the older paradigm. Fernando Calderón, Alejandro Piscitelli, and José Luis Reyna claim that "to a great extent the state is no longer the 'object of attraction'" (1992, 24) for social movements, which are looking for a "new system of political institutions" (29); but they also recognize that "the state is a referent for almost all social movements" (25). This same tension arises in an essay by María Pilar García, who first describes "the emergence of forms of social action that are independent from both the political parties and the state" but then admits that "at certain times they confront the state; at others, they ally with it, depending on the problem" (1992, 159). Arturo Escobar (1992, 83) resolves the issue more satisfactorily: "Social movements are somewhat exterior to the state, and if it is true that the state is a key interlocutor for the movements, these latter cannot be reduced to the logic of the state."

19. The "developmentalist" state used the policies of "Import-Substitution Industrialization" (ISI) to promote economic development. The goal of ISI was to produce goods formerly imported into the country; and meeting this goal required significant state involvement in building infrastructure, supporting and protecting industry, and mediating the demands of different social sectors. For further description of ISI, see Haggard 1993; Todaro 1994, 491–500.

Davis 1994; Foweraker 1995) and is particularly useful for studying the development of social movements within the process of democratization. Political opportunity structures can be applied to transition politics by modifying the "cycles of protest" version of the approach. Tarrow posits that general social mobilization increases when new external political opportunities allow for it. More movements join in, coalescing around a "master frame" of the common goals of different organizations until a peak of mobilization is reached. At a certain point differences arise between participants over the content and tactics of the general mobilization, and it declines. The activities of movements may leave new institutions in their wake, but movements will not reappear until political opportunities allow for the start of a new cycle (Tarrow 1991b, 51–54; 1994, 155–58).

Analysts have directly mapped the cycles of protest concept onto Latin American regime change (G. Munck 1991; Foweraker 1995). Reflecting the description of social mobilization outlined in the democratization literature, the protest cycle is seen to begin its ascent when authoritarian regimes begin to liberalize. It peaks at some point in the transition and declines as the space for social mobilization is closed off. Gerardo Munck (1991) finds that both the length of the transition and the emerging party structure determine how long movements continue to develop, a view that supports the arguments in the first section above. He posits a "trade-off between the 'window of opportunity' allowed for the emergence and consolidation of social movements and the degree of state democratization" (13). Crucially, he notes that social movements lose their primacy as the focus of political organizing turns to electoral politics and political life is reoriented around parties.

However, Munck repeats two errors of the political opportunity structure/cycles of protest approach: ignoring the emphasis on context when discussing the decline of social movements, and assuming that movements' visible rise and fall comprise the full extent of their activity. In his conclusion, he first reaffirms the importance of social movements: "Democracy is the fruit of various factors"; although state form, political parties, and constitutions are all fundamental, "the pressure of civil society, in the form of social movements, is equally indispensable" and is "an arm for democracy" (1991, 15). But in describing how new democracies might reverse the seemingly inevitable decline of social movements, Munck discusses only factors internal to the movements: their inclusiveness, their ability to engage in strategic interaction, and their consistency in action.

Munck highlights the problematic interaction of parties (and other forms of institutionalized politics) and social movements in the transition stage. But he repeats a common error made by cycles of protest analysis: the assumption that cycle decline is wholly due to factors internal to the movement. Tarrow also argues that the competition between social movement organizations at the cycle's peak is seen to result in "sectarian involution . . . and goal displacement. . . . Between them, *these effects combine to conclude the cycle*" (1991b, 54, emphasis added). This line of reasoning contradicts the political opportunity structure emphasis on the political environment. If political opportunities are responsible for movement emergence and development, they must also at least influence movement decline.

But what this "decline" (or, for that matter, the "rise" and "peak") of social movements entails is itself open to debate. Aspects of mobilization, such as strikes and other protest demonstrations, do rise and fall visibly. But as Alberto Melucci (1988) convincingly argues, collective action can also be seen as an ongoing process of transformation, based on "networks submerged in everyday life." These networks do not cycle, but they form the basis upon which visible manifestations periodically erupt:

> Within these networks there is an experimentation with and direct practice of alternative frameworks of sense, in consequence of a personal commitment which is submerged and almost invisible. . . . The "movements" emerge only in limited areas, for limited phases, and by means of moments of mobilization which are the other, complementary, face of the submerged networks. . . . [T]hese networks make possible such mobilizations and render them visible in a punctual manner: that is, at the moment when there emerges a confrontation or conflict with a public policy. (248)

Thus, even as political opportunities change, the activity of social movements continues through ongoing interactions among actors and the spread of new meanings, resulting in political learning that often informs the next visible "cycle."[20]

The political opportunity structure approach allows for an assessment of the impact of political context on social movement development during democratization. But it does not allow for an understanding of the specific dynamics of women's political organizing in the transition to democracy. General claims that social movement activity emerges only after an initial re-

20. See S. Alvarez (1997), and Alvarez, Dagnino, and Escobar (1998) for further discussion of social movement networks or "webs." Morris and Mueller's (1992) work on resource mobilization also pays attention to the importance of ongoing interactions among social movement actors in forming a collective identity.

laxation of authoritarian rule neglect women's opposition, which frequently begins before political liberalization. Furthermore, democratization theorists' focus on the benefits of party politics in the transition and consolidation of democracy overlooks the marginalization of women's social movement–based organizing. The political opportunity structure approach has been used to make women's organizing strategies more visible (Katzenstein and Mueller 1987; Costain 1992). But even this improvement does not explain why these opportunities have an impact on women's ability to organize politically *as women*. What is missing is an understanding of the gendered nature of political opportunities, especially the political institutions of democracy.

The Gendered Opportunities of Democratization

Understanding the impact of political context on women's organizing calls for an examination of the influence of gender relations on political thought and action: how ideas about the proper social relations between men and women are incorporated into political practice. This section first discusses the meaning of gender relations and the need for gender analysis. It then shows how feminist theorists have used gender analysis to reveal the gendered nature of the theoretical discourse of democracy. In examining political institutions, however, much remains to be done. Most studies of Latin American women in democratization do not focus on institutional factors. The research on "gender and politics" (or "women and politics") focuses on institutions but does not use gender analysis, and it neglects the importance of women's organizing. In contrast, this section argues that gendered political institutions form much of the context that conditions women's mobilization, often impeding it.[21]

21. The claim that political institutions are gendered in a way that can marginalize women is not meant to imply that the founders of such institutions consciously sought to privilege men's participation. However, in designing political mechanisms with the traditional actors of politics in mind, they ended up creating ones into which women did not "fit." Similarly, discriminatory political discourse should not be seen as deliberately biased against women, but rather as the outcome of a long history of assumptions that men, not women, belong in political life. Examples of this type of unconscious discrimination abound in social life, for example, the former strength and endurance qualifications for US firefighters. Because firefighters were originally all men, these qualifications were based on men's physical capacities—to which women were unable to conform. When challenged, the requirements for firefighting itself were proven to be of a different order, but one that could not be seen as long as men were assumed to be carrying out the activity.

Gender Relations and Gender Analysis

Contrary to much current usage, the term *gender* is not a synonym for biological sex (male/female), nor does it refer exclusively to women. Gender denotes the *socially constructed significance* of biological sexual difference, or how society assigns male and female bodies the different expectations, obligations, and rights associated with masculinity and femininity. Consequently, the feminine gender cannot be understood in isolation from the masculine gender; they are inextricably intertwined. Only in relation to one another can the various characteristics assigned to each gender be distinguished. Thus *gender relations* is a more useful concept than the term *gender* alone.

But the concept of gender relations, like class relations, implies more than socially attributed difference. Because of men's historical dominance over women, gender relations contain socially ascribed *value,* which is apparent in the nearly universal ascription of superiority to the masculine over the feminine gender. Moreover, this ranking is invoked in some way in every significant social structure, making gender relations a "primary way of signifying relationships of power" (Scott 1988, 42).[22]

Because gender relations are socially determined, their manifestations in social life are not static. A general association of masculine gender with the public sphere of work and politics stands in contrast to the linking of feminine gender with the private sphere of family and household. But there is no establishing, once and for all, the myriad roles and expectations every man and woman is expected to fulfill, nor their inherent value. Every context reveals multiple renderings of gender relations in private and public life.

But gender relations do not float freely above the complex interactions of daily life and power politics, open to revision. To the contrary, gender relations are firmly rooted in political, economic, and social structures and actions. Because gender hierarchy is one of the fundamental ordering processes of all known societies and is imparted to children from birth, the relations constructed on it are not easily altered.[23] Moreover, they are often deeply embedded in institutions through the repeated application of norms and rules based on a particular configuration of gender relations.

However, gender relations are subject to change. Their hierarchy can be

22. I am indebted to Karen Booth for helping to clarify the definitions of, and distinctions between, gender and gender relations. Joan Scott's examples include analogies between political structure and the marital relationship and the legitimation of war through appealing to notions of manhood (1988, 46–50).

23. While Nancy Chodorow (1974) has been taken to task for her cultural essentialism, her assessment of the impact of family structure on the development of children's gender identity has been widely accepted.

explicitly challenged or affirmed through organized activity such as feminist, queer, antiabortion, or prochoice movements. The daily interactions of individuals within institutions ranging from the family to the armed forces also implicitly modify or reinforce patterns of gender relations. Thus, "gender is not fixed in advance of social interaction, but is constructed in interaction" (Connell 1995, 35). Given that much of this interaction takes place in institutions, the ways in which these reflect gender relations also can be altered, albeit with considerable difficulty.

Political analysis commonly has used *gender* as a synonym for *sex role*, usually that of the female sex, seeking comparative or case study information about women as political actors. While this information has contributed to the illumination of empirical factors that strengthen or weaken women's ability to participate in political life, it has added very little to the conceptual understanding of why women are subject to exclusion from the political realm—and why men have access to it.[24] In order to explain why women have experienced inequality in the political realm, analysts must go beyond examining women's actions. They must subject the political realm itself to scrutiny for its reflection of gender relations, through the use of gender as a primary category of analysis (Silverberg 1990).

The study of women in politics can be an endeavor distinct from research using gender as a primary category of analysis. The first does not necessarily consider gender relations, and the second does not necessarily involve women. For example, compare a study of women's voting behavior in the 1996 U.S. presidential elections with an examination of how the configuration of U.S. welfare programs has made it difficult for many fathers to participate in rearing their children. The first gathers statistical information on the voting patterns of women as a group but may exclude consideration of gender relations. The second is premised on the effects of gender relations, though it does not focus on women. It examines how a particular social construction of masculinity, which excludes hands-on parenting because of its association with femininity, is reflected in, and reinforced by, a governmental policy.

In order not only to describe but also to theorize about women's political organizing, analysts must use both methods. Because political activity has been assumed to be a masculine endeavor, women's organizing has yet to be made visible in many contexts. But once it is brought to light, it cannot be explained as the behavior of merely one among many excluded groups. The

24. R. W. Connell (1995, 26) finds role theory inadequate because it "exaggerates the degree to which people's social behaviour is prescribed. But at the same time, by assuming that the prescriptions are reciprocal, it underplays social inequality and power."

incorporation of assumptions about masculine and feminine behavior into political thought and action means that women will face distinct problems and possibilities in their attempts to be politically active. These can only be understood by revealing the gendered nature of politics.

Gendered Political Discourse

Western feminist theorists of democracy have pointed out that the discourse of democratic politics is predicated on gendered understandings of the political roles of men and women. Women's serious and persistent underrepresentation in the formal institutions of consolidated democracies has led these scholars to seek explanations in the underlying premises of Western democratic theory as it has been formulated from Greek times to the present. In doing so, they have found that canonical political theorists systematically excluded women throughout their constructions of political life by assuming that the democratic citizen would be a man, usually a man of some means.

Aristotle, who while not a theorist of democracy per se is frequently taken to have first described the ideal of participatory citizenship, premised that ideal on the assumption that the male citizen had a wife and slaves at home. It was only because these noncitizens could take care of the household economy, including both intra- and extradomestic business, that the citizen could devote himself to the public affairs of the polity (Okin 1979; Phillips 1991). John Locke formulated a social contract that included contract making only between brother citizens in public life, while naturalizing male dominance in the private sphere (Pateman 1989, 1994). Even John Stuart Mill, who recognized the injustice of women's exclusion from political life, believed that given the choice between public and private activities, women would—and should—choose to concern themselves primarily with the home, forming their children into moral citizens (Okin 1979; Shanley 1991). In this century, John Rawls has taken for granted that male heads of households will be the citizens deliberating principles of justice in the hypothetical "disinterested" (and disembodied) "original position" and thus has neglected to extend these principles to family life (Okin 1989b).[25]

Western feminist theorists have gone beyond revealing how democratic theory excludes women as political actors to demonstrate the centrality of gender relations to political discourse. Carole Pateman has described

---

25. As described in Rawls's *A Theory of Justice* (1971, 12), among the "essential features" of the "original position" are ignorance of one's class position, social status, natural assets or abilities, intelligence, strength, conceptions of the good, and psychology. Gender and race are not mentioned.

how liberal democracy is in fact premised on women's exclusion. In her discussion of two types of "rights of man" (1994), she groups the familiar civil and political rights of the public realm as one type, and contrasts them with the invisible patriarchal rights—the rights of men over women in the private realm. It is these rights, she argues, on which liberal democracy is based. Pateman describes how they "disappeared" into social acceptance (1988, 1989). In the movement from a politics based on the patriarchal divine right of kings over subjects to one founded in a social contract between two equal citizens, one king was kept on the throne: the husband. Patriarchalists had legitimated the political rights of kings by comparing them to a man's rights over his wife and children, making a direct link between private and public rule. Social contractarians, looking to replace the rule of the father king with a contract between brother citizens, sought to free the sons to be equal to their father. But they were left with the problem of what to do with the wife (and daughters), whose equality they were not seeking. In order to maintain the gender hierarchy they had no interest in disturbing, they created distinct arenas of private and public dominion. This allowed them to disassociate men's egalitarian interaction in public from their now "naturalized" control over women in private. While men's rational, intellectual minds suited them for public activities, women were linked through their procreative bodies to all that was natural, irrational, and private. This made women conveniently unfit for contract making in the public sphere. As a result, "the civil body politic created through the fraternal social contract is fashioned after only one of the two bodies of humankind" (Pateman 1988, 34).

Liberal democracy's very foundation in the "patriarchal division between the private family and public, civil society" (Pateman 1988, 44) materially and ideologically blocks women's participation. As Anne Phillips explains, "The caring responsibilities that most women carry in relation to the young, the sick and the old—not to mention the able-bodied men—act as a powerful practical barrier to their political involvement; while the cultural constructions of politics as primarily a matter for men work to disadvantage those women who still put themselves forward" (1994, 96). As long as the requirements of democratic politics do not take into account women's responsibilities in the private sphere, where the demands of home and family reduce time and inclination for political activity, women will not be able to make full use of their formal political rights.[26]

Western feminist theorists of democracy have shown how certain con-

---

26. Susan Okin (1989a), Anne Phillips (1991) and Iris Young (1990) have all suggested policies, ranging from flexible working schedules to political representation for women as a group, that would help to ensure women's ability to participate in democratic politics.

figurations of gender relations form the foundations of democratic political discourse. Clearly, the content of the political discourse of Western democratic theory does not determine the experiences of women in all political contexts. Critics of Western feminist theorists have questioned the dichotomy between public man and private woman in several ways: by citing the fact that some women manage to participate vigorously in public life (usually by passing on their domestic duties to other women); by pointing out that other social categories, such as race and class, affect the participation of citizens of either gender;[27] and by showing how women's actions have never been, and certainly are not now, wholly without public content.[28]

That a strict public/private division does not hold in practice is undeniable. However, that the gender relations based on it continue to inform contemporary political discourse is also evident. As shown by scholarship on Latin American women's organizing in transition politics, gender continues to be a salient category of analysis—and a source of political and social identity.

This scholarship at first seems to contradict the finding of feminist theorists: it shows that women's protest activity has in fact been facilitated by their association with the private sphere. It was when authoritarian rulers prevented women from carrying out their traditional duties in the private sphere, violating the human rights of their family members and denying women the resources needed to run their households, that they responded by organizing in human rights organizations, neighborhood associations, and feminist groups. Although violating women's rights in practice, the heads of governments operated within a discourse that, while assuming the public sphere to be the realm of men, regarded women's private activity as laudable—and apolitical. So while men's political activity was repressed, women's organizing was allowed to grow (at least initially), enabling women to take an active part in opposition politics. In doing so, they too operated within a political discourse that ignored their political identity. They claimed to be "above" the corrupt politics of the regime and only to be asking for the restoration of their traditional rights.

Notwithstanding women's active opposition to authoritarian regimes, their fate in the transition to democracy reflects the finding of feminist analysts that women's association with the private sphere ultimately results in their political marginalization. Women's stand against authoritarianism did

27. On the inadequacy of focusing on gender as the determining element in analysis, see Mohanty, Russo, and Torres 1991; Emberley 1993.
28. See Stephens (1997, esp. 271–75) on how the public/private dichotomy does not accurately describe women's lives in contemporary Latin America.

not involve a fundamental change in political discourse. This led many men, and women as well, to expect that women who had become politically active would withdraw from the public sphere once "normal" politics was restored. It also resulted in discrimination against those women who chose to remain active (Feijoó and Nari 1994; Waylen 1994).

How can women's private duties account for and also impede their political participation? Feminist scholarship regularly finds that women's association with the private sphere "nonpolitical" activity conditions their political participation, and this finding clearly applies to the experience of Latin American women. To show why this association produces different outcomes in different contexts, it is necessary to specify how the political discourse in any given regime is gendered, with what results.

The impact of gender relations on the political discourse of transitions is an important consideration. It cannot be considered in isolation, however. As shown above, political institutions also have considerable impact on social mobilization. What needs to be examined is how the key institutions of the political opportunity structures of democratic transition are gendered and how they condition women's organizing throughout the process.[29]

Gendered Institutions

To say that an institution is "gendered" is to understand that the formal and informal rules that make it up are both based on, and reproduce, gender relations.[30] "The term 'gendered institutions' means that gender is present in the processes, practices, images and ideologies, and distributions of power in the various sectors of social life" (Acker 1992, as quoted in Kenney 1996, 446). The paradigmatic research on gendered institutions has been done in the field of the sociology of work. Early studies assumed that workplace organizations were "gender-neutral" phenomena (Kanter 1977). But more recent

---

29. Sonia E. Alvarez has gone the furthest in this respect, though her gender analysis is deeper when discussing the state than when applied to other political structures, such as parties (1986, 1990). Annie Dandavati (1996) also focuses on how transition politics affected the Chilean women's movement. The most systematic study of the gendering of transition politics is that of Waylen (1994), who provides a thorough overview of the subject and suggests some of the reasons for women's exclusion during democratization in both Latin America and Eastern Europe. However, because her focus is on the impact of democratization on gender relations rather than on how gender relations affect democratization, she does not show how gender is a crucial aspect of the obstacles to women's inclusion during regime change.

30. Feminist institutionalists often use Douglass North's definition of institutions, which also differentiates between institutions and organizations. "Institutions are not organizations—although they embrace them—but are best understood as a set of formal and informal rules, which are administered by organizations" (Goetz 1995, 5; see also Ackerly 1997).

scholarship shows gender relations to be embedded in the organizational logic and materialized in the rules, contracts, directives, and other "documentary tools" used to run organizations (Acker 1990, 147). A given job is based on the abilities of a supposedly gender-neutral "universal worker"; but the closest approximation to this worker is usually a man whose life is assumed to center "on his full-time, life-long job, while his wife or another woman takes care of his personal needs and his children . . . 'a job' already contains the gender-based division of labor and the separation between the public and the private sphere" (149). As a result, a woman can only become a "universal worker" by becoming "like a man," often relying on other women to take care of domestic tasks. Even so, she may still face the assumption that women are more inclined to put private above work-related priorities, and she may find her advancement at work impeded by phenomena familiarly known as the "glass ceiling" and the "mommy track."

The concept of a gendered institution can be usefully extended to the arenas of representation and decision making of the political opportunity structures of democratization. In the state structures of both authoritarian and democratic regimes, men's interests usually predominate. Feminist theory has explained this outcome by portraying the state as a single actor representing the interests of men (patriarchy), the dominant classes (capitalism), or some combination of the two.[31] Radical feminist theory has taken issue with the liberal assumption of the state as a neutral actor capable of mediating the demands of all citizens. Instead, it is seen as one of the primary mechanisms for ensuring women's continued subordination to men. State policy and national legal systems reinforce male dominance in the family and the workplace (MacKinnon 1989), and state bureaucracy is made up of, or at least controlled by, male actors (Ferguson 1984). In contrast, Marxist feminists claim that state welfare policies are, most fundamentally, efforts by states to ensure women's continued—and cheap—reproduction of workers, thus ensuring the success of capitalist economic development (McIntosh 1978). Socialist feminists argue that the welfare state as a whole is constructed in order to allow women to add the role of worker to that of mother/reproducer—or carry the so-called double burden—without altering men's roles (Lewis and Astrom 1992).

Changing trends in the empirical study of the state have had an impact on theoretical analysis. Particularly relevant has been the shift from conceiving of the state as a single actor to examining the capacity of different agen-

---

31. For comparative analyses of feminist theories of the state, see Rhode 1994; Baldwin 1997; Waylen 1998.

cies within the state to mediate political demands via distinct processes and policies (Evans, Rueschemeyer, and Skocpol 1985; Franzway, Court, and Connell 1989). For example, studies that focus on the impact of particular welfare policies on women have found that, far from ensuring women's subordination, welfare support has increased some women's life options (Borchorst 1994). Historical research has also revealed that women have been crucial participants in the development of welfare policies (Mink 1990; Sarvasy 1992; Skocpol 1992). These actually existing policies present a challenge to theories based on assumptions that the state represents or reproduces the unitary interests of (and opposition between) men and women, capital and labor.

Instructed by such research, postmodern feminist analysts see the state, instead of as a monolithic actor, as a "collection of practices and discourses" that are historically and contextually constructed and defined—and reconstructed and redefined. As a result, "what intentionality there is [in state practices] comes from the success with which various groupings are able to articulate their interests and hegemonize their claims" (Pringle and Watson 1992, 63). Such a perspective, which focuses particularly on gender, reveals that there is a "dynamic relationship between gender and the state" where state practices and gender relations are mutually constituting (64).[32]

Thus states are not in some fundamental, essential sense male dominated or "patriarchal." More accurately, "the state is *historically* patriarchal, patriarchal as a matter of concrete social practices" (Connell 1994, 163). Moreover, the state "represents *both* class and patriarchal interests," the upholding of which can lead to certain contradictions that may further gender-based demands (S. Alvarez 1990, 30–31). For example, the authoritarian Brazilian state, by simultaneously improving middle-class women's education (but not their employment opportunities) and depriving working-class and poor women of the resources needed for their families, provided the conditions in which feminist and "feminine" movements could spread across the country (1990, chap. 2). Other authoritarian governments, by closing down traditional channels of political representation that had been dominated by men and promoting traditional gender and class ideology, have often unwittingly opened up space for women's protests.

In the transition to democracy, many states have provided institutionalized spaces for women's issues that also reflect gender relations. In her work on national women's agencies, Anne Marie Goetz compares women

32. As with other postmodern claims, these present the challenge of avoiding an exclusive focus on the discursively given microlevels of power relations to the neglect of the material structures of oppression and dominance.

entering into institutions to new players entering a game: "When new participants—women, for example—participate in institutions, the rules of the game may be stacked against them, structured around the physical and social needs and capabilities and the political interests of those who designed them in the first place" (1995, 5). To give a striking example of rule-based discrimination, the position of state women's agencies often reflects the pattern of feminine subordination, remaining peripheral within the larger state organization of which they are a part (Franzway, Court, and Connell 1989, 31). Nevertheless, these agencies have often facilitated—as well as sometimes complicated—women's organizing in civil society (S. Alvarez 1990; Lind 1992; Chuchryk 1994; Stetson and Mazur 1995).

Not only the state but political parties as well are gendered institutions that have contributed to women's demobilization in the transition because the increasingly important parties, like states, often reflect gender relations in ways that result in women's marginalization. Again, as with state structures, this reflection is not automatic; it depends on parties' historically constituted practices. For example, in most cases the requirements of leadership positions in parties and elected bodies are well known for their discriminatory aspects, demanding a devotion to political life that few women can offer, or be seen as offering, because of their association with domestic responsibilities.

Another relatively unexamined but particularly problematic gendered structure within many political parties is the party women's bureau or department. Although women may participate in party life through other channels, the women's bureau is a mechanism set up to facilitate their incorporation into party life as women. The weakness of the women's bureau is well known, yet it remains understudied. It is often briefly mentioned[33] or discussed in very general terms: "The parties' distrust of women's organizations, and their reluctance to give them any real measure of autonomy, are probably not inspired by deliberate sex discrimination. They are simply particular instances of a general tendency to prevent the development within the party of more or less autonomous groups which might lead to rivalry and division" (Duverger 1955, 109).

But while other groups might suffer from a lack of autonomy stemming from their incorporation into party life, no group receives fewer benefits in return for their participation than women. Marginalization through women's

---

33. Writing about Venezuela, Coppedge (1994, 112) notes that the women's departments are among those that have never been "important vote brokers owing to their small size and lack of disciplined organization." Looking at the development of Costa Rican parties, Deborah J. Yashar (1995, 84) mentions that "the women's section, akin to a women's auxiliary . . . had local representatives at the cantonal level, but was not a very powerful group."

bureaus in the early formation of political parties, often accompanied by a decline in women's autonomous organizing, has been noted in Peru (Chaney 1971), Chile (Gaviola Artigas et al. 1986; Kirkwood 1986; Muñoz Dálbora 1987), and other countries, both in Latin America (S. Alvarez 1986) and outside of it (Nelson and Chowdhury 1994). In contrast, the women's suffrage movement in Brazil "could not be relegated to 'women's sections' of competing parties" only because of the absence of coherent national parties in that country (Hahner 1990, xv).

The weakness of women's bureaus is not "inspired by deliberate sex discrimination." It is due to the incorporation of gender relations within party structures.[34] While other sectoral bureaus serve as channels for the representation of group interests, including the promotion of sectoral leadership, the women's bureau ends up reflecting women's traditional responsibility for the reproductive tasks of the private sphere. It houses the "housekeepers" of the public sphere who carry out the reproductive tasks of politics. "Keeping house" (hosting meetings, making coffee and copies, throwing fundraising parties, and running raffles) and "raising the children" (turning out the vote during elections) have been typical duties. As a result of their marginalization through the women's bureau, some women have demanded its dissolution (Erickson 1993; Simms 1993). Others have sought alternative forms of interest representation, such as those described below.

Those who have suggested changes in order to increase women's representation in party politics as democratization progresses have not focused on altering the ways in which the mechanisms of party politics can reflect gender relations. Instead, they have sought primarily to gain more seats for female candidates and more party offices for female members. Studies of countries, most with established democracies, offer summaries of the most and least "woman-friendly" designs of electoral systems and party structures (Lovenduski and Norris 1993; Rule and Zimmerman 1994). These studies conclude that the electoral system least likely to promote women is simple plurality/first-past-the-post voting, particularly in countries where there are a small number of representatives per district. Because of the dependence of electoral success on a single candidate, any bias against women will be reflected in discrimination against their candidacy. Proportional representation by party list, especially where there is a high number of representatives per district, is the system most favorable to women. Parties are more inclined to offer a diversity of choices on their lists, including women, if all their eggs are

---

34. As Chilean feminist Julieta Kirkwood (1986, 150) writes, "Because patriarchy is universal, it also affects political parties."

not carried by a single candidate.[35] High competition for elected positions and high rates of incumbency hurt women's chances for much the same reason. If the party system is comprised of several parties, there may be more room for those supporting women's advancement.[36] Parties themselves also restrain or encourage women. As mentioned in the first section, well-organized national parties are most successful in promoting women and their issues, given an egalitarian gender ideology and a significant lobbying effort on the part of women.[37]

The most effective solution to women's underrepresentation in both party hierarchies and elected bodies seems to be "positive discrimination," most often through the creation of a minimum quota for women's representation. Its purpose is to correct for the discrimination women have experienced within parties on the basis of their gender, and it may be implemented in recruitment, party directorship, placement in "winning positions" on party lists, and so forth. The potential for quota adoption is the basis of Pippa Norris's (1993) evaluation of the party structure most likely to promote women, and much of the positive assessment of party list/proportional representation electoral systems in electing women assumes the prior existence of quotas for the lists.

The most successful use of quotas in a newly democratized Latin American country is Argentina's 1991 quota law, which specifies that 30 percent of all candidates on party lists for the lower chamber of congress be women and that they be placed in electable positions. With its implementation in 1993, women's representation in the lower chamber jumped from 5 percent to 21 percent, reaching 28 percent in the 1995 elections (Jones 1996). Quota laws have also been passed in Bolivia, Brazil, Costa Rica, the Dominican Republic, Ecuador, Panama, Peru, and Venezuela (Htun 1998, 15).[38]

---

35. Wilma Rule (1994a, 691) notes that women are more likely to be elected in multimember districts even with first-past-the-post voting; this is also attributable to the increased number of candidates.

36. Rule (1994b, esp. table 2.3) also recommends steps to increase the effectiveness of smaller parties, which may offer more access to women: a low threshold for election of party representatives, easy formation of new parties, and voting formulas that reward small parties. However, Richard E. Matland and Michelle M. Taylor's (1997) study of Costa Rica argues for larger parties, which are more likely to make room for women on their lists because they have higher numbers of representatives per district.

37. In considering what form of party might most benefit women in consolidated democracies, Philippe C. Schmitter (1998) echoes this conclusion. While he does not make the last two crucial caveats, he does point in a footnote to the unwillingness of "historical" parties (with more traditional gender ideologies) to include women. Because the return of such parties in the transition to democracy is a common occurrence, the issue of ideology is crucial.

38. The effectiveness of quotas is further discussed in Chapter 7.

The preceding methods have proved effective means for increasing women's formal political participation, but they do not address the gendered dynamics of party politics. Consequently, most of these criteria for increasing women's participation could be applied to any excluded group. Thus the criteria, however valuable in themselves, do not address women's exclusion explicitly. However, gender analysis is implicit throughout the studies on which they are based. Beate Hoecker (1994, 75) mentions how in Germany the prerequisites for nomination for the Bundestag are "geared largely to the male political biography." Miriam Feldblum and Kay Lawson (1994, 86) note that women's greater presence in local, as opposed to national, elected bodies in France is partly due to women's expecting "to carry out traditional domestic roles while joining the workforce in ever greater numbers," an expectation that can be accomplished more easily while holding local office because it does not require leaving home for long periods of time. Similarly, Joni Lovenduski (1993, 12–13) notes that the political requirement for membership in the Swedish legislature, local elected office, has helped Swedish women gain the largest percentage of parliamentary seats in the liberal democratic world, thanks to their significant presence in local politics. Finally, Mark Jones warns that "where political parties continue to be dominated by men . . . there will be a strong tendency for the implementation of the [quota] law to be minimalist" (1996, 90). Ultimately, the success of any measure for improving women's participation in party-based decision making depends on the extent to which the embeddedness of gender relations in party politics is confronted.

Besides the lack of explicit gender analysis, another problem with most of the scholarship on women and party politics is that it focuses exclusively on promoting women's leadership. It does not question the assumption that women's leadership will automatically lead to the representation of women's interests. While "mirror" representation and critical mass arguments in favor of promoting women have some merit,[39] studies show that a further element is necessary to ensure that women's concerns are raised: the organized pressure of women outside as well as inside of political institutions. Lovenduski and Norris's (1993) volume comparing women's experiences in party politics in developed countries shows that the pressure exerted by female activists inside and outside of parties is a crucial factor both in assuring women's party leadership and in incorporating women's issues into party platforms.[40] Even

39. Mirror representation is the concept that elected bodies should reflect the makeup of the electorate in equal proportion; critical mass arguments hold that it takes a critical mass of underrepresented actors to achieve their effective representation in political bodies.
40. One of the most successful examples is Sweden, where the united efforts of women

the women's bureaus of parties have worked in women's favor when responding to a women's movement in civil society.[41] Studies of state agencies for women also reveal the importance of women's activism from outside of the state both in establishing such agencies and in ensuring their effectiveness (Stetson and Mazur 1995). Research on Latin American countries confirms the importance of women's organized pressure for their improved political representation (Jones 1996; Matland and Taylor 1997; Htun 1998) as well as their increased access to the state (S. Alvarez 1990; Chuchryk 1994; Waylen 1996b).

Despite the crucial importance of women's collective pressure in promoting their leadership and interests through political institutions, the process of women's organizing is often slighted in research, which focuses on tracking its more easily measurable results. But the results cannot be fully evaluated, sustained, or propagated if the process itself is not examined. Such an examination requires analysis of women's organizing around their shared and differing interests.

Women's Gender Interests and Organizations

Women are far from passive in their response to gendered opportunities, as is shown by the rich history of women's organizing in Latin America, especially over the last few decades.[42] This history is notable for the diversity of its actors, including autonomous feminists and party leaders, workers and peasants, and Afro-Latin and indigenous women. Such diversity points to two central and interrelated aspects of any analysis of Latin American women's collective action: women do not have a single set of shared interests, nor do they use one model of organization to address them. Gender is crosscut by

---

within parties and in organized interest groups exerted sufficient pressure to put gender equality issues on party platforms and increase the numbers of women candidates and officer holders (Sainsbury 1993).

41. This has been the case in certain developed countries—see Appleton and Mazur 1993; Guadagnini 1993; Kolinsky 1993; Norris and Lovenduski 1993.

42. The following represents a sample of works on the issue. For historical perspectives, see Macías 1982; Gaviola Artigas et al. 1986; Hahner 1980, 1990; Stoner 1991; Miller 1991; Luna and Villarreal 1994; Lavrin 1995; Smith and Padula 1996. For more contemporary analyses see Chaney 1979; Andreas 1985; S. Alvarez 1990; Jelin 1990; Saporta Sternbach et al. 1992; Fisher 1993; Radcliffe and Westwood 1993; Jaquette 1994a; Léon 1994; M. Randall 1994; Basu 1995; Dandavati 1996; Waylen 1996b; Smith and Padula 1996; Leitinger 1997; Stephen 1997; S. Alvarez 1998; Jaquette and Wolchik 1998; Craske 1999.

other social characteristics, such as class and race, and all are mediated by particular political processes. Thus differently situated women have very different experiences of the intensity or centrality of gender relations in their lives. As a result, women's organizations and movements address a wide range of interests and develop a wide variety of structures. While these differences in aims and methods often translate into separate struggles, women have also built alliances around particular issues.

Women's Gender Interests

Although gender is one of the primary categories of social difference and hierarchy, it is not the only one. Class, race, ethnicity, religion, sexuality, age, and disability are also relations of power inequality. Since all women take part in social relations in addition to gender, no one set of interests applies to all women at all times. All women do have "gender interests," that is, "those that women (or men, for that matter) may develop by virtue of their social positioning through gender attributes" (Molyneux 1985, 240). But because women have such a wide range of social positioning, the gender interests of differently situated women may conflict directly. The degree of conflict depends not only on structurally given positions but also on how these positions have been manifest in different contexts.

As a central example among Latin American women, the interest of middle-class professional women in hiring cheap domestic labor so that they are able to balance the demands of career and home life conflicts directly with the interest of the working-class or poor women hired as housekeepers to make a livable wage with sufficient benefits.[43] While this illustration is explicitly based in class differences among women, it also implicitly illustrates other aspects of interest formation, such as the impact on women's personal and political lives of their challenge to gender norms in joining the workforce. Because of such differences, women's organizing cannot be expected to be geared to an immutable set of shared gender interests in spite of the widespread nature of women's subordination on the basis of their gender (Razavi and Miller 1995).

Class is, in fact, the basis of some of the starkest differences among Latin American women. With a poverty rate of over 35 percent, the region has one of the worst income distributions of the world: the income share of the richest 20 percent of the population is more than fifteen times the share of the poorest 20 percent in many countries (Todaro 1994, 147; UNDP 1995,

---

43. On the situation of domestic workers in Latin America (and the Caribbean), see Chaney and García Castro 1989.

26). Poverty has a particularly harsh impact on women because of their pre-dominant employment in the low-paying service sector (73 percent) and the fact that they earn three-fourths of the salaries men earn for comparable work, coupled with their general responsibility for dependent children (Valdéz and Gomáriz 1995, 79, 65). In most countries more than 10 percent of indigent nuclear families are headed by a woman, with rates rising if extended families are taken into account (34). Not surprisingly, women's organizing has been greatly shaped by their class position.

To theorize about how Latin American women's political activity has been informed by their class differences, Maxine Molyneux (1985) proposed the dichotomy of "practical" and "strategic" gender interests. In her study of Nicaraguan women's organizing, she found that poor and working-class women were generally mobilized around practical gender interests: such basic needs as health care, running water, and affordable food and shelter for themselves and their families. Advancing these interests did not directly challenge women's traditional association with the private sphere of domestic duties or the gender subordination usually accompanying it. In contrast, middle-class women, whose practical needs had been met, could "afford" to organize around strategic gender interests, such as the right to birth control and child care, and an end to violence against women. Acting on their interests did directly challenge gender subordination, specifically as it was manifest in the gendered division of labor associating women with domestic duties.

The practical/strategic dichotomy has been widely accepted as a way to categorize Latin American women's organizing and has also been applied in research and policy making on gender and development (Moser 1993). But as studies of such organizing, and the organizing itself, have evolved, this dichotomy has been subject to some criticism (Lind 1992; Radcliffe and Westwood 1993; Wieringa 1994; Hays-Mitchell 1995; Waylen 1996b; Craske 1999). The use of the terms *practical* and *strategic* has been criticized for obscuring the fact that poor women might be strategic in seeking to fulfill practical interests, and that these interests themselves might change through the process of demand making (Jaquette 1994a, 226). The distinction also obscures the fact that middle- or upper-class women's strategic interests might be practical to them—that is, that they constitute the most immediate demands they need met in order to thrive. Moreover, issues such as control over fertility, access to childcare, and ending domestic violence are of practical significance for women of all classes (Craske 1993, 132). The distinction cannot account for the presence of both types of interests in women's organizing or admit the challenge to gender subordination—at some level—present in all women's organizing (Stephen 1997, 272). Finally, the distinction ignores the increasing interaction between women of different classes and the resulting cross-pollination of movement thought and action (Saporta Sternbach et al. 1992; Jaquette 1994a; Waylen 1996b). Such cross-pollination is not unidirectional. There is no clear, linear progression from practical to strategic interests on the part of poor women under the influence of middle-class feminists.

Fundamentally, the dichotomy of strategic and practical gender interests stumbles over the danger inherent in fixing categories of interests on social or economic class position, which assumes an objective and transhistorical relationship between socioeconomic position, political consciousness, and action. This practice ignores the political processes, including the changing nature of political opportunities as well as women's own demand making, by which some elements come to be defined as the interests of certain women at certain times. Women's own actions have shown their interests to be far from fixed.[44] As Molyneux herself has argued in response to the way in which her context-specific analysis of Nicaraguan women's organizing has been adopted as a static framework for understanding women's interests, "Claims about women's objective interests need to be framed within specific historical contexts since processes of interest formation and articulation are clearly subject to cultural, historical and political variation and cannot be known in advance" (1998, 233). The importance of context becomes clear when we examine the changing interests of historically situated women, such as those who have organized in this century in Latin America.

One clear thread runs through the development of women's gender interests in the history of Latin American women's organizing: the centrality of motherhood—and more generally, women's association with private life—to their political practice. This centrality stems from the historical development of gender relations in Latin America.[45] Some have traced Latin American women's central identification with family life to the inheritance of colonial times, when Spanish colonizers would start new families in the colonies, only to abandon them when they returned to Spain or maintain them on the side when a more "suitable" Spanish wife arrived in the New World. Indigenous

44. For example, Alvarez (1990, 112–14) describes how poor women's groups in Brazil added "strategic" interests to their "practical" demands, influenced by feminist organizations and their own political practice. Some went on to assert "the most radical gender-specific issues" at the first Sao Paulo Women's Congress in 1979. Lynn Stephen's work on grassroots women (1997) focuses on the transformation of women's interests through their collective organizing.

45. For the purposes of my discussion, I am giving a very general overview, which should not be taken as capturing the specific nuances of gender relations within the different historical and cultural contexts of the Latin American region, such as those of indigenous and Afro-Latin communities.

and *mestiza* (mixed race) women were thus left to fend for their children alone, and sons were brought up with the model of the absent (or shared) father—a model many went on to follow in adulthood (UN 1992). This dynamic has led to a long history of de facto female-headed households. Yet the cultural precepts of male dominance in the family continue:

> In the Latin American cultural tradition, the subordination of women is anchored to the strongly cohesive family group that constitutes the base of the whole system of social relations. The patriarchal family is seen as the natural unit around which daily life revolves. . . . Women are in charge of the domestic tasks associated with the private sphere of reproduction and maintenance of the family; men are responsible for tasks related to the public sphere of social and political life. (Jelin 1990, 2)

The patriarchal family is often said to be reinforced by (if not based on) the norms of Catholicism, the historically dominant Latin American religion. In a widely cited work, Evelyn Stevens (1973) relies on the concept of *marianismo* (the contrary of *machismo,* or men's cultural dominance over women) to explain the ideology of Catholic womanhood. She describes *marianismo* as a "cult of female spiritual superiority" that views women as "semi-divine, morally superior to and spiritually stronger than men" (91). María Elena Valenzuela (1987) discusses how this idealization purports to offer women spiritual salvation in exchange for this-world subordination. The Latin American woman is supposed to be the perfect mother, taking care of myriad household duties, rearing her children, and looking after her male partner— or accepting his absence with long-suffering patience.

However, the concept of *marianismo,* like its complement *machismo,* is very problematic.[46] Although Catholic norms have an undeniable influence on Latin American gender relations—as, it might be noted, they have on those of many countries in Europe as well as particular communities in the United States—they cannot be captured in a static category. For one thing, the power of the church varies from country to country in the region. For another, the history of women's activism in Latin America, as well as the conditions that have given rise to it, are a clear indication that women do not stoically endure this-world subordination in exchange for next-world salvation. Nor, it hardly needs saying, are they universally treated as "semi-divine." The record on domestic violence alone shows this starkly: despite

---

46. Thanks to Sonia Alvarez and Marysa Navarro for useful discussion on this point.

estimates as high as one in five women suffering from "conjugal violence," until quite recently only two countries in the region penalized intrafamilial battery (Valdéz and Gomáriz 1995, 191–92). Furthermore, Tracy Ehlers (1991) suggests that those women whose attitudes seem to be influenced by the concept of *marianismo* may, in fact, have no alternative but to accept their partners' irresponsible behavior because they have limited access to economic resources.

Without returning to static analyses of gender relations, it is still possible to analyze how deeply embedded the association with private life and exclusion from public affairs has been for women in Latin America. Indeed, it is reflected in the very language, as is illustrated by the definition of the phrase *mujer pública*. Its literal translation is "public woman," but it means "prostitute" in Latin American Spanish. Public women are not those who take part in civic life, but those who openly sell the use of their private bodies.

Feminist historians have found that Latin American women's private responsibilities were both motivation and justification for their organizing to achieve social and political democracy (Hollander 1977; Hahner 1980; Miller 1991; Stoner 1991). As in Europe and the United States, in Latin America middle- and upper-class women's struggles for suffrage, civil rights, and societal reform were premised on bringing feminine perspectives to the masculine sphere of politics. Although her work has focused on the history of French feminism, Karen Offen's classification of "relational feminists," those who "emphasized women's rights as women (defined principally by their childbearing and/or nurturing capacities) in relation to men" applies to these Latin American activists. That is, they challenged gender *hierarchy,* not gender *difference* (1988, 136).

Relational feminists demanded that as mothers, workers, and citizens women be made socially, economically, and legally equal to men; but they rarely questioned the difference between women's and men's social roles. They "insisted on *women's* distinctive contributions in these roles to the broader society" and made claims based on those contributions (Offen 1988, 136). This did not prevent them from making radical demands within their own contexts. They took on such issues as suffrage, prostitution, and sex education, and they asserted a woman's right to control her own children and property. But they made these demands in accordance with their view that women had a "different mission" from men (Miller 1991, 74).

Latin American women explicitly distanced themselves from English and U.S. "individualist" feminism, which is based on the assumption that women and men are equal individuals and as such should receive the same rights and benefits regardless of gender. The emergence of this strand of feminism, which surfaced in the United States and England in the early 1900s, was dependent on a growing group of economically self-sufficient single women (Offen 1988, 143). Early Latin American feminists, however, faced a different economic climate, as well as a cultural milieu heavily influenced by the traditional gender relations promoted by the Catholic Church. As a result, Brazilian and Chilean feminists presented their claims for women's suffrage as differing from "English style" suffrage. They stressed woman's role as man's ally, not his competitor (Gaviola Artigas et al. 1986, 27; Hahner 1990, 153). They were not alone: "Cuban women were loath to portray themselves as similar to U.S. suffragists; rather, like elsewhere in the region, feminists stressed their maternal values, their cooperation with men, and their concerns with Cuba's moral and social welfare" (Ali 1995, 7). This need for cultural differentiation also extended to activists' debates over whether even to identify themselves as "feminists."

The "relations" of early relational feminists extended beyond the domestic sphere. They frequently allied themselves with socialist or other progressive movements working for more equitable class relations in the early part of the twentieth century, and some supported the guerrilla movements inspired by the Cuban revolution in the 1960s and 70s. However, these movements were not especially responsive to women's demands. As a result, some activists turned to the transnational arena, hoping to influence recalcitrant governments from above (Miller 1991, chap. 4). This arena has continued to be a key source of support in the most recent decades, particularly as it has developed through the UN world women's conferences during the Decade on Women (Mexico City, 1975; Copenhagen, 1980; Nairobi, 1985) and afterward (Beijing, 1995).

In struggles against authoritarianism in the post–World War II decades, three types of women's organizations emerged: human rights, urban poor, and feminist. Rapid urbanization and increasing poverty led poor and working-class women to interact with governmental agents and agencies in order to secure the goods and services necessary for family survival. The rise of authoritarian governments in the 1960s and 1970s spurred other types of women's organizing. In the best known of the movements, working- and middle-class women participated in human rights groups that protested the disappearance of their children and partners (Feijoó and Nari 1994; Waylen 1994). By entering into politics on the basis of their domestic duties, those women who brought mothers' and housewives' perspectives to political action were seen as redefining politics and the concept of the political actor. In their "militant motherhood" (S. Alvarez 1990) women challenged even the most authoritarian of governments, simultaneously forming the image and the backbone of opposition movements.[47] Considered in historical perspective, this transformation is not a surprise, but is another manifestation of the impact private claims can have on public actors. However, the more overweening and idealized assertions of the virtues of the private sphere— women's claim to be above politics, or to be able to purify it—have worked against them when they try to engage in democratic politics (Kirkwood 1986; Feijoó and Nari 1994).

The other strand of women's organizing that emerged during the repressive periods was the reemergence of feminist groups among middle- and upper-class women. In part inspired by ideas brought home by former exiles in Europe and the United States, feminist protests against dictatorship critiqued the patriarchal underpinning of authoritarian politics. Their experiences in left-wing opposition movements that often subordinated women also confirmed that patriarchy was deeply embedded in society. Feminists served as focal points for women's oppositional activity, helping to unite women in political action to change the structures of both private and public arenas of inequality (Chuchryk 1994; Waylen 1996b). However, because they delivered a clearer challenge to gender difference as well as to gender hierarchy, a challenge that continues to be associated with the imposition of "foreign" ideas about appropriate gender relations (Basu 1995b, 6), these feminist groups in Latin America tended to have a small base of support.

With the transition to democracy, groups formed under the previous regimes have been joined by women organizing around such issues as race, sexuality, health, and domestic violence, as well as to promote women's leadership in politics and other arenas of public participation such as unions. Cross-fertilization among organizations has led to "a new kind of feminist practice" by women from the lower classes, which combines the interests of women with and without children, confronting both political and economic repression, empowering women from all classes, and politicizing the issues of everyday life (Jaquette 1994a, 6; S. Alvarez 1990, chap. 10). In their struggles for equity, even elite women often rely on an identification with home and family to justify their emergence into public life (Chaney 1979; Valenzuela 1987).[48] Women's continuing association with motherhood and private life in their organizing has led to the call for a "rupture with the traditional form of

47. There is a considerable literature on this dynamic. See M. Navarro 1989; S. Alvarez 1990; Jelin 1990; Radcliffe and Westwood 1993; Jaquette 1994a; Waylen 1994.

48. As Chaney (1979, 52) writes: "The most successful women carefully maintained the boundaries set by woman's universal mothering role and legitimized their activities as forming natural extensions of it."

constructing knowledge for feminist thinkers, and their praxis," in order to acknowledge the power of this association that links historical and current activism (Huggins Castañeda 1992, 17). This call serves as a reminder to those studying women's activism that individualist feminism is not the only possible type:

> In order to fully comprehend the historical range and possibilities of feminism, we must locate the origins and growth of these ideas within a variety of cultural traditions, bearing in mind that feminism both as a movement and ideology for sociopolitical change is based on a critical analysis of male privilege and women's subordination within any given society. . . . Focusing on [individualist feminism] alone blinds us to the range of effective arguments used to combat male privilege in the Western world during the past few centuries, and even to arguments put forth today by women and men in economically less-privileged countries, where women's aspirations to self-sovereignty are often subordinated to pressing short-term political and socioeconomic necessities. (Offen 1988, 138, 151)

Women's Organizations

Because women's gender interests have varied considerably over time, no single type of organizing has been used to express them. Women's organizations also show the influence of their gendered political opportunities. In particular, their innovations attest to women's frequent exclusion from formal politics. Analysis of the effectiveness of such innovations in the context of Latin American democratization is taken up in Chapter 7. Here such key organizational considerations as internal structure, external linkage, membership, and coalition building are briefly delineated.

Organizational form has been a subject of much experimentation among women's groups. Often reacting to their exclusion from, or marginalization within, the highly centralized, hierarchical, and formalized institutions of political representation, women have sought to build loosely knit, decentralized, and highly participatory structures. These organizations seek to foster a more inclusive environment where women can discover and act upon their own needs and desires. Their less rigid nature has been thought to make them more resilient during times of political upheaval (Jaquette 1994a). Frequently, however, the absence of a clear distribution of responsibilities has led to co-optation from without or domination from within, leading to group dissolution (Siriani 1993; Phillips 1991).

Degree of linkage to formal institutions and other organizations is another issue of crucial importance. Women's organizations and movements in Latin America advocate everything from complete independence from the state and organizations in civil and political society to complete integration within them (S. Alvarez 1990; Jaquette 1994a). Internal debates among participants rage over the benefits and drawbacks of collaboration with political parties, state offices, community associations, funding organizations, the church, and other women's groups, whether local or international. Forging connections with other organizations is often a matter of trading independence for access or giving up control over agenda setting and actions to order to gain increased support, whether political, social, or economic.

Policies regarding who may belong to an organization often touch on issues of linkage as well as on socioeconomic difference. Grassroots groups of poor and working-class women generally reject the idea of having well-connected elite leaders, though they often rely on advisors from parties or feminist groups who help to channel resources their way (Carrillo 1990). Latin American feminist groups focused particularly on women's issues have been predominantly middle-class, though as noted above, contact with low-income women's organizations has been increasing. Women of all classes have debated the advisability of membership in groups outside of their own, for fear of co-optation. Often individual women will choose to do "double militancy" in order to bridge the gap between groups. The term originally indicated having a role in both feminist and partisan organizations to ensure the representation of feminist issues in party politics and vice versa. Recently it has been extended to indicate participation in both feminist and grassroots organizations (Saporta Sternbach et al. 1992).

Because of women's varied gender interests and forms of organization, ongoing, widespread, and coordinated collective action is not likely, nor are permanent overarching associations practical. Reflecting on the Brazilian case, Sonia E. Alvarez has suggested instead that "a variety of political action arenas, loosely coordinated by conjunctural coalitions, may prove to be the best way to advance the multiple goals of socially, politically, and ideologically heterogeneous movements" (1990, 237). In fact, some sort of "conjunctural coalition," whether formally or informally aggregated, can be seen undergirding many of the successful moments of Latin American women's mobilization during both dictatorship and democracy (S. Alvarez 1990, 1998; Chuchryk 1994).

In summary, theorizing about the influence of gender on the transition to democracy reveals that the political opportunities of different regime phases incorporate gender relations, thus conditioning women's mobilization. As a central example, the dominance of party politics at the moment of transition not only inhibits the inclusion of former opposition movements into an active civil society, but it also can lead to the entrenchment of an institution that may structurally impede women's participation, depending on the way in which gender is incorporated into party organization. This is not to say that women can never take advantage of political party representation, which would contradict the evidence from many consolidated democracies. But the sequencing of transition politics is crucial. The possibility of women's external as well as internal mobilization to pressure parties to promote women's interests and leadership may be thwarted by the demobilizing dynamics of democratization and gender-biased party structures. Thus the decisions made by those guiding the transition, as well as women's responses to them, are crucial in determining the nature of women's participation.

However, democratization does not start or end with the transition phase. In both the preceding decline of authoritarianism and the ensuing consolidation of democracy, gendered institutions and discourses also have an impact on women's organizing. If democracy is lasting, women's innovations in organizational form, responding to their gendered opportunities and mediated by their own political learning, can result in the promotion of a wide range of women's interests.

The following chapters use the theoretical framework developed above to analyze the history of women's organizing in Venezuela. From its beginnings in the mid-1930s, a movement emerged that has evolved through two transitions to democracy, a dictatorship, a period of democratic consolidation, and most recently, a crisis in its democracy. Its trajectory can only be understood in the context of its political opportunities, both general and gendered. Often this context includes structurally embedded obstacles to women's political participation. Nevertheless, over the past six decades women's rights advocates and activists have sought to deepen democracy through an alternative set of practices and institutions.

THE PARADOXICAL RISE AND
FALL OF THE WOMEN'S
MOVEMENT IN THE FIRST
TRANSITION TO DEMOCRACY
(1936–1948)

Notwithstanding its absence from accounts of Venezuelan politics and Latin American women's history, women's organizing formed a distinct part of the explosion of civic activity following the death of the dictator General Juan Vicente Gómez in December 1935.[1] In the subsequent period of liberalized authoritarianism under General Eleazar López Contreras and General Isais Medina Angarita (1936–45), a decade-long women's movement prospered. It drew predominantly from the first and second generations of middle- and upper-class educated and professional women.

Started by the pioneers who founded the first women's rights association in October 1935, the movement began to take shape a mere two weeks after Gómez's death, when women published an open letter to president-elect López Contreras outlining their demands on the new government. These efforts grew rapidly as women's civic, feminist, charitable, and cultural organizations sprang up across the country. In 1940 several hundred women came together at a national women's conference to consolidate their positions on issues ranging from sex education to suffrage. In the next five years women mounted national campaigns involving thousands of women to gain

1. Beyond a brief mention of the organizing in Martz (1966), Venezuelan political history ignores women's activity in this period. The most comprehensive history of Latin American women, Francesca Miller (1991), also overlooks this activism. For example, Miller claims that in Venezuela, "postwar democratic openings supported broad reform movements within which women as well as men expanded their political rights" (142). However, the movement for women's suffrage movement began before and continued throughout the war, as shown below. No other historical reviews of women's organizing in Latin America mention the Venezuelan case (see Ali 1995).

equal rights in the home and the polity. But following the October 1945 coup that began the *trienio,* the three-year-long experiment with democratic politics, the women's movement disappeared. Women's organizing would resurface only when the next dictatorship began, and then in a quite different form.

Why did women's organizing thrive during the liberalization of authoritarianism, only to decline with the first glimmer of democratic politics? Answering this question not only sheds light on the paradoxical experience of women in this period but also foreshadows what was to come with the more durable democratic transition of the late 1950s. While some political opportunities of liberalized authoritarianism (or, later, even dictatorship) permitted the growth of women's mobilization on their own behalf, the change in opportunities with the brief transition to democracy blocked women's continuing efforts. Throughout, women's organizing was conditioned not only by the general structure of political opportunities of each regime but also by their particular manifestations of gendered political institutions and discourses.

The principal political institution conditioning social mobilization in the period following Gómez's death (1936–45) was the state, which remained in the hands of conservatives. Gómez's successor, his minister of war, López Contreras, ruled over a congress comprised of former supporters of the dictator. He allowed only sporadic independent political organizing. Parties began to form, seeking mutual support but remaining largely clandestine. They grew in strength when López Contreras's successor, Medina Angarita, liberalized politics under the influence of the Allies during World War II and legalized party formation.

The gendered institutions of this political opportunity structure included the state, made up exclusively of male actors, and political parties. While beginning to reach out to women, these two institutions remained largely male-led. In political discourse women were primarily associated with private life, though their presence was noted in some arenas of public interaction. The congress and the president proposed little legislation directed primarily at women but revised the Labor Law to provide for limited maternity leave and child care. These provisions were not often implemented. The new political parties promised women political and civil equality; however, party weakness meant these promises could not be kept easily. Finally, a regional women's suffrage movement contributed to raising consciousness about women's political rights.

Women's response to their opportunities was mediated by their varied gender interests and forms of organization. Mainly middle- and upper-class women organized, and not surprisingly, the policies they advocated reflected their particular perspectives. By tying women's activism firmly to their roles as actual or potential mothers, they attempted to challenge the gender hierarchy that supported male dominance in the family and the polity without challenging gender difference or class hierarchy. Their acceptance of both would continue to influence the development of women's organizing.

Not subject to the sporadic restrictions on overt political organizing, women's organizations flourished. As liberalization progressed, so did the development of women's coalitions to press for what they called their "civil" rights, principally their rights within the family, and their political rights to vote and to hold office. These coalitions allowed women to come together around a particular issue at a particular moment despite their different political orientations. Such "conjunctural" coalition building would prove to be a key advance in organizational strategy in the decades to come. But the coalitions did not prove to be wholly successful during this period, and women's legal gains remained limited.

With the transition to the democratic experiment of the *trienio* (1945–48), the political opportunities changed, though not in women's favor. The social democratic party Democratic Action (Acción Democrática or AD) took power through a reformist military coup, though its leaders were determined to found a political democracy. Its dominance of political organizing resulted in the incorporation of many social sectors even as it alienated important elites. However, women were only incompletely included in the primary channel of democratic representation. Because their founders assumed that men would be the primary participants, parties such as AD privileged men's participation through the gendered structures of leadership and membership, marginalizing women's participation.

This chapter begins with a history of women's political participation up to 1936 and a description of the socioeconomic position of women between 1936 and 1950. It then shows how the development of the interests, organizations, and campaigns of the women's movement under liberalized authoritarianism depended on the regime's general and gendered political opportunities, as well as on the characteristics of the women themselves. The second half of the chapter explains how the shift in opportunities with the transition to the *trienio* brought to the fore the gendered institution of party politics, which put an end to women's independent organizing. However, the lessons of the period would not be lost but would inform women's future activism.

Women's Participation and Status Before 1936

The beginning of the twentieth century found Venezuela a country still rent by the bloodshed of the civil wars that followed independence from Spain in 1821. Political control was dominated by *caudillos* (strongmen), who held particular regions under their sway. The centralization of political power began with the *caudillo* Cipriano Castro, who marched down from the Andes into Caracas and proclaimed himself president in 1901. He was followed in 1908 by Juan Vicente Gómez, who continued to centralize power and to reap the benefits of the discovery of oil in the 1920s.

Gómez ruled as a dictator and neglected the needs of the general population. The first significant challenge to his rule came in 1928 from a group of radicalized students at the central university in Caracas, the Student Federation of Venezuela (Federación de Estudiantes de Venezuela or FEV). Known as the "Generation of '28," many of these student leaders would go on to form the first significant political parties following Gómez's death. But it was during the February 1928 "Students' Week," a series of events designed to raise money for a dormitory, that they first spoke out for political liberty. The leadership was incarcerated for its efforts. But it had struck a chord in the general populace, which held massive demonstrations to demand the release of the jailed students. Upon their release they joined with a reforming element of the military to stage a coup in April. However, its failure brought on increased repression and exile for many of the plotters.

Though not yet organized on their own behalf, women opposed the Gómez dictatorship as they would oppose the next dictator, who came to power in 1952 (see Chapter 3). Not yet acting as movement organizers, they supported the opposition by facilitating communication among male leaders, caring for male prisoners and their families, raising money, and distributing propaganda (*La Mala Vida* 1985). It was only when men were not available, often jailed or in exile, that women and girls organized demonstrations (CIS-FEM 1992, 216). Women were also active in organizing against Gómez from abroad. In 1928 Ana Esther Gouverneur, a social worker living in exile in New York, founded the Patriotic Society (Sociedad Pro-Patria) both to serve as a mutual aid society for exiles and to raise U.S. awareness about the dictatorship. The society routinely picketed the Venezuelan embassy, and it used the media to protest against the situation of political prisoners under Gómez (de Leonardi 1983, 388; La Mala Vida 1985).

Women's other role in the struggle against dictatorship was as a symbol of liberty. During the most open protest against the dictatorship, the 1928 "Students' Week," a student queen, Beatrice I, was elected. The events at which she was fêted were seized as opportunities for student activists to declare their political positions, and she was transformed into the "ethical, rebellious metaphor for the people's yearnings for freedom" (Lerner 1984, 32). This can be seen most clearly in the poem addressed to her at one ceremony by Pío Tamayo, who would go on to become a well-known poet. After telling her about his own lover, he continued:

Trembling in shadows I loved her in fear.
In my veins ran fears for her life.
And one day they stole her from me,
And one day they took her away . . .
. . . and the name of this lover is much
like your own:
She was called Liberty.
(quoted in Levine 1973, 20)

In addition to these nascent forms of political activism, many of the socioeconomic structures that would define Venezuela took shape under Gómez's rule. Venezuela became the world's largest exporter of petroleum by 1930. The exploitation of petroleum had a powerful effect on the country's economic and social organization. Agriculture was slighted for the development of the oil sector and its related industries, commerce, and services, causing a rural-to-urban migration that led to the majority of the population becoming urban by 1950. An urban middle class developed through employment in the expanding public sector and the oil companies.

From the turn of the century on, middle-class women began to enter professional life and higher education; many working-class women were already employed as domestics and some in small manufacturing. In 1911 the first and mainly female Teachers' Training College (Escuela Normal) opened, followed in 1912 by the Women's Trades College (Escuela de Artes y Oficios de Mujeres) and in 1913 by the predominantly female Nurses' College (Escuela de Enfermeras) (Ministerio Público 1990). The professions open to educated women reflected the gender relations of the time. Educating the next generation and taking care of the sick could be seen as an extension of women's mothering role and were thus considered acceptable tasks for women. In 1936 women constituted 2.3 percent of university students, most of them going on to become lawyers and journalists (de Leonardi 1983, 201).

With the increasing urbanization and employment generated by the oil industry, the development of urban commerce, and the growth of government bureaucracy came the further entry of women into the labor force and education. Although they still remained largely segregated by sex, women made up 18 percent of all workers by 1950, with the vast majority in the service sector (42 percent). Only 9 percent of all women called themselves "professionals" (OCEI 1961). Steadily advancing in higher education, university women increased their numbers from 35 in 1936 to 362 in 1946, making up 10 percent of all students (Ministerio de Educación 1936, 1946).

Women in the "female" professions, especially teachers, constituted the logical basis of the women's movement in Venezuela, since they were all over the country. They shared the new experience of the potentials and problems of public activity, which made them aware of their lack of rights and the need to fight for them (Chaney 1971; Gaviola Artigas et al. 1986; Hahner 1990; Miller 1991). But their organizing was conditioned by the particular political context in which it emerged.

The Political Opportunities of Liberalized Authoritarianism, 1936–1940

A political opportunity structure that somewhat favored women's organizing on their own behalf began with the death of Gómez in 1936. There was a general explosion of political and organizational activity in which many sectors began to form their own organizations, ranging from unions to women's groups. Significant among these were the fledgling leftist parties. The most prominent were the Republican Progressive Party (Partído Republicano Progresista or PRP), a prior incarnation of the Venezuelan Communist Party, and the Venezuelan Organization (Organización Venezolano, or ORVE), forerunner of Venezuela's most powerful party, Democratic Action. The state was headed by the new president, General Eleazar López Contreras, who alternated between toleration and repression of organizational activity, and a conservative congress, still full of *gomecistas* (supporters of Gómez).

To advance their demands for further political liberalization and improved labor relations, the parties made several attempts to band together. The first was the April Bloc (Bloque de Abril), which lasted until López Contreras cracked down following a general strike in mid-1936. Suffrage, already limited to local and congressional elections, was restricted to literate males over twenty-one years old, effectively excluding the great majority of potential voters (in a country with 50 percent women and 70 percent illiteracy).

The left-wing parties continued to cooperate, forming the National Democratic Party (Partido Democrático Nacional or PDN) in October 1936 to promote democratic political rights, social justice, and economic nationalism (Bergquist 1986, 231). These goals came together in the PDN's support of the December 1936 strike of the oil workers in Western Venezuela. This was the high-water mark of the period's protests, which "sounded the death knell for the legacy of Gómez and presaged a new era in Venezuelan history" according to Charles Bergquist (1986, 230). The coalition of political activists and oil workers, and the exposure of the alliance between the Venezuelan government and foreign oil companies (which reaped the majority of the oil profits, thanks to their control over extraction), raised political consciousness. The strike forced the oil companies to negotiate with their workers, pressured the government to consider social and economic concessions, and increased labor and political activity in the area. But López Contreras ended the strike in January 1937 and refused to legalize the PDN. Although a few of its adherents won congressional seats in the next elections, most of these victors were promptly jailed or exiled.

López Contreras's manipulation of political organizing made certain opposition leaders realize that their approach to winning power through electoral means would not work until they had a mass base of support. Thus party building became their top priority. It was carried out clandestinely by establishing party cells and affiliated occupational branches. Most of the branches were based on legally organized unions, beginning with the oil industry and spreading into construction, transportation, services, and agriculture. But by 1938 the former allies of the PDN had split over whether to organize along class lines. The PRP insisted that workers should remain the principal targets of organization, while ORVE championed a multiclass perspective.

Gendered Opportunities

Both the liberalized authoritarian state and nascent political parties reflected gender relations in structure and discourse. State policy mainly addressed women in their role as mothers. López Contreras's 1936 and 1938 National Plans called for improved maternal and infant health, and increased maternal education (Suarez Figueroa 1983, vol. 1). The July 1936 reform of the Labor Law did take women's new roles as workers into account, providing for a six-week pre- and postnatal maternity leave, onsite nurseries, and equal pay for equal work. However, while this law was "on paper . . . among the most progressive and comprehensive in Latin America" (Bergquist 1986, 229), it was rarely enforced. As a result, women's demands for Labor Law enforcement would become a central feature of their later organizing.

The new parties also accommodated women in their platforms, going beyond state policy to demand civil and political rights for women. Since its (clandestine) founding in 1931, the Communist Party had pronounced itself in favor of equal pay for equal work and paid maternity leave (Suarez Figueroa 1983, vol. 1), a goal it continued to uphold as the PRP (Magallanes 1973, 278–80). The offshoot National Democratic Bloc (Bloque Nacional Democrático) promoted the protection of pregnant workers as well as the improvement of women's legal, social, and political status (1973, 290). The short-lived National Republican Union (Unión Nacional Republicana), a middle-class party, also supported women's suffrage (1973, 266). Although there was nothing explicit regarding women in ORVE's first program,[2] the program it helped write for the PDN coalition in October 1936 included equal civil and political rights for women (Mijares 1980, 76) and equal pay for equal work (Magallanes 1973, 300).

Beyond holding positions in favor of women's rights, from the outset the most significant parties established some form of sectoral bureau for the incorporation of women. In 1936 the PRP had a women's secretariat *(secretaria femenina)*, and both ORVE and later PDN had a women's movement secretariat *(secretaria del movimiento femenino)* (Magallanes 1973). Those women who were interested in explicitly political activity generally joined parties through these sectoral organizations (de Leonardi 1983, 397; Herrera 1991).

The Expansion of Women's Organizing Under Liberalized Authoritarianism (1936–1940)

The eruption of women's mobilization came with the general social upheaval following Gómez's death. It was the first time women had organized independently:

> What happened in Venezuela was like a miracle, that which came to pass with . . . the pioneers of the women's movement, because here there hadn't been [organizational or ideological] preparation, because it hadn't been possible to work. There was clandestine work in political parties . . . but for the movement there was

2. This may have been due to ORVE's general reluctance to proclaim itself a political party with an explicit program for fear of persecution (Martz 1966, 30).

nothing. There were no examples . . . and so began our awakening. Without organizational or cultural background, nevertheless this group of women brought about an incredible movement, which hasn't been repeated in Venezuela. These women succeeded not only in bringing together the women of the capital but also in beginning a movement in the interior of the Republic.[3]

Capitalizing on the political opportunities made possible by the uneven liberalization under López Contreras, middle- and upper-class women organized in many groups that fought for women's civil and political rights other issues. Those women who joined the new parties cooperated with the women's groups, often holding membership in both and serving as conduits for women's issues within the parties. Women's organizing was conditioned not only by general opportunities—more freedom to associate, publish, protest, and lobby—but also their reflection of gender relations. Although parties experienced periodic repression, women's organizations, not seen as a political threat, were left to promote their own interests. But their lack of relevance to political institutions and the fact that few women held important positions in the parties would prevent them from achieving significant goals.

The internal development of the women's movement reflected the gender interests of their middle- and upper-class leaders. They differed in their approach to politics, but they all challenged male dominance while maintaining women's maternal role as the center of their activism.

Women's Gender Interests

In both their early organizations and later conjunctural coalitions, activists developed their gender interests by contesting gender hierarchy but largely accepting gender difference. Like many of the "relational feminists" of the period, they claimed their rights in the home and polity while maintaining their primary association with private life, especially motherhood.[4] They also maintained a certain amount of class privilege. Because mainly middle- and upper-class women led the movement, their perspectives clearly marked its strategies and goals, even when working-class and poor women were the object of their activities.

The establishment of an ideology that promoted the equality of women

3. Interview with Ana Senior, former member of the first women's group, the Women's Cultural Association (ACF, Agrupación Cultural Femenina).

4. See Chapter 1 for an analysis of the widespread nature of relational feminism in early Latin American women's movements.

and men without challenging the difference between men and women's social attributes was a constant theme in the movement. Activists debated the use of the term *feminism* because of its association with the suffrage movements in England and the United States, which both women and men in Venezuela perceived as mistakenly seeking to eliminate gender difference. In his defense of women's civil rights in a national newspaper, *Ahora*, on 22 May 1937, one male writer assured his readership that granting civil rights would not pervert Venezuelan womanhood: "We ought to make women's horizons broader without fear of English-style suffragists, the mythical Amazon warriors. Woman can enter fully into civil life, in dynamic modern life, without renouncing her exquisite femininity to do so." The initial priority that women activists gave to obtaining civil, not political rights was partly due to the movement's fear of association with these "mythical Amazons." Moreover, when women did identify themselves as feminists, they were careful to specify that their goal was not to "replace men" but to improve women's lot. This distinction was reinforced by activists' constant justification of their organizing as making women better mothers and improving the lives of their children. Whatever their method, these activists' tireless work on behalf of women's advancement qualifies them as feminists in the broad sense of the term.[5]

Like many other women's movements around this time, the Venezuelan movement solved the dilemma of opposing male dominance without a full-blown challenge to traditional gender relations by asking the state to intervene on women's behalf.[6] They proposed numerous legal and social changes, from shared legal responsibility for children to sex education, which depended primarily on state action rather than on altered male behavior.[7] But because the state was in the hands of men, this strategy would have only limited impact.

The relations taken up by Venezuelan relational feminists reflected their position not only in the family but also in the wider society. Most of them were educated women from the upper classes; those who worked outside the home were teachers and professionals. Because the nascent parties sought to organize the middle and working classes, those women who were influenced by the parties gave working women's[8] issues priority and pro-

5. Linda Gordon (1994, 8) offers a cogent defense for using the term *feminist* to describe those working for both women's equality with men and the improvement of women's lives.

6. A "social role" for the state was also the demand of early women's rights activists in Cuba (Smith and Padula 1996, 16).

7. For examples of women's involvement in constructing state welfare policies directed at women and families, see Gordon 1990; Koven and Michel 1993.

8. In Spanish the terms *mujeres trabajadores* and *obreras*, which translate as "working women" or "female laborers," are usually taken to mean blue-collar or working-class women.

moted union organizing and strike support. Groups formed by upper-class women and those who did not work outside their homes were largely focused on maternal/child issues and charitable works. Yet despite their claim to have working and poor women's interests at heart, the leaders of the women's movement did not recruit them in any consistent manner. They also kept decision making to themselves. This class bias prevented the movement from gaining a mass following, a problem that would continue to affect women's organizing in subsequent periods.

Despite their common exclusion of women of the lower classes, more elite women did not agree among themselves as to who was most suited to lead the movement. The different perspectives of upper- and middle-class feminists were clearly laid out in an exchange of views printed in the newspaper *Ahora* on 12 March 1937. One woman began the debate by defending wealthy women as the most able leaders of the women's movement. She acknowledged that currently most of them spent their time in idle chatter and society life and as a result were considered incapable of understanding important issues. But she argued that once led to think seriously, their superior resources and inherent intelligence would make them most suited to lead:

> It is from the upper class that the cultural movement should start, because its economic situation, free time, and other factors enable its members to undertake the work.
>
> Later, the members of the upper class will motivate and morally and materially help the middle and proletarian classes, which lack—especially the latter—the economic resources and most elementary comprehension.

This proposal did not sit well with women from the middle class. In a rapid return of fire, a middle-class woman responded that despite their resources, wealthy women were ignorant of the importance of the struggle for women's advancement because their economic well-being and lack of work experience kept them far removed from the preoccupations of the majority. Nothing was ever demanded of them, so they had no reason to fight. In contrast, it was the middle-class woman, because of her education and exposure to the world, who was the most fit to be in the vanguard of the women's movement:

> It is precisely this woman, whose intellectual level is higher than that of working women or peasants and so can appreciate it more, to whom the problem is presented at a basic level, and therefore it

must be she who is called to understand social concerns more clearly. The necessities of her condition have obliged her to widen her horizons, and she no longer moves in a very restricted and familiar circle, and has encountered a multitude of reasons which make her interested in improving her condition and the condition of all her sisters. It is the teachers, the office workers, the students, the employees, who can best . . . improve themselves and those who can most interest themselves in improving the conditions of life of the other women and of humanity in general. (*Ahora* 14 March 1937)

But Olga Luzardo, an early leader of the communist party and union organizer in the Western Venezuela oil fields, argued that the classism of these women demonstrated why feminism had nothing to offer working-class women, who found work far from emancipating. She had written earlier (*Ahora,* 25 October 1936) that in her opinion they would be better served by fighting alongside their oppressed male partners in an anti-imperialist popular front. She responded to the debate between the middle- and upper-class feminists by declaring that women could not be freed unless the class system itself was overturned:

Feminism will not be capable of resolving the problem of working women as some of us idiotically thought at the beginning. We women will gain nothing by occupying the same places as men, as long as the women of the masses will always be the women of Juan Bimba[9] and the position of governors or generals will be given to the ladies of the dominant classes. What would the comrades of the soap and perfume factories, the polishers, the seamstresses, say [to the idea] that we ought to pull woman from her idleness and push her into work? Wouldn't they laugh at such an unbalanced way of thinking?

The feminist premises, thus, cannot be the premises of the struggle of working women, who are interested in the improvement of all of the exploited sector, and not in the participation of women in a battle which would give the positions of responsibil-

9. Juan Bimba is a cartoon character who symbolizes "Mr. Ordinary Citizen, who in Venezuela is an illiterate peon" (Fergusson 1939, 65). While AD often used him in early campaigns to represent the average citizen whom it was going to empower, Juan Bimba remains today in Venezuelan political cartoons a caricature of the most victimized citizens—whose oppressors now include the political parties.

ity to women interested in sustaining a state of things which is notably prejudiced against the social sector to which we belong.
(*Ahora* 13 July 1937)

Because of the greater numbers of elite women involved in the movement, overturning capitalist oppression would not become a priority. Nevertheless, movement leaders would claim to represent all women as they
worked on issues that they linked to women's supposedly shared experience
of motherhood. But the two major coalition efforts of the period were clearly
oriented to the interests of women of a higher socioeconomic status. Because
the demand to reform the Civil Code, the laws governing intrafamilial relations, clearly could be justified as a claim to improve motherhood, women
most easily came together for this purpose. The more contentious suffrage
campaign was clearly class-biased, seeking the vote only for literate women.

Women's Organizations

The first and most influential women's rights group to form was the Women's
Cultural Association (Asociación Cultural Femenina or ACF). It was
founded on October 15, 1935, at the house of Cecelia Nuñez Sucre, a member of the "Generation of '28," a future founder of Democratic Action (AD),
and a teacher at the Escuela Normal, where she was a role model for young
women students. Called the *pólvora* (gunpowder) of the ACF, Nuñez Sucre,
along with other women who had been active in the student movement of
1928, inspired the next generation of women activists. Many were teachers
and came from Venezuela's emerging middle class (de Leonardi 1983, 391).
      The political activism of the founders influenced the ACF: although ac-
cording to its statutes its objective was "elevating the cultural level of the
Venezuelan woman" (ACF n.d.), one founding member claims that the group
was a "front" for women's political action at a time when such action was forbidden (Mercedes Fermín interview). Many of the *acefistas* (members of the
ACF) joined either the PRP, forerunner of the Communist Party, or ORVE,
which would become AD. Their goals mirrored the aims of those parties:
uniting across classes and improving the status of workers. Although they
couched their efforts within the political discourse that associated women
primarily with motherhood, their limited contestation of gender norms,
combined with an increasingly overt leftist political orientation, earned them
some opposition.
      The ACF's view of women's interests took into account the changing
nature of women's activities during the period but always in the context of

women's potential motherhood. In one of its first press statements, the ACF argued for improving women's education because "in the woman is the mother, in her the base and principal foundation of the family" (*Ahora* 22 January 1936). On the basis of their own experience and that of the women they saw around them, the *acefistas* were aware of the problems facing women who had to combine motherhood with paid employment. They sought better hours and pay, enforcement of the 1936 Labor Law, and improved education and health care for women and children. But because the *acefistas* also wanted to improve the civil and political status of all women, they also promoted the reform of the Civil Code and women's suffrage. Reflecting the diverse nature of the group, cultural activities—literary, artistic, and musical—also formed an area of emphasis. These priorities shifted as the political opportunities allowed and according to the internal debates of the ACF.

Because both PRP and ORVE were focused initially on organizing the emerging working class, these women's political connections led them to be primarily concerned with the situation of women workers.[10] Immediately after founding the ACF, members established the Working Women's Center (Casa de la Obrera). There they sponsored skills training, a job placement center, and a clinic. Members also helped to promote women's unions through the center. Because of the influence of educators in the group, the ACF was committed to providing women workers with access to education. The ACF headquarters housed a library, and the group offered basic education through night schools.

Four night schools were established by early 1936, and more were added over the following years. Promoted by *acefista* Mercedes Fermín, a pedagogue as well as a staunch supporter of ORVE and later of AD, the night schools were held in primary school classrooms. However, after seven programs had been established, the principal of one school where the classes were being held overheard Fermín discussing the need for family planning and publicly accused her of promoting free love. The schools were temporarily shut down, although the Ministry of Education soon adopted the idea of adult education and reopened them.[11]

But women workers were not the only focus of the ACF's attention. It decided on its priorities democratically and published them widely. In the

10. The Chilean "first wave" of feminism was also influenced by its association with leftist parties. See Kirkwood 1986; Silva Donoso 1987; Gaviola Artigas et al. 1986.

11. In their volume on women's contributions to state welfare policy, Koven and Michel (1993, 30) note that women's initial, private efforts at welfare provision have often served as a model for later state programs. On the United States, see Gordon 1990.

first tumultuous years, women arrived at the weekly or bimonthly meetings brimming with ideas, which would then be debated and put to a vote. Perhaps their most important contribution to the women's movement as a whole was the publication, from 1938 through 1945, of a weekly page called "Women's Culture" ("Cultura de la Mujer") in *Ahora,* the daily newspaper with a national circulation of over 10,000.[12] "Women's Culture" served as a key means of communication for country-wide activism. According to *acefista* Ana Senior, it was "the light for the women of the interior." Because there was a rotation of editors, the focus changed over the years. Besides the regular features—including a weekly editorial, ACF's programs and transcripts of talks given at its headquarters, letters, and reports from women's groups in the interior—there were articles on laws, work, education, divorce, prostitution, health, child rearing, sex education, single mothers and their "illegitimate" children, psychology, women's organizing in other countries, and the effects of both national and international issues (war, economics, elections) on women. There were also occasional profiles of famous women and translations of the work of women's rights activists such as birth control pioneer Margaret Sanger and First Lady Eleanor Roosevelt. Arts-related items included poetry and book and music reviews. In addition to publicizing issues through *Ahora,* the *acefistas* also broadcast radio programs and sponsored lectures and discussions of women's social, cultural, legal, medical, and political concerns. Committed to political pluralism, they invited representatives of all of the nascent political parties, as well as doctors and literary figures, to speak.

Through its effective communication, the ACF became a model for other women's organizing. Affiliated associations were formed in cities in the interior. The ACF was also a motor for general organizing for women's rights, undertaking the organization of a national women's conference in 1940, and participating in lobbying the congress to reform the Civil Code and grant women suffrage.

Beyond their work for women, the political orientations of many *acefistas* led them to participate in more general political organizing. This was usually undertaken as an extension of their home-based activities. They were active in the *barrios* (poor urban neighborhoods) around Caracas, where they would sell wholesale food at cost from the backs of trucks— concern for the high cost of living was easily defined as within the purview of women. They also joined in protests supporting the Spanish Republic

12. The dates usually given for "Women's Culture" are 1937–48. While there were articles on the ACF and women's issues prior to mid-1938, a close review of *Ahora* did not turn up the weekly page until that time. During the *trienio* (1945–48), it appeared only irregularly.

and in local strikes, most crucially in the Maracaibo oil workers' strike of December 1936.

This particular action provides a good example of how the ACF took advantage of the political opportunities of the period from a basis in women's maternal role. The strike "shook Venezuelan society to its foundations . . . reveal[ing] the strength and long-range political potential of the social and ideological forces galvanized by oil workers in their struggle" (Bergquist 1986, 230). Its widespread support was particularly symbolized by one event, the transporting of the oil workers' children to Caracas for care during the strike:

> In early January [1937] oil workers and their allies hit on a brilliant tactic to symbolize the meaning of their struggle and consolidate the multiclass national coalition emerging in support of the strike. They announced a plan to send children of strikers to live in middle-class homes in Caracas for the duration of the conflict. The idea caught on immediately. Invitations from Caracas and other cities in North-central Venezuela flooded into Maracaibo. Scores of children prepared to leave their homes in the oil zone for the capital. A steamship company offered the children free transportation; a commission of well-to-do *caraqueños* [Caracas residents] visited Zulia to arrange for the transfer. The children were given medical examinations, their parents provided with the names and addresses of their children's sponsors. A few days before the settlement of the strike, thousands of cheering oil workers and their supporters gave the first 50 *"niños petroleros"* [oil workers' children] a rousing sendoff. The children's arrival in Caracas was greeted by another public demonstration and ample press coverage. (1986, 234–35)

The founder of AD also mentions this important solidaristic event in his history of Venezuelan democracy: "The sons of the galley slaves of petroleum slept on linen sheets in rich men's homes when hundreds of them were brought to the capital city for care during the difficult economic times in the oil camps" (Betancourt 1979, 57).

By ignoring the identity of the brilliant tacticians who came up with this plan, these descriptions form part of the long tradition of making Venezuelan women's actions invisible. The unspecified "allies" of the oil workers were not the "rich men" on whose linen sheets the children slept, but the *acefistas,* the middle-class women who organized to care for the children of the striking workers. They gathered themselves into a women's committee of the Committee to Support the Families of the Western Oil Workers (Comité ProFamilias de Obreros Petroleros de Occidente), sought volunteers to take the children into their homes through articles in *Ahora* in early January, and notified the pledged families when the children arrived in Caracas at the end of the month. They were the ones to organize publicity around the event. They gave regular updates on the children's health and well-being for the time they were in Caracas and reported on their journey home in February (*Ahora* January–February 1937; Clemente Travieso 1961, 18; Hernandez 1985, 28; Ana Senior interview).

Through their work for women's rights and their political involvement, the *acefistas* stretched the socially acceptable boundaries of their gender and their class. As a result, they aroused some enmity from certain sectors. There were some who thought that "it was incredible that women of a certain social standing took to the streets fighting for women's rights, helping unions, supporting the Spanish Republic; and so they came to brand us as a group of crazy women, prostitutes" (Ana Senior interview). These comparisons clearly referred to the ACF's transgression of accepted standards of gender and class relations by labeling them as women who violated conventional behavior. The church was at the forefront of this opposition. It criticized the ACF regularly in a column in the paper *La Religion*. Erna Fergusson, a U.S. woman who published a book about her 1937 tour in Venezuela, noted the ACF's "radical" reputation:

> A conservative friend had warned me against that institution as radical and not altogether in good favor with the Church. Members of the club have actually encouraged working women to join unions. . . . They are so unladylike as to demand the municipal vote for women, and reform of the Civil Code which now gives a woman no rights whatever against her husband, either personal or financial, even no right to her own child. They demand laws to regulate child labor and white slavery. Many little girls of twelve and thirteen—they mature young in the tropics—have been sold by their mothers to pimps or have drifted, unguided, into a house which specializes in virgins.
>
> Such knowledge has stirred Venezuelan women quite out of their traditional role. They are not only at work to change such conditions, they speak out about what they know. The Venezuelan gift of forceful expression is not limited to men. . . . [I]n social novels, in newspaper and magazine articles, in pamphlets, and as

editors, Venezuelan women are outlining their policies and making their demands. One or two have come out so definitely Left-
ish as to be tapped on the shoulder by the police, though none has
yet joined the young men radicals in exile. (Fergusson 1939,
312–13)

While the ACF challenged class and gender norms in its more overtly
political work, the other significant women's group of this time, the Venezuelan Association of Women (Asociación Venezolana de Mujeres or AVM)
stayed closer to a wholly maternalist perspective. Mainly made up of upper-
class women and keeping its distance from political parties, this group focused principally on maternal/child health, public hygiene, and charitable
works. However, even their mild activism proved too challenging to accepted
notions of gender relations.

In the tumultuous first weeks after the death of Gómez, the future
founders of the AVM, Ada Pérez Guevara de Bocalandro and Luisa de Valle
Silva, took immediate action to make their voices heard on behalf of women,
publishing the "Message from Venezuelan Women to General Eleazar
López Contreras" (*La Esfera* 30 December 1935). They began by claiming
that their interest in the progress of the country stemmed from a "profound
sense of actual or future motherhood," because "the hope of the whole
country is in the child, the future citizen." To ensure children's proper up-
bringing, the adequate preparation of women and the effective cooperation
of the national government were necessary. The two authors made specific
demands that they deemed necessary for children and women. For children,
they asked for milk, playgrounds, daycare, low-cost boarding schools, or-
phanages, and an end to child begging. For women, they sought education
for child rearing, lay schools for pregnant and "wayward" girls, training and
health certification for domestic workers, pregnancy leave, prenatal check-
ups, prenuptial medical examinations to prevent the spread of venereal dis-
eases, and sex education. Although some of these requests were daring by
the standards of the time, couching them in language implying that they
would contribute to the promotion of responsible motherhood helped to
draw the support not only of the ACF but also of the more conservative
Catholic Ladies (Damas Católicas) and Infant Protection Society (Sociedad
Protectora de la Infancia) (*La Esfera* 8 January 1936; Clemente Travieso
1961; de Leonardi 1983, 393).

But this set of demands seemed too radical or impractical to many male
elites. Catholic priests objected to the idea of prenuptial medical examinations, which were intended to catch venereal disease before the mainly male

carriers could infect their brides, on the grounds that they would "discourage matrimony and so increase immorality" (Fergusson 1939, 309). The health of women and children was not foremost in their minds. While not explicitly disagreeing with women's demands, an *Ahora* editorial disparaged their priorities as more suited for a utopia than for the practicalities of everyday Venezuelan life:

> Our women have sketched out a social-benefit action program that is too vast. They have revealed themselves as theorists, outlining issues that are not in accordance with the current and concrete necessities of our situation. . . .
>
> Thus, we advise our women—if our voice merits your hearing—that they situate themselves in the Venezuelan reality and therefore limit their aspirations to putting to work their desire for social cooperation beginning with those problems which demand an immediate solution and which should be well known to them. Programs such as that which they have elaborated—which we believe well-intentioned and generous—[are] social utopias which do not reflect the truth of our situation and run the risk of becoming sterile as a whole. (20 January 1936)

The mothers of the "Message" denied their sterility by founding the AVM on 11 February 1936 to fulfill their ideas. Ten days later, López Contreras included the protection of mothers and children in his first political program, though with little concrete detail (Suarez Figueroa 1983, vol. 1). Over the next two years the AVM widely publicized their own efforts to promote the well-being of women and children. Their work included the establishment of an orphans' home, a prenatal clinic, child-care centers, and preschools, as well as the sponsorship of hygiene campaigns and a public lecture series on women and civil law.

The ACF and AVM shared concerns for poor and working-class women and children but differed in their approach to traditional politics. *Acefista* Fermín claims that the main motivation behind the formation of the AVM was upper-class women's desire to participate in the social ferment of the time, not any coherent political ideology.[13] The AVM itself explicitly stated that it was interested in working with groups that were "not politi-

---

13. This motivation has also been identified in the Chilean case, where the involvement of upper-class women in the women's club movement was attributed to their fear that politically

cal"—that is, did not have an agenda that could be seen as promoting a particular political ideology. Although the AVM went on to participate in the effort to reform the Civil Code, suffrage would become a divisive issue for the group, which split in the mid-1940s over whether to join in the movement for female enfranchisement.

Other women's groups formed around the country, reflecting a range of political and social motivations: civic, feminist, charitable, and cultural. "Every town of any importance has its women's clubs devoted to specific tasks in aid of women and children. Most of them are aware of the need of better laws, though not all are active campaigners for them" (Fergusson 1939, 311). Articles in *Ahora* in 1936–37 found an ACF in Cúmana and self-described feminist groups in Lara, Apure, Carora, and Tovar, among others. There was a Venezuelan branch of the Union of American Women (Unión de Mujeres Americana or UMA), whose goal was the region-wide incorporation of women into socioeconomic development and political life. Besides the Catholic Ladies and the Infant Protection Society, which publicized their prochurch, anticommunist, and prosocial-improvement stances in the magazine *Nos-Otras* (1939, 313), other Caracas-based groups included the Inter-American Cultural Association (Asociación Cultural Interamericana), which promoted women's literary achievement; the Ateneo, a cultural center that routinely sponsored women's events; and the national Venezuelan Federation of Teachers (Federación Venezolana de Maestros or FVM), which often participated in women's organizing efforts. Support for women's issues also came from women organized in the Neighborhood Development Councils (Juntas Pro-Fomento de los Barrios) and the unions and associations of feminized occupations such as textile manufacturing and nursing. At the end of the decade, the Housewives' Association (Asociación de Amas de Casa) was founded to address the high cost of living.

Women also organized within the emerging political society through the party women's bureaus. Initially these groups were nurtured by the civil society-based women's organizations, particularly the ACF, and took on many of the same issues. "The ACF, PRP and ORVE operated in parallel, the first connecting with the others through common members, who . . . oriented their activity to political matters, without excluding educational and social activities" (de Leonardi 1983, 395). The first program of ORVE's women's bureau took up the demands of the ACF in great part. Concerned with women's roles as mothers, wives, and citizens, they wanted to train mothers to become quali-

---

active middle-class women would gain more stature. In both cases, however, this rivalry had the positive effect of enlarging the movement as a whole (Kirkwood 1986).

fied educators of the future citizens of Venezuela and to have women assume their responsibilities as "partners with men." Thus they called for women's participation in political organizations, civil equality between husband and wife, women's political rights, equal pay for equal work, and maternity leave. They also promoted the study of children's and working women's needs; public day-care facilities; more maternity hospitals, schools, and libraries; and U.S.-style Parent-Teacher Associations (Clemente Travieso 1961, 37–38).

Thanks to the influence of the parties' cooperation in the April Bloc and PDN, the unification of leftist organizations from 1936–38, as well as the parties' inability to dominate political life due to their periodic repression, women's joint efforts to achieve their common goals were not impeded by their political affiliations:

> On the ACF's benches sat women representing all the political parties. And there was a spirit of understanding that has not been repeated in Venezuela. Each one of us knew who was who. For example, each party had representation there, but with a great independence. It was not that we came to give a [pre]determined position. . . . [I]f there was a proposal, a motion about something that was good for the country, even if one of the women was not in agreement with it, but knew that the majority accepted it, she worked for it with the same fervor as if she had [made the proposal]. (Ana Senior interview)

But even early on there was foreshadowing of the divisions that party politics would create among the women activists. ACF's Fermín recalls that Rómulo Betancourt, founder of ORVE, requested her to help form the women's bureau in order to trade in the "political club of well-dressed ladies for a 'work organization'" (de Leonardi 1983, 397), a clear dismissal of the work of the women's organizations as merely a hobby of elite women.[14] Moreover, as the political parties that were once unified to pressure López Contreras went their separate ways in their clandestine organizing efforts, women began to orient their activities within party priorities and away from unified goals (1983, 399). But political differences would not block women's own organizing efforts until the parties were fully able to control political life. Meanwhile, these efforts grew larger and more collaborative.

14. Fermín had a close working relationship with Betancourt and asked his advice on orienting her ACF activities. This is attested to in her letters in Betancourt's papers, Vol. 6, 1940.

Coalition Building Begins

The coalitions built to promote women's rights in the late 1930s and early 40s reflected women's political opportunities as well as the gender interests of the more elite activists who headed the campaigns. These interests and the strategies used to promote them were developed at the first national women's conference.

The Preparatory Conference of the First Venezuelan Congress of Women (1938–1940)

From late 1938 to 1940, the *acefistas* organized the first national women's conference. They sought to recapture the momentum that had declined somewhat from the first years of organizing. The June 1940 gathering brought together several hundred women to discuss the main issues of the women's movement, from civil rights to sexuality. Although mainly middle- and upper-class women organized the conference, they clearly sought women's unity across classes. Their main strategy to preserve gender harmony was to ask the state, not individual men, to share the responsibility for women's double burdens (as mothers and workers) and to improve women's legal status.

As the PRP and ORVE went their separate ways following the dissolution of the PDN in 1938, class conflict and the demands of rival political allegiances began to weaken women's early organizing efforts. However, the ACF, whose members straddled the divisions, was not content to let the more unified struggle dissolve. In reaction to the diverging of interests, *acefistas* began to organize an explicitly multiclass, multisector national women's congress at the end of 1938. They were inspired by their belief that women shared a common goal of "improvement":

> May this congress be the first step so that the hidden energies, the potentials that until now only have emerged in isolated moments of profound crisis, are directed toward methodological, daily, organized action, which alone is capable of bearing the best fruit and achieving great undertakings.
>
> Are these qualities and excellencies of which we have spoken the exclusive patrimony of determined classes, castes, or individuals? No. Who thinks thus suffers from an incomprehensible short-sightedness or an insulting egoism. The problems of our women are one: their material and moral improvement, their dignification. The weapons to arrive at this goal are possessed by all

Venezuelan women: the student and the worker, the employee and the schoolteacher, the mother and the artist, and also—why not?—the [wealthy] "good girl" who until now has been in the most atrophying idleness, but who may secretly yearn for a greater ideal, for a noble activity which will put an end to the pallor of her vegetative existence. (*Ahora*, 19 November 1938)

By July 1939 preparations for the congress, to be held in December, were in full swing. August brought a call for the participation of women workers. But the already apparent dispersal of women's energies was reflected in ACF's September report on the internal disorganization and funding problems that were slowing its efforts. Although women from all over the country continued to pledge their support for the meeting in letters reprinted in "Women's Culture" in November, December came and went with no congress, and 1940 began without the weekly page. When it reappeared in March, the ACF apologized for its absence and explained that the members had decided that it would not be possible to hold the congress because full representation of all women had not been achieved. They had been promised participation by many women, but it was "never enough so that in a Congress the great majority of women of the Nation would be authentically represented" (*Ahora*, 9 March 1940).

The *acefistas* clung to their commitment to inclusivity, but they refused to give up on what they saw as an essential undertaking to rekindle and unify women's energies. Instead of the full congress, they proposed to hold a "preparatory" conference. The Preparatory Conference of the First Venezuelan Congress of Women (Conferencia Preparatoria del Primer Congreso Venezolano de Mujeres) finally took place 13–16 June 1940 in the Ateneo. One hundred and fifty-five women registered by organization and were joined by "a good number" of others who attended the sessions (*Conferencia* 1941, 11). While the attendees may have not been the "authentic representation" of the majority of Venezuelan women, they represented a wide range of interests. Sixty-nine groups registered, including cultural groups, women's rights organizations, neighborhood associations, teachers' and nurses' organizations, student groups, charities, and unions.

Emphasizing the urgency of uniting women's efforts, *acefista* Ana Luisa Padra decried, in her opening remarks, the lack of a solid base in society for the women's movement and called particular groups to task for the failure to spread their views more widely. In her view, the exclusively maternity-oriented AVM did not have broad enough appeal, the more leftist ACF had lost "cultural content" in its effort to organize workers, and the activist

FEV had not tried hard enough to retain its membership. The aim of the conference was to determine the issues that united women and publicize them in a document that would be distributed nationally in order to build a movement worthy of the convening of a full congress.

While she acknowledged the different backgrounds of the attendees, Padra held the common middle-class position that class should not be an obstacle to gender unity: "We have different interests, but a common problem: the conquest of our rights for which we ought to [fight] together without rancor or distinctions" (*Conferencia* 1941, 19). To achieve these rights, she advocated a broad-based "Women's Front" (*Frente Femenino*) with a common platform combining women's equality and devotion to motherhood: equal pay for equal work, reform of discriminatory laws, suffrage under the same conditions as men, an end to discrimination against children born out of wedlock, and the simplification of civil marriage and divorce proceedings.

Throughout the document produced at the conference, the participants justified their demands as appropriate for their gender. As a result, the term *feminism* was used gingerly. In the preface the Venezuelan "feminist" movement was described as revolving around a single principle: protection of Venezuelan mothers and children. While the conclusion claimed that the conference was "of women and never feminist," that was taken to mean "we have not been able and are not trying to replace men" (120).

But in keeping with the relational feminism of the activists, the acceptance of gender difference was combined with a clear challenge to gender hierarchy. The demand for laws to end discrimination against women, while justified as protecting future generations, explicitly involved punishing irresponsible fathers. The "total absence of moral responsibility in men" (5) and men's extremely advantageous situation under Venezuelan laws were both cited as reasons for women's subordinate position. To facilitate the maintenance of gender difference in the face of such subordination, conference presenters held the state accountable for resolving women's problems.

Improving women's rights within the family was a major concern of conference presenters, reflecting their class position: marriage was far from universal among working-class and poor women, and their children had little to inherit.[15] Panchita Soublette Saluzzo of the AVM argued in the section on "Civil Rights" that while women had taken on increased duties and responsibilities, their rights lagged far behind. Married women were classified as legally incapacitated, like idiots or "degenerates," and their husbands given

---

15. Judith Ewell (1984b, 736) notes that in 1941 only 24 percent of all Venezuelans over 15 were married.

absolute control over their property and children. Moreover, children born out of wedlock could not claim any support from their fathers. She asked, not for new rights, but for those taken away from women at marriage.[16] The sections on "Maternal Rights," and even "Women and Culture," emphasized the importance of guaranteeing women's civil rights for the sake of making them more able mothers—and to give upper-class women a sense of their own worth in order to encourage their cultural development.

The frequently mentioned demand for state implementation of the 1936 Labor Law, particularly in the sections on "Maternal Rights" and "Working Women," shows that the interests of working-class women were not ignored. More specific demands, such as that the state be responsible for providing social security during maternity leave, were asserted to help women fulfill their "Maternal Duties" and improve the situation of "Working Women." Equal pay for equal work was seen as a mechanism to help women avoid "Prostitution." In the section on "Women Workers" labor activist Eumelia Hernandez of the ACF went beyond urging that the state take action and called on unions to incorporate women into their ranks, and on business to improve its training and shorten the work day. The only profession that had a section devoted to it was that of "The Woman Teacher," indicating the importance of this sector to the women's movement. Here Mercedes Fermín of the ACF called for the improvement of teachers' work environment, pay, training, career opportunities, and organization.

Various presenters also called on the state to take steps to address the pathologies associated with sexuality, which they saw as threatening the family unit. A primary preoccupation was stopping the transmission of venereal disease so that women could rear healthy children. The section on "Civil Rights" called for stricter laws penalizing adultery by men to stop the spread of venereal disease. One of women's "Maternal Duties" was ensuring that the fathers of their children were not infected. In this effort conference participants called for state support for programs ranging from sex education to prenuptial certification. Sex education itself was recognized as a contested issue. It was described as ideally a matter to be taught to children in school, once "certain prejudices are overcome" (*Conferencia* 1941, 59)—such as the ones that forced the closure of the ACF's night schools. In the meantime, it was urged that parents be provided with information that they could teach their children at home.

With respect to mothers, the state was urged to provide financial support for single mothers, child care, and *puericultura* (child-rearing training),

---

16. Single women did have control over their property and children.

and to institute legal paternity testing. Financial support was among the "Maternal Rights" regarded as essential for single mothers to help them avoid "Prostitution." Child care and *puericultura* would enable women to fulfill their "Maternal Duties." Paternity testing was seen as a way to discover those men who led women into "Prostitution" as well as those who sexually exploited "Working Women," both of which groups were to be punished.[17]

In keeping with the conflict among women's groups over suffrage, political rights received less attention than other issues. They were brought up only twice by *acefistas*, primarily in one section. In "Political Rights" Josefina Juliac explained how industrial society had introduced women to the world of public interaction, changing their social but not their legal situation. Some restructuring of the patriarchal family had come about as a result, but political rights would have to be fought for through the disciplined efforts of women's organizations in combination with political groups that upheld equal rights.

The essence of the different sections was agreed upon as a whole by the conference participants, and women's cooperation was affirmed again in the repeated call for a united organization. But only the conclusions of the section on women's civil rights, signed by conference delegates, were sent to Congress. Women were pragmatic, taking advantage of the opportunity presented by the presence of a commission to review the Civil Code. However, their attention to the Civil Code was also a de facto compromise of the more challenging gender- and class-based demands for suffrage and better working conditions.

Despite women's pragmatic compromises, the male authorities governing the state were not prepared to grant women's demands, no matter how class- and gender-appropriate. A month after the meeting, the "Women's Culture" editorial, in a highly ironic comparison of the previous congressional session with the women's conference, noted the lack of results from women's efforts to lobby Congress on their civil rights. Judging by what the men discussed (nothing of great importance, and certainly not the women's rights demands presented to them), the women must have been mistaken— there couldn't possibly be any problems to solve in Venezuela. "*Compañeras?* We must repent. Let us return to our houses, devote ourselves to preparing the favorite dish of the man of the house or fetching him his slippers. The men do not need us—for anything. The destiny of the country is safe in their hands. Venezuela will continue to be always, always, always the best of all possible worlds" (*Ahora*, 28 July 1940).

17. As was made clear in the section on "Civil Rights," paternity testing was illegal at that time. In order to guarantee inheritance within the legal family unit, there was no consideration given to the claims of children born out of wedlock (or their mothers).

While the women's movement did not achieve legal reform as a direct result of the conference, it met its goal to unite women to debate their interests. Under the leadership of elite women, the struggle for women's rights was clearly underway, and a network assembled that would carry it into the streets and the halls of Congress.

The Political Opportunities of Liberalized Authoritarianism (1941–45)

With the ACF generally at the helm, women's groups brought together coalitions for two major campaigns during the decade: the reform of the Civil Code and women's suffrage. Both efforts reflected women's general and gendered opportunities, which were modified with the further liberalization of authoritarian rule. In 1941 López Contreras's minister of war, General Isais Medina Angarita, came to power. Under the influence of cooperation with the powers allied against fascism in World War II, Medina Angarita liberalized social and political policies. He established limited social security, insisted on more control over foreign oil companies, and allowed press and political freedoms, including the return of political exiles and the legalization of political parties.

Liberalization resulted in increased political activism, especially through political parties. Legalized in September 1941, Democratic Action (AD) began its goal of "not a single district, not a single town without its party organization" (Betancourt 1979, 64), under the visionary leadership of Rómulo Betancourt. Taking into account a population on the move from the dislocations of a changing economy, AD leadership set out to form a multiclass party that would integrate every sector into its ranks. Its success made it the model of political organization for other parties (Martz 1966, 148).

As AD grew stronger, its leadership was increasingly unhappy operating in what they saw as an insufficiently democratic environment. The 1941 presidential candidacy of AD's Rómulo Gallegos was largely symbolic. Suffrage was quite restricted, and the president was still appointed by the congress. Although other political parties, particularly the Communist Party (now called the Partido Comunista de Venezuela, or PCV), were willing to go along with the Medina government's plans for gradual liberalization,[18] AD

---

18. The Comintern at this time directed national communist parties to participate in national coalitions to strengthen the pro-ally war effort (Alexander 1969).

continued to push for universal suffrage and direct elections. Medina Angarita's supporters and AD first agreed on a compromise presidential candidate for the 1945 elections. But after their choice became too ill to participate, they could find no other universally suitable candidate. Meanwhile, elite sectors worried about Medina's concessions to popular forces began to coalesce in an effort to return López Contreras to power. When a group of reformist military officers concerned about the threat of López Contreras's return came to the AD leadership to propose their participation in a coup, they agreed. On 18 October 1945, a half-military, half-AD directorate took power after relatively little opposition.

Gendered Opportunities

While the general political opportunities shifted somewhat in this period, the gendered aspects stayed much the same. Several congressional committees, still all male, oversaw the reform of the Civil and Commercial Codes, changing some of the references to women's civil status. Political parties continued to recruit women through the mechanism of the women's bureau. A contributing factor to women's activism, especially around the issue of suffrage, was the growing network of regional women's rights activists. However, the presence of other suffrage movements was not wholly beneficial. The contention around advocating suffrage was partly based on its association in political discourse with demands for gender equality, a radical concept to Venezuelans.

The First Campaign of the Women's Movement:
The Movement for Civil Code Reform (1940–1942)

Reforming the Civil Code on behalf of both married women and illegitimate children had been a leading demand since the emergence of the women's movement in 1936. It was justified as women's gender-appropriate advocacy on behalf of mothers and children. Over the next several years the reform movement expanded, gathering force from the support of all the women's groups. They hung on doggedly through six years of delay by the congressional commission responsible for the reform, repeatedly publicizing the reform as necessary for all women and unthreatening to the stability of the family. They also introduced new justifications linked to changing political opportunities. Yet although women mobilized nationwide for the reform, few of their suggestions were included in the final version.

The reform was on the ACF's initial agenda and introduced the AVM founders' "Message" to López Contreras, which began, "In view of the lack of attention to the civil rights of women—the legal protection of married women or women in common-law marriages—and by extension the situation of minors, women have decided to send a public message to President López Contreras" (Palumbo 1988, 8). Individual women who had promoted the 1936 reform of the Labor Law included suggestions to improve the legal status of married women and illegitimate children. These were sent to the Congressional Codification Commission established in June 1936, but it took no action for several years. Nevertheless, women's pressure continued, both in lobbying and in public debate. On 14 September 1937 the ACF, AVM, and UMA again sent the Codification Commission a petition supporting the improvement of married women's and illegitimate children's legal status. While this petition still had no effect, the ACF and AVM continued to publicize the issue in the newspapers *Ahora* and *El Universal* (AVM 1942).

To support women's civil rights activism during a time of social upheaval, an ACF editorial expanded upon a quote from the poet Gabriela Mistral, "Women's real patriotism is perfect motherhood": "We cannot consider a perfect mother one who is obliged like a slave to endure the yoke of anachronistic institutions in this time of renovation, besides her burden of motherhood and sacrifice: without having in exchange, as a citizen, the right to participate in the elaboration of laws which decide her own future and that of her children" (*Ahora*, 16 April 1937). As the years passed, the reform was repeatedly presented as beneficial for all women because of their common link with motherhood: "All women are before everything else women, actual or potential mothers, and we find ourselves in the same unprotected situation, needing adequate protection from the State, from laws and from society" (*Ahora*, 24 March 1939).

The agreement made at the 1940 Preparatory Conference on the need to reform the Civil Code and the opportunity to lobby a reconstituted Codification Commission sparked the formation of the Movement for Civil Code Reform (Movimiento Pro-Reforma del Código Civil). The Codification Commission provoked conference organizers by not responding immediately to their suggestions, but it finally circulated a reform proposal in 1941. Women from the Movement for Civil Code Reform, including members of the AVM, ACF, Ateneo, and the Interamerican Cultural Association, returned a detailed critique of the proposal, objecting to its lack of attention to gender bias in several areas. It did not change the inequity of regarding any type of adultery by the wife, but not by the husband, as grounds for divorce, or improve the legal status of common-law wives or the economic situation

of single mothers and children born out of wedlock, or institute the requirement of prenuptial medical certification (AVM 1942; Palumbo 1988, 9).

Meanwhile the *acefistas* continued to promote the formation of a unified front to achieve their reform goals. Under the title "We Must Organize
Ourselves, Venezuelan Women," they editorialized: "As long as there does
not exist a truly structured, real women's movement, we will never achieve a
legislative reform that will convert our desires into reality" (*Ahora*, 23 February 1941). More women joined the reform movement. Supporters wrote to
"Women's Culture" from the interior, and seventy-five women signed a letter to Congress in support of women's and men's equal parental rights, sim-
plified divorce laws, and the right of illegitimate children to inherit parental
property.

The ACF also used the opportunity presented by the 1941 presidential
elections to promote the reform. On 20 April, responding to the ACF's request that the candidates make their positions known with respect to
women's rights, Gallegos, the essentially symbolic candidate of the Left,
came out in support of women's civil and political rights. But in his inaugural
address in May, the new president, General Isais Medina Angarita, continued
to give only lip service to women's demands. He went no further than his
predecessor in again promising the vague "maternal and child protection."
Women's efforts were also limited by the pace of the Codification Commission, which delayed yet another year in its deliberations.

In 1942 women continued to seek the reform on the basis of their
shared role as mothers—"The Venezuelan woman, molder of citizens, guider
of infancy . . . the current civil code subjects to a guardianship worthy of the
Middle Ages" (AVM 1942, 9)—but also brought up new justifications based
on the changing political context. Responding to the proposal that women's
rights be put on hold for the more important business of wartime, the April
and May issues of "Women's Culture" entreated legislators to end discrimination against women precisely because they had shown their equal worth in
wartime efforts and because the reform would be another democratic advance in the face of fascism. Advocating a faster pace in legal change to catch
up with the progress they perceived in elite women's rapidly changing role in
society, the ACF wrote: "The shackles which the current code imposes on a
woman are five years behind, when a woman, confined in the four walls of
her house, did not undertake any economic activity that would force her to
act in a way that would be different from the established mode. But today,
when a woman is a doctor, a lawyer, an educator, etc., it is absurd that an ar-
bitrary legislation limits her activities" (*Ahora*, 17 May 1942). One of these
"shackles" was the right of husbands to have a confinement order issued

against their wives seeking to leave home for any reason. Activists sought to supercede it with a law guaranteeing a women's right to temporarily leave the house for study or work reasons (*Ahora*, 21 June 1942).

The reform of the Civil Code was finally passed in July 1942, but it proved a limited victory for women. Married women were given control over their own property (though not its profits or products), and women in proven common-law marriages had the right to shared child custody and shared control over communal property. But the legal status of illegitimate children, marriage and divorce procedures, child support, and the parental rights of mothers were largely ignored (La Mala Vida 1985). Although women organized for their own and their children's rights within the framework of gender difference, the men in power were not ready to uproot gender hierarchy and allow women to assume equal civil rights. The full reform would wait for another forty years and another broad-based women's coalition using some of the same justifications. But this time it would be led by women with considerably more social and political power in a different political opportunity structure.[19]

The Second Campaign of the Women's Movement: The Suffrage Movement (1941–1947)

While women's rights activists could agree on the need for a reformed Civil Code that would grant mothers the rights they needed to raise future generations, suffrage was a more contentious issue. The ACF debated suffrage from the founding of the group. Articles in "Women's Culture" initially subordinated political to civil rights, claiming that if a woman "does not have voice or vote within the boundaries of her home, it would be laughable that she would be granted the vote within the boundaries of her country" (*Ahora*, 24 March 1939). But priorities were not the only consideration. Activists clearly felt substantial pressure to disassociate themselves from the English and U.S. suffragists, whom Venezuelans saw as demanding an unacceptable equality with men. Later, however, the ACF recognized the suffragists' efforts and announced its support for women's political equality. However, in the case of AVM, contention over the issue of suffrage resulted in the group's division. Although the AVM's rejection of politics could be relaxed when it came to lobbying legislators for women's civil rights, to lobby for the right to choose these legislators was too great a leap.

The suffrage struggle began in 1941 and got fully underway in 1943,

19. The 1982 Civil Code Reform is discussed in Chapter 4.

quickly gathering national support. Its partial success—the granting of municipal suffrage in 1945—showed that women had achieved some degree of effectiveness in their united organizing. But even more than with the reform of the Civil Code, this effort was clearly designed to benefit certain classes: the vote was sought only for literate women.

Responding to an article that claimed that Venezuelan women were indifferent to suffrage, the ACF in late 1938 identified a primary focus on political rights with the "individualist" feminism of those women who sought complete equality with men.[20] But at the same time it argued that not indifference, but a sense of priorities was leading the group to focus on other demands:

> It's true that in Venezuela there have never existed exclusively feminist groups. But we have determined that this, instead of being an indication of the backwardness of our women, is more likely an indication that they clearly understand that the simple aggressive feminism of the 19th century will not get them anywhere. [I]f it is true that [the women's groups of the country] have been misunderstood a little on the issue of the women's vote, it is not because they are not interested but rather because—including this demand among their aspirations—they have dedicated themselves first to achieving the most urgent and immediate women's demands. (*Ahora*, 16 December 1938)

At this point the members believed the vote would come "automatically" on the heels of social and economic reforms, with no need to resort to a suffrage campaign. "When in Venezuela the feeling of democracy and justice is affirmed, when the equality of women in the law and the society becomes a fact, when the article of the Labor Law which stipulates: 'For equal work, equal salary' becomes a reality, when the single mother is not considered an affront to society, the women's vote in Venezuela will be achieved automatically, without the need for a campaign to obtain it, nor of feminist groups to ask for it," the *Ahora* article continued.

Early in 1939 *acefista* and writer Carmen Clemente Travieso discussed the reasons why women needed to achieve civil equality before political equality, explaining that although she did not deny the desirability of women's suffrage, the winning of basic civil rights seemed to be more essential. But the need to differentiate the Venezuelan struggle from the suffragists who supposedly sought to replace men clearly influenced her reasoning:

20. See discussion of "individualist" feminism in Chapter 1.

It would seem incongruous, if not to say pathetic, that our women would be given the right to vote, for example, when they lack representation and personhood within the home; or when they are denied the defense of their children, as mothers, or the defense of their dignity as women. When a woman in Venezuela does not have voice or vote within the boundaries of her home, it would be laughable that she would be granted the vote within the boundaries of her country. It is thus a question of logic, to begin to fight for that which our women most need; [the Venezuelan woman] does not want to present herself before the Venezuelan man as a suffragist nor as a rival; nor with the desire to attribute to herself the rights which correspond to men, but rather [she] simply begins by asking, with justice, for her equal rights before the law; her rights as a human and conscious being; the rights which correspond to her as a part of a civilized and democratic society. (*Ahora*, 24 March 1939)

With the focus on the 1940 conference in the pages of "Women's Culture," the issue of suffrage diminished in prominence. It resurfaced in 1941, when the ACF again affirmed that suffrage would not be used against men but would be used to fight social problems alongside them (*Ahora*, 9 February 1941). In an article in May, the ACF recognized that it was now calling for the same reform as suffragists in other countries, and it explicitly acknowledged its own feminism. But the ACF continued to insist that it did not seek to end gender difference:

The ACF is not feminist, but if that which our *compañeras* defended so brilliantly is feminism, or forms part of some feminist plan in the meaning which is generally given to this word, the whole Association, from this moment, declares itself feminist. If to struggle so that women acquire culture, so that the mother has rights over her children, for a more broad protection for the Venezuelan mother and child, is feminism, we declare ourselves feminist. But we are not nor never will be feminist to appropriate places which don't belong to us nor to dispossess the man of his rights. We want to be at the side of men, reclaiming the right which humanly and socially belongs to us, in our condition as beings conscious of their rights and duties. (*Ahora*, 1 May 1941)

The Civil Code campaign took up the energies of the *acefistas* for the next year, interrupting the debate on political rights. But the unsatisfying results of the reform no doubt helped to bring them back to a consideration of suffrage. Responding to the fears of some liberal legislators that women would use the vote to promote conservative ideology, Luisa Amelia Pérez Peroso, the first Venezuelan female political scientist, wrote in December 1942 that women deserved the vote because they made up half of the nation. If they voted conservative, that preference would simply reflect the will of the nation.

In early 1943 the ACF declared a national organizing drive to have women's political rights considered by Congress in April. Its first step was to circulate a petition that defended these rights against claims that they were a threat to the family. To the contrary, it claimed that as citizens women were justly due these rights. They would allow Venezuelan women the same respect accorded women in other countries and would enable them to become an example to their children, for whose moral formation they were responsible (*Ahora*, 10 May 1943).

While *acefistas* could couch their demands in ways that did not threaten gender difference, they could not get around the class status quo. They asked for the vote "in the same conditions as men." Because only literate males voted, female suffrage would be similarly limited to those mainly elite women who were literate. Eleven thousand signatures were collected, and in May the petition was taken to Congress. Although the government party had declared itself in support of women's "incorporation into political life" (Suarez Figueroa 1983, vol. 2), the petition was passed to the Commission for Internal Affairs and put on hold, ostensibly because of the war.

The suffrage movement continued into 1944 with editorials, petitions, and organizing directed at pressuring state and national legislators. Coordinated by a new group formed in mid-1943, the Committee for Suffrage (Comité ProSufragio), it circulated another prosuffrage petition throughout the country and continued to link women's rights to their duties as mothers—to "permit us to fulfill par excellence our mission of mother-citizens" (*Ahora* 30 January 1944). For the first celebration of International Women's Day, March 8th, the Committee for Suffrage sponsored a national meeting in Caracas. The minister of education and the president of Congress as well as party leaders attended and used the opportunity to affirm their support of women's rights (Hernandez 1985, 30).

This second petition for suffrage, signed by more than 14,000 women across the country, was introduced to Congress on 8 May 1944 to coincide with the beginning of a constitutional reform effort. It received support on the floor of Congress from several parties, but it was not passed. *Acefistas* continued to publicize their demands in *Ahora,* always stressing that women's enfranchisement would only serve to improve society, not to make women into men's rivals or change the structure of the family. Moreover, they employed the justifications used with the Civil Code reform: women deserved equal rights because of their contribution to wartime efforts and to the economy.

Facing a recalcitrant legislature, women continued to amass support. They drew not only on national but also on regional resources. Members of the AVM who decided to join the movement collaborated with the ACF and others in June, forming Women's Action (Acción Femenina), a new organization whose sole goal was to gain the vote (CISFEM 1992, 220). The idea for forming Women's Action almost certainly came from contact with the OAS's Inter-American Commission of Women (IACW), which was promoting the formation of groups with that name throughout the region, starting at the 1938 Conference of American States in Lima (Miller 1991, 115). Lucila Palacios, a prominent women's rights activist in Venezuela, corresponded with the IACW throughout the campaign (1991, 262, n. 22).

While women were gearing up for a more prolonged suffrage movement, they continued to serve in a time-honored capacity as the symbol of political freedom. Only this time, instead of standing for liberty as the 1928 student queen Beatrice I did, the new queen represented the growing hopes for political democracy. The contest to elect the queen of the Seventh World Series of Amateur Baseball, originally meant to be a small promotional gimmick for the event, was turned into a primer for universal suffrage (Henriquez 1989). In September, newspapers announced that the contest would be national and that anyone over fifteen could vote. The finalists were Oly Clemente, daughter of the presidential secretary, and Yolanda Leal, a poor schoolteacher. The class rivalry and its political implications were made explicit in the slogan of Clemente's supporters: "Oly Clemente for the respectable people, Yolanda Leal for the common folk" *(Oly Clemente para la gente decente, Yolanda Leal para la gente vulgar).* Each candidate had a national campaign team, and as many as 10,000 people turned out for rallies held all over the country. The election was publicized as a model for the coming municipal elections: "If people went with the same enthusiasm to other elections, the genuine leaders of the people would be elected" *(Ahora,* 24 September 1944).

As the campaign drew to a close, it made headlines. Both women's pictures were prominently featured on the covers of *Ahora.* On election day the "polls" were besieged by voters, both men and women, not all of whom were able to cast their "ballots." People put pictures of their favored candidate in the windows of their cars, and the city was abuzz with news of the "election." When Yolanda won overwhelmingly (17,834 to 6,009), her victory made the first page of *Ahora* (2 October 1944). For a week afterward, the paper reported on her activities. A poem, "Yola, Venezuela's Sweetheart" (*"Yola, Novia de Venezuela"*) was published, comparing her victory to that of David's over Goliath. The "daughter of the people" *(hija del pueblo)* had won, in the most democratic election in Venezuela's history.

Having participated in one mock election, women continued to press for political suffrage. They organized inside and outside of the state. They sent the presidents of the different state legislatures their petition in January 1945 and held the Second Preparatory Conference for the Venezuelan Women's Congress (II Conferencia Preparatoria del Congreso Femenino Venezolano[21]) with 200 delegates, again on International Women's Day. There they reaffirmed their desire for suffrage and addressed issues ranging from the national economy to the situation of indigenous women.

Women's efforts paid off—in part—when literate women were granted municipal suffrage in the constitutional reform of July 1945. However, this did not satisfy the suffragists, who realized that they would have to improve their methods and broaden their struggle outside of Caracas. Women's Action, with a membership of 1,500, took the lead, publishing the *Correo Cívico Femenino (Women's Civic Courier)*; broadcasting radio programs; and publishing a pamphlet on civic activity, the "Civic Primer" ("Cartilla Cívica"), explaining the different aspects of suffrage.

The *Correo Cívico Femenino* was published monthly from August 1945 to January 1947, circulating 81,000 copies for the price of postage alone across the country. It clearly sought to reconcile women's role as mothers with their desire for political citizenship, while reflecting the values of the class of women allowed to vote. The paper focused on civic education—including women's rights, what the vote meant and how to use it, and information about the constitution—as well as news on women's political advances in other countries. It combined these with tips on child rearing and recipes, always ending with a songsheet. The class of women voters to whom the paper was directed was made clear by the reiterated reassurances that the act of voting would not take women away from their daily lives. They could go dressed in the latest fashions, they could take their babies with them, and it would take no longer than a game of cards or a gossip session with the next-door neighbor.

Women's Action and its constituent groups (ACF, AVM, UMA, and the new Women's Association for Civic Education [Asociación Femenina de Edu-

---

21. The full congress did not take place until 1974; see Chapter 4.

cación Cívica]) capitalized on their suffrage coalition to pressure for a reform to the Commercial Code. On 22 June 1945, the reform was passed by Congress. It allowed married women to exercise a commercial profession independently of their husbands and to have legal control over their own property, including that which they bring into a marriage (Clemente Travieso 1961, 27–28).

The suffrage movement continued even after the beginning of the democratic *trienio* period. It ended only when AD, the dominant party of the coup coalition, decreed universal suffrage for all citizens over the age of eighteen, regardless of gender or literacy. In the elections for the Constitutional Assembly of October 1946, the strength of women's activism was confirmed by the election of twelve women, six of whom were prominent figures in the women's movement. Universal suffrage was enshrined in the constitution with the reform of July 1947.

Because AD had supported women's suffrage since 1936 and granted it along with the general extension of social benefits in the *trienio*, it is difficult to judge the success of the movement from the final passage of full suffrage. However, it is clear that women recognized the importance of gaining the right to vote and had mobilized widely—and successfully—for municipal suffrage. This mobilization had another effect: the election of twelve women to the Constitutional Assembly in a country that had never allowed women to hold national office. Women's limited demand for the vote "in the same conditions as men," which enfranchised only literate women, may be interpreted as sacrificing gender solidarity for class solidarity, or a matter of making conservative compromises in an attempt to achieve success.[22] But it is also likely that the decision to ask for the vote only for literate women was intended to assure men that women were not seeking to displace them or challenge them directly. To ask for universal suffrage for women in a context of men's restricted suffrage would have done just that.

The Political Opportunities of the Transition to Democracy (1945–1948)

With the "Revolution of October" that brought AD to power in 1945, women's political opportunities changed radically—and paradoxically. As parties increased their dominance of Venezuelan political life, these channels

22. Hahner argues much along these lines with respect to the Brazilian suffrage movement (1990, xvi, 129).

for interest representation impeded women's independent mobilization. It is not surprising that women, like men, turned to the parties to channel their political activism. The parties were actively recruiting different sectors and had been cooperative with the women's movement in the past. Now that women had the vote, they had every opportunity to make their voices heard through the normal channels of politics. But with the business of democratic politics firmly underway, women's incorporation into party politics resulted in the deprioritization of their issues and the marginalization of their actions.

While relational feminism worked to women's advantage in mobilizing for and achieving limited rights under liberalized authoritarianism, it would prove to be a difficult basis on which to organize when political opportunities changed.[23] The gendering of political discourse remained similar to that of the authoritarian period: men were regarded as fit for politics, women for domestic life. But this discourse took on more weight as it became institutionalized within the gendered structures of party politics. Women were incorporated into parties that formalized masculine gender privilege in politics and marginalized women. There was nowhere left to turn: women's organizations disbanded as their members went into different parties or left off organizing altogether.

General Political Opportunities

The political opportunity structure of the transition largely stemmed from party politics, especially the structures and actions of AD. Its dominance of *trienio* politics was facilitated by its high degree of organization. It was "democratic centralist," based on a tightly organized hierarchy that was both vertically and horizontally integrated (Levine 1973). To integrate vertically, the founders of AD built an organization with a clear chain of command from the national down through the local levels, with corresponding organizations (conventions, executive committees, and disciplinary tribunals) at each level.

Horizontal integration of AD was established through the mechanism of sectoral bureaus,[24] the institutionalization of the occupational branches

23. Kecia Ali argues that the problems with "social motherhood" have been overemphasized by historians of Latin American women's history, leading to a neglect of the power of maternalist rhetoric in gaining women perhaps the only foothold available to them in politics at the time and thus a crucial justification for claims to increased political power. However, my evidence supports what these historians have found. In the long term, "[W]ithout challenging traditional gender roles—and thus moving from the domestic into the public or political sphere—women's quest for enhanced social power and status is doomed" (1995, 12).

24. Bureaus are also known as "wings," "departments," or "branches." In Spanish, they are called *buros* (bureaus), *secretarías* (secretariats), and *frentes* (fronts).

that had been formed during clandestinity. The sectors multiplied over time, soon including not only the predominant labor and peasant sections but also youth, professionals, and women. The bureaus were integrated into the hierarchical party structure: each had a national secretary on the national executive committee, and there were representatives of the bureaus on every other level. They were supposed to serve as two-way communication channels, providing a means of party penetration into a given sector of civil society as well as a way for the sector to advance its issues within the party (and within the government, if the party was in power).

In practice, the penetration of civil society was greatly facilitated by the fact that parties helped to organize the major societal interest groups with which their sectoral bureaus interacted.[25] AD consolidated its hold over labor as a result of the events surrounding the Second Workers' Congress, convened in 1944 to establish a confederation (Martz 1966; Alexander 1969). After having its proposal to share the leadership equally with its communist rivals rejected, AD withdrew, leaving the new confederation linked to a political party, which was illegal. Medina Angarita then outlawed the confederation and all the unions that had participated in its founding. AD moved in on the now leaderless organizations, eventually tying them to its own structure. Facing no similar challenge within peasant unions, AD had little trouble establishing its dominance over peasant organizing by 1945 (Powell 1971).

Although the monopolization of sectoral representation of peasants and labor worked to the advantage of the sectors, producing favorable legislation and participation in political leadership, party efforts to control the student movement resulted in its loss of autonomy and unity. This decline was typified by the decimation of the student federation FEV. It first divided in 1936, when Catholic students, angered at the secularism of the group, left to form the rival National Student Union (Unión Nacional de Estudiantes or UNE). UNE formed the basis of what would become the Independent Electoral Committee (Comité Independiente Electoral or COPEI party), AD's main opponent in later years. With the legalization of parties under Medina Angarita, AD and the PCV fought for control over what remained of the FEV through their respective student bureaus, gradually incorporating students into the party youth branches (Levine 1973, 30–31). From then on, students would organize largely along party lines to achieve party goals rather than those of the students themselves.

In the *trienio* AD oversaw general improvements in social welfare, in-

25. For more information on AD's involvement in the founding of the principal labor federation, see Coppedge 1994, 31–35. For its involvement in the national peasant union, see Powell 1971.

cluding education, health, housing, transportation and infrastructure, food and clothing subsidies, prolabor legislation, agrarian reform, and industrial diversification. It also passed the so-called fifty-fifty legislation, mandating that foreign oil companies split their profits with the government. These advances further consolidated sectoral allegiance to AD as labor and peasant organizing was encouraged and the middle class benefited from government-sponsored education, employment, and services. Finally, AD oversaw a transition to political democracy. It proclaimed universal suffrage for all citizens over eighteen regardless of gender or literacy. Three elections took place during the *trienio*—for constituent assembly, for president and national and state legislatures, and for municipal councils—in all of which AD's candidates were the most successful. However, by 1946 other major parties had emerged. Besides AD and the PCV, COPEI and the Democratic Republican Union (Unión Republicana Democrática or URD, a personalist vehicle for the former president of FEV, Jovito Villalba) were constituted in 1946.

Despite its many successes, AD was not able to consolidate its democratic rule. Its policies created losers as well as winners. Economically, wealthy landowners were upset by agrarian reform; business was worried by concessions to labor; and foreign investors feared that the party would become increasingly radical in its policies. Socially, the church objected to AD's secularism, especially when it came to state regulation of education; and some elites were caught in AD's campaign to bring to trial those accused of corruption under former regimes, which many saw as AD's vengeance against those who had hurt its members in the past. Politically, the other parties claimed AD held too much power. But the most important source of opposition turned out to be the military, which objected to its loss of power during the *trienio*. After AD candidate Rómulo Gallegos was elected president in early November 1948, the military presented him with demands, including the appointment of more officers to the cabinet and the exiling of Betancourt, the head of AD. When these demands were not acceded to, the military took over on 24 November 1948.

Gendered Discourse

Political discourse in the *trienio* continued to be used in such a way as to associate women with private life, even within their political activity. Parties employed this rhetoric to varying degrees, with COPEI, the Christian Democratic party, most receptive to it:

The Venezuelan woman, underappreciated at times and misunderstood at others, has demonstrated in the civil struggle and in COPEI's activities her great capacity and her purifying civicism. Without abandoning her home, which makes the most primordial claim on her; without trying to deform her particular role in the world, masculinizing herself; conserving herself wholly feminine and vocationally home-loving, the *copeyana* [female COPEI] woman has demonstrated that she knows and can fight for the country, for her convictions, and for her ideals.[26]

Women's strategy to challenge gender hierarchy while accepting gender difference resulted in the limited gains of women's early mobilization. But virtuous and "vocationally home-loving" women were not the obvious players in politics. The very different virtues needed in political life may in fact have discouraged women from participating once they were granted suffrage (Kirkwood 1986) and discouraged men from encouraging them. But while discourse had equivocal effects on women's ability to organize, the institutionalization of gender difference in the mechanisms of politics during the transition was more definitively detrimental to women's activism.

The Gendered Institution of Party Politics

Gendered discourse alone did not account for women's marginalization in democratic politics. The embeddedness of gender relations in the powerful political parties of the *trienio* ensured that women would have difficulty advancing through the principal channel of representation. Because parties were built on the assumption that men would be the primary political activists—not only in leadership but also in membership—the leaders accommodated the masculine gender within the very structure of the parties. The requirements of leadership ensured that only with great difficulty would women rise to the top. But the masculine-oriented sectoral bureaus were the central culprit. While the women's bureau had historical usefulness in bringing women into party politics at their foundation, under democracy it turned into a women's ghetto, leading neither to the expression of women's interests nor to the promotion of their leadership. Instead, it led to their becoming the housekeepers of the public sphere.

26. "Essence and Future Projects of COPEI, September 1946," in Suarez Figueroa 1983, 2:106.

Leadership

The highly organized parties of *trienio* centralized policy decision making and party administration, including selection of candidates for party and elective positions, in the hands of a small group of leaders (the National Executive Committee—Comité Ejecutivo Nacional—or CEN), which transmitted decisions down through a highly organized structure to the base.[27] The CEN fiercely guarded this power to control party workings, including the power to nominate internal and external candidates.

It was no accident that until 1988 no major party had more than three women on the CEN and elected women representatives remained below 5 percent of Congress (Huggins Castañeda and Dominguez Nelson 1993; García Prince 1993; Valdéz and Gomáriz 1995). These positions were designed for someone of the masculine gender. To move into higher levels of party structure or be nominated for elective office, one's devotion to party life had to be a priority. A woman could not devote herself to the party if she was expected to fulfill the myriad demands of private life. When asked in an interview why so few women rose as high as she had in AD, Mercedes Fermín responded that there were not women in a position to dedicate their lives completely to the party as she had done. Discussion with current female party leaders indicates that little has changed since the first transition to democracy: few of them have significant home-based responsibilities, and those that do have full-time help.[28] They can take on leadership roles only if they can give up domestic duties or have others take them over.[29] Moreover, many of the women who have achieved significant party positions are attached to highly placed men, either as family members or lovers, and are often known as "women of" (*mujeres de*) particular men.[30] This phrase reinforces the idea that legitimate leaders are men.

Membership

Parties used the mechanism of sectoral bureaus as a means of influencing different social sectors and attracting members. This interaction was greatly

27. For more on Venezuelan party structure, see Martz 1966; Coppedge 1994; Kornblith and Levine 1995.

28. Interviews with Isabel Carmona, Paulina Gamus Gallegos, Isolda Salvatierra, and Ixora Rojas, and informal conversation with other women in leadership positions.

29. This statement is not meant to imply that all men are able to devote themselves to politics full time, but men's work schedules on the whole allow for party duties better than women's, which usually include a range of domestic tasks to be carried out throughout the day, whether a woman works for pay or not.

30. This finding is not limited to Venezuela. Mala Htun (1998, 13) notes that frequently in Latin America, "women who have achieved power in government are relatives of male politicians."

facilitated by the fact that parties had helped to establish the peak organizations representing these sectors. Thus most groups—from unions to student councils, peasant leagues to professional organizations—held internal elections in which the candidates were chosen on the basis of party affiliation.[31] Groups that tried to remain aloof from party politics rarely succeeded.[32]

Organized labor and peasants were the primary beneficiaries of this form of party organization, receiving in return for promoting party interests within their sector an array of rewards: party posts, representation in both executive and legislative branches, favorable legislation, and material benefits. This exchange underwrote a class compromise. The working class received "compensation" for agreeing to bargain with middle-class party elites instead of forming a significant class-based movement. Thus, overall, Venezuelan civil society was organized along party lines, with ideological adherence leading to successful clientelistic relationships for the party faithful.[33]

Women were given their own bureau, as the parties followed the historical rationale for its existence from the 1930s when many of the women parties targeted for inclusion did not have an association outside of the home but were housewives.[34] Several female party leaders, including two who had been heads of AD's women's bureau in the 1940s, agree that initially a dedicated bureau was necessary to reach women, who had had little exposure to politics.[35]

In the transition to democracy, however, the women's movement, like the student movement before it, was largely absorbed into the parties without garnering the benefits that accrued to other sectors through their respective bureaus. Women received few leadership positions and gained little elective representation, favorable legislation, or material advantage. Scant at-

31. Coppedge (1994, 28) mentions rumors that even beauty contests are decided along party lines. I heard of at least one instance in which a party organized a beauty contest, though the party affiliation of the winner was not known.

32. The main examples of this tendency have been the neighborhood associations *(asociaciones de vecinos)*, often looked to as the best hope for nonpartisan citizen mobilization in civil society. The parties, however, have attempted to infiltrate this movement as well, creating parallel neighborhood organizations or running candidates for existing organizations' boards who have the advantage of party resources to distribute (see discussion in Chapter 7). Party dominance of civil society led Coppedge to claim that "parties in Venezuela have a preoccupation with controlling social organizations that borders on obsession" (1994, 29).

33. For an analysis of party dominance of civil society, see Coppedge 1994, chap. 2. For further consideration of the obstacles this situation posed for deepening the later democratization of Venezuela, see Brewer-Carías 1988; García 1992; Salamanca 1995.

34. Some women were employed as nurses and teachers (de Leonardi 1983, 201). Those in the second category did enter parties through the "professional" bureaus as they developed (Mercedes Sandoval Marcano interview).

35. Mercedes Fermín and Ana Esther Gouverneur, in Petzoldt and Bevilacqua 1979; interviews with Paulina Gamus Gallegos, Evangelina García Prince, Isolda Salvatierra.

tention was paid to the demands women had raised during the period of liberalized authoritarianism.

The ineffectiveness of the parties' women's bureaus stemmed from the nature of sectoral bureau membership, which (much like leadership positions) was designed to facilitate men's participation. Because the dominant party model was multiclass, most of the sectors, or interests, that parties sought to organize were based on some functional derivation of class position—the laborers and peasants of the working class, and students and professionals of the bourgeoisie. These positions happened to correspond to what were traditionally men's various occupations in the public sphere. Each of these occupations had one or more organizations associated with it—its particular unions, leagues, or associations, whose internal elections were the main point of entry for party penetration. Parties could thus manipulate the workings of the sector, but each sector also had a basis from which to make demands on party leadership. This arrangement allowed for the successful co-optation of the interest groups based on masculine gender into partisan political life.

But women were incorporated on the basis of their gender identity—simply *as women,* whose primary association as a group was with private life. Because the sectoral grouping of women was not derived from a class position or socioeconomic function around which they could unite to advance common interests, there was no "women's union" in which to hold partisan elections and in whose name they could in turn claim party favors, such as leadership positions, candidacy for elective office, material benefits, and influence on policy. Because parties did not perceive women as an interest needing attention, they did not encourage such organization.

Moreover, it is doubtful that even if a "women's union" had existed, it could have played the role that the other interest groups took on. While the women's bureau was clearly established to incorporate one of many social sectors into party life, it was chronically weak—always underfunded and understaffed, and never given the prominence of the other branches. The neglect of the women's bureau shows that its goal was capturing a part of the electorate, not representing "women's interests" in policy or promoting women as party representatives, the two goals of the other bureaus. Women's "private" demands—based on either gender equality or gender difference—were a challenge to the whole structure of masculine politics and were not sought out. Politics was to remain an area reserved for men.

The Decline of Women's Organizing in the Transition to Democracy (1945–1948)

Women had been ostensibly included in the structure of politics—what were they to do that would not challenge male dominance? Instead of leading to the promotion of women and women's issues in party life, the women's bureau fulfilled women's traditional gender role: it carried out the reproductive tasks of the political sphere.[36] If women had entered politics on the basis of their mothering role, they were marginalized by it within the parties, becoming their "housekeepers." "Keeping house"[37] (hosting meetings, making coffee and copies, throwing fundraising parties and running raffles) and "raising the children" (turning out the vote during elections) became the primary duties of the first women's bureaus.[38] AD's bureau continued to teach women to read and write, but increasingly with an eye to insuring their political indoctrination (de Leonardi 1983, 403). When women's issues were addressed in party politics (a rare event), they were inevitably issues related to their maternal role: promoting *puericultura*, breast-feeding, student nutrition, vaccinations, health, and social security (CISFEM 1992, 222).

Outside of the parties, women's organizing declined precipitously. The various women's groups that existed were destroyed by partisan politics. Even before the transition to democracy but after Medina Angarita legalized parties, political schism had already begun to affect women's organizing. The gendered unity celebrated at the Second Preparatory Conference for the Venezuelan Women's Congress, for example, was not entirely stable: "The unity of women was weakened by party activism to the point where, in the [conference] welcoming remarks the president of the meeting, Panchita Soublette Saluzzo, directed conciliatory words 'to the delegates of different ideologies' to exhort them to maintain a more unified conduct 'because we all need each other,' a clear reference to the political ruptures which were taking place" (CISFEM 1992, 223). Already split along lines of class and political affiliation, the associations found it too difficult to continue their ongoing

---

36. Alvarez has found a similar outcome in other cases of party recruitment of women: "Partisan courtship of new female constituencies . . . reinforced political power imbalances between the sexes by replicating and institutionalizing existing gender power arrangements within the party organizations themselves. I emphasize the word 'courtship' because male dominated political parties typically assigned women a 'special' place within partisan ideologies, platforms and programs, and organizational infrastructures—and that place was quite compatible with dominant female stereotypes and with women's continued confinement to domestic roles, or at best, with extension of those roles to the political arena" (1986, 105).

37. In Venezuela the party headquarters is known as the National House (Casa Nacional) of the party.

38. Alvarez (1986) calls women "the reserve army of electoral labor."

work on women's behalf as parties came to power. During the *trienio* the Working Women's Center closed, and the ACF, the most powerful motor of the women's movement, was stilled: "The Center died when democracy began. Because then each of the women had located herself in her party, and that nucleus which was formed by all the women of the different parties had begun to languish. The parties had been founded already at that time, and of course, each women went, locating herself in her specific group, and the Association started to decay" (Ana Senior interview).

Despite the granting of suffrage and women's election to the Constitutional Assembly, a victory in itself, the more basic issues of civil rights that women had fought for over the previous ten years received little attention during the *trienio*. In early 1947 a new women's organization, the Venezuelan Women's Union (Unión Femenina Venezolana), was formed to circulate another petition, directed this time to the Constitutional Assembly, on matters such as paternity testing, prenuptial medical certification, and paid maternity leave. They received no response. Meanwhile, women would wait another forty-two years before the election of the same number of representatives as they gained in 1946, an achievement that would come about only with the resurgence of a cross-party women's movement in the 1980s (see Chapter 5).

Venezuelan women learned for themselves what many other women's movements had experienced before and would continue to experience after: trading in their own organizations and orientations for that of male-dominated institutions resulted in the scattering of their energies with little to show for their efforts.[39] Democratic politics did not make a difference in this regard. Indeed, the institutionalization of gender bias in the very channels promoted for democratic citizen participation excluded women even as they were incorporated into party politics. Moreover, the dissolving of women's own organizations resulted in the loss of political space they had claimed under authoritarianism. The gendered nature of the transition to democracy harmed women's potential to achieve their own goals.

This chapter has analyzed the paradoxical rise and fall of the early Venezuelan women's movement during the first transition to democracy. In the explosion of civic activity following the death of the dictator Juan Vicente Gómez, predominantly elite women organized in women's groups. Justifying their activity as part and parcel of responsible motherhood, they drew to-

---

39. Estelle Freedman describes a similar outcome for the U.S. suffrage movement: "When women tried to assimilate into male-dominated institutions, without securing feminist social, economic, or political bases, they lost the momentum and the networks which had made the suffrage movement possible" (1979, 524).

gether in campaigns to end discriminatory family legislation and to be granted the vote. Their activism was conditioned by the political context. Allowed more room to organize because they were not seen as politically threatening to the regime, women at the same time faced a political discourse that took little account of their rights and a congress made up of conservative male politicians. Consequently, their legal gains were limited to a partial reform of the Civil Code and municipal suffrage. Activists' class biases also limited the extent of their popular following, a problem that would continue to affect their organizing in the future.

Instead of encouraging women's participation, the transition to democracy short-circuited the development of their autonomous organizing, throwing into question the extent and meaning of democratization. Although the AD party gave women the national vote, suffrage alone did not make women into a viable political force. The political institutions of democracy, especially political parties, proved to be undemocratic when it came to gender relations. The institutionalization of gender bias within the very structures of political parties effectively pushed women out of political life, restricting their leadership and the channels for their issues.

However, the *acefistas* and others laid down important groundwork for future activists to build upon. Their coalition-based strategies for achieving both a reform of the Civil Code and women's suffrage would be repeated. Particularly during a second and more successful drive to reform the Civil Code in the early 1980s, women would again rely on unified organizing, petition drives, and the strategic use of gendered political discourse. In doing so, they would continue to develop the alternative form of political participation devised by early activists.[40] Women would challenge the soon-to-be dominant method of political organization by building on their experience of exclusion and significantly restructuring the mechanisms of participation.

But it would be several decades before women's organizing on their own behalf successfully reemerged. Meanwhile, the return of authoritarian rule in 1948 brought a new set of paradoxical opportunities for women's participation. Women's continuing overall association with private life made them a valuable asset to the newly clandestine political parties, and as a result women were incorporated into opposition activity. During the dictatorship

---

40. Saluzzo's perceptions notwithstanding, at the closing of the Second Preparatory Conference, the president of Congress, invited to address the attendees, explicitly differentiated between the growing partisan struggles of male-dominated politics and women's ability to unite: "The women are teaching us as men that it is possible to overcome petty personal and political ambitions, when it is a matter of establishing a common front to achieve a cherished ideal" (*Ahora* 11 March 1945).

itself, they further developed both gender interests and organizational strategy, including conjunctural coalition building. With the second transition to democracy, however, the particular paradox of political parties reappeared: the gendered institutions of strong parties along with a highly centralized state again forced women to the sidelines of democratic politics.

WHY "*MACHISMO* WAS
STRONGER THAN A MILITARY
DICTATORSHIP":

*Women's Organizing in the
Second Transition to Democracy
(1948–1973)*

On International Women's Day, 8 March 1958, ten thousand women gathered in the largest stadium in Caracas to celebrate the fall of the dictatorship of Major Marcos Pérez Jiménez (1952–58) and to honor the many women who had taken an active role in opposing it. Sponsored by the women's committee of the coordinating council of the opposition, this gathering was the first mass meeting following the demise of authoritarian rule. Despite the array of political views represented in the audience and on the dais, unity was stressed by every speaker. Women had been united in their struggle against the dictatorship, and united they would promote their own rights in the fledgling democracy. Yet within a year, the women's committee was disbanded, and as a result, women's organizing declined precipitously in the new democracy. Women did not hold another large-scale nonpartisan meeting for sixteen years, and then only when the United Nations' International Women's Year in 1974 galvanized the two thousand participants.

What happened to women's unity? As had occurred in the previous transition, the paradoxes of political opportunity led to women's mobilization under authoritarianism and demobilization with the advent of democracy. During the dictatorship the general opportunities of an opposition movement run primarily through clandestine parties were also gendered. The male-dominated parties were unable to operate without the help of seemingly nonpolitical actors—women—who were thus identified in the political discourse of Pérez Jiménez. Like his predecessors, López Contreras and Medina Angarita, he continued to associate men with political life and women with the home. Thus party leaders took advantage of women's nonpolitical role, recruiting them into some of the more visible aspects of the opposition, both as individuals and in separate women's groups.

In contrast to its original construction, which relied on a masculine hierarchy and male-oriented membership, the gendered nature of political parties was now modified. Individual women's contributions were circumscribed by the still-operative masculine hierarchy. But in their group actions, women regendered the housekeeping role of the party women's bureau. These groups also relied on assumptions about women's lack of association with politics to help disguise their activity. However, their partial autonomy allowed women to take on leadership roles and develop an awareness of their common interests in ending gender-based discrimination both inside and outside of the parties.

With the uniting of the opposition toward the end of the dictatorship in the Patriotic Council (Junta Patriótica), another general opportunity presented itself: united organization. It too was gendered; as with the parties, the leadership of the Patriotic Council was all male. But drawing on their growth as political actors during the dictatorship, women included themselves by forming a linked group, the Women's Committee (Comité Femenino), to encourage women's participation in the opposition. Like the women who had been active a decade or so earlier, the Women's Committee formed a coalition across political parties. It grew in strength, eventually sponsoring the first mass rally following the downfall of the dictatorship. The ten thousand women who attended and the speeches that were given attested to a promising role for women's organizing in the new democracy.

But before they could establish a firm foothold, women's unity was fractured by both the general and gendered opportunities of the transition to democracy. Like the Patriotic Council, the Women's Committee fell afoul of the "pacted" transition agreements. These agreements excluded the Communist Party and privileged both party- and state-based interest representation. When women either entered into the resulting Communist-led guerrilla movement or rejoined the legalized parties, they again experienced marginalization because of the gender-biased structures of these opportunities. But the experience women had gained through their clandestine organizing efforts was not wholly lost. The network formed by those who had been active under the dictatorship became the basis on which women began to come together again to discuss their common goals at the end of the transition period.

This chapter begins with the demographic changes women experienced during dictatorship and the transition to democracy. It then offers a description of the general and gendered political opportunity structure of the period of dictatorship (1948–58) and shows how it led to parties' use of women's activism and women's organizational development. The second half of the chapter explains how the shift in opportunities with the transition to democracy and beginning of democratic consolidation (1958–73) led to women's incomplete incorporation into the guerrilla movement, the restoration of gender-biased party structures, and a new form of discriminatory representation through the state. Although these opportunities largely blocked women's independent organizing, at the end of the period women were still struggling to assert their unified demands.

Women's Status, 1950–1970

As the urban population of Venezuela increased in the period between 1950 and 1970 (hitting 72 percent by 1970), women as a demographic group underwent significant changes. They had fewer children, while increasing their educational levels and labor force participation, albeit in "feminized" occupations. Between 1950 and 1970 the number of children per woman declined from 6.5 to 5.1 (Huggins Castañeda and Dominguez Nelson 1993). With the increased emphasis on education in the democratic period,[1] women's high school enrollment grew from 32.7 percent in 1950 to 39 percent in 1961 and reached 50 percent in 1970 (Ministerio de Fomento 1968; Huggins Castañeda and Dominguez Nelson 1993). Women remained above 80 percent of those enrolled in teachers' training colleges during the period. They were also catching up at the university level: in 1946 women constituted only 10 percent of university enrollment, tripling to 31 percent in 1960, and rising to 43.7 percent by 1972—though this figure represented only around 40,000 women (Ministerio de Educación 1960; Huggins Castañeda and Dominguez Nelson 1993).[2]

Women's participation in the labor force rose from 17.7 percent in 1950 to 22.4 percent in 1970. Throughout the period women were primarily employed in the low-paying service sector (around 44 percent of all working women), forming 70 percent of those employed in menial jobs such as housekeeping, laundry work, and waitressing. Women's employment in agriculture declined, as did men's, from 10 to 5 percent of working women. At the same time, female "professionals and technicals" increased from 9 to 19 percent. This increase was not as transformative as it might sound because it included

1. Secondary and university enrollment doubled in the first four years of the democracy (Ewell 1984a, 142).
2. Not all the statistics on university enrollment are disaggregated by sex, making an exact figure hard to come by.

the large category of schoolteacher, a profession traditionally practiced by women. Moreover, women as a percentage of the entire sector of "professionals and technicals" did not increase during the period. Office work became a significant occupation, and the percentage of female office workers rose from 6.2 to 18 percent of all working women (an increase also reflected by their representation in the category, which rose from 30 to 44 percent). Women also moved into sales, increasing from 4 to 9 percent (from 8 to 15 percent of the total sector) (OCEI 1961, 1971).

It has been hypothesized that such demographic changes form the underpinning for women's organizing on their own behalf (Klein 1984). However, as noted above, Venezuelan women's organizing declined during the second half of this period. To understand why, we must examine how the political opportunity structures of dictatorship and democracy affected women's organizing.

The Political Opportunities of Dictatorship (1948–1958)

The political opportunity structure of the Pérez Jiménez dictatorship was characterized by personalistic rule justified by the need for economic development and made possible by a repressive security apparatus; it was opposed by clandestine political parties. The opposition was divided at first by the parties' different strategies. But toward the end of the decade, they coordinated their efforts and joined in an all-party council that oversaw the increasing mobilization of civil society sectors, whose combined efforts brought about the downfall of the dictator and the transition to democracy.[3]

Venezuela's first experiment with democratic politics, the three-year period known as the *trienio,* was abruptly ended by a military coup in 1948. An all-male provisional military *junta* (council) took over; and within two years it banned the former ruling party, AD, its affiliated unions, and the PCV.[4] At first the *junta* promised to restore democracy. But after the murder

---

3. This section draws from accounts of the dictatorship in Stambouli 1980; Avendaño Lugo 1982; and García Ponce and Camacho Barrios 1982.

4. In 1944 the Communist Party split into two factions, known as the "Red" and the "Black" communists, over support for the government of Medina Angarita. The "Red" faction, which became the PCV, went on to give limited support to AD during the *trienio,* while the "Black" faction, which eventually called itself the (Communist) Revolutionary Proletarian Party (Partido Revolucionario Proletario [Communista] or PRP-C), opposed AD. Unlike the PCV, the PRP-C did not openly oppose Pérez Jimenéz and remained legal for most of the dictatorship. Toward the end, however, certain PRP-C leaders joined with the PCV in fighting against the regime (Alexander 1969, chap. 1).

of *junta* president and former minister of defense, Carlos Delgado Chalbauld, in November 1950, Major Marcos Pérez Jiménez, a hard-liner, became the most powerful *junta* member. After the 1952 elections he accused the winning party, the Democratic Republican Union (URD), of collaborating with the banned parties and claimed victory for himself and the government party. The URD leadership was sent into exile. They were joined by leaders of the other party that had participated in the elections, COPEI. Although COPEI itself was never officially banned during the dictatorship, its leadership spurned the dictatorship for its repressive political tactics.

The goal of the Pérez Jiménez dictatorship, expressed through the doctrine of the "New National Ideal" *(Nuevo Ideal Nacional)*, was to promote national development through a transformation of the physical environment—that is, the construction of infrastructure. Telecommunications and transportation, iron manufacturing and irrigation, recreational facilities and oil refining were all expanded during the period as state-led industrialization boomed. Although the regime's propaganda, as illustrated by publications of the new social security administration, claimed that all citizens benefited from this transformation, the priorities were clear. The "human environment" was the "essential complement" to the transformation of the "physical environment" (Instituto Venezolano de Seguros Sociales 1957).

Armed repression was employed to control those who valued bodies over buildings. At first Pérez Jiménez relied on the military to ensure order, but he soon established a private police force, the National Security Force (Seguridad Nacional or SN), whose brutality led it to be nicknamed the *gestapo criollo* (native gestapo). Thus, although the period of authoritarianism started under the rule of a military council, it soon degenerated into a personal dictatorship.

Most of the opposition to Pérez Jiménez was carried out by AD and the PCV in clandestinity and from exile. To try to escape detection, the parties retreated from mass mobilization to their original networks of small "cell" structures whose members rarely knew each others' real names. Initially AD focused on fomenting armed rebellion by establishing contacts among the procivilian-rule military leadership, while the PCV attempted to rebuild a mass movement. Their different objectives, as well as the anticommunist beliefs of AD's exiled but still effective leadership, precluded the establishment of a unified opposition. Both parties suffered heavy losses as their cell-based organizations were rooted up and crushed again and again by the ruthless SN. Opposition waned as hundreds were jailed, many repeatedly, and some were interned in a concentration camp established on disease-infested Guasina Island in the Orinoco Delta in eastern Venezuela. AD was dealt a severe blow when its clandestine secretary-general, Leonardo Ruiz Piñeda, was assassinated in 1952 and his successor, Alberto Carnavali, died the following year.

After several years of severe repression, the reduction of opposition forces led to more cooperation between the parties. A new generation of leaders, including students radicalized over the decade of dictatorship, replaced those killed and sent into exile and forged a unitary movement. In June 1957 they established the multiparty Patriotic Council to coordinate the opposition. Mobilization increased when Pérez Jiménez announced a plebiscite on his rule, as well as general elections, for December. Joined now by professional organizations, the middle class, and even the business sector,[5] the Patriotic Council took to the streets. Reflecting the new makeup of the opposition movement, huge student strikes were mounted toward the end of November. In reaction to Pérez Jiménez's claim to victory in the plebiscite, an estranged sector of the military attempted a coup on the first of January 1958. Insufficient coordination resulted in a lack of support for the uprising, but the rest of January was turmoil, with continuous riots, school closings, and the open circulation of prodemocracy propaganda. The Patriotic Council called for a general strike on 22 January, and the army joined in to bring down the dictatorship the following day.

The Gendering of Opportunities Under Dictatorship

The political context of the dictatorship included a gendered institution and discourse that served to promote female participation: the repressed male-dominated parties and the association of men, not women, with political activity. Pérez Jiménez sought to repress traditional political activism, which meant eradicating the parties founded in the mid-1930s and expanded in the *trienio*. His idea was to raze society's institutions almost literally and to build new ones. Known political activists had no place in his plan. As his principal ideologue Laureano Vallenilla Lanz explained: "The tractor is the government's best collaborator, the exact interpreter of the elevated and noble aim of transforming the physical environment. . . . The tractor, that symbol of the fatherland and of the government, destroys many things, even the political clubs called parties and their representatives" (cited in Stambouli 1980, 94).

The information available suggests that Pérez Jiménez did not consider women to be political actors, at least initially. "The problems which present

5. Business was disgruntled by Pérez Jiménez's squandering the oil wealth of the country on grandiose building projects to the point of running up debts with nationally based companies.

themselves in life should be resolved by men," he told his biographer. "Women, although they might be the best companions, have their concerns with family life" (Tarnoi 1954, 197). The dictator had little else to say on the subject.[6]

Opposition party leaders took advantage of Pérez Jiménez's association of men with politics by organizing women to do clandestine work.[7] Unlike the dictator, they were quite aware of women's potential for activism from their history of organizing, some of which had taken place through parties. Many of the women who took part had some previous contact with the parties, either personally or through family members.[8] Interviews with former activists routinely highlight party sympathies, if not membership.[9] Many were teachers or students, coming from environments where political activism, albeit clandestine, was a common experience.[10] The majority of these participants were young women without children, some unmarried, who were available for work outside the home. Like their activist foremothers, most came from middle-class backgrounds, although there were some notable exceptions among members of the Communist Party.

Most accounts of the opposition published after the fact have ignored women's participation (Levine 1973, 1989; Stambouli 1980; Avendaño Lugo 1982).[11] But women played a significant role. *Libro Negro 1952: Venezuela bajo el signo del terror* (The 1952 Black Book: Venezuela beneath the sign of terror), a collection of clandestine documents published and circulated by the

6. A review of governmental publications during the dictatorship and analyses of the period reveal no other significant references to Pérez Jiménez's views on women.

7. Besides the textual material cited in this chapter, much of the information on women's participation is drawn from seventy interviews with participants in the opposition. Fifty-four of the interviews are collected in two works, Petzoldt and Bevilacqua (1979), and Farías Toussaint, de la Cruz Mejías, and Rodríguez Sánchez (1985). I also conducted interviews with sixteen participants in 1994–95. Some of the participants were interviewed in more than one study. Quotations are drawn from these interviews, listed with their dates in the bibliography, as well as from the other two works.

8. Forty-seven percent of the interviewees (see note 7) cite family influence as crucial in their political development. This evidently carries into later periods: according to a 1975 survey, Venezuelan women were more liable than men to be influenced by family members on political matters (cited in Montero 1987, 32).

9. Almost all the interviewees were either clandestine party members or sympathizers during the dictatorship: 54 percent were with AD, 37 percent with the Communist Party (PCV), 7 percent with COPEI, and 1.4 percent with the Democratic Republicans (URD).

10. Several interviewees were members of the Venezuelan Teachers' Federation (Federación Venezolana de Maestros or FVM), one of the most active associations to take part in the early opposition. Alcira Colmenares and Mercedes Sandoval Marcano mentioned that the FVM, reflecting the makeup of the profession, was around 75 percent female, though not led by women.

11. Martz (1966), writing soon after events, did not ignore women's contribution, but mentioned it briefly. The attention Martz paid to women's participation in politics, unique among

AD during the dictatorship, lists 110 women known to have been imprisoned or exiled between 1948 and 1952.[12] The editors of *Nosotras también nos jugamos la vida* (We too risk our lives), a collection of interviews with women who fought against the dictatorship, assembled the names of 275 women remembered as having participated in the struggle (Petzoldt and Bevilacqua 1979). While these numbers no doubt underrepresent women's participation, the lists and other descriptive materials indicate that women's activism was valued at the time both by the male clandestine party leadership and by the female activists themselves.

Party leadership incorporated women both as individuals and in groups. Although they accomplished crucial tasks, individual women largely carried out the infrastructural duties of the opposition, or exposed the abuses of the regime, according to the directives of the male leadership. But their experience in groups led women to modify the formerly passive nature of the party-linked women's branches. Under dictatorship, women in party-linked groups gained leadership experience and developed networks. The knowledge and skills they acquired would continue to foster gender-based activism in later years. However, because women's mobilization as a whole was predicated on their association with the private sphere, it did not form a basis on which they could develop sustained public activity when confronted with a new set of opportunities in the transition to democracy.

Engendering *Enlaces*: Women's Incorporation as Individuals

By incorporating individual women in clandestine work, male party leaders used gender relations strategically. For one thing, they disguised women's political work as nonsuspect activity, "designat[ing] for women jobs which their female condition itself allowed them to accomplish" (Farías Toussain, de la Cruz Mejíias, and Rodríguez Sánchez 1985, 97). For another, they drew on assumptions about the "weaker sex" in publicizing the eventual persecution of women to demonstrate the extent of dictatorial abuses, which extended to "defenseless ladies." Individual women found a certain level of acceptance from the leadership. But the masculine hierarchy of the parties re-

---

analysts of Venezuelan politics, probably stems from his friendship with Mercedes Fermín, a prominent member of AD since its founding (Fermín interview).

12. This represents 3.4 percent of the total named in the *Libro Negro* (3,147 men are also listed).

mained in place, leading some women to recognize that they were not receiv-ing the same kind of training as men for future political activity.

Women undertook many of the same duties as men but were called upon especially for certain tasks. One of the principal ones was acting as an *enlace*—a combination of liaison and "gopher"—for men in the opposition leadership.[13] *Enlaces* undertook a range of activities, such as transmitting daily messages to and from key contacts, finding "safe houses" in which the leaders could hide, setting up meeting sites, and running errands for the lead-ers.[14] Often women were entrusted with crucial information. For example, Regina Gómez Peñalver was the only other person besides the male secre-tary-general to know the names and hiding places of AD's clandestine lead-ership in the early years of the opposition (Petzoldt and Bevilacqua 1979, 253). Providing personal protection was also part of women's responsibility. They often chauffeured party leaders or accompanied them on foot or on public transportation.

Taking care of communications and propaganda distribution were other regular duties. Women passed secret messages to male prisoners in food or while greeting them with an embrace. A woman pretending to be the im-prisoned AD leader Alberto Carnavali's sister smuggled him the gun that he used in an escape attempt. Women also carried notes in their clothing and leaflets in furled umbrellas. When the wife of AD's clandestine secretary-general Ruiz Piñeda was forced into exile following his assassination, she stuffed her daughters' teddy bears with documents. Women also put their houses at the disposition of the parties, facilitating meetings and hiding those who could not risk being seen. Socorro Negreti noted that clandestine radio broadcasts were transmitted from her house (Farías Toussain, de la Cruz Mejías, and Rodríguez Sánchez 1985).

Examination of the assignments that individual women carried out re-veals how women's tasks were facilitated by their gender. Women's mere presence effectively disguised the political escorting of a male leader as a ro-mantic stroll. As Clarisa Sanoja explained, "Many times they needed a woman, not as a driver, but at their side to appear as though they were a couple out walking in the street" (Petzoldt and Bevilacqua 1979, 125). Pris-oners were expected and allowed to get visits, packages, and embraces from their "sisters," "sweethearts," "wives," and "mothers." Items of women's clothing, such as the undergarments and maternity smocks that most sug-

---

13. *Enlace* literally means "connection" or "linkage."
14. The *Libro Negro* itself was delivered to the publisher by one of the AD secretary general's key *enlaces*, Carmen Veitia (*Libro Negro 1952* 1983, vi).

gested their gender, were used for transporting messages, as were their children's toys.

Party leadership benefited from the activities women could accomplish under the cover of their nonpolitical gender. Simultaneously, they used gender relations to publicize the fact that the dictatorship violated gender norms in persecuting those same women. The dictatorship did come to recognize that women as well as men were taking part in the political opposition, and to treat them similarly to the male activists. One woman who had been imprisoned was greeted by her interrogator with a slap and the words "Here women don't have a sex" (*El Nacional,* 12 March 1980, C-1). Many women were interrogated, imprisoned, and exiled; some were brutally tortured. But some treatment remained gender-specific. Activist Yolanda Villaparedes recalled how she was threatened with rape by her jailers: "As [women] pretend not to know anything, and are enemies of the government, we are going to make them pregnant by the government to see what they will do with the children" (Petzoldt and Bevilacqua 1979, 298).

Secretary-general Ruiz Piñeda, writing to Luisa Velásquez, an author and the *enlace* responsible for collecting material on women for the *Libro Negro* (Black Book), demonstrated the party's interest in showing that women in particular had been mistreated by the Pérez Jiménez regime:

> I have an important job for you. . . . Right now we are preparing
> a pamphlet[15] about the violations of the regime against public liberties, a type of indictment which we hope to issue in the course
> of the next month. I want it to be you who works on everything
> referring to offenses against women. To this end I suggest you: a)
> Draft a central report, a sort of history of police violations against
> Venezuelan women since November 1948. This report should be
> extensive, it doesn't matter how long. You should do an inventory
> of searches, ill-treatment, detentions, exiles, imprisonments, etc.
> You should describe whatever facts you know; b) [Include] complementary documents referring to the women's struggle against
> the dictatorship. . . . [W]e will also need graphic material: photos
> of abused, arrested, imprisoned and exiled women. (Ruiz Piñeda
> Papers)

Velásquez came through. Details on the treatment of women are scattered throughout the text of the *Libro Negro.* Women are clearly considered

---

15. The *Libro Negro,* in preparation at that time.

part of the opposition, as shown by the repeated use of the phrase "men and women" in descriptions of the general actions of participants. But the gender hierarchy is equally clear: in discussions of leadership, only "men" is used. Moreover, women's "normal" gender roles are emphasized for effect. Although portrayed as active participants, women are simultaneously seen as weak and victimized: "Defenseless ladies (*Damas indefensas*) have been jailed and thrown into prison cells, in outrageous proximity to criminals, and, afterwards, forced into exile" (*Libro Negro* 1983, 59).[16] The section on the methods of persecution and terror contains a subsection on "Exiled, Imprisoned and Hunted Ladies," against which "the most brutal and unusual police aggression has been committed" (122). Attacks on women are cited along with references to the Guasina concentration camp and torture to indicate the full extent of the persecution employed by the dictatorship.

The exiled founder of AD, Rómulo Betancourt, also named the abuse of women as the worst violation of the dictatorship: "What passed all previous limits in Venezuela and probably in all Latin America for savagery was the imprisonment, indignity, and torture inflicted upon numerous women" (Betancourt 1979, 258). He found it a trespass against proper gender relations that mothers, female professionals, schoolteachers and students, and the female relatives of male opposition leaders were imprisoned:

> This was a new horror introduced by the worst despotism in Venezuelan history. It has been a national tradition, inherited in part from the courtly Spaniards, to always respect the female sex. In the terrible nineteenth century, with its cruel wars and authoritarian governments, jail and exile were reserved for men. Even Juan Vicente Gómez respected the female sex. The Pérez Jiménez regime, so closely akin to fascism, violated the limits which had been set by the most barbarous autocracies of the past. Great numbers of women passed through the jails, often tortured and kept for years behind bars. (259)

Despite its fervor, the outrage over the persecution of women only respected the sex of certain women. In both the *Libro Negro* and Betancourt's account, the imprisonment of female activists alongside prostitutes and other criminals is cited as evidence of degrading treatment (*Libro Negro* 1983, 110,

---

16. Many of the women who fought in the early opposition describe how they were forced into exile after they had become too visible. They continued to work in communities of fellow exiles in Latin America, Europe, and the United States to bring pressure against the Pérez Jiménez government (Petzoldt and Bevilacqua 1979).

122; Betancourt 1979, 258). As was the case during their organizing efforts in the late 1930s and early 1940s, women themselves were divided on this issue in a manner that reflected their class affiliations. On the one hand, Olga Luzardo of the Communist Party mentioned teaching "common criminals" how to read, write, and sew during her imprisonment (Petzoldt and Bevilaqua 1979, 188). On the other hand, Isabel Landaez of COPEI remembers a friend protesting to the prison director that they were from "good families" and so should not be kept with the other prisoners (Petzoldt and Bevilacqua 1979, 358).

Some female activists felt that their participation was valued on its own merits and that they did not experience discrimination at the hands of the leadership. The first two clandestine secretaries-general of AD surrounded themselves with female *enlaces*. Ruiz Piñeda reportedly said to Carmen Azopardo, "What will we do with all these valiant women the day that we come to power? We'll put [their names] in huge letters in all the newspapers so that all the world will know how they acted" (Petzoldt and Bevilacqua 1979, 217). When asked about his and other leaders' attitudes toward women, those women who had worked closely with the leadership claimed that they never discriminated between the sexes (Petzoldt and Bevilacqua 1979, 199, 216, 247). Other interviewees also felt that "being a woman was never an impediment" and that they were allowed to take part in the clandestine activity "like any man" (Alcira Colmenares and Mercedes Sandoval Marcano interviews). Women also recognized that some participated in less direct ways, making contributions that went unrecognized at the time because they were not seen as political "risk-work." Esperanza Vera elaborated:

> Not all the women were messengers; look at Olga Luzardo, for example. Not all were cooks for the prisoners. We could not expect the number of [female] participants to be high. What percentage of women were studying then? How many women were there who could leave their children in daycare? No, the participation cannot be measured in terms of leadership-work or risk-work only. All the jobs were risky, and nevertheless it is a participation that has been given very little value. How many women had to raise their children alone while their husbands were fighting? How many had to pass day after day on the staircases of the National Security Force waiting for Pedro Estrada [the head of SN] to grant them permission so that at the end of two or three years they might catch a glimpse of their husbands? I understand this also as participation. This also can be called Resistance! (Petzoldt and Bevilacqua 1979, 271)

Individual women made specific contributions to the opposition, and individual leaders treated them fairly. But women were rarely included in the more important decision-making or organizational activities of the opposition. AD's clandestine structure had no women in its national leadership, nor were any to be found in regional, union, or youth directorship positions. Only a few women were included in the communist leadership (García Ponce and Camacho Barrios 1982, 84–88).

Some women recognized their exclusion from the party hierarchy and the resulting lack of political training. AD activist Elia Borges de Tapia reflected: "Although it appears that in clandestinity we are all equal—like when we die—it must be recognized that the women did not participate in leadership. Women's jobs were very risky. They took on great responsibilities and accomplished rather dangerous missions. Only at the hour of making decisions, at the moment of designating those who ought to lead, they continued to be the stone guests (*las convidadas de piedra*)" (Petzoldt and Bevilacqua 1979, 336). Another female activist made the connection between most women's roles in the opposition, as helpmates to the leadership, and women's lack of political development. As Isabel Carmona explained,

> Women organized as women but continued to play the role, contributing in the space that was destined for them. . . . We have to recognize that, in the political struggle, they enrolled certain women in the work of being *enlaces* of the leaders, who brought them the papers, who ran that type of risk which was as great as that which a person ran who placed bombs, because the punishment was the same. But the development wasn't the same. Because the person who placed the bomb was in a part of the movement which had a more direct role in action and was in contact with the force where . . . power . . . was centered. But the person who brought the paper was like a courier, a messenger, who didn't read the paper, thus was not able to grow—she was growing in her morals, in her ethics, in her devotion, but perhaps she wasn't able to develop in her thinking because she did not engage in direct confrontation. All [the work] was valid and important, and the [women] grew in terms of courage, of risk-taking, but from the point of view of fostering political thinking, this was not the best work. (Isabel Carmona interview)

The reliance on women's nonpolitical identity, while leading to the participation of individual women in the clandestine struggle, would have detrimental consequences for women's participation in the new regime. Because women were viewed as private actors who facilitated political activity when men could not take part as easily or were used to illustrate the extent of authoritarian abuses, they were not trained to continue political activism after the danger surrounding men's participation had passed. That some women did continue to be active, within the parties or on their own, is a tribute to their individual efforts—and the lessons they learned in women's groups of the opposition.

Gendered Growth: Women's Group Organizing

Party leadership also took advantage of women's ability to participate by organizing them into women-only groups. In contrast with the *enlaces,* the women who led the groups had autonomy with respect to decision making. As a result, they developed organizational skills and political awareness—including a recognition of their subordinate position within party life. This indicated a change in the gendering of party structure. Although individual women were still subordinated to a masculine hierarchy, the formerly "auxiliary" women's bureaus of the legal parties were replaced in large part by groups that allowed for some prominence of women's role in the opposition, as well as for growth in women's capacity to organize.[17] Moreover, women's experience in party-linked groups led them to make use of the new opportunity provided by the opposition Patriotic Council: they formed the multiparty Women's Committee (Comité Femenino). This women's group served as the catalyst for the expansion of women's cross-party organizing, whose effectiveness was manifested most visibly in the huge rally of women following the downfall of Pérez Jiménez. The success of this group both mirrored women's history of conjunctural coalition building in the 1940s and foreshadowed what they would accomplish in the future.

Both principal parties of the opposition started young women's groups to facilitate organizing above ground. The PCV sponsored the longest lasting all-female group during authoritarian rule, the Young Women's Union (Unión de Muchachas). Active between 1951 and 1954, it was initially organized within the framework of the Communist Party strategy to "emerge to the surface" and make connections with the masses.[18] The Communist Youth

17. The few references to surviving women's branches during this period indicate that they mainly served to coordinate *enlace* work (Petzoldt and Bevilacqua 1979).

18. The details on the formation of the Young Women's Union come from García Ponce and

bureau (Juventud Comunista) initially started a group to attract young work-ers. It failed because the workers were unwilling to risk unemployment. The Communist Youth then turned to organizing among female students, most of whom had familial financial support and were thus more willing to engage in political activity. The Young Women's Union became the only branch of the Communist Party to have legal status under dictatorship. Around the same time, AD founded the Young Women's Association (Asociación Juvenil Fe-menina), a group modeled on the Young Women's Union.

Party leaders' sponsorship of women's groups, much like the incorpo-ration of individual women, took advantage of the fact that women's activi-ties initially did not arouse suspicion. The head of Communist Youth, Guillermo García Ponce, who came up with the idea for the Young Women's Union, explained in an interview: "At this time it was supposed that young women did not become involved in this [type of] struggle. They were [as-sumed to be] occupied with young women's affairs." This sentiment was confirmed by Isabel Carmona, the founder of AD's young women's group: "[This] organization counted on the support of the party because it saw [the group] as a tool for the legal struggle; women who were not known as acting in politics were a very expeditious peripheral tool to do things that men could not."

Unlike the *enlaces,* women in the Young Women's Union and the Young Women's Association led their own organizations. In at least the for-mer case, this was a deliberate strategy on the part of a male leader to foster women's development. García Ponce claimed that another reason for setting up the Young Women's Union was that "if the young women directed their own organization, they would have more possibilities to develop politically, as organizers, and to act with much more initiative and liberty." Communist Youth had recognized that in the presence of young men, who had had more political training and were prone to take control in group situations, young women had less chance to develop. Therefore, the leadership of the Young Women's Union, while following the general line of the PCV to make contact with the masses, was allowed independence in its work. Crucially, it was given control over strategy.

In keeping with the class perspective of the Communist Party, the Young Women's Union organized working-class and poor young women in the factories and *barrios* (low-income neighborhoods) of Caracas, holding history and craft classes, sponsoring sporting events for young women, and

Camacho Barrios (1982) and an interview with Guillermo García Ponce, head of the Communist Youth bureau during the dictatorship.

even starting a medical clinic.[19] Members kept a lookout for potential recruits for the party but claimed that the main purposes of the group were to maintain a legal presence and organize young women from the lower classes. They clung tenaciously to their mandate, never giving in to party pressure to make the Young Women's Union more overtly oppositional.

Notwithstanding its explicitly nonoppositional strategy, as the Young Women's Union gained in membership and visibility, the government recognized that the group was actively organizing women. According to María del Mar Alvarez, it "realized . . . that it was not the work of crazy girls *(muchachas locas)* but rather political work." The regime began to track down the leaders. After sponsoring a sporting event for more than a thousand young women, the leaders were imprisoned and interrogated. Although these women were eventually released, governmental repression prevented the Young Women's Union from continuing its activities. After three years of operation, the group dissolved.

Yet the Young Women's Union left behind women who had discovered that they could lead movements and had recognized some of the obstacles confronting them as women.

> [The work for the Young Women's Union] awoke in us, in all who were party activists, [the realization] that we had a problem which was greater than the attention that we were giving it. In seeing the situation of the women in the parties who were those who sold the raffle tickets, those who cooked when there was a meeting, those who washed the dishes, you began to understand that in the work of the party meetings the women were the ones who were selling and making things. . . . [T]hus we began to ask, why were we so foolish? Why do we sell? Why don't [the men] sell? That sort of thing. [We were able to see this from being in the Women's Union] because [there] we were only women. We met and made decisions. . . . We had independence in our work. . . . And I believe that this helped us a great deal. . . . We realized that we had abilities and that we were not sufficiently esteemed in the party. (María del Mar Alvarez interview)

The leaders were not the only women who gained from the experience. The Young Women's Union's founder, Esperanza Vera, noted that participat-

---

19. The description of the work of the Young Women's Union comes principally from interviews with its founder, Esperanza Vera, and a member of the leadership, María del Mar Alvarez.

ing in the group allowed the young women in the barrios to justify doing something outside of their homes. By coming together and discussing their similar situations, they had what she saw as a feminist realization: "My problems aren't only my problems. They are the problems of many. And that to which I aspire, others also aspire to. That which I can do can be shared." Thus women's experience of group organizing during the dictatorship made possible their development as political leaders and activists on their own behalf. Such an outcome was not fostered by individual participation.

Women Unite Against the Dictatorship

The benefits of group organizing were not confined to women acting within their parties. Female leaders made connections across parties to foster women's solidarity, which eventually led to a new attempt at coalition building. Although the Young Women's Union was a party-based initiative, it was helped in its formation by the first women's rights organization, the nonpartisan Women's Cultural Association (ACF). Founded sixteen years earlier (see Chapter 2), the ACF provided the members with resources and a meeting space. The Young Women's Union in turn was the inspiration for other groups, such as the National Women's Union (Unión Nacional de Mujeres), a short-lived group (1952–53) founded to educate adult women in the *barrios* on their rights, first aid, and neighborhood improvement.[20]

Founders of these organizations continued to use the strategy of disguising women's activism as apolitical (often cultural) endeavors. The National Women's Union was founded under the guise of an essay contest to honor world-renowned Venezuelan pianist Teresa Carreño on her birthday. Similarly, the AD-based Gabriela Mistral Center took the Nobel Prize-winning poet's name in an effort to mask the political hall as a cultural center.[21] But the ubiquitous SN appeared at the inauguration of the center, either tipped off or at that point suspicious of any new organization. The Gabriela Mistral Center was immediately closed.

Party women also helped to coordinate mass women's protests, most of which drew on women's identification with the private sphere.[22] In June 1952,

20. The organization was forced to disband after the suspicious SN found out that many of the members of the National Women's Union were linked to AD and the PCV.

21. Several interviewees confirmed that the strategy of establishing "cultural centers" or clubs was a common one to use for clandestine organizing, especially within the university. The information on the Gabriela Mistral Center comes from an interview with Elia Borges de Tapia, one of the center's founders.

22. Although the extent of direct party influence in these actions is unclear, the signatures on the protest letters include those of many well-known female party activists.

141 women signed a widely distributed letter protesting the conditions under which their relatives were being kept at the Guasina concentration camp (*Libro Negro* 1983, 191–93). Women collected five thousand signatures protesting the dictatorship and attempted to deliver them to participants attending the 1954 conference of American Secretaries of State held in Caracas. They had already placed copies of the *Libro Negro* on these officials' desks and demonstrated publicly outside the conference (Petzoldt and Bevilacqua 1979, 88, 164, 294). On 17 January 1958, 338 women signed the "Mothers' Manifesto" calling for an end to police abuse of school-age children. (Police repression had reached into the high schools by this time.) The signers distributed this document from house to house (Umaña Bernal 1958). Women also staged mass demonstrations, as described by Yolanda Villaparedes: "We held actions of women dressed in black in front of the National Congress when an important personality came to the country. These demonstrations that we prepared were silent actions. . . . [W]e also disguised ourselves as students, joined in the obligatory parades organized by the dictatorship and shouted slogans against it. Or we held 'lightning' actions[23] to denounce the tortures" (Petzoldt and Bevilacqua 1979, 293–94).

The most significant cross-party organizing among women came toward the end of the dictatorship. By this time, many women activists had met through clandestine efforts or in prison and were in a position to take advantage of the political opportunity presented by the unified opposition. Seeing that the leadership of the broad-based organizing group, the Patriotic Council, was formed entirely of men, two women who had led women's groups, Argelia Laya of the National Women's Union and the PCV, and Isabel Carmona of the Young Women's Association and AD, organized a committee to coordinate women's participation in the opposition.[24] They recruited two other women from COPEI and URD, and on 23 September 1957, founded the Women's Committee of the Patriotic Council.[25]

The determination of the leaders of the Women's Committee to fight women's exclusion by forming their own multiparty organization indicated the growth of women's ability to undertake independent political activity. Its formation drew on the experience of women's conjunctural coalitions in the

23. Lightning actions (*actos relámpagos*) were quick public denunciations of the dictatorship made in crowded streets or plazas.

24. Isabel Carmona claims that she was entitled to a position on the Patriotic Council for her role in mediating the rapprochement between the PCV and AD youth leadership, but at the last minute it was given to a man.

25. Information on the Women's Committee of the Patriotic Council comes from interviews with its two founders, Isabel Carmona and Argelia Laya, as well as Umaña Bernal (1958).

1940s for legal reform and suffrage, an experience now adapted to the current situation. Carmona cited the name of the Women's Committee as evidence of women's continuing subordination to male leadership: "Look at how we had a tendency to devalue what we ourselves were doing! It was given the name of the 'Women's Committee of the Patriotic Council'. . . as if we were a committee of the men!" But in calling themselves the "Women's Committee," the founders clearly sought to take advantage of a political opportunity, strategically connecting themselves to the major coordinating body of the opposition while maintaining autonomy for their own organization.[26]

Members of the Women's Committee also used their gender to their advantage. They encouraged participation through propaganda distribution and demonstrations deliberately directed at women. Their major pamphlet, "Carta a las Mujeres Venezolanas" (Open Letter to Venezuelan Women), solicited women's opposition to the dictatorship. Forty thousand copies were issued. Demonstrations were held where women were most likely to be found: outside of churches after mass on Sundays and in the marketplaces. The committee also collected money for Christmas presents for the children of political prisoners (Umaña Bernal 1958).

By these means, the Women's Committee unified women's opposition. The journalist Lucila Palacios claimed that its demonstrations were multiclass, involving women from the *barrios,* secretaries, students, professionals, and wealthy women (Umaña Bernal 1958). The demonstrations grew larger and more audacious as the opposition gained in strength. For example, in the beginning of January 1958, according to Gudrun Olbrich, "a women's demonstration was convened in the Museum of Fine Arts Plaza to plead for the freedom of political prisoners. Everyone remembers this demonstration because an impressive number of women were brought together" (Petzoldt and Bevilacqua 1979, 324–25). When the women started singing the Venezuelan national anthem, the approaching SN stopped in its tracks. Seeing the success of this tactic, the protesters sang for several hours until a superior officer arrived and ended the demonstration by ordering his men to use their billy clubs against the women.

The Women's Committee was so successful that it continued organizing with considerable momentum after the fall of the dictatorship, staging the first mass rally of the new democracy. Harking back to historical tradition, it set International Women's Day as the date to bring women together in a massive demonstration to celebrate the end of the dictatorship.[27] Along with their

26. I am indebted to Brooke Ackerly for helping me to clarify this point.
27. Women's groups had sponsored mass meetings of women on International Women's Day in 1944 and 1945 to promote suffrage, among other demands (see Chapter. 2).

male counterparts, the women's leadership was riding high on the unity achieved by the opposition, as illustrated by the ads run in the national daily *El Nacional:*

> Everyone come celebrate International Women's Day! The Women's Committee of the Patriotic Council calls all women of Caracas to come together en masse at the New Circus[28] Saturday, 8th of March, at 7 p.m. (*El Nacional*, 7 March 1958, 8)

> United we will achieve stability of the conquests gained in the political arena. United we will achieve the solution of all the problems which plague our country. United we will achieve a better future for our children. Unity has always been the slogan of the Women's Movement of Venezuela for the Celebration of International Women's Day. (*El Nacional*, 8 March 1958, 36–37)

Under the headline "Ten Thousand Women Attended the First Unitary Assembly Last Night," *El Nacional* emphasized the remarkable unity of the endeavor.[29] The article reported that representatives of all four parties—AD, the PCV, COPEI, and URD—began the celebration that morning by offering flowers at the tomb of Simón Bolívar, the hero of the liberation from Spanish rule, and at those of two Venezuelan women of letters, Luisa Cáceres de Arismendi and Teresa de la Parra. Throughout the day in Caracas, female party members and nonaffiliated women gave speeches that "insisted on the need for Venezuelan women to organize themselves." They also honored the women who had been imprisoned and exiled during the dictatorship. That night ten thousand people, mostly women, attended the rally. Invited guests from women's groups, political parties, and cultural groups were on the platform. Each speaker emphasized the success of the united struggle, the proof the meeting itself provided that women could continue to work in unity, and the necessity for women to remain united under the new democracy.

Ironically, the new democracy itself would dissolve women's unity.

To summarize, women's opposition to the Pérez Jiménez dictatorship, as individuals and in groups, was evidently facilitated by the regime's gendered structure of politics. But their individual actions, while crucial to the success

---

28. The Nuevo Circo, the largest amphitheater in Caracas at that time.

29. The article in *El Nacional* was republished in the *Historia Gráfica de Venezuela* (1958, 81–83). Because this publication reprints articles on the most significant political happenings, the appearance of this piece therein is another indication of the meeting's historical importance.

of the opposition, did not provide women with the opportunity to develop leadership and organizational skills needed to participate in political life. It was in the semiautonomous women's groups that women improved their own capacities for organization, recognized the discrimination that had kept them from maturing as political actors, and further developed the form of organizing used in achieving women's previous successes: conjunctural coalition building. The women involved in the Women's Committee would become lifelong allies and go on to work together in campaigns to benefit women—but only after experiencing substantial demobilization. In the second transition to democracy, the pressure of the political polarization between noncommunist and communist parties would fracture women's unity. As in the first transition, political structures would again exclude women on the basis of their gender.

The Political Opportunity Structure of the
Pacted Transition to Democracy (1958–1973)

Once the dictatorship fell, the political opportunity structure of the transition was characterized by the results of the "pacted" transition process. A series of agreements drawn up by certain elites established the dominant patterns of democratic interaction for the next few decades: elite settlement of the most pressing economic and political issues through party control of a strong centralized state, and the redirection of mass participation through these new channels of interest representation. The exclusion of the Communist Party from this process led to the other element of opportunity: the development of the largest guerrilla movement in Latin America until that time.

   Immediately after the fall of Pérez Jiménez, the unity of the successful opposition seemed durable. The Patriotic Council pronounced itself in favor of a unified front, and all the parties involved declared a political truce to continue working toward a stable democracy (*Historia Gráfica de Venezuela* 1958, 37). But unity, at least with the communists, had never been AD's long-term goal. The AD leadership in exile had agreed to unite with the PCV for strategic purposes only. In the international atmosphere chilled by the Cold War, such an alliance could not be maintained.

   Various sources confirm the instrumental approach to unity with the communists of AD-in-exile. In January 1957, as the clandestine parties drew closer together, the AD youth bureau in exile stated that it "ratifies the goal that the party act as champion of unity. But it considers that this unity should be managed tactically, that is to say, in a realistic form oriented concretely to the overthrow of the dictatorship. . . . Taking into account the national and international political situation an exclusive alliance with the communists would cause prejudice against the Organization and slow down the solution of the Venezuelan problem."[30] AD's exiled leadership in Mexico agreed that strategically an antidictatorship front was desirable, but the PCV should be recognized as "the major rival for the masses" and untrustworthy for its obedience to directions from abroad and early cooperation with the dictatorship.[31] The Mexico group explicitly warned against linking with the communists in anything but the most provisional of agreements.[32]

AD's founder, Rómulo Betancourt, in exile from the beginning of the dictatorship, dismissed the idea of ongoing participation with the communists in a speech before the Carnegie International Center in New York in January 1957.[33] On 27 January 1958, a mere four days after the overthrow of Pérez Jiménez, Betancourt sent a memo to the internal party leadership advising it to hasten the termination of the Patriotic Council:

> This organism carried out a great undertaking in the final struggle to bring down the dictatorship. . . . But I think that the preliminary steps ought to be taken so that the organism stops in its functions. Since the political parties are already acting, the persistence of a super-party organism of this type is not justified. Moreover, it is evident that we, and I presume that the other two national parties, will only lose if the common and concrete objective of overthrowing the dictatorship having disappeared we continue in a de facto alliance with the Communist Party.[34]

While the AD leadership was obviously anxious to overcome a potential rival, their interest in shaking loose from the communists was based on other considerations as well. From their short experience in governing during the *trienio*, AD leaders had learned that a stable political democracy would be better based on the appeasement of a wide range of sectors. In the atmosphere of suspicion that characterized U.S. foreign policy during the Cold War, these inevitably included the local dominant superpower, anxious not to see the spread of communism in its hemisphere, and excluded an opposition ally.

30. Betancourt Archives, Vol. 34, Annex C, 179.
31. See note 4 for a discussion of the alliances of the Communist Party during this period.
32. Betancourt Archives, Vol. 33, 90–91.
33. Ibid., Vol. 34, 74.
34. Ibid., Vol. 35, 187.

To attend to both the demands of those sectors newly empowered in the political realm and the threats from more entrenched interests to return to authoritarianism, the three noncommunist parties (AD, COPEI, and URD) signed the Punto Fijo Pact (Pacto de Punto Fijo) and the Declaration of Principles and Minimum Program of Government (Declaración de Princípios y Programa Mínimo de Gobierno). These consisted of a series of economic and political accords that mollified the sectors most threatened by the new regime—military, church, and business—and rewarded potential (or actual) party supporters: labor, peasants, and the middle class. The distribution of power among noncommunist parties and their political dominance was also ensured as they agreed to coalition governing.

The continuance of "import-substitution industrialization" (ISI), the economic development model popular throughout the region at this time, was also ensured through the pacting process, underwritten by the profits of the oil industry. This model called for heavy state involvement in promoting the development of national industries that could produce "substitutes" for imported goods, thereby making countries less beholden to external markets and capital.[35] While pact makers shied away from direct redistribution of income, ISI was accompanied by a more than doubling of social spending (from 11.4 percent of the national budget under Pérez Jiménez to an average of 28 percent between 1958 and 1973) to insure the middle and working classes' adherence to the democratic regime (Karl 1997, chap. 4).

After assuring their dominance over politics through the Punto Fijo Pact, the parties faced the challenge of rebuilding an effective structure on shaken foundations, following the murder, torture, and exile of many activists during the dictatorship. Survivors had to be reintegrated and new members indoctrinated (Martz and Myers 1986, 123). In the view of party leaders, everything depended on reestablishing central control to guarantee discipline and attract followers.

Thus party leaders returned to the "democratic centralist" model based on a hierarchical leadership and sectoral-based membership developed before the advent of dictatorship (see Chapter 2). Parties quickly dominated interest representation. Organized labor and the peasantry continued to be the primary beneficiaries, as before receiving benefits ranging from party posts to material resources in return for partisan support.

But with the advent of democracy, parties were not the only channel open to interest representation, which could be now facilitated through the state. The transition to democracy did not unseat the large, centralized state

35. For further description, see Haggard 1993; Todaro 1994, 491–500.

developed since Gómez's rule. Rather, it replaced the largely personal channels of influence with a formalized network of commissions and organizations. Capitalist interests were the ones most served by this network, but organized labor also benefited (Kornblith 1995; Karl 1997, chap. 4).

While the policies of the political pacts established a stable foundation for the democratic regime, its degree of democracy is questionable. The sectors included in the pacting process had access to the channels of power. But the various mechanisms put in place to ensure access for these sectors further inhibited the mobilization of constituencies that had not participated, resulting in "selective mobilization according to the logic of the situation and . . . demobilization of the masses" (Salamanca 1995, 200).

Betancourt made clear which groups he was interested in incorporating in a statement made in 1960 justifying the repression of a demonstration by the unemployed: "The people in abstract is an entelechy which professional demagogues use in seeking to upset the social order. The people in abstract does not exist . . . the people are the political parties, the unions, the organized economic sectors, professional societies, university groups" (quoted in Levine 1973, 49)—precisely those groups that were successfully co-opted by the parties and the state. While this selective inclusion would have even greater ramifications later on, it produced immediate repercussions: "The agreement to exclude important social forces and organizations led to serious struggles within Acción Democrática. . . . Betancourt abandoned the mobilizational tactics of the past, purged leaders of peasant and labor organizations who insisted on further reform, and stopped trying to organize and mobilize previously unorganized groups" (Karl 1990, 85).

Along with the economic austerity measures that Betancourt applied after becoming president, its exclusion from pact making alienated the Communist Party as well as the more left-leaning youth bureau of AD, which had been risking life and limb against the dictatorship while Betancourt was in exile. Frustrated by the foreclosing of possibilities for establishing a social and economic and not exclusively political democracy, the entire youth bureau of AD split from the party and joined the PCV, whose demands for radical social transformation were neither invited by, nor acceptable to, the elite groups who negotiated the pact (Peeler 1992).[36] Inspired by the recent Cuban example, this group then formed the largest guerrilla movement in Latin America up to that time.

36. A similar process took place in contemporary Chile, where the Communist Party played a significant role in the opposition to Pinochet, only to be excluded in the transition to democracy (Schneider 1992).

The movement turned out to be too radical for its political context.[37] Between 1960 and 1962 its leadership concentrated on staging urban riots, hoping that high unemployment combined with discontent over AD's economic policies would spur action among the poor. However, the urban poor generally did not support the guerrilla movement. They were more interested in the AD's promise of social services than in revolution, and they were put off by such guerrilla tactics as killing policemen, who usually came from impoverished backgrounds. The movement next tried its luck in the countryside, turning to rural organizing between 1963 and 1967. While some peasants joined, most had been or hoped to be helped by AD's land reform policies, and many were members of this party that had started organizing them in the 1930s.

On their own the urban intelligentsia (mostly university students) were not strong enough to maintain the movement. Moreover, it did not promote sufficient organization between those urban and rural poor who were mobilized, and it made no inroads in the military. The movement showed weakness all along: in 1963, despite the guerrilla threats against those participating in national elections, 90 percent of the electorate went to the polls. By 1965 the Communist Party was already discussing reincorporation into democratic politics. The party split the guerrilla movement by preparing in 1967 for the next year's national elections. The left misjudged the extent to which society was already organized by parties, with no room left to establish the necessary base for a successful uprising.

While sporadic student protests continued during the late 1960s and early 1970s, by the late 1960s the democracy was consolidated. There had been three democratic turnovers in political leadership, and there were no serious contenders for power that refused to abide by democratic political procedures. The "democratic exclusion" of the pacted democracy would only become destabilizing as the mismanagement of the oil-driven economy gradually eroded the initially substantial middle class and relatively well-off working class of the early years of democracy.[38]

Women's Opportunities Contract in the New Democracy

Despite the ideal of a more inclusive politics under democratization, women's mobilization was fragmented by the new political opportunity

37. Information about the guerrilla movement in Venezuela comes from Levine 1973 and Wickham-Crowley 1992.

38. In 1970 the lowest 40 percent of the population earned only 8 percent of national income (Ewell 1984a, 182).

structure of the transition period. The dissolution of the Women's Committee was linked to the dissolution of its parent, the Patriotic Council. While its tie to the council gave the committee political legitimacy under the dictatorship, with the disbanding of the council the committee suffered as well:

> The Women's Committee of the Patriotic Council had the same luck as the Patriotic Council as a whole. The unity of the people, stitched together through these organizations, upset those leaders who came out of exile and returned to the country to conduct the process. ... So they divided the people who had united and formed a unity in their own way. ... [T]he Patriotic Council had to disappear so that the traces of a fight in which [the returning leaders] had not participated might disappear. ... Thus from that moment the democracy belonged to them and not to the forces who had acted to liquidate the dictatorship. (Isabel Carmona interview)

Because the unity on which women had based their successful activism involved many communists, exclusion of the left in the transition confounded women's organizational strategy. Although female activists struggled to maintain some form of separate, multiparty organization, this effort was defeated by partisan politics.

Other groups as well as women were demobilized in the process of the pacted transition.[39] But the extent of women's "democratic exclusion" far exceeded that of other groups because of the reflection of traditional gender relations in the structure of political opportunities. Some women left politics altogether, guided by the assumption that once the crisis passed, men would again become the primary political actors.[40] Other women chose to stay in politics, only to find their incorporation impeded. Those on the left who had

39. The effects of this process are summed up in López Maya et al. (1989, 77): "The measures of the coalition government of President Betancourt were oriented with the priority of consolidating the political system which emerged from the pacts of '58, delimiting the quotas of responsibility and participation which the different social actors would have according to the positions which they occupied in the hegemonic model. In the process the fundamental political parties were constituted and consolidated, at the same time that those groups which did not conform to, or were not contemplated within, the sociopolitical project were suppressed, weakened, or marginalized."

40. Most of the interviewees continued to participate in politics following the transition. Little information is available on those who chose to stop, but a few reflections are suggestive. As Clara Herrera (1991, 22) quotes a participant, "It was thought that the women had been 'loaned' to the political activity and when the democratic movement was consolidated, the governmental-level and party positions were monopolized for the male activists of the struggle; in contrast the women in their majority withdrew to home life, in time forgetting how they figured in [the

joined the guerrilla movement found that its radical egalitarian theory tolerated discriminatory practices. Perhaps most tellingly for the future of
women's activism, the reconstruction of the parties marginalized women as a
group within this dominant channel of interest representation. State structures also hindered women's ability to function as an interest group.

The Impact of General Opportunities on Women's Organizing

Following the celebration of International Women's Day, the Women's Committee set up an office and looked toward continued activism in conjunction
with the Patriotic Council.[41] The Women's Committee was allowed its own
representative to the council, Isabel Medina, the widow of the former president. But the group's attempts to operate under the new democracy were
foiled by the ideological struggles of the transition.

Women's united activism represented a threat to the pacting process,
whose goal was to isolate the communists and channel all political activity
through the parties. Women in AD had ignored their leaders' request not to
participate in the International Women's Day celebration, but the pressure
was increased considerably afterwards. When AD's Betancourt returned from
exile, he was furious to hear that the celebration had been a massive event involving women from all the parties, including the communists. He called the
heads of the other noncommunist parties, Rafael Caldera of COPEI and
Jovito Villalba of URD, into his office and demanded to know how they could
have let women from their parties join with communist women to celebrate "a
communist day."[42] Such solidarity was not to be tolerated.

So from the *cúpulas,* or very top of the parties, came the order to end

---

overthrow of the dictatorship]." Although some men and women forgot about women's contributions, other former participants suffered under a restored division of labor. Yolanda Villaparedes remembered, "[My husband] was the man and I annulled myself as a human being. I left
political activity and became a housewife and nanny. At first I rebelled, but later I became lazy
until I was converted into the typical housewife. As I had acquired a consciousness of my duties,
of my rights, in this new situation I became neurotic." She went on, "There were waves of
women [participating in the opposition] . . . if I put myself to remembering names, well then! It
seems that we did not know how to appreciate our effort and that it has not been valued. The majority of participants got married, made their lives. Each one dedicated herself to finishing her
studies, to her family, to her own [life]. No, I feel frustrated" (Petzoldt and Bevilacqua 1979, 303,
304).

41. Information on the decline of the Women's Committee is from interviews with Isabel
Carmona and Argelia Laya.

42. International Women's Day has been associated with communism since it was first proposed by the socialist Clara Zetkin in a resolution before the Second International and was promoted by the communist-linked International Democratic Women's Federation.

women's pluralist organizing. In the middle of the first meeting that the Women's Committee called to discuss its transformation into a fully autonomous women's group, Mercedes Fermín, a well-known AD spokeswoman, stood up and exhorted all AD members to leave. Many did. When approached about the matter, URD's Villalba said he could not let the women of his party participate because "the communists will end up winning them over" (Argelia Laya interview).

The women who stayed in the Women's Committee, primarily those associated with the PCV and small leftist parties, attempted to reorganize it under the name of the National Women's Union from the dictatorship period.[43] It acquired an office and enrolled thousands of members all over the country. Again it focused on poor urban women, organizing around issues of legal reform, economic justice, and social activism such as establishing clinics, daycare centers, and summer camps. Organizers claim that their campaign directed at Congress was responsible for the inclusion of a clause in the constitution of 1961 barring discrimination on the basis of sex.[44]

This attempt to organize women across parties also succumbed to the pressures of the political conflicts of the time. Because many of the leaders were known to support the guerrilla movement, the police repeatedly raided the National Women's Union's office, making organizing difficult. The guerrilla leadership was eager to absorb the Women's Union as an auxiliary. But leaders knew that if they attached themselves to the armed struggle they would become what Esperanza Vera termed "a small closed group which wouldn't respond to the expectations that women had of [such] an organization." The pressures on the Women's Union became too great, however. As Isabel Carmona explained, "The guerrilla wanted to use the organization to build the guerrilla, those who were against the guerrilla denounced the organization for helping the guerrilla, and so within this confrontation of interests, which was of the parties and not of the women, their organized strength died." Neutrality was not possible. Women's unity fell victim to the larger political struggle.

Gendered Guerrillas

After the Women's Union disbanded in 1961, many of its leaders joined the guerrilla movement. Here again, women played a crucial role. They repeated

43. Information on the National Women's Union comes from Clemente Travieso (1961, 34) as well as from an interview with Argelia Laya.

44. Article 61 of the constitution includes the stipulation "Discrimination based on race, sex, creed, or social condition will not be permitted." The preamble also refers to the prohibition of sex discrimination.

the traditional women's tasks of the political opposition, including working as *enlaces*, helping political prisoners and their families, and forming human rights committees. Some of them also fought alongside the men.[45]

As in other guerrilla movements in Latin America, gender ideologies and their reflection in political structures impeded women's incorporation.[46] In the Venezuelan guerrilla movement, women conformed to traditional gender relations in most of the infrastructural or "housekeeping" tasks they were assigned. But they were also given the apparently radical egalitarian chance to fight alongside their male comrades. However, discriminatory attitudes prevailed. Guerrilla commander Argelia Laya recalled one exchange with a fellow commander who sent her a note requesting her to send nine women guerrillas to his battlefront. "What kind of women guerrillas—explosive experts, propaganda experts, organizers?" she inquired. "Just send us some girls," came the reply (*New York Times*, 24 September 1990, A4). When such "girls" were sent along with men into the hills, sexual intrigue quickly became an obstacle to movement discipline. But the mostly male leadership decided that it was the women's distracting presence that caused the problem, rather than both sexes' behavior. Commanders refused to continue to train women (Argelia Laya interview).

Thus even within a structure of radical equality, women were the ones to be excluded. Revolution, it seemed, was to be limited to the political arena. Guerrilla leadership assumed that women were responsible for allowing the temptations of private life to subvert revolutionary political goals. Angela Zago, another guerrilla leader, commented on a meeting where she observed the continuing reluctance of male peasant supporters to allow their female family members to participate in the movement: "How strange these communists who want their country to be communist, but not their women and children!" (Zago 1990, 207).

Women Respond to the Resurgence of Gender-Biased Parties

It is not surprising that many women chose to continue participating in political parties with the advent of democracy. Parties were the structure on which the clandestine struggle was built, and the old rival parties AD and COPEI quickly dominated democratic politics. However, as had happened during the first attempt at democratic transition, women were marginalized

45. For a description of one woman's experience in the guerrilla movement, see Zago 1990.
46. In a comparative article on women's participation in Latin American guerrilla movements, Linda Reif (1986, 151) notes that there are both "ideological and organizational" obstacles to women's incorporation.

through the gender-biased structures of party organization, principally through their subordinate housekeeping role in the women's bureaus. Although women soon reached 50 percent of active party membership, they only held one or two positions on party directorates and formed less than 3 percent of the national legislature and no more than 6 percent of the state legislatures in the first decade of democracy (Briceño Caldera, Brito Salazar, and Faria 1977; CSE 1984). Women as a group would wait until 1974 for the creation of an (unfunded) advisory commission on women's affairs. They would wait until 1982 before any substantial legislation was passed promoting women's equality. But because women had begun to challenge their subordinate role in their fight against dictatorship, they also continued to contest their exclusion under democracy.

Early on in the democracy, Mercedes Fermín, who had founded one of the first women's bureaus in AD's predecessor ORVE, objected to its reinstatement. In the transition to democracy "it was time to go beyond that nonsense" (Petzoldt and Bevilacqua 1979, 74) and incorporate women at every level of the party.[47] Unless they were incorporated throughout the party alongside men, she felt, women would be included for ornamental value, "like someone who is setting the table and forgets a vase. And so says, oh, I'm forgetting the vase! Let's put it here—that's the woman" (Mercedes Fermín interview).

Acknowledging this objection, AD did not include a women's bureau in the party in 1958. But within a few years a women's commission (later department) was reestablished as the mechanism by which to incorporate women into the party.[48] From its inception the more traditional COPEI had some form of women's bureau whose marginal position was indicated by the fact that it was not written into the party statutes until 1965. As the leftist parties returned to legal activism following the pacification of the guerrilla movement, most established women's bureaus.

The different ways in which the women's bureaus led to discrimination based on gender can be gleaned from the reflections of current and former female party members several decades after the transition. Women's relegation to reproductive roles was noted by one long-time AD member, Clarisa Sanoja, who claimed that because of the women's bureau, male party leaders "always look at us as something domestic" (Petzoldt and Bevilacqua 1979, 133). COPEI leader Isolda Salvatierra said in an interview that "it turns women into the housewives within the party (*amas de casa dentro del partido*)."

47. Also see Martz 1966, 202.
48. The full women's bureau was reestablished in party statutes in 1985.

The assumption that women would not be primary political actors was made clear in the limited access women gained to party decision making through their bureau. AD leader Elia Borges de Tapia claimed that while she had not felt personally discriminated against, she was aware that "there are talented women, with vast training, with a serious political conscience, and they are relegated to the women's type of organizations within the parties or attending to household duties. The parties, they utilize them and underutilize them! The woman is marginal in society, in the family, and within the parties" (Petzoldt and Bevilacqua 1979, 336).[49] Moreover, as Salvatierra pointed out, women ended up fighting over "one directorate position in eleven possibilities."

According to AD supporter Evelyn Trujillo, little political training took place in the bureau, with the result that the most successful women tried to enter traditionally male bureaus. The situation was no better in parties of the left, despite their claims to promote gender equality. As Lilia Henríquez observed, "Unfortunately the political parties maintain the same attitude as the man in the home. The parties that called themselves progressive and which try to take into account women's situation, turn to women only when they need them. . . . [W]omen's struggle should not be in the women's bureaus of the parties, which are a form of discrimination. The just thing is to incorporate in a party and occupy one's position in it as one more person" (Petzoldt and Bevilacqua 1979, 313).

Given the gender-based construction of opportunity, one might ask if things could have been different had the Women's Committee been able to transform into a multiparty women's rights organization. Could it have then become the peak organization from which women could have made demands on their parties through their women's bureaus? The historical experience of the Women's Committee indicates that it could not. Why was this unitary group destroyed instead of co-opted by the parties? The idea that it fell victim to the centrist parties' efforts to marginalize the left is not sufficient, because the left failed to take over the committee. A unitary women's group could not be effectively co-opted because unlike the corresponding groups for laborers or peasants, its demands could not be channeled within the gender-biased structures of parties. As Aurelena de Ferrer concluded, "To obtain our full liberation we would have to stop being women" (Petzoldt and Bevilacqua 1979, 113).

---

49. Ruth Lerner de Almea echoed this sentiment:

My condition as a woman never was an obstacle. I accomplished [my tasks] and continued on. . . . I evaluate the participation of women in that time as something very positive, but still given in an unjust form. We were allowed to participate, but not in

The inclusion of women as women would have required restructuring the parties to adapt them to the intertwined nature of the private and public in women's lives, but this effort could not be considered, given the continuing reliance on conventional gender relations during the transition. Moreover, as women's interests were crosscut by class as well as other factors, their shared interests would be considerably harder to aggregate than those of the other traditional interest groups successfully represented through party structures.

Gender Bias in the State and Political Discourse

Parties were not the only channel available for interest representation with the new structure of opportunity of the transition. Class-based interest groups also had mechanisms within the centralized state to insure their access to resources and representation outside of the electoral arena. The state-based representation primarily of workers and capitalists was facilitated through a "semicorporatist" network within the Decentralized Public Administration[50] and state advisory commissions (Kornblith 1995, 79).[51] This mechanism was a crucial channel of communication for particular sectors' demands because it provided a source of direct access to the powerful administration (Rey 1989; Crisp, Levine, and Rey 1995). But as was true in the case of political parties, the incorporation of sectors in this manner assured the representation of certain class "functions," or economically defined groups. This fact helped exclude women as a group based on gender identity.[52]

---

relation to women's professional preparation. And with respect to legislation, nothing doing. It is completely retrograde and unjust.... I have the impression that much more is asked of us women than of men in similar situations. It is very difficult for a woman to get to occupy high posts. It seems to me that there is an underutilization of women's talent and capacity. They are used at the base, but for social tasks, for the food baskets, for selling tickets. That is to say: to collect money!

However, I disagree with all types of women's committees. Nothing works with women alone. All has to be with men. We cannot be fighting against men, but with men to obtain the objectives that we propose. (Petzoldt and Bevilacqua 1979, 206–7)

50. According to Crisp, Levine, and Rey (1995, 154), the Decentralized Public Administration is a state bureaucracy made up of over four hundred bodies including "the governing boards of universities, regional development corporations, credit and finance agencies, and state-owned industries. Their independent legal status gives them substantial (although varying) degrees of autonomy with respect to income and expenditures."

51. Schmitter (1993) defines "corporatist" interest organization as state recognition of one peak association per interest group and its incorporation into the decision-making process on policy in relevant areas. The Venezuelan state is not as limited in its incorporation of interest organizations, leading Kornblith (and others) to refer to it as "semicorporatist."

52. Economically defined groups (primarily capital and labor, but also including middle-class professionals) have been significantly overrepresented on these commissions; surveys of the

The political discourse manifest in the National Plans of the first three democratic presidents also reinforced the neglect of women as an independent sector.[53] The small amount of attention paid to women by the powerful executive branch through 1968 focused on their potential contribution to the labor force, their literacy, and their reproductive functions. Betancourt rarely referred to them on their own in his early speeches as the first president of the new democracy. In the 1960–64 National Plan, women are only mentioned as the principal population through which to increase the labor force. There are no particular strategies for their incorporation (CORDIPLAN 1960). In the 1963–66 National Plan, even a reference to women's employment is absent; the only table that disaggregates by sex is that of the illiterate population, in which women are disproportionately represented (38 percent to men's 30 percent). Again, no specific strategies are given as solutions to this problem, despite the recognition that it indicates "the situation of cultural inferiority in which the Venezuelan woman still finds herself" (CORDIPLAN 1964, 306). In all of the collected speeches of Raúl Leoni, the second president, the only time women are mentioned is with respect to the need for family planning (*40 Años de Acción Democrática* 1981). The word *woman* never appears in his National Plan (CORDIPLAN 1966).

As a candidate, Rafael Caldera, who would become the third president and the first from the Christian Democratic party COPEI, was more preoccupied than his predecessors with women's role. But he was mainly concerned with how to keep it traditional in the face of social change. Unlike the relational feminists, he did not seek to help women integrate their roles as mothers and workers, but to encourage them to return home. In his campaign platform he celebrated women's increasing enrollment at the university level (up to 32 percent by 1965) but blamed working women for the decay of the family, made evident by an increase in divorce and the continuing problem of out-of-wedlock births. To address these issues and restore the family as the "base of society," he claimed he would promote "family policy." The cornerstone of the policy was to grant "family loans" to help women devote themselves to their true calling: homemaking.

---

different types of commissions established between 1958 and 1989 reveal that in the public law entities only 4 percent of the participants were representatives of noneconomically defined groups (such as religious, human rights, and environmental groups); on the consultative commissions they were also outnumbered by five to one (Crisp, Levine, and Rey 1995, 155).

53. The National Plan is prepared by all presidents at the beginning of their terms to outline the administration's plans for the country. While it is rarely fully implemented, it reflects the preoccupations and priorities of administrations.

The family loans will help the mother to give attention to her home, which is her central focus. The work of women outside of it disintegrates and separates the family, translates into the neglect of the health and feeding and clothing of the children, and damages their emotional development and moral education. At first glance, thus, the extreme importance of applying norms of family policy is obvious in Venezuela, whose nuclear families are characterized by their high birth rates, low marriage rates, precarious levels of economic sufficiency and the progressive augmentation of women's professional employment. (Caldera 1968, 45)

The policy also included a "Home Bank" through which poorer households would be able to buy labor-saving devices to help women care for their homes and families, a national volunteer program, a national secretariat of housewives, and a commission to study the condition of working women. However, by the time Caldera took office, he seems to have forgotten about his family policy; his National Plan contains none of the ideas he presented as a candidate but follows in the tradition of scarcely mentioning women (CORDIPLAN 1971).

Thus women were effectively excluded from political participation by the gendered institutions of the political opportunity structure established during the transition to democracy. The clandestine organizations that women had sometimes led, and in which they had begun to take political initiative, were closed down. Their legal successors had little room for women's meaningful participation. The rebuilt parties and channels of access to the powerful executive branch were based on structures that privileged men's access to "democratic" politics.

Women Begin to Reunite

As a result of the way in which transition politics excluded them, women undertook little activism on their own behalf until the late 1960s.[54] However, beginning in 1968 women slowly built on their experience under the dictatorship and the period that preceded it. As the tensions of the transition phase receded with the waning of the guerrilla movement, in May 1968 women again attempted to unite for their common interests across parties

---

54. One group, the Venezuelan Federation of Women Lawyers (Federación Venezolana de Abogadas or FEVA), which had been established in 1956, was restructured in 1965 (de Leonardi 1983, 431). It would play a crucial role in reinvigorating women's organizing in the early 1970s around the second reform of the Civil Code (see Chapter 4).

and generations. At the instigation of Margot Boulton de Bottome, a member of the Venezuelan Association of Women from the 1930s, the First Seminar for the Evaluation of Women in Venezuela (Primer Seminario para la Evaluación de la Mujer en Venezuela) was held to assess how far women had come since they were granted the vote in 1947 and what the current challenges were. Women who had participated in women's groups during the 1940s were joined by others politicized during the struggle against Pérez Jiménez, from almost every political party. COPEI threatened to boycott if the communists attended. But Boulton maintained, "If I have a seminar about the rights of women, I cannot discriminate." No members of COPEI came, but five hundred women attended, calling as they had in 1940 and 1958 for unified action on women's behalf (*El Universal,* 14 June 1968; Hernandez 1985).

Once again women assembled a common platform that reflected their historical demands: implementation of the 1936 Labor Law, eradication of discriminatory legislation, and state assistance to balance women's roles as mothers and workers. A new demand was for the creation of a state agency to implement laws concerning women and children (*Primer Seminario* 1968).

No immediate results came from the First Seminar, but within two years another attempt at unification was made by women from leftist parties (the AD offshoot People's Electoral Movement [Movimiento Electoral del Pueblo]), URD, and the PCV) who had been active in the clandestine opposition. Founders recognized the need to organize women separately, away from the discriminatory parties: "It was not possible to organize through political party representation because this was an obstacle. . . . [T]he political parties did their work for women simply to use women" (Argelia Laya interview). Claiming their antecedents in the National Women's Union, they organized the Women's Legion (Legión de Mujeres) "to achieve the full enjoyment of women's rights [and] to incorporate women in the political and social life of the country." But again the effort failed in the face of political pressures: "The political differences of the parties ended by smashing the Legion" (Hernandez 1985, 23).

Despite the destructive consequences of partisan rivalries, women never stopped meeting altogether. They continued to innovate in their autonomous organizing. Drawing strength from their long history, certain activists kept in touch. At one meeting of a small group of such activists, Perspective of Today's Woman (Planteamiento de la Mujer de Hoy), the new proposal from the First Seminar that women would benefit from having representation directly in the state as did other groups was resurrected (Isabel Carmona interview). This suggestion turned into a campaign to urge the 1973 presidential candidates to take a position on the establishment of a national women's agency. Its backers were finally rewarded when the new president, Carlos Andrés Pérez, founded the Presidential Women's Advisory Commission (Comisión Femenina Asesora de la Presidencia or COFEAPRE) in 1974. While COFEAPRE would not oversee great changes itself, the establishment of this first national women's agency would begin the transformation of the way in which gender relations were reflected in the state, one of the central institutions of the political opportunity structure. It would help to promote women's organizing as democratization progressed.

Why Machismo Was Stronger Than a Military Dictatorship

> It would seem that we came to have more strength [during the dictatorship] than has been recognized in legal democracy. Because the parties have not come to recognize women as equals. They acknowledge [us] in declarations but don't put them into practice. The party continues not to be aware of its own history, where it saw us not betraying secrets under torture in prison, where it saw us leave prison without crying and without giving up the fight but instead returning to it and then being captured again and then returning to the struggle again. (Isabel Carmona interview)

How do we explain the paradox that women's organizational strength rose during authoritarianism, only to decline under the new democracy? Women's ability to participate during the different phases of the transition to democracy was determined not only by the general political opportunities of the transition, but also by how the opportunities reflected gender relations. The gendered political discourse of the dictatorship period and its subversive use by clandestine parties facilitated women's participation in the struggle against dictatorship. Women participated as individuals mainly through their role as nurturers, caring for political prisoners and the clandestine leadership. However, in the women's groups affiliated with parties, women learned to lead. They also came to understand the importance of unified and at least semiautonomous organizing. Their experience led to the formation of a multiparty women's organization that held the promise of continued women's activism in the new democracy.

But the unity that women had developed under dictatorship was broken apart by the "democratic exclusion" of the pacted transition to democracy. Many women left politics altogether. Others found the gender equality of the guerrilla movement a sham. The rechanneling of interest representation through the gendered institutions of the parties, especially as manifested in sectoral organizing and state structures, left women with only a small part to play in democratic politics. Commenting on why women were "defeated" by democracy, clandestine activist, longtime feminist, and former socialist party president Argelia Laya put it succinctly: "In the case of *machismo,* it was stronger than a military dictatorship! Because it is a problem . . . of thousands of years in the minds of women and men." The legacy of *machismo,* or male dominance, was (re)institutionalized in the transition to democracy.

However, the lessons learned from women's semiautonomous and united action would not be forgotten. Thanks to their repeated encounters through the earlier period of organizing as well as during the dictatorship, a network of women's rights advocates was clearly in place by the 1970s. Because of their experiences of exclusion, women would continue to innovate organizationally, challenging masculine dominance both in the state and in party structure. This innovation would lead to a new period of relational feminist activism in the decades to come. But the tension in determining what constituted women's "shared interests" would also persist in the future as they struggled to advance their nontraditional interests through and around traditional channels of interest representation.

REGENDERING POLITICAL
OPPORTUNITIES:

*The Growth of Conjunctural
Coalition Building Under
Democratic Consolidation
(1974–1982)*

With the consolidation of democracy in the early 1970s, women became more proactive on their own behalf by substantially regendering their political opportunities. Remarkably, they did so at a time when party control over society remained quite strong. Working in and around the increasingly dominant executive branch, highly competitive parties, and alternatives to traditional party politics, women made structural innovations in various arenas. These innovations allowed them to debate their gender interests and organize a significant nationwide campaign. The growing international awareness of women's issues, spread by activities focused on the UN Decade on Women (1975–85), and the diffusion of "second-wave" feminism influenced women's national innovations. But they were also clearly building on their own history.

Women simultaneously experimented with new forms of organizing in the state, political society, and civil society. Within the state, women made use of the two first national women's agencies, the Presidential Women's Advisory Commission (Comisión Femenina Asesora de la Presidencia or COFEAPRE, 1974–78), and then the Ministry for the Participation of Women in Development (Ministerio Para la Participación de la Mujer en el Desarrollo, 1979–83), to unite women across parties and sectors on specific campaigns. In political society, the new Socialist Party provided women on the left with a chance to incorporate women's issues into party life on their own terms. They first attempted to do so through a linked women's movement, Socialist Women (Mujeres Socialistas, 1972–77). They continued the effort through the party-based Feminist Front (Frente Feminista, 1981–86).

In civil society, feminists and women from the urban slums formed their own organizations, including feminist groups and the low-income women's group Popular[1] Women's Circles (Círculos Femeninos Populares). The small, exclusively feminist groups, which started in the early 1970s, peaked around 1979–80; while the Popular Women's Circles continued to expand.

Women's common attempt to assert a measure of autonomy for gender-based activism characterized these various organizational efforts. Although the organizations had different approaches to the inclusion of men (socialist women sought to enlist men in their groups, whereas early feminists focused on female activists), they were all seeking some degree of separation from traditional gender-biased politics. This was manifest particularly in their relations with political parties, which for so long had marginalized women's activism.

This experience of marginalization formed the basis of women's search for structural transformations to enhance their participation. State-based organizing gave women an entry into the powerful executive branch, formerly reserved for the representation of traditional interests. Within the Socialist Party, women activists modified the sectoral mechanism for representing women—the women's bureau—at first sponsoring an affiliated women's social movement organization, then attempting to work from inside the party. In civil society, feminists and women from the *barrios* rejected parties altogether and formed wholly different organizational structures to represent their own interests. As elaborated in this chapter, these different strategies led to differing results in each arena, but they produced one clear success: the second reform of the Civil Code, achieved by a coordinated effort across all the arenas.

On 6 July 1982, Congress passed a reform of the Civil Code fulfilling demands women had been making for over forty years. Both the content and the timing of the reform defied precedent:[2] it was a substantial revision by an almost all-male congress of a set of laws that had upheld traditional gender

---

1. Synonymous with "urban poor." Analysts of Latin American class structure often use the term *popular* to indicate that this class contains the majority of the region's citizens, whose experiences are the most common to Latin Americans as a whole.

2. Sonia E. Alvarez notes the difficulty in altering the Civil Code, arising from the threat such reform posed to middle- and upper-class men:

> Demands for reforms of the civil code, for greater legal autonomy for married women, for divorce laws or for the legalization of contraception, have rarely fallen on receptive ears in partisan arenas dominated by men of the upper- and middle-classes. Such demands, if conceded to, might significantly alter social relations of production and reproduction, as well as power relations between the sexes within the domestic sphere. Thus, the platforms and programs of political parties gradually incorporated some of the political claims raised by women's movement organizations, but only those which

relations, and it came at a time when the congressional accord of the two major political parties previously achieved by pact making had broken down. Eight previous attempts at reform since 1970 had failed to bring results. Nevertheless, in 1982 the Civil Code was finally reformed to ensure that women had legal rights equal to those of men within the family and to eliminate all legal discrimination against children born out of wedlock.

The combined efforts of women active both inside and outside of the state, drawing on the progress they had made during the 1970s, produced this reform. The Venezuelan Federation of Female Lawyers began the process, joining forces with the state agency for women in 1979. Through their campaign, women contested the party-driven nature of politics by refusing to rely on these traditional channels for representation. Instead, they continued to develop the strategy of conjunctural coalition building. They also carefully constructed a reform discourse that, as had been the case in the first period of women's rights activism, linked women's advancement with their roles in the family. Like the first relational feminists, they challenged gender hierarchy but not gender difference.

This chapter focuses on the organizational and interest-based innovations women made during the first period of democratic consolidation. It begins by noting women's changing status and discussing the new political opportunities—both general and gendered—of the period. It then takes up women's advances in the three arenas of political interaction: the state, political society, and civil society. Finally, it shows how women drew on these accomplishments in their campaign to reform the Civil Code.

Uneven Advances in Women's Status (1974–1984)

Women of the middle classes benefited from the expansion of educational and professional opportunities made possible by the still-wealthy and now democratic Venezuelan state. Women's participation in higher education rose from 44 percent of all university graduates in 1972 to surpass men's enrollment by 1984 at 54 percent (Huggins Castañeda and Dominguez Nelson 1993). Although there was a 5 percent dip in women's participation in one of the most prestigious occupational categories, "professional and technicals," between 1961 and 1971, by 1981 they constituted 55 percent of the category.

would not significantly compromise the social, economic, and political roles which dominant ideologies and institutions had assigned them. (1986, 117)

Women continued to enter the public sphere as their percentage of the labor force increased from 21 to 28 percent between 1970 and 1981 (OCEI 1971, 1981). Higher earnings and more education were also correlated with lower birthrates, which declined between 1970 and 1985 from an overall average of five children per woman to four children per woman (Huggins Castañeda and Dominguez Nelson 1993).

However, many of these advances were limited to a small number of women. Even a generous estimate reveals that only 8 percent of all women of the appropriate age bracket were enrolled in the university by the mid 1980s. The majority of women were employed in sex-segregated, low-paying service and manufacturing jobs. Not surprisingly, the poorest and least-educated women had the largest number of children (Huggins Castañeda and Dominguez Nelson 1993).

Because professional women were often dependent on other women's work in their homes and offices, cross-class organizing on the basis of gender was never much more than a faint possibility. The partisan loyalties that had inhibited past attempts continued to make such organizing highly unlikely, making the unity women achieved in the fight for the Civil Code reform that much more remarkable. The strategies developed for its success reflected the opportunities of the period.

The Political Opportunities of Democratic Consolidation

Democratic consolidation was attained upon the defeat of the guerrilla movement in the late 1960s and the first alternation of power in a presidential election with the 1968 victory of COPEI's Rafael Caldera. As developed through the pacted transition process, the polity was characterized by a strong executive branch dominating the state and by powerful centralist parties channeling representation in both political and civil society. However, the nature of party politics shifted during the first decades of consolidation. The major parties grew less cooperative and were challenged by a newcomer.

The constitution of 1961 ensured the political dominance of the executive branch (Oropezo 1986; Levine 1989), whose power was increased by *adeco* (AD party member) President Carlos Andrés Pérez's further centralization of political authority during his 1973–78 administration. The state-based representation of functional groups such as workers and capitalists continued to be facilitated through the semicorporatist network of executive-branch commissions and the Decentralized Public Administration.

Relations between the two most powerful parties, never wholly without conflict, became strained as the cooperation of the transition period
gradually gave way to sharp partisan divisions. Under the exigency of controlling the massive inflow of state revenue due to the 1973–74 oil boom,
President Pérez asked for and received special powers from an AD-domi-
nated congress. COPEI saw this request as a violation of the formal and informal interparty agreements in force since 1958.[3] The major parties began to
cooperate less, as was illustrated by COPEI's both opposing the congressional bill calling for the nationalization of petroleum and boycotting the nationalization ceremony in 1976 (Karl 1997, 153). Such partisan divisions led,
among other problems, to less oversight of the investment of the crucial oil
revenue. While income was still plentiful, its chronic mismanagement would
lead to increased dependence on foreign loans and an unmanageable debt.

By the late 1970s, the model of political cooperation had clearly deteriorated. Calls for the decentralization of political power became more frequent. Emergent groups, especially neighborhood associations, sought more
local autonomy from the centralized and societally penetrative parties. However, these groups met with little success at this time.

Although AD and COPEI dominated political life, they were not without challengers. The most significant development in party politics during
the first period of consolidation was the founding of the Venezuelan Socialist
Party, Movement Toward Socialism (Movimiento al Socialismo, or MAS), in
1971.[4] It arose as the result of a largely generational split in the Communist
Party following the pacification of the guerrilla movement. Younger members, who had taken the most active role in the guerrilla struggle, were dismayed at the older leaders' eagerness to return to traditional politics. Those
combatants who had gone into exile in the late 1960s had seen the problems
with "real-existing" socialism. Most significant among these was the Soviet
Union's crushing of Czechoslovakia's Prague Spring, which deeply affected
the few who had experienced it in person. As a result, the exiles returned determined to build a nationally oriented socialist movement.[5] They found eager allies in the student movement that, swept up in the international wave of

3. Although the election of a COPEI president in 1968 brought an end to formal coalitional
governments, AD and COPEI continued to share power through the informal power sharing
arrangements set out in an "institutional pact" in force until 1983. This agreement established
that the president's party would name the president of the Senate, and the other party, the president of the Chamber of Deputies. The parties also agreed to reach consensus on nominating
supreme court justices and other governmental officials (see McCoy 1989, 65).

4. The description of MAS is principally drawn from Ellner (1988), the definitive work on the
party.

5. A principal founder of MAS, Teodoro Petkoff, was denounced by Brezhnev at the Twenty-

student activism of the late 1960s and early 1970s, had begun a process of "renovation" to gain more of a voice both on campus and in political parties. These developments led many members to leave the Communist Party and organize MAS.

The founders of MAS had been exposed to more than the usual set of Venezuelan political experiences. As a result, they initially experimented with both party ideology and structure. Inspired by the new left movement and contrary to traditional Marxist doctrine, the founders held that a socialist revolution could be begun by an intellectual vanguard before the achievement of certain "objective conditions"—that is, the preparedness of the working class for its own liberation. The MAS leadership also drew on its experience in the failed guerrilla movement in deciding that revolution could not be predicated on armed struggle. Instead, social transformation would take place through a Gramscian "war of position," the largely intellectual battle for the hearts and minds of society. Thus, MAS focused on mobilizing middle-class professionals, especially intellectuals, and students.

In order to gain followers, MAS began a new form of organization. Fully aware that AD and COPEI between them controlled the leadership of most civil society groups, the party decided to approach from below. Instead of forming a traditional party, MAS implemented the concept of a "Movement of Movements." The goal was to seek unity within certain sectors through a base-level social movement rather than focusing on top-down organizing. The role of party activists, moreover, was to unite the sectors around issues that were of vital importance to them instead of urging them to follow a particular party line.

But MAS soon found that the pattern of political participation established by AD and COPEI was too deeply ingrained to modify. The 1973 elections gave the combined dominant parties 85 percent of the vote, a clear indication of their control of the electorate. Moreover, party affiliation was too firmly entrenched to be broken through by issue-based organizing. The MAS-mobilized "movements" never developed as planned into autonomous structures "disassociated from political parties. In practice, they often took on the form of leftist 'fronts' whose leaders responded to the directives of their respective parties" (Ellner 1988, 176). Thus, in the mid-1970s MAS dropped the "Movement of Movements" concept and began to restructure the party along traditional lines, increasing hierarchy, central-

---

fourth Congress of the Communist Party (1971) for his "nationalistic tendencies" (Ellner 1988, appendix).

ization, and sectoral organization in hopes of becoming a significant electoral contender.[6] This replacement of social movement-focused organizing with a more traditional party structure led to its becoming the electoral alternative to AD and COPEI, although it would not garner more than 10 percent of the vote in presidential elections until 1988.[7]

Gendered Opportunities

Women took advantage of the consolidation of democracy to begin to regender their opportunities. As time passed and they became aware of the discrimination built into democratic procedure, they responded in various ways. They made organizational innovations that permitted either their entry into male-dominated institutions or their creation of alternative ones in the state, political society, and civil society. In these arenas women debated their interests and goals. The result of women's simultaneous activism on different fronts during this period was the building of one of their most successful conjunctural coalitions: the second campaign to reform the Civil Code.

As described in the previous chapter, the first Venezuelan national women's agency, COFEAPRE, was founded at the insistence of veteran women's rights activists during the consolidation. The history of their own largely thwarted struggle for inclusion in the democracy begun in 1958 had revealed the need for an agency that would promote women's issues within the powerful executive branch. Because Venezuelan political life was to a great extent carried out through semicorporatist bargaining, women recognized that they had little chance at promoting substantial gender-based legal or social reform without such a resource. Thus they began a campaign to pressure the 1973 presidential candidates to promise to create a national women's commission.

Their efforts were aided by the changing international attitudes toward women's issues. In 1967 the United Nations promulgated the Declaration on the Elimination of Discrimination Against Women, followed by the Programme of Concerted International Action for the Advancement of Women in 1970. The impact of these documents on governments' willingness to devote attention and resources to promoting women's social, economic, and

6. It should be noted, however, that MAS still maintained a greater degree of internal democracy than the traditional parties by legalizing instead of repressing party factions and by holding internal elections for party positions instead of filling them by appointment (Ellner 1988, chap. 10).

7. Ellner (1988, chap. 8) notes that this concern with electoral politics has often impeded the ability of MAS to focus on more long-range planning, including strategic coalition building within the left.

political development was greatly increased by the declaration of 1974 as the United Nations International Women's Year, which would begin the UN Decade on Women (Miller 1991, chap. 7).

The final factor in the establishment of the state agency for women was the particular configuration of the Venezuelan state during this period. President Pérez came to power after a landslide victory, a congress with his party in the majority, and an oil boom that more than tripled fiscal income between 1972 and 1975 (Karl 1997, 120–21). Building on his already considerable executive power, he proceeded to expand state jurisdiction in all directions. His major focus was the development of economic capacity. But social welfare was also on the agenda; for example, he oversaw the establishment of a national home-based day-care program. Overall, it was a time in which international influences coincided with national opportunities for the creation of new state entities. Pérez established COFEAPRE in 1974.

COFEAPRE both reflected and challenged the influence of gender relations on institution building. Its position within the state reflected a traditional gender hierarchy: because it represented women, it was never given the full status of a regular ministry, was rarely funded, and was only allowed to propose, not execute, policy.[8] But insofar as COFEAPRE represented a new channel for women's representation at the highest level of government, it also challenged the executive-branch representation of traditional, male-dominated interest groups. After a weak beginning, the women's commission would go on to serve as a key mechanism for women's access to national politics. Its first major accomplishment was the organization of the long-delayed First Venezuelan Congress of Women, at which were introduced the changing gender interests and organizing principles that would guide women's activism on their own behalf over the next decade.

At the same time as changes were taking place in the state, women on the left were attempting to alter the gender-biased nature of political society. The initial innovations of MAS resulted in the alteration of the male-oriented membership structures. Unlike the traditional democratic centralist model of Venezuelan political parties, the sectoral organizing of this new party was not dependent on the takeover of social groups through their incorporation into party bureaus, a process that privileged the recruitment of men of different classes through work-based organizing. In contrast, the social movement-based organizing of MAS provided women with the opportunity to organize *as women,* who had no defining workplace or class, but did have an identity

---

8. Franzway et al. (1989), Alvarez (1990), Jaquette (1994), and Goetz (1995) have all noted the parallel between women's subordination to men and the low status of political institutions focused on women's issues.

to represent. As a result of its innovation, women were among the groups MAS organized most successfully, along with students and professionals.

Women took advantage of the new model of activism to organize as a sector. Moreover, they articulated a feminist perspective on socialism that had an impact on MAS as a whole. Although temporarily thwarted by the reversion of MAS to traditional organizing in the late 1970s, feminist members continued to try to use the women's bureau of the party to further their own interests. They were joined by women in other left-wing parties, and they succeeded in some adoption of their demands in party platforms. But their organizational innovations had limited impact within the parties. Women faced ongoing resistance on the part of male leaders, and they learned, in addition, that their own outreach efforts were too weak to achieve long-lasting change.

As some women struggled to create new organizational forms within the dominant institutions of state and political society, others availed themselves of the marginal spaces in democratic civil society. Both middle-class feminists and poor women attempted to establish alternative forms of representation. They explicitly rejected state influence and party-related organization. In their own groups, they sought more "women-friendly" structures in order to present their distinctive points of view. While the embeddedness of traditional structures and gender relations would prove resistant to these nascent challenges, both groups articulated important ideas for the future.

Women's Organizing in the State

The main accomplishment of COFEAPRE in its four-year existence was to hold the First Venezuelan Congress of Women (Primero Congreso Venezolano de Mujeres). After a thirty-year hiatus following the Preparatory Conferences of the 1940s, the congress was held 21–25 May 1974 and drew 1,805 participants. Its goal was to address four main themes reflecting both the history of Venezuelan women's organizing and the new priorities of the UN Decade on Women: women's legal position, women's social situation, women and development, and women at the international level.[9] The official

9. The official publication of the First Venezuelan Congress of Women, *Acta Final* (Final Summary), reports the conference proceedings, including the keynote addresses and a detailed list of proposals from each section. In summary, conference proceedings show the legal section made the familiar calls for reforming the Civil and Penal Codes and the Labor Law, but it also

conference proceedings and unofficial reports attest to the opportunity the state commission provided for women to debate gender interests and women's organizing strategies. But progress was held up by the ongoing problem of partisan rivalries that marked the period. The parties' disagreements were played out by their women activists: no *copeyanas* were included in COFEAPRE, and partisan rivalries reduced the potential of the long-awaited congress.

Contesting Gender Interests

The issue of motherhood illustrates both the continuity and change in perspectives on gender relations manifest at the congress. In the opening address, First Lady Blanca de Pérez harked back to the relational feminist perspective of the 1940s. Again inclined to challenge gender hierarchy but not difference, she considered women mainly in their role as mothers: "We ought to protect women legally and economically, together with their children." As would become common in much commentary on women's issues during this period, she saw a threat in the challenge to traditional values embodied by the still nascent women's liberation movement, and she defended those values behind the shield of motherhood: "The only way that we can understand Liberation is to train [women] to better accomplish [their] high mission" (Primer Congreso 1975, *discursos*).

The first lady's statements reflected the accomplishments of her husband's administration. One significant innovation under Pérez responded to the appeal for state intervention to ease women's child-care responsibilities—albeit in a manner that reinforced the association of women and children. The centerpiece of President Pérez's social policy was the Daily Care Homes (Hogares de Cuidado Diario), a home-based child-care program for low-income mothers.[10] It was effective. By 1978 state spending for subsidized day

---

addressed the new issues of abortion and the collectivization of housework in poor neighborhoods. The section on women's social condition stressed the importance of balancing women's roles as homemakers and workers by implementing policies such as day care and flextime. It also addressed the need to provide family planning programs for both men and women, to consider abortion legislation, to end sex role stereotyping in the media and in textbooks, and to provide state assistance to single mothers and their children. The section on development was clearly influenced by the priorities of the upcoming UN Decade on Women (1975–85), covering topics such as: women's incorporation into state planning, education and production; adequate nutrition; and the situations of rural, indigenous, and young women. The section on women at the international level stressed international cooperation and issued a statement in support of women imprisoned in Chile for opposing the dictatorship of Pinochet (Primer Congreso 1975).

10. Linked to the larger effort to provide *barrios* with the services necessary for integrated

care had quadrupled, and the number of children in programs quintupled. The program was seen as so successful that UNICEF promoted the model in other developing countries, and it was adopted in Colombia and Ecuador (Fundación del Niño 1979). But while coming to the aid of mothers, the program continued to link women, and not men, with child rearing. It also reflected and reinforced a discriminatory sexual division of labor: the *madres cuidadores* (mother-caretakers) had supervisory authority over the children of others, but they worked for very little money and had no voice at all in the state administration of the program (CFP 1994).

In their discussions on motherhood, congress participants also introduced new ideas about gender relations. These ideas began to challenge gender difference, not just gender hierarchy. Abortion was a hotly debated issue. As in most Latin American countries, in Venezuela the procedure was illegal unless the life of the mother was at stake.[11] The resulting clandestine abortions were estimated in 1972 to be responsible for over a third of all maternal deaths (Alvarez T. 1989, 153). There was vigorous opposition on the part of Christian Democratic women to any easing of abortion restrictions. A contingent of *copeyanas* protested discussion of the topic by confiscating the information on therapeutic abortion from the chair of the panel on family planning and walking out of the final assembly when the issue was brought up (Hernandez 1985, 59; Argelia Laya interview).

The majority of conference participants, however, were interested in some form of compromise on the issue. As a result, abortion was discussed in two sections of the final document. The section on legal reform called for a sentence reduction by half for those women accused of aborting and the providers who assisted them.[12] The family planning section recommended against the legalization of abortion as a "free and indiscriminate" practice.

---

development, the Daily Care Homes program took a model of child care from the area itself: "The previous existence in the *barrios* of some women who take charge of the care of the children of the neighbors serves as a material platform for the installation of the Daily Care Homes." The program was administered through the Children's Foundation (Fundación del Niño) started in 1964 as the Children's Festival Foundation (Fundación Festival del Niño) to coordinate a national event in celebration of children. It then expanded to seek funding for social projects directed at children, vacation programs, TV shows, children's books, and so forth. Support for children of low-income parents only began when Pérez took office in 1974 (Fundación del Niño, 1979).

11. There is another rather unclear exception in the cases where the male head of household approves the procedure if the pregnancy is due to a "violation of proper conduct," i.e., the rape of his wife or daughter (Article 436, Venezuelan Penal Code). Of the Latin American countries, only Cuba has legalized abortion.

12. At that time, for women the term was six months to two years; for those who assisted in abortions, one year to thirty months.

But recognizing that the procedure was subject to "anachronistic norms and national laws," the section urged scientific investigation of the problem. It also proposed an executive-sponsored commission to regulate abortion "so that it might not be realized in an anarchic form without control," such as was already causing the tragic and avoidable deaths of so many women. Reflecting the priorities of the UN Decade on Women, which included the promotion of birth control as a means for women's advancement, the section went even further on the subject of fertility regulation. It recommended that access to birth control be enshrined in the constitution and encouraged men's education on issues of fertility and parental responsibility.

Organizational Development

While debates on motherhood would continue without resolution throughout the decade, another issue introduced at the congress would take on great importance in future organizing as it had in the past: using the united force of women outside of male-dominated institutions as a strategy to alter men's historic domination of public life. One argument in favor of gender-based autonomous organizing came from a regional reflection. The Colombian UNESCO consultant on the International Women's Year, Dr. Esmeralda Arboleda de Cuevas, argued that region-wide, women's autonomous organizing was a crucial political strategy to confront and change male-dominated structures, especially political parties:

> The Latin American woman finds herself within a historic development that has resulted, more than in other parts of the world, in the masculine character of the social structure. The evolution of feminism in Latin America has been slower than in other regions because of the very strength of traditional institutions. . . . Autonomous women's movements that take into account Latin American characteristics ought to continue. They are indispensable to call into question already out-of-date social structures; and so that political parties might know the true aspirations of women and respond to them. (Primer Congreso 1975, *discursos*)

Because of the strength of such "traditional institutions," especially parties, in the Venezuelan context, de Cuevas's remarks were echoed by local leaders. Ensuring autonomous action through the construction of a mass organization of women was the subject of closing remarks by Isabel Carmona, the coordinator of the committee that oversaw the national implementation of International Women's Year. As a founder of the Women's Committee of the Patriotic Council, the united women's organization from the end of the Pérez Jiménez dictatorship that disintegrated under the pressure of partisan organizing during the transition to democracy, she could see the stride forward that had been made with the establishment of a state commission for women. But from her experience, Carmona also knew the importance of women's continuing pressure from outside the state. She argued that "the positive disposition of the State [was] not enough; if [COFEAPRE were] not backed by the vigilant action of popular mobilization and the pressure of a mass organization, which brings together women from all sectors around their specific objectives," it would not succeed in maintaining the mobilization of women evident at the congress and achieving women's demands (Primer Congreso 1975, *discursos*).

Carmona's remarks reflected an awareness of how the corporatist-type commission women had acquired in the state functioned. It was powerless without a corresponding mass movement of the sector it was established to represent. Much like the parties' women's bureaus, the commission by itself would not allow women to advance in participation and decision making, especially because it too was in a subordinate structural position. But while women in political parties could count on the assistance of the parties' women's bureaus in organizing at least on a partisan basis, mobilizing women to make demands on the state would require the construction of an extra-party organization of women.

To promote a mass organization of women, Carmona exhorted the nearly two thousand congress participants to reflect on the problems they had encountered in their previous experiences with politics. They should think "if they will put up with continuing to struggle only through political organizations, which up to now have not fulfilled their aspirations in practice."[13] She pointed out that only a mass organization would be able to represent women's demands to the predominantly male political leadership:

> We know that even when here in this Congress we have concluded today with the acknowledgment that we ought to reform laws to guarantee the equality which the Constitution proclaims, tomorrow, if the Parliament, in its majority constituted by men, does not pay attention to our requests, no one will be able to make any effort so that they might happen unless it is the sector

13. Carmona included labor unions in her critique, citing the recent refusal of the Seventh National Congress of the national labor confederation to include women's demands.

of organized women itself, with its own mass following, which cannot be replaced by the women's bureaus of the political parties, seeing that it must be broader, because not all the women of the country are incorporated into political parties and the problems which we are defending are of all the women, and not of the women in the vanguard. (Primer Congreso, *discursos*)

But the general and gendered political opportunities would not permit the construction of such crucial mass organization at this juncture. In general, partisan divisions separated the female members of different parties just as it did the males. Carmona herself acknowledged the "reasons of a political nature" that had prevented the congress from taking place earlier, and the *diablillo* (little devil) of sectarianism that plagued the proceedings.[14] Esperanza Vera, the women's rights activist from the dictatorship-era Young Women's Union of the PCV, explained in an interview that a unified group could not have emerged from the congress. Party influence would have led to female members' attempts to capture such a group as a means to promote their own leadership:

I think that one of the obstacles which has not been overcome is the resistance of the political parties which translates as a hostile position of their women toward the creation of organizations of this type. . . . There are messages which may not be spoken out loud but which exercise a determining influence over actions. We here in Venezuela had in 1975 a marvelous opportunity to create this large women's organization. We held a conference where there were more than 2000 women present of all the political parties, of all the religious beliefs, and the possibility of leaving there with a unitary organization was put forward, and the women from the parties of greatest influence rejected [the idea]. And it has not been achieved to this day. . . . The women from the parties, what they want to offer to their parties is a group where these women have control so that by means of this control their parties recognize them as leaders.

In summary, the first women's agency, resulting from the confluence of women's activism, international opportunity, and an expansive state, pro-

14. In an interview, Evangelina García Prince, a longtime member of AD who attended the 1975 congress, affirmed that there "the criterion of party loyalty prevailed over gender solidarity."

vided a space for women to debate issues. These issues included the need to organize themselves outside of the state to ensure pressure potential. The establishment of COFEAPRE thus introduced the idea that gender issues could be legitimately addressed through state-based activism.

However, partisan differences worked against the realization of concrete plans. Given women's limited ability to organize outside of their parties, were there resources inside them? The gendered nature of the dominant parties meant that internal party structures were biased against the representation of women's interests, with the women's bureau still functioning more in service to the party than to women. But the early 1970s gave rise to a new form of party-based organizing with somewhat more room for women's organizing.

Autonomy in Political Society? Socialist Women

The 1971 founding of MAS, the Venezuelan Socialist Party, gave women on the left a new opportunity to alter the gender-biased nature of partisan politics. When MAS first embraced the "Movement of Movements" concept, these women rejected the traditional women's bureau. Instead, they founded a MAS-linked women's movement group that held tightly to its autonomous decision making and promoted what its members saw as women's interests. When MAS reverted to a more traditional structure, socialist women slowly adapted to it, still holding onto their mandate to represent women's interests. But now they sought a feminist transformation of the women's bureau. However, not only the political institution of MAS but also the actors who formed it provided gendered opportunities. The predominantly male leadership of MAS never wholeheartedly endorsed women's activism on their own behalf, and this lack of support exacerbated the weakness of women's organizing.

Organizational and Ideological Innovation

The women's group inspired by the "Movement of Movements" concept that MAS promoted was Socialist Women (Mujeres Socialistas), founded in 1972.[15] It not only included women who left the PCV in the split that led to the formation of MAS but also, in line with the party's class orientation, at-

15. Information on Socialist Women is compiled from internal documents and interviews

tracted journalists, intellectuals, and students, many of whom had begun to identify themselves as feminist. "Second wave" feminism, the second global wave of mobilization for women's rights that was nurtured by civil rights–based, antiwar, and nationalist movements of the 1960s and 1970s, had reached Venezuela in the early 1970s. Feminist books and debates filtered into the country, brought by women who had either been in exile following their participation in the guerrilla movement, emigrated, or studied abroad; and feminist influences began to be felt in left-wing politics. The explicit attention to women's issues within a socialist party attracted women who had been active in small parties such as the Socialist League (Liga Socialista) and the Revolutionary Left Movement (Movimiento Izquierdo Revolucionario, or MIR).[16]

The activists who joined Socialist Women were determined to avoid repeating their various experiences of discrimination within their respective "revolutionary" contexts. Thus they rejected the traditional mechanism for women's incorporation, the women's bureau. Instead of settling for a marginalized structure that did not promote women or their interests, they took advantage of the "Movement of Movements" concept to establish a semiautonomous women's movement linked to a political party. Following the MAS strategy of organizing movements as opposed to affiliating partisan supporters, Socialist Women stipulated that its members had to join the group as individuals, not as members of parties. The organization reserved the right to work with parties if there were a coincidence of objective and method (Mujeres Socialistas 1973, 9). In order to assert its independence of partisan control, it demonstrated financial self-sufficiency by paying for its locale and staff (Ellner 1988, 186).

Its semiautonomous status allowed Socialist Women to formulate its own views on women's gender interests, following a socialist-feminist ideology. This combined the struggle for workers' and women's rights, as illustrated by the motto "Neither exploited by a boss nor chained to a stove" (*Ni explotadas por un patrón, ni arrinconadas en un fogón*). The group saw capitalism and patriarchy as an intertwined system ensuring the reproduction of workers through the gendered division of labor in the home. In order to address oppressive class and gender relations, freeing both the working class (all of which was oppressed by capitalist relations of production) and all women

---

with MAS members (and former members) Ofelia Alvarez, Fernando Aranguren, Gioconda Espina, Argelia Laya, and Magdalena Valdevieso.

16. MIR was formed by those activists who had left AD in the early 1960s to join the guerrilla movement.

(who despite their different class positions were similarly oppressed by patriarchy), not only economic and political but also social models had to be transformed.

Maintaining a contextual view of women's oppression in Venezuelan society, the group recognized as its principal object the many women from the urban poor who were single mothers with children from different and mainly absent fathers. Unlike middle-class women, poor single mothers often worked at the most exploitative jobs as well as carrying out domestic duties. However, Socialist Women claimed that all women, regardless of class, suffered from the legal, economic, and social entrenchment of the ideology of *machismo,* which justified male dominance as natural and eternal, the logical product of biological difference.

In challenging *machismo,* Socialist Women went beyond rejecting gender hierarchy to suggesting that gender *difference* might also be a problem. Both views were incorporated into the 1973 MAS party platform. It listed five "basic conditions" that a socialist government had to guarantee in order to ensure women's liberation: (1) state attention to maternity and infancy; (2) technical, scientific, political, and cultural preparation of women so that they might have the same opportunities as men; (3) political participation of women at every level; (4) legal equality of the sexes; and (5) the emergence of a "new cultural reality" based on the eradication of the dominant male-chauvinist, capitalist ideology. These conditions were to be achieved through strategies including collectivization of housework, state protection of maternity and infancy regardless of the civil status of the mother, equal pay for equal work, education for domestic workers and prostitutes, and the modification of the Civil and Penal Codes (Acosta and Espina 1982).

Some of these strategies merely repeated the "basic conditions" and did not directly address every pertinent issue.[17] But the feminist advances of Socialist Women were evident: the group incorporated the social, economic, and legal equality of women as an integral part of the socialist revolution. Socialist Women elaborated on its ideology at its public presentation before the MAS general assembly in 1974. If socialism were to succeed, women's oppression, "the ultimate capitalist contradiction," had to be eliminated. But women's liberation would not come as "a mechanical fact or change as a consequence of an economic revolution," nor be effected through the "simple presence" of women at different levels of the struggle (Acosta and Espina 1982, 6, 5). Women themselves had to be active participants in the decision making and execution of the socialist project, which had to take certain reforms to heart.

17. Mayita Acosta and Gioconda Espina (1982, 10) mention the complete absence of women's control over their fertility, among other neglected topics.

Most of the reforms Socialist Women promoted were those advocated by the 1940s women's movement: equal pay for equal work and the end of other work-related discrimination, access to education, eradication of prostitution, improving the rights of domestic servants, implementation of sex education, increased child care, improved health care, and legal reform. Family planning was added to the list. But in this latest version of women's activism, Socialist Women insisted that it was not promoting "reformism," but it was undertaking the first steps to permit women to join in revolutionary transformation: "As long as women don't acquire their economic independence and just demands, they cannot really integrate themselves and participate actively in the struggle for liberation" (Acosta and Espina 1982, 15).

Gendered Opportunities Thwart Attempts to Bridge the Gender Gap

Socialist Women's defense of its combined activism for society's and women's liberation, especially its members' insistence that they were not mere "reformists," was clearly addressed to the potentially hostile audience of male socialists—the actors on whom women's new opportunities depended. From its inception, the group was eager to include men. They were seen as fellow victims of the "values of the dominant culture." Thus, although the movement "came from women for women and society," it sought the incorporation of both men and women who were willing to challenge the dominant modes of production and reproduction (Mujeres Socialistas 1973, 7). This attitude was reiterated in the 1974 presentation, which stated that one of Socialist Women's immediate goals was to have men understand and participate in the struggle for women's liberation. This liberation was again explained as one that benefited both genders and could only be interpreted as detrimental to men's interests by those who held the macho attitudes produced and supported by capitalism. Moreover, men were assured that the group was not promoting the "arid discussions" of nonsocialist feminists, who were assessed at that time to be neglecting the class struggle.

Despite Socialist Women's overtures to men, the group faced considerable hostility from male members of MAS. Its influence on the 1973 platform notwithstanding, this new form of party-linked women's activism encountered opposition from within the party from the outset. Argelia Laya, the veteran women's organizer and a founder of Socialist Women, reflected on many men's first response to the women's use of new organizing tactics: "The debates with the *compañeros* were terrible; [but] they could not prevent us from organizing this movement of socialist women because MAS was 'something else' *[otra cosa]*." In Socialist Women's presentation to the 1974 MAS general assembly, the sense of exclusion was already a palpable undercurrent in members' remarks. Several times they mentioned how women's dual oppression was a well-worn path or a simple refrain (*camino trillado,* or *refrán simple*), but one that nevertheless needed to be repeated. Although women's concerns had been included "theoretically" in platforms for action, they had not been implemented in practice (Mujeres Socialistas 1974, 7). Members darkly referred to "a list of concrete facts . . . at times certainly negative" that they had learned from, but would not elaborate upon, because "it is not our interest to resent, chastise, or demand anything" (5). They defended their struggle as one that was "real and should be continued" and "cannot be isolated nor delayed by any organization which struggles or ought to struggle for the same ends," i.e., complete socialism (5). Yet the group anticipated and accepted its fate. "Probably alone, or [perhaps] accompanied," it would continue to do its "simultaneous and isolated" work (6). Members recognized that even socialist revolutionaries tended to repeat certain dominant patterns of discrimination. To overcome these patterns would require a revolution in gender relations as well as in class relations.

Despite open opposition to its existence, Socialist Women hung on tenaciously for three more years, hosting three national conventions. It was only with the change in political opportunity that the group disintegrated. While the reversion of MAS to the traditional party structure in the late 1970s led to its greater showing at the polls, it also introduced traditional gender-biased aspects of that structure into this formerly innovative party. This had a direct negative impact on women's organizing: Socialist Women broke up in 1977. In an internal memo to the group's leadership, Argelia Laya explained that not only was the group subject to the general ideological, political, and organizational problems of MAS, but there were also "disturbing relations" between the party and the movement. In an interview, Laya elaborated on the change following the transformation of MAS: "The party wanted to give [Socialist Women] the instrumental treatment which was given to the other organizations"—that is, turning the movement into a minor sectoral appendage in true *adeco/copeyano* style. This restoration of traditional gender relations within the party was evident in preparation for the 1978 national elections for president. Although the party did not organize a traditional women's sectoral bureau, it held unauthorized meetings in the name of Socialist Women and manipulated the group into supporting one of the two choices for the socialist candidate.

Socialist Women's reaction to this manipulation by MAS was sharp. Laya, angered at the subordination of women's issues to party priorities once again, reminded the group's leadership in her memo that they had voluntar-

Fig. 4.1
Argelia Laya, prominent activist
against the Pérez Jiménez dictatorship,
guerrilla commander, founder of
Socialist Women, and former president
of the Socialist Party (MAS).

ily undertaken this work "because life and studies have shown us that the
Venezuelan path to socialism is pure blah-blah without work specifically directed at raising the consciousness of women." She closed by saying that she
would continue to fight for the cause of socialism and women—for her the
same cause—"with MAS or without it." Many members decided to go without and left to form the completely autonomous feminist groups of the late
1970s. As a result of the dissolution of Socialist Women, the analysis of
women's oppression received much less attention in the 1978 MAS electoral
platform than it had five years earlier. Unlike the 1973 platform, that of 1978
focused on legal discrimination against women and excluded all elements of
the societal critique proclaimed in 1973 (Acosta and Espina 1982).

MAS was not the only party on the left that gave insufficient support to
women's organizing on their own behalf. The coalition building of leftist parties around the municipal elections of 1979 spawned a Coordinating Committee of Leftist Women (Coordinadora de Mujeres de Izquierda), including
women from MAS, PCV, MIR, the Socialist League, several other small parties, and nonaffiliated feminists. Like Socialist Women, the Coordinating

Committee of Leftist Women declared itself in favor of legal reforms to end discrimination against women as the first step toward a more just socialist society. It also fought on behalf of the most disenfranchised. In September 1979 the coordinating committee held the first street demonstration of the new presidency of *copeyano* Luis Herrera Campins to protest the high cost of living.

Gioconda Espina, a feminist columnist for the leftist newspaper *El Nuevo Venezolano*, reported on the discrimination that men from the left continued to perpetrate during the women's march:

> They belonged to different leftist organizations but in the Plaza del Venezolano [the rally site] they found, finally, a reason to unite: they were men, and thus ought to sacrifice their "serious" differences (that is, their political differences) to assume the leadership of [the women]: those eternal minors who that day were accompanied by minors given birth to (and surely supported by) the women themselves. . . . To be from the left does not signify, by any means, to be clear about everything. It does not signify not being as sexist as any *adeco* at the hour of believing that someone should make decisions for the poor defenseless women. (10 November 1979)

Male party activists directed the march, deciding which groups could hand out literature (some parties, but not feminist groups), and the order of the marchers (putting themselves in front of many women). Espina presented this example of male dominance as yet another reason to continue strengthening women's activism. However, the Coordinating Committee of Leftist Women soon faltered as an organizing force because of the lack of ongoing contact among its members. It came to life again two years later, though only briefly, during the Civil Code campaign, berating the almost-all-male leadership of the left for its exclusive preoccupation with the upcoming elections and demanding that it come out in support of the reform (Coordinadora de Mujeres de Izquierda 1981).

Building from Within

The women who remained active in campaigning for women's rights within MAS did not stop trying to incorporate their own perspectives. Their experiences in Socialist Women showed them that organizing somewhat outside of the party did not give them enough of a voice. But they also found their specific demands diluted when they worked through the traditional structures adopted by MAS in the mid-1970s. Therefore they decided to try to integrate women's particular perspectives into the general struggle by working for gender-specific demands within the party. Turning from a linked organization to an internal mechanism, party activists started the Feminist Front (Frente Feminista) of MAS in 1981. The name itself reflected their determination to reclaim the sectoral bureau for women: the traditional women's bureaus was often named the "Women's Front" *(Frente Femenino).*

The Feminist Front criticized MAS for being ideologically oriented toward, and structured on behalf of, male activists. In preparatory documents for the Fourth Conference of Socialist Women,[18] the front faulted MAS for its continuing refusal to incorporate women's issues in its platforms and promote women's leadership. It exhorted the party to promote discussion of women's issues, including the long-sought demands for legal reform, and to encourage feminist projects such as public women's centers (Rugeles 1981, 1982; Valdevieso and Castejon 1981; Valdevieso 1982). To reform the masculinized structure, the front proposed internal changes to party organization to allow women to participate fully: day care should be regularly offered during meeting times; funding of the Feminist Front should be on a par with that of comparable party bureaus; and quotas should be established for women's participation at decision-making levels of the party.

Finally, the Feminist Front recognized the need to promote different forms of organizing, particularly social movements of women. They were most likely to be incorporated on the basis of "social activism," the locally based community advocacy in which they tended to be involved (as opposed to party-based political activism) because it took place near the home. The front also actively promoted the idea of a mass nonpartisan women's movement, which it saw as crucial for the liberation of all women.

As the 1983 presidential elections approached, MAS seemed to welcome the Feminist Front's ideas. In 1982 MAS founder and presidential candidate Teodoro Petkoff publicly stated that the party should define itself as feminist as well as socialist. The National Council of MAS also promised that at least 15 percent of the members of MAS's electoral slate would be women (Ellner 1988, 186). This promise was particularly innovative, coming about a decade before quotas were regularly discussed as a way of guaranteeing women's inclusion in Latin American parties. The front's activism also resulted in the inclusion of the first "Women's Policy" *(Política Hacia la Mujer)*

18. Although it was the Feminist Front's first conference, organizers called it the Fourth Conference out of respect for the work Socialist Women had done previously, including its three national conferences.

Fig. 4.2
Cover of Feminist Front
pamphlet describing
MAS's "Women's Policy."

section of a party platform. This section advocated many of the reforms proposed by Socialist Women, from the collectivization of housework to equal pay for equal work. But it also specifically mentioned the liberalization of abortion restrictions (Frente Feminista 1983).

The Feminist Front saw the 1983 developments as more than just an election-year gimmick; they were to lead to the invigoration of MAS-based and beyond-MAS mobilization of women. In its bulletin *A Pesar de Todo* (Despite Everything), the front stated its two goals: to solicit women's vote *and* to build a women's movement that would continue beyond the election year.

But the lack of such a movement, coupled with the relatively weak organizational status of the Feminist Front—marginalized as a women's bureau—led to another disappointment: the women's bureau and their issues were exploited for electoral ends and then ignored. MAS failed to fulfill its commitment to have 15 percent representation of women on party slates. In 1985 only two women were elected as permanent members of the national party leadership. Moreover, despite its promise in the 1983 platform, MAS congressmen did not support the legalization of therapeutic abortion in the next congressional sessions. Finally—in a more symbolic form of MAS's betrayal—its leadership pressured the Feminist Front into a name change: the Women's Work Front (Frente de Trabajo Hacia la Mujer). "It was argued that the word *feminist* had been largely discredited and that the party would be more effective if it appealed to women in their condition as members of a household and as workers rather than feminists" (Ellner 1988, 187).

La Mala Vida (The Dissolute Life), a feminist publication to which MAS supporters contributed, declared the party guilty of a sellout, charging that it had never been feminist in more than name and that it was only interested in organizing women "to send more pants [i.e., men] to the city council." After all, how could the party be different when like all the others it was controlled by men and a few women who imitated them? (*La Mala Vida*, May 1984). To add final insult to injury, in 1985 party leadership unilaterally moved the Feminist Front into MAS's "Area of Unconventional Social Movements" without explanation (O. Alvarez 1987).

What the activists who attempted to organize on behalf of women through a party learned was that not only male-oriented structures but also the sexist attitudes of party leadership could prove to be an obstacle. The experience of the women of MAS illustrated what Chilean feminist theorist Julieta Kirkwood (1986, 103) described as "a fantasy of realization through invocation," (*la fantasía de la realización por invocación*)—or more colloquially, "giving lip service." To the women who believed firmly that socialist revolution would be incomplete without women's liberation, its mere recognition by party leadership led them to assume that women's issues would be incorporated into the socialist struggle. But the male leadership never fully accepted or promoted gender equality, as proved by its unwillingness to follow through on its promises after the 1983 elections.

In addition, during the course of their attempts at organizing while maintaining some affiliation to a party, MAS women did not put enough emphasis on the important mobilizational principle they might have learned from the history of Venezuelan women's organizing, which had been resurrected at the First Congress. Women had to develop some form of women's activism *outside of* male-dominated political structures. This was crucial both to help those struggling to reform structures from the inside and to promote women's interests in general. But certain groups did attempt to build such civil society–based activism during the first period of democratic consolidation. They achieved advances in political strategy, even if their efforts did not appear immediately effective.

Autonomy in Civil Society: Feminist Organizing and the Popular Women's Circles

In a direct response to their manipulation by political parties during democratic consolidation, women from two classes decided to organize autonomously in civil society: middle-class women through the feminist movement, and urban poor, or "popular" women in grassroots community organizing. In both of these endeavors, women challenged assumptions about their interests. They also rejected the organizational forms through which their political participation had been marginalized. But their success was limited by the structure of opportunities. Party-based activism was too strong a force to allow for effective alternatives in this period. Moreover, although women of both classes formulated similar strategies, class differences largely impeded their fruitful interaction.

Feminist Organizing

Experience with party politics gave a distinctive character to the small feminist movement that developed in Venezuela in the 1970s. A negative experience with party politics, particularly the left's insistence on putting class before gender liberation, was pivotal in the construction of many such movements in the region (S. Alvarez 1998, 296). But the entrenched power of parties in the Venezuelan context had perhaps an even deeper impact, simultaneously stimulating and hobbling the development of feminist activism.

From their particular history of marginalization, feminist activists offered the most forceful argument for women's politically autonomous action.[19] Feminist groups initially drew their membership from the university population and female professionals, but the groups grew with the defection of those women who had been disillusioned by their experience in MAS (*El Nuevo Venezolano*, 13 March 1980). While espousing many socialist tenets, they recognized from past experience in a male-dominated party that women would have to rely on themselves for their advancement. The membership profile was reflected in the types of activities most common to the movement: small encounter sessions, occasional public meetings, and a stream of published work, most commonly in the form of journals and newspaper ar-

---

19. Information on feminist organizing is drawn from groups' internal documents, newspaper reports, and interviews with Fernando Anaguren, Laly Armengol, Isabel Carmona, Nora Castañeda, Gloria Comesaña, Franka Donda, Gioconda Espina, Argelia Laya, and Esperanza Vera.

ticles. Although they articulated an important dimension of women's organizing, feminists would not develop a widespread alternative to party-based activism. Their structures were no match for the entrenched parties, nor was their message of gender equality well received in general.

One of the very first feminist groups, the Women's League (Liga de Mujeres), understood the need for autonomy from party politics from firsthand experience. Founded at the Central University of Venezuela (Universidad Central de Venezuela) in 1972, the Women's League began its own journal. Clearly inspired not only by feminist but also by socialist principles, league members campaigned against the Miss Venezuela pageant, declaring that "this type of spectacle reflects the denigrating position that women have in the capitalist system" (*Al Margen*, July 1972). However, the group split in 1974 when the Socialist League Party, in a takeover move, sent all of its female members to join the Women's League. This resulted in its adoption of a more general political agenda: to free political prisoners, participate in hunger strikes, take part in demonstrations protesting the high cost of living, and generally agitate on behalf of "democratic freedoms." Founding members of the Women's League were sympathetic to these demands, but as one remarked, "By our way of seeing things [they] didn't have anything to do with the goals which a feminist movement should have, that is the struggle for the specific problems of women in a dependent capitalist society like our own" (cited in Briceño Caldera et al. 1977, 152).

As a result of the Women's League's "colonization" by the party, those women who did not want to be associated with the party formed a new feminist group, Toward a New Woman (Hacia la Nueva Mujer). They declared it to be completely autonomous from party politics and focused primarily on what activists claimed to be issues affecting all women, taking class position into account only secondarily.

Many of the former members of Socialist Women as well as of smaller leftist parties were attracted to this perspective. Inspired by example, in 1978 women in Caracas founded three groups—The Spell, Person, and the Wednesday Feminist Group (La Conjura, Persona, and Grupo Feminista Miércoles)—to focus on women's consciousness-raising through group discussion, journal publication, and video production. Feminist groups also started in Mérida and Maracaibo, two large cities in the interior of Venezuela, and eventually spread to other areas.[20]

20. Gloria Comesaña, the founder of the Feminist League (Liga Feminista) of Maracaibo, credits Jean Paul Sartre for its existence. While writing her dissertation on Sartre's philosophy in Paris, she had the opportunity to interview him several times. At one such interview she expressed how much she was going to miss her Parisian feminist group when she returned to Venezuela, and Sartre suggested that she start one of her own.

As explained in a statement of principles by the Wednesday Feminist Group, autonomous activism was a key principle of feminist organizing. Autonomy was the strategy by which women could develop an awareness of their need for liberation, an essential process for any oppressed group:

> The movement for women's liberation . . . should be an AUTONOMOUS movement, that is, should allow for women's autonomy regarding their specific organization. The movement ought to be autonomous, and the women's groups are tools of this struggle because they are a favorable environment where women can affirm themselves, understand themselves, speak freely, and build self-confidence; they allow the search for a new identity, leaving behind the constructed image in which women are imprisoned and oppressed; they facilitate the break with the traditional relations of subordination-domination, seduction, etc. which privileges *machismo* to the detriment of women; and the group allows the move from personal to collective consciousness, the same as the class consciousness of any oppressed group. (Grupo Feminista Miércoles 1979)

Reflecting many members' former involvement with MAS and other leftist parties, the Wednesday Feminist Group explained that although women's liberation would only be made possible through a socialist revolution, socialist revolution would only be realized with women's liberation. Women's activism on their own behalf, now through separate efforts, was explained as an integral part of the socialist project: "The organization of women's struggle does not divide the struggle of workers, peasants, and the proletariat in general, it strengthens it, and just as those struggles liberate those most involved, the liberation of women will be the work of women themselves" (Grupo Feminista Miércoles 1979).

Through their publications and meetings, feminists sought to raise general consciousness—at least among educated women—of women's specific oppression. Although never enlisting great numbers, the movement made itself heard inside and outside of the country. In August 1979 The Spell proposed the first Latin American Feminist Encounter, which eventually took place in Bogotá, Colombia, in July 1981 (Saporta Sternbach et al. 1992, 238, n.23). The movement held its own feminist meeting in Caracas in 1979 (which would be repeated for several years), producing a document that continued to link older demands for ending gender hierarchy and newer ones challenging gender difference. Feminists called for a coordinating group of women's

QUE ES EL FEMINISMO RADICAL?

El Feminismo radical es un movimiento de mujeres, revolucionario, materia-
lista y autónomo.

Se propone una transformación total de la sociedad. Adhiriendo a los prin-
cipios del Materialismo Histórico, los lleva hasta sus últimas consecuencias, al
politizar la categoría de la sexualidad y al poner de relieve la situación espe-
cífica de opresión que vive la mujer en tanto que sexo.

La revolución feminista será la más radical, ya que no sólo busca la eli-
minación de un sistema económico (lucha contra el Capitalismo), sino la transformación total de las relaciones humanas al transformar las relaciones entre la mu_
jer y el hombre (lucha contra el Patriarcado).

El Feminismo no divide ni resta fuerzas a la lucha revolucionaria: la amplía
y la profundiza.

El Feminismo es autónomo porque corresponde a las mujeres, como a todo gru_
po oprimido, luchar por su propia liberación.

Después de siglos de temor, pasividad forzada y timidez, la mujer debe apren_
der a tomar la palabra, a reflexionar sobre sus propios problemas y a luchar so-
lidariamente junto a sus hermanas.

MUJER!

La opresión que sufres en el hogar, la oficina, la fábrica, la calle
el taller, la Iglesia, la escuela, la Universidad, el liceo, la ciudad, el país,
el MUNDO; es un problema SOCIAL. Sola no puedes liberarte. Descubre la amistad y
la hermandad de las otras mujeres. Unete a ellas, forma grupos de reflexión y lu_
cha allí donde vives, trabajas o estudias.

Liga Feminista de Maracaibo

Maracaibo 4-9-79

Fig. 4.3   Flier distributed by the Feminist League
of Maracaibo defining "Radical Feminism."

Fig. 4.3   English translation

WHAT IS RADICAL FEMINISM?

Radical feminism is a revolutionary, materialist, and autonomous women's movement.

It proposes a total transformation of society. Adhering to the principles of Historical Materialism, it takes them to their ultimate consequences, by politicizing the category of sexuality and by putting into relief the specific situation of the oppression lived by the woman on account of her sex.

The feminist revolution will be the most radical, because it does not only seek the elimination of an economic system (the struggle against Capitalism), but also the total transformation of human relations through transforming the relations between woman and man (the struggle against Patriarchy).

Feminism does not divide or reduce forces for the revolutionary struggle; it augments and deepens them.

Feminism is autonomous because it corresponds to women, as to all oppressed groups, to fight for their own liberation.

After centuries of fear, forced passivity, and timidity, the woman ought to learn to speak, to reflect on her own problems, and to struggle in solidarity together with her sisters.

WOMAN!

The oppression that you suffer in the home, office, factory, street, shop, Church, school, University, high school, city, country, WORLD, is a SOCIAL problem. Alone you cannot liberate yourself. Discover the friendship and sisterhood of other women. United with them, form groups for reflection and struggle there where you live, work, or study.

organizations, increased child care, an end to workplace discrimination, minimum wage for domestic workers, and the eradication of sexist portrayals of women in the media. But building on some of the work of the First Congress and Socialist Women, they also challenged the assumption of maternity as women's "function" by seeking the legalization of abortion (*El Nuevo Venezolano,* 20 December 1979).

Such ideas were spread further through new women's studies programs, the feminist magazine *La Mala Vida,* and groups inspired by feminist ideals. These included the longest lasting private family planning organization, the Venezuelan Association for an Alternative Sex Education (Asociación Venezolana para una Educación Sexual Alternativa, or AVESA), which has focused on reproductive health, sex education, and rape crisis intervention from 1984 until the present.

But notwithstanding feminists' claims to autonomous action, the shadow of party activism fell over feminist organizing. Feminists brought their struggle with partisan politics out into the open: in the celebrations for International Women's Day 1979, members of The Spell held a banner claiming "Mujer: Tu Unica Militancia es con el Movimiento de Mujeres" (Woman: Your Only Activism is with the Women's Movement), deliberately using the word *militancia,* usually applied to party activism, to encourage women's activism. But the groups could never escape completely from the legacy of the parties, which they recognized as affecting feminists throughout Latin America and in Europe—any place women had been active in democratic centralist parties like those that characterized Venezuelan politics. Party priorities influenced feminists even as they tried to focus their attention on other issues, and party organization was reflected in their new forms of mobilization.

> Daily we are subjected to accusations that we have substituted women's struggle for the class struggle. . . . Many feminist activists find ourselves—some with excessive frequency—interrogating ourselves whether, in truth, [our] struggle might not be postponable, as the *compañeros* of the leadership of the mixed organizations say. Many times we ask ourselves if it might not be better to sacrifice ourselves, one more time, to honor a more general struggle, even if this signifies returning to silence and obedience to the line of the leader (a necessarily macho leader, even if she wears a skirt). (*El Nuevo Venezolano,* 13 March 1980)

Yet even as they attempted to reject it, feminists found their political train-

ing incorporated into the new groups: "It is not possible to abandon traditional activism, because all the ideological baggage is carried along to the
feminist collective" (Persona 3/13/80). Thus feminists found themselves reproducing the same gendered roles of party politics in their new groups:
"feminine" deference to a "masculine" leader on decision making and execution of tasks.[21]

While the feminist movement made the most articulate case for the
need for autonomy in order to achieve women's liberation, their organizing
never gained a large following. One estimate numbers not more than fifty
"active" feminists at the height of this period of the movement. Their idea of
small consciousness-raising groups could scarcely be widely implemented in
the face of the control that mass-based parties had over most sectors of civil
society. Feminists themselves were plagued by the vestiges of party-based
political indoctrination. Furthermore, party incorporation of women activists continued apace, and with the exception of the early MAS, along traditional lines.

Beyond their different organizational style, these feminists' challenge
to gender difference and hierarchy threatened social norms upholding the
importance of conventional gender roles. Autonomous feminist action to
achieve women's equality was a separation not only from traditional politics
but also from men. In reaction, as one activist explained it, many people accused feminists of being either lesbians or prostitutes—women who trans-
gressed the boundaries of traditional gender relations. How deeply
entrenched was the objection to feminism by powerful sectors of Venezuelan
society would become quite evident during the reform of the Civil Code.
Meanwhile, feminists' perceived rejection of traditional gender relations and
focus on educated women also prevented them from effective outreach to
what might have seemed a logical constituency, women organizing on their
own behalf in the poorer neighborhoods.

The Popular Women's Circles

In the early 1970s women from the Caracas *barrios* started what would turn
into the largest politically autonomous women's organization, the still-exist-
ing Popular Women's Circles (Círculos Femeninos Populares, or CFP). Despite the economic and social differences between popular women and those
from other classes, they were similarly affected by the encroachment of party

21. Lynn Stephen (1997, 279) notes a similar struggle with "socialization" among women's
grassroots groups seeking to transform political culture in Brazil and El Salvador.

politics on their organization. The experience of partisan manipulation also led the CFP to advocate autonomous activism. It sought to express its own challenge to traditional gender relations through a new, nonhierarchical model of women's organizing.

At least initially, so long as the challenge to gender relations by the CFP did not prioritize the theory of women's liberation, this innovation was supported by a larger community organization. During this period, the members promoted a practical struggle against class and gender oppression to resolve their day-to-day problems. This difference in outlook from the feminists' made it difficult for women to organize across classes. But it also revealed an analysis crossing "strategic" and "practical" lines of interest.

In Venezuelan *barrios*, mothers with children from multiple and absent fathers were the central adult figures (Dalla Costa 1995, 96). They were the concrete embodiment of the large number of both households headed by a woman, which formed 22 percent of all households in 1976, and out-of-wedlock births, which amounted to 53 percent of all births in 1974 (Huggins Castañeda and Dominguez Nelson 1993, 33; Ministro de Estado 1983, 137). While single mothers were the subjects of programs such as the Daily Care Homes, state attention never provided sufficient relief for the quarter of all families that lived in poverty (Huggins Castañeda and Dominguez Nelson 1993, 18).

To address the problems of poor urban women, in 1974 a few women living in a Caracas *barrio* suggested to community organizers from the Popular Action Service Center (Centro al Servicio de Acción Popular, or CESAP), Venezuela's largest and most successful community organization, that it establish a project specifically focused on their needs. In response, CESAP sponsored the Popular Women's Circles (CFP) to organize *barrio* homemakers. The CFP initially gave small classes or workshops in self-esteem, health issues, child rearing, and microenterprises, using a "popular education" model. Following the teachings of Paolo Freire, it built on the knowledge that the students themselves brought to the subject from lived experiences. By 1978 there were seventeen circles in Caracas and nineteen in other states; in 1982 the national CFP organization began its own publication, *Mujeres en Lucha* (Women in Struggle).

A New Form of Organizing

The CFP regendered the opportunity of party-based representation. It rejected the party women's bureaus and offered an alternative specifically geared to the needs of poor urban women, whether material or, eventually, representational. Unlike the centralized models that dominated Venezuelan political activity, the structure of the CFP was decentralized and nonhierarchical, much closer to a social movement than a political party. Each local circle was based on a structure of concentric circles. The inner circle was made up of four coordinators who oversaw the areas of formation, organization, solidarity, and financing. The second circle included the regular participants; and the third circle, the wider community. The local circles met in yearly statewide and national meetings run by small elected coordinating teams.

The contrast with party organizing became even more striking with the explicit rejection of party politics by the CFP. Within a few years of the group's founding, the coordinators at every level of the organization were forbidden to be active members of political parties. A national coordinator of the CFP explained that early on, political parties tried to "capture" the local organizations for electoral ends. After the CFP had achieved a national presence, it also experienced political pressure around the 1978 presidential election. These experiences led members to pass the nonpartisan rule (Juana Delgado interview).

The difference between the parties and the CFP is also emphasized in its first brochure, *¿Qué son los Círculos Femeninos Populares?* (What are the Popular Women's Circles?). In explaining why the CFP was established, the authors note how local organizations had been politicized to the point of impeding community-based organizing: "Organizations exist like the Neighborhood Council, or Communal Committee, which is in the hands of some political party and functions only for the interests of the party, dividing us even more" (Orellana and Ortiz n.d.).

The profound influence of party politics, and women's rejection of it, is again made clear when the authors explain the need for women to organize. After a paragraph describing how popular women's needs had prepared them to mobilize on behalf of their children and their communities as well as for themselves, a cartoon depiction of an older woman responds, "That's what I've always said." She is answered by a young mother holding a crying infant: "Yes, granny, but a single tree doesn't make a mountain. And to understand and fight for our rights as women and as a people, we have had to organize ourselves, to start to open our eyes and keep ourselves very alert in the Popular Women's Circles." To which the grandmother replies with an angry expression, "What is that *guarandinga* [whatchamacallit]? Have you all invented another party?"

The political independence of the organization kept it from traditional sources of funding. Beyond the support of its members (20 percent of the

Fig. 4.4   Cartoon from CFP pamphlet.

dues of each local organization and 10 percent of the revenue from production workshops was provided to support the national organization), the CFP was dependent on outside funding.[22] This was in significant contrast to many local organizations, which often engaged in party-based clientelism. Having affiliated with one or another party, they were assured some form of regular income as long as their members supported party programs and promoted candidates during elections.

Beyond the training offered by the local circles, as it expanded the national body began to serve as a means of representing popular women to a state that had largely ignored them. In this process, the CFP effectively made an end run around the political parties that sought to capture the group for electoral purposes. In 1979 the membership sent their own petition to President Herrera Campins, demanding a voice in social policy making but insisting on respect for their political autonomy. In 1980–81 the CFP coordinated protests against the high cost of living for *barrio* residents, conducted a survey to show how few of them could afford the *cesta básica* (the "basic basket," a measurement of the cost of staples), and coordinated bulk buying clubs.

22. These funders have included the Inter-American Foundation, the Global Fund for Women, the United Nations Development Programme, ILDIS, and other private European and Venezuelan foundations.

Popular Women's Gender Interests

Despite the CFP's autonomous activity and defiance of party manipulation, the common experience with other women's groups did not lead to an easy alliance. Individual middle-class women who devoted their energies to organizing in the *barrios* were welcome collaborators. But as a whole, the group saw their interests differently from those expressed by the largely middle-class, educated feminist groups in Venezuela, as well as those of party activists who took on women's issues. The popular women's orientation came from their practical, not theoretical experience of the intertwined nature of gender and class oppression:

> The CFP differs from those theoretical approaches used by some feminist groups and other political organizations which underestimate work with women, housewives, in their family and community spheres and which, moreover, consider that this work only introduces "reforms" and does not produce transformations which have repercussions throughout society. The experience of the Circles, much to the contrary, proves that it is precisely through reflection on her daily family and community life that a woman from the popular sectors, with more harmony and greater profundity, introduces changes in her daily tasks, democratizes authoritarian and patriarchal family and community relations, starts to question the structures of power, and develops actions whose significance and extent is of great relevance and social transcendence. (Paredes and Tapia 1989, 38)

The CFP stressed the need to address the effects of discriminatory gender relations within the context of popular women's daily lives, thus combining "practical" and "strategic" interests.[23] Their context was made up of a complex interaction of forces, including, but not limited to, the problems associated with *machismo*. The group made clear that popular women worked within their communities, not somehow estranged from them:

> The problem of *machismo* and the subordination of women is an integral phenomenon in the sense that it has to do with the family as a whole (parents, daughters and sons, etc.) and the community. [It must be addressed] in such a way that the understanding of

23. The division between practical and strategic interests is problematized in Chapter 1.

these problems and the educational actions which are undertaken to improve women's condition do not a priori exclude the work which must be undertaken with all of the family, the neighborhood, the *barrio,* the community, etc. In this way, the feminist components are taken on within a more complex whole which has important relations with the social distribution of power, the economic capacity of popular women, the education and formation of children, etc. (Paredes and Tapia 1989, 41–42)

Yet popular women's gender interests were not static. In the early 1980s, the CFP showed a notable repositioning. In 1979 it described itself as "a popular women's organization which seeks to articulate women's participation in the solution of the problems of the popular class in general and not a feminist organization which works only for women's rights." But in 1981 it produced an internal evaluation, noting that it was not focused enough on the problems of sexism and women's subordination (Orellana 1991, 116). One of the more significant causes of this development was the CFP involvement in the mobilization to reform the Civil Code. In this campaign deliberate attempts were made to strategize around issues common to all women.

Conjunctural Coalition Building Reemerges:
The 1982 Reform of the Civil Code

The 1982 reform of the Civil Code came about as the result of the regendering of political opportunities during democratic consolidation. It fulfilled women's forty-year-old demands for equality between men and women in family decision making and for equal legal status for all children. After eight previous attempts during the 1970s had failed, in the final, successful campaign, first a professional women's organization (the Venezuelan Federation of Female Lawyers) and then the minister for women's affairs, Mercedes Pulido de Briceño, took the lead. They built a conjunctural coalition that relied on women's capacity for autonomous organizing across partisan differences and political arenas, using an explicitly nonfeminist, profamily rhetorical strategy. The result was a reform of the Civil Code supported by women from a wide range of backgrounds and from every political party.

In the 1980s version of conjunctural coalition building, women activists profited from, and made advances over, the experiences of their 1940s foremothers. The result was a more radical reform of the Civil Code than the one attempted in 1942. As in the earlier effort, women's groups in civil society were of considerable importance, again using the strategies of national petition campaigns and election-based issue promotion. These efforts increased in effectiveness because they were now employed under a democratic (not liberal authoritarian) regime, which paid considerably more attention to citizen-based activism. The new mechanism of women's state-based representation, giving women a foothold in the powerful executive branch, proved indispensable to the success of the campaign. Pulido de Briceño was a well-connected Christian Democrat whose leadership was the sine qua non of the reform effort. It also helped that this second reform took place during the UN Decade on Women, a time of increased international attention to women's issues.

In the campaign, women also drew on lessons from their organizing experiences during the 1970s. Women's experience in MAS showed that even in the most innovative of parties, leadership and organization were still gender-biased, indicating that party-based activism could not be relied upon as the primary locus of women's organizing on their own behalf. Moreover, the resistance to feminist ideals showed that a political discourse that challenged gender difference could not easily promote women's interests. Instead, women found ways to go around the parties, through state and civil society, and to frame the reform as an issue of "democracy in the family."

The Rebirth of the Reform: Women Lawyers Take the Lead

The ideological orientation of the Venezuelan Federation of Female Lawyers (FEVA), the most significant women's professional association in Venezuela, largely explains its central role in the reform struggle. FEVA, dedicated to "the study of the social, economic and juridical problems of women, minors and the family" (FEVA 1987, 1), was the contemporary reincarnation of the nonpartisan, relational feminist groups that formed the broad-based women's movement of the 1940s. FEVA was founded in 1956 by women active in the first initiative to reform the Civil Code. These activists included Luisa Amelia Pérez Perozo, Venezuela's first female lawyer, and Panchita Soublette Saluzzo, whose presentation at the 1940 Preparatory Conference formed the basis of the first comprehensive petition sent to Congress in favor of the reform.[24] Obliged to keep a low profile during the Pérez Jiménez dic-

---

24. Information on FEVA's role in the Civil Code reform comes principally from de Leonardi (1983), Prince de Kew (1990), and an interview with Ana Luisa García Maldonado, president of FEVA during the reform process.

tatorship, the group reemerged in 1965. Restarting the reform effort was its major focus. In the early 1970s, the membership of FEVA increased, benefiting from women's access to professional education made possible under the democratic regime. With growing strength, the group began a series of meetings to publicize the discriminations legislated by the current Civil Code.

The work of FEVA was supported by the national attention paid to women's issues under democratic consolidation. The group participated in the lobbying of presidential candidates for the 1973 elections in order to get the theme of "women, minors and the family" on the election-year agenda. In 1974 the attorney general proposed the first modifications of the Civil Code to Congress, a move repeated by a small independent group of lawyers in May 1975. These efforts resulted in the establishment of a congressional committee to study the issue. Meanwhile Dr. Helena Salcedo, the coordinator of COFEAPRE, called upon FEVA members to participate in its legal commission. Through COFEAPRE, the members sent their first reform proposal to Congress in April 1975. When no response came, FEVA repeated the proposal in October, now strengthened by the support of the First Congress of Women. Their submission was seconded by another proposal in November sponsored by the small MIR party.

Beyond benefiting from national organizing, the efforts by FEVA were helped by international opportunities. The observation of International Women's Year motivated COFEAPRE to hold the First Congress of Women, and the Plan of Action of the 1975 UN International Women's Year meeting in Mexico City paid crucial attention to the family. The Plan of Action stated that "the institution of the family, which is changing in its economic, social and cultural functions, should ensure the dignity, equality and security of each of its members" through measures resembling the proposed reforms of the Civil Code. These included equal rights for wives and husbands with regard to community property and divorce laws, and equal treatment for children, whether born in or out of wedlock (*Action Survey of IWY* 1976, 82–83).

Responding to growing international influence and internal pressure, the administration finally took action on the reform. In November 1976 President Pérez's legal consultant presented a version of the reform bill to Congress. However, the reforms proposed in this bill had been watered down to the point that FEVA members found themselves opposed to its passage. The administration's proposal continued to grant husbands final say in matters concerning children as well as in the location of the domestic residence. Most importantly, it did not end discrimination against so-called "natural" children. The author of the FEVA proposal, Yolanda Poleo de Baez, called the bill "worse than nothing." The then-president of FEVA, Ana Lucina García Maldonado, recalled that "if we'd accepted that this would be it for reforming the Code, it would be as though they'd said: 'Here's a candy, now hush!'" Instead of being quiet, the leadership of FEVA immediately gave press conferences in which they accused the administration of making fun of them (*"Burladas las Juristas"*) and called the new legislation "a juridical monstrosity" *(mamotreto jurídico) (El Nacional,* November 1976). With the reform's major supporters in active opposition to the bill, it was tabled.

Tired of having their issues ignored or misrepresented, the lawyers of FEVA updated mobilizational tactics from the 1940s, while taking advantage of the new opportunities of democratic consolidation. To insure that their reform proposals would not suffer the same fate as the preceding efforts, essentially ignored by Congress over the last five years, they organized another petition campaign. However, under democracy, the petition had more legal relevance than before. Enshrined in the 1961 Constitution was article 165, which provided that one of the five ways a law could be directly introduced in Congress was through a popular initiative signed by 20,000 citizens. The first group ever to implement this initiative process, FEVA began to solicit signatures for its proposal to reform the Civil Code.[25]

Meanwhile FEVA kept the pressure on national leaders, using the elections of 1978 as an occasion for raising the issue of the reform, just as the activists in the 1940s had asked candidates for their support on women's issues. This agitation by FEVA bore fruit. The campaign literature of both major contenders, *adeco* Luis Piñerua Ordaz and *copeyano* Luis Herrera Campins, specifically mentioned attention to the family as a priority, including the necessary modification of existing legal structures (Prince de Kew 1990, 42–46). The winner of the race, Herrera Campins, even went as far as to promise in his program that "educational action [to improve the situation of Venezuelan women] . . . will be complemented with legal measures, especially in that which refers to civil legislation, and to the family, in which aspect one can see Venezuela is unfortunately lagging behind" (Herrera Campins 1978, 122).

25. In an astonishing example of the widespread ignorance of women's organizing, a 1986 book analyzing the 1961 Constitution published by the highly esteemed Venezuelan Academy of Political and Social Sciences (Academia de Ciencias Políticas y Sociales), claimed that "this form of participation of the people in legislating . . . has scant resonance in Venezuela, as is shown by the fact that there has not been at any time even tentative steps toward the exercise of the right of initiative in the laws on the part of the electorate" (Oropezo, 447). A surprising conclusion, given its highly publicized use in the process of the 1982 reform!

The author of the proposals, Yolanda Poleo de Baez, was privy to the candidate's commitment following a public meeting of presidential candidates in 1978 to discuss the reform: "When it was all over and everyone had gone, we were still on the dais; he collected his three proposals and put them in his bag and said, 'Yolanda, this can be done and I offer to you that I will push this as much as I am able so that it gets through [Congress].'"

FEVA expanded the movement for reform by involving women inside and outside of parties in their signature drive, foreshadowing the strategy of multi-arena organizing that would lead to the reform's ultimate success. Branches of the organization throughout the country collected signatures, spreading the idea of the reform beyond Caracas. They were joined in this effort by women from different political parties. Former members of Socialist Women, who from its inception had supported a reform of the Civil Code, took an active part, as did other parties' women's bureaus. They collected signatures in union halls, professional organizations, government offices, businesses, markets, and other public places.

The drive was an overwhelming success. FEVA and its supporters collected over 35,000 signatures and caught the public's attention. On 18 May 1979, FEVA presented the initiative, which by then had acquired the signatures of both former President Carlos Andrés Pérez and current President Herrera Campins, to Congress.

As this campaign for the reform proceeded, it took on a different character from its historical predecessor. It was not promoted as a reform on behalf of women's rights, but one that would benefit all of society. FEVA president García Maldonado explained that the first reactions to the organization's efforts in the early 1970s were that their proposals were "crazy"—that is, "feminist." Feminism continued to have pejorative connotations, even before the expansion of the contemporary feminist movement in the late 1970s. FEVA was anxious to disassociate its work from that of feminist activists, whose more active challenge to gender difference brought them ridicule and rejection. Thus the initiative petition itself stated that the proposed reforms were "far from strident" and "were not those of a feminist group" (Despacho de la Ministro de Estado 1984, 101–2). When she presented the initiative to Congress, Maldonado reaffirmed this perspective: "This is not a feminist undertaking, or one only of legal experts. It concerns a theme which transcends both dimensions to constitute itself as a problem whose solution interests everyone" (*El Nacional,* 17 May 1979). The need to disabuse the public of the notion that the reform of the Civil Code was a "women's rights issue" or somehow "feminist" would be a constant preoccupation as the campaign continued.

State Support for the Reform: The Women's Ministry and Its Minister

After years of agitation and its petition drive, FEVA was able to get a publicly supported bill before Congress. But the movement still faced the problems that had led to the failure of all previous attempts: the lack of both leadership from within the powerful executive branch dedicated to seeing the reform through, and an ongoing nonpartisan coalition of women inside and outside of government to keep up the pressure.[26] Both needs were answered through the reconfigured national women's agency.

Because of its founding by executive decree, the future of the first national women's commission, COFEAPRE, had become unclear as the 1978 elections drew near. But activists were determined to maintain it. At the suggestion of the lawyer Clarisa Sanoja, an activist from the days of the Pérez Jiménez dictatorship, representatives of all the major parties and independent feminists created the Committee for the Defense of Women's Rights (Comité de Defensa de los Derechos de la Mujer) to entreat presidential candidates to promise to retain the commission. They found a sympathetic ear in the eventual winner, Hererra Campins, who went beyond previous candidates in his support for women's political incorporation: "The country has heard me speak about the necessity of incorporating women fully in the responsibilities of public life, to participate in government, to achieve legal equality with men, and to try to make into reality the conviction that I have expressed many times, that equal opportunity ought to be offered to equal ability" (1978, xvi). Herrera Campins made good on his word by including six women in his cabinet, the highest number ever.

Furthermore, when he took office, President Herrera Campins raised the level at which women's issues would be considered in his administration by replacing COFEAPRE with a ministry, the Ministry for the Participation of Women in Development (Ministerio Para la Participación de la Mujer en el Desarrollo). Like his predecessor, Herrera Campins was also influenced by the international dynamics surrounding women's issues. The title itself was a reflection of international priorities: the UN's International Women's Year and Decade on Women focused on the integration of women into development efforts.

Initially, the ministry's mission was rather vague; it was intended to cover any issue, from education to health to political participation, seen to

26. Still another ineffective reform attempt had been made by the attorney general in January 1979 to have the Supreme Court nullify many of the discriminatory aspects of the Civil Code (Despacho de la Ministro de Estado 1984).

have an effect on women's participation in development. Like COFEAPRE before it, the ministry had few resources (no funding of its own or permanent staff) and a subordinate position within the executive: it was allowed to offer policy suggestions but had no executive authority.

A clear difference between the first and second women's agencies could be seen at the level of leadership. While COFEAPRE had no clearly identified leader, Mercedes Pulido de Briceño was well-positioned both professionally and socially to lead the Ministry for the Participation of Women in Development. Her background in social psychology gave her insight into how Venezuelan society functioned and how to communicate about difficult issues effectively. Her family connections through an ambassador father and bishop uncle firmly tied her to the world of elite politics and religious hierarchy. Having gone into exile with her family during the Pérez Jiménez dictatorship, she had close ties to other exiled elite members of both major parties. Ironically, as Pulido's assistant Giovana Palumbo argued, her lack of prior advocacy of women's issues also turned out to be a benefit for their promotion: "Not being able to associate her activity with women's or feminist struggles was a type of guarantee of seriousness. It is not that the actions undertaken by women up to that moment had not been done with seriousness, but they were catalogued as 'women's affairs,' which disqualified them almost automatically" (Palumbo 1988, 20). Moreover, Pulido's advocacy for women, coming from a staunch Christian Democrat, could not be rejected as the undertaking of a radical feminist activist.

The reform of the Civil Code was not an initial priority of the ministry. But when the new minister held open meetings for those interested in women's issues, activists eager to promote the reform made full use of the reestablished political opportunity to make their demands. Feminists published articles exhorting the ministry to take up the reform (*El Nuevo Venezolano*, 28 February 1980). Poleo de Baez of FEVA remembers long debates with Minister Pulido over the different strategies for combating women's subordination. These were finally resolved in favor of focusing ministerial efforts on the reform of the Civil Code.[27]

Once won over to the reform side, Pulido formed what she called a "model of negotiation" to achieve the goal.[28] She began by organizing a na-

27. By the time of the publication of the National Plan, the administration was openly committed to the need to end the discrimination against women legislated in the Civil Code, and this reform was explicitly named as the responsibility of the Ministry for the Participation of Women in Development (CORDIPLAN 1981, 103).

28. Information on the minister's role in the campaign comes principally from interviews with activists in the campaign and with former president Luis Herrera Campins.

tional debate over the reform issues to increase people's awareness of what was at stake. Much necessary contact with the mass media was easily established; by now several of the major radio stations and newspapers had reporters assigned to cover women's issues. Pulido also took advantage of the popularity of TV soap operas, serving as a consultant on the production of four short dramas, each about a problem that was at issue in the reform proposals—children's legal status, administration of community property, family unity, and parents' responsibility for children. The ministry also sent every one of the 752 parishes in Venezuela bimonthly reports on the progress of the reform. These reports described the issues, the opposition, and the arguments. Regardless of whether they were ill or well received, these updates became the subject of many sermons, further enlarging the debate over the reform. Finally, between 1980 and 1982, Pulido, her staff, FEVA, and other reform proponents held over one thousand forums country-wide to explain the reform. In neighborhood schools, hospitals, and community meeting halls, they kept the issue a topic of widespread discussion. As journalist and frequent forum panelist Rosita Caldera described these meetings, "People brought up their specific concerns and [the panel] would discuss how they would be treated under the old and new codes, very specifically. This showed people how the law affected their own lives."

Given the severe fracture along party lines among political elites that characterized the political opportunity structure of the time, Pulido had to go beyond publicizing the issues. She also had to solve the problem of garnering nonpartisan congressional support. Thus, as well as turning to her own personal contacts, Pulido ensured that parties were widely represented in the state-based elements of the reform effort. The congressional subcommission on the reform established by Pulido's congressional supporters Deputy[29] Orlando Tovar and Senator Pablo Herrera Campins was multiparty, not *copeyano*-dominated. As coordinated by the ministry, the subcommission's technical commission, which was in great part responsible for writing the legislation, included members of the legal community (especially members of FEVA) who were volunteers "from all the parties . . . with great technical credibility" (Palumbo interview). At crucial moments in the debate, Pulido made personal pleas to acquaintances in both major parties, avoiding partisan lobbying by "touching on the personal" to neutralize the attitudes of members of the reform opposition (Palumbo and Caldera interviews). In an interview, *copeyano* President Luis Herrera Campins himself, reflecting on the reform in an interview, argued that it was "not a *copeyano* reform," and that

29. "Deputy" (*Diputado/a*) is the title for members of the lower house of Congress.

it was passed under his administration precisely because it was not made into a "political cause."

The Discourse of the Debate: Women's Rights in a Democratic Family

The framing of the reform as a nonpartisan effort was not limited to the organizing of multiparty congressional support. It also depended on a rhetorical strategy that had broad societal appeal, especially to a male-dominated congress.[30] While the less successful reform activists from the 1940s promoted women's rights in combination with the rights of children, the contemporary campaign largely rejected a women's rights discourse in favor of promoting the reform as a family issue. In their advocacy of a "democratic family," however, reform proponents essentially continued in a relational feminist vein. They too sought to end gender hierarchy, but they left gender difference intact in associating women's rights with their position in the family.

The muting of women's rights language can be understood in light of the opposition reform proponents faced, which made clear how threatening the gender equality advocated by feminists had become. The loudest rejections came from two sources: conservative legal professionals based in the Academy of Political and Social Sciences (Academia de Ciencias Políticas y Sociales, or ACPS) and conservative *copeyanos*. Both groups feared that the reform, by changing legal norms, would do damage to the "sanctity" of the family. The Christian Democrats blamed feminists in particular for creating this threat.

The objection from the ACPS came a year after it was asked for its opinion on the reform. In 1981 it presented an alternative reform proposal to Congress that did not extensively restructure of the Civil Code. The proposal warned of "the danger that the modification of the basic structures of Venezuelan Family Law, contained in our Civil Code, without sufficient meditation and contemplation, represents" (Despacho de la Ministro 1984, 546). An ACPS member, a lawyer of considerable reputation, explained this danger: "There are areas of communal life, which have a great stability and permanency . . . which do not allow for precipitous legislative reforms. [These areas include] all that is related to the regimen of the family, because in it is rooted and found the base itself of society. . . . Haste, in this delicate and sensitive area of human relations, can cause irreparable damage." He went on to question the need for reforming the hierarchy of the male-headed

---

30. In 1982, 95.5 percent of the senators and the deputies were men (Huggins Castañeda and Dominguez Nelson 1993, 96).

family, because "the typical Venezuelan husband is not the pathological husband, the sick husband, but the husband preoccupied for the future of his partner and his children" (*El Nacional,* 8 March 1981).A pro-reform congressman answered this claim ironically with a more accurate assessment of the behavior of the typical Venezuelan husband: "If the husband by overwhelming majority rule comports himself as a good father of the family, from where come the single mothers, children without last names, abandoned minors, promiscuity, juvenile delinquency, unfulfilled claims for child support and all that we lawyers are familiar with and whose enumeration would be tedious?" (*El Nacional,* 1 April 1981).

The *copeyano* deputies who made public their rejection of the reform agreed that it posed a threat to family authority. Deputy Douglas Dáger spoke out against the reform in the initial debates: "Many of the articles of this proposal are conceived under completely feminist criteria according to which all vestige of authority in the heart of the family ought to be abolished, criteria according to which there ought not to be unified leadership in the family, criteria according to which the family should not have direction [at all]" (*Diario de Debates* Tomo XI, 1:63). In a paid ad taken out a week after the reform was signed into law, another *copeyano* showed the depth of conservative objection to what he saw as feminist, antifamily, and anti-Christian plotting to destroy the family: "[The reform] is not a desire felt or shared by the majority of the Venezuelan people. At the most it is shared by small noisy groups of divorced and feminist radicals. . . . [W]ith the Code reform they have made the most radical attack ever seen in our country, and only in a few other parts of the world, on the stability of marriage, on the constitution and the traditional regimen of the family. . . . [The philosophy of the reform] is radically anti-Christian" (*El Nacional,* 4 August 1982).

Confronted by an antifeminist, profamily opposition, as well as a history of neglect for women's concerns at the national level, Pulido (a *copeyana* herself) and other reform advocates steered as clear as possible from any association with feminists' explicit challenges to traditional gender relations.

Securing women's rights was never seen as a goal in itself by the ministry. In its first year, none of the national events it sponsored, few of the international events in which it participated, and few of its publications were about or directed at women per se (Ministerio de la Secretaria 1980). This pattern continued throughout its history. At the national meeting it sponsored on women's participation in the labor force, which took place at the end of her term, Pulido claimed that policy directed at women should be viewed as part of general social policy. It should not be seen as separate, because women were just one of the new subjects of national planning. Moreover, she saw women's advancement as linked with the family, not separated from it, and explicitly opposed the feminist idea that the family could be an obstacle to women's development (Pulido de Briceño 1982, 94, 117).

Pulido rejected feminist formulations of the problems family structure created for women, and directed little of her public commentary to the need for men to take on more familial responsibilities. However, she did recognize that the family would have to be based on more equality of participation in order to serve as an adequate model of democracy for future citizens:

> The principles of justice and social equality have their roots in the democratic vision of the world. The family, without a doubt, is the fundamental and continual support of democracy. For that reason policies . . . which assist in the necessary sharing of responsibilities in economic matters, in education and in attention to the children and decision making related to the family should be identified and developed. . . . The family structure, however it is organized, must be protected by any women's policy or social policy. (Pulido de Briceño 1982, 117–18)

In line with Pulido's perspective, the strategy developed to advance the potentially "feminist" Civil Code reform was to pitch it as promoting "democracy in the home" *(democracia en la casa)*, and not as a women's rights effort.[31] Reform supporters promoted it as the moral imperative of a democratic polity. It would end unjust authoritarianism at the most basic level of society, the family, where women were legally subject to their husbands and the majority of Venezuelan children were denied legal rights. Not women's equality but a democratic family would be the outcome of the reform. Of course, a democratic family would be one in which both parents had equal rights, and thus women would be given the same rights as men. But these rights would be granted in the context of women's roles as wives and mothers and reinforced by attention to the rights of all children. This strategy had the effect of making those who did not support the reform look "like troglodytes, like throwbacks who didn't want to modernize society," said reform analyst Carmen Prince de Kew in an interview.

This nonfeminist, family-oriented discourse was evident in many aspects of the reform campaign. In the first of two congressional addresses

---

31. This has become a common slogan in women's organizing throughout the region. Most notably, during the Pinochet regime in Chile, the Chilean feminist slogan was "democracy in the country and in the home" *(democracia en el país, y en la casa)*.

Pulido made in support of the reform, she argued, "This is a project which popularly has been known as a women's rights proposal, but which those of us who have worked on it consider necessary to clarify is a proposal which aims at the consolidation of one of the basic institutions of society, which is the family" (*Diario de Debates* Tomo XII, 1:26). The banner that women held during the second march in support of the reform read: "For Equality in the Family, Unite!" (*El Nacional*, 5 March 1982). Finally, the full-page report on the signing of the reform by President Herrera Campins was headed, "The historical importance of the reform is that it eliminates the difference between children" (*El Nacional*, 27 July 1982).

On the basis of this appeal, the minister and her supporters gained the support of two key sectors: the church and the military. The importance of the church support was made clear by Deputy Orlando Tovar. Introducing the reform in Congress for the first time, he made specific reference to the fact that abortion was not mentioned in the text,[32] and that the reform did not propose anything that altered "the morality which the saintly mother church obliges us to follow" (*Diario de Debates* Tomo XI, 1:46). But beyond not offending Christian morality, the reform was crafted so as to appeal to church leaders. The family rhetoric served well in this regard: as Poleo de Baez of FEVA put it, "We mixed [the equal rights of women with the equal rights of children] because if we had left them separate, the church would have dropped out." Palumbo recognized this as well, noting that "from a philosophical point of view, the church could not oppose [the reform]; the equality of children is equivalent to the equality of all people." This strategy, in combination with Pulido's personal connections among the church hierarchy, succeeded in enlisting powerful ecclesiastical support. Bishops—even the archbishop of Caracas—made statements to the press in favor of the reform, albeit with reservations about specific changes in divorce law.[33]

Pulido also received backing from the military by stressing the measures that would eliminate discrimination against those born out of wedlock. In doing so, she tapped the discontent over the discrimination against the many soldiers who were prevented from advancing to senior positions be-

32. As noted previously in the controversy over abortion at the First Congress and within MAS, abortion is a contentious issue in Venezuela. One interviewee explained it thus: "It's done, but it isn't touched [politically]" *(se hace, pero no se toca)*. There is a small but socially powerful right-to-life movement that currently has effectively stopped any move toward liberalizing restrictions on abortion.

33. Evidently the easing of divorce procedures that was legislated in the reform was accomplished by introducing it just before the final vote to avoid extensive debate (Prince de Kew interview).

cause of their "illegitimacy." Because these soldiers came from small towns, mobilizing their support was crucial to the spread of reform support.

The Reform Succeeds Through Coalition Building

The compromise discourse of the reform led to unity across a spectrum of women's groups and produced a coalition movement of women inside and outside of government. This phase can be dated from 8 December 1980, when Argelia Laya, then a MAS city council member, presented Congress with a resolution signed by all the female council members of the capital district, urging action on the reform. They called on community, political, women's, and cultural groups to join in the reform effort (*El Nacional,* 5 and 8 December 1980). Drawing in preexisting networks of neighborhood organizations and professional groups, Pulido, a few dedicated female politicians, supportive journalists, and FEVA members coordinated marches, picket lines, and a constant presence at Congress.

In February 1981 planning began for a march in support of the reform. This effort served as a catalyst for the participation of new groups, particularly women in unions and professional organizations. One particularly striking example of the new support was a well-publicized call by members of the organizations for all women to be allowed to leave work early to join in the march. On the by now historically significant International Women's Day, hundreds of women marched across town to Congress. In a show of gender solidarity, party members agreed not to display their affiliations, and a group of uniformed policewomen led the march. When they arrived, they presented Pulido and the president of Congress with petitions from many organizations supporting the reform.

Much of the reform support came from middle-class women. But reform proponents also made an effort to include women from the popular sectors. Most of the reform provisions reflected a middle- or upper-class perspective—for example, because poor women rarely got married, they would not benefit from a changed divorce law, and their partners usually did not have property to share or inheritance to leave. However, many poor women did have children out of wedlock, so the emphasis on equalizing all children's legal position ensured their mothers' support. Moreover, these women had an interest in sharing legal responsibility for their children with the fathers.[34] Rosa Paredes, a founder of the CFP and former student of Pulido's, helped forge the link between the reform movement and popular

---

34. This class analysis of the reform was affirmed by interviews with feminist activist Gioconda Espina, CFP advisor Inocencia Orellana, CFP founder Rosa Paredes, and Poleo de Baez.

women. She coordinated CFP-sponsored reform workshops in *barrios* that inspired popular women to take part in the general mobilization for the reform.

The attention to children also caught the interest of nonfeminist middle-class women, who wanted to gain more effective authority in their homes, their principle arena of activity. Housewives in Action (Amas de Casa en Acción) supported the reform because it promised "the equality of children and the equality of the rights of spouses in making important decisions in the home" (*El Nacional,* 15 April 1981).

Despite the explicitly nonfeminist reform discourse, feminists and feminist groups were equally galvanized by the reform campaign. From her difficult experience promoting women's organizing through MAS, long-time feminist Argelia Laya recognized that a women's rights approach would not get the necessary support: "If we presented the proposal as only a women's issue, we weren't going to have enough strength [to get it passed]; we had to make it so that the men who were opposed to women's rights felt as though they too would benefit from the reform." Other feminists, recognizing the weakness of their movement, agreed that compromise was necessary:

> Although we would have preferred to include more radical ideas, it was not the historical moment, nor did we have the necessary force to include these ideas, and we recognized that in that climate it already was radical enough to share inheritance, recognize consensual unions, eliminate the difference between children—it already was superradical and revolutionary for Latin America. And for now [we felt] we ought to accompany [the other women] in this struggle. (Interview with Gioconda Espina, feminist journalist and member of the Wednesday Feminist Group)

The effectiveness of women's unity came through in incidents such as the protest pickets outside of Congress:

> During the [congressional] debate there were some terrible tropical thundershowers, so there we were, twelve people with our hair plastered down by the rain, without umbrellas. . . . We held placards with the central slogans, such as "Eliminate the difference between children"—with the rain washing away the letters! More than pressure on public opinion, it was pressure on the deputies. Because each time that they went in, they met the women right there. . . . Once someone said that the women were

blocking the entrance to the Congress . . . that the deputies were angry because they couldn't pass through the rain with the women there. So the female deputies of AD and COPEI . . . went outside, grabbed the placards, and also got wet with us. So when [the objectors] came and saw that these deputies [were outside], they shut their mouths. (Espina interview)

During times of most intense debate, women across the political spectrum increased the pressure outside and inside Congress. Feminist activists doing street theater and local politicians giving speeches in the nearby Plaza Bólivar joined the picketers (*El Nacional,* 18 July 1982). The day the ACPS introduced its rival proposal, Argelia Laya denounced it in the press as "more proof of the existence of *machismo* and of the backward conceptions regarding rights and the relations between human beings" (*El Nacional,* 9 October 1981). She, along with members of FEVA and women from the CFP, went to congressional leaders to express their displeasure in the morning and then spent the afternoon with the picketers. *Adeca* congresswomen blocked debate on the measures inside both chambers, and the rival proposal was subsequently dismissed.

The success of the reform movement was due to a combination of tactics—institutional and personal appeals, forums, marches, and pickets—but more than anything else, broad-based coalition building around the idea of giving support to the democratic family. The women's triumph was affirmed by a deputy during the closing session of the reform debate:

The approval of the reform of the Civil Code demonstrates one more time that it is not the product or fruit of the gracious gift of the parliamentarians, of political parties, of deputies or senators of good heart. It involves, solely, the dominating strength, potent and eminently firm, of a group of women who, located in different political tendencies, fought a tenacious battle over a long time, a tenacious struggle in this epoch in which the mobilization of the masses does not seem to be of hundreds of millions of people, but of five or six humble and firm fighters who stationed themselves at the doors of this parliament to demand, to pressure for the passage of the reform. (*Diario de Debates* Tomo XII, 1:609)

On 6 July 1982, Congress passed the reform with a packed audience watching from the balcony. Deputy Dáger, who had led the opposition to the reform, felt compelled to recant his views publicly, declaring that with the same sincerity and vehemence with which he had opposed the reform, he now supported it.[35] Because he clearly did not agree with the reform—in an interview ten years later he stated that the Civil Code did not have much to do with the "normal" life of a family, which should be guided by a single authority with "the last word"—this public declaration made clear the change in public opinion that he felt it best to support.

Mercedes Pulido also took the floor on the day of its passage, to the last moment framing the reform as an issue of democracy in the family. She thanked the previous generation of women's rights activists, of whom she had ended up being a descendant, for opening doors that had led to "this achievement for the Venezuelan woman, but more than for just the Venezuelan woman, for the Venezuelan family." And she congratulated Congress for finally recognizing a reality that organized women had led them to: "Democracy is perfectible, democracy is participatory, there are no ideological differences when Venezuela is present" (*Diario de Debates* Tomo XII, 1:610).

There is little doubt that the democracy was well represented that day. When the president of Congress announced the debate over, the whole audience broke into the Venezuelan national hymn. Eumelia Hernandez, a veteran member of the Communist Party and founder of the Women's Cultural Association, which worked on the reform proposals in the 1940s, dropped a banner over the side of the balcony—an action strictly forbidden inside the congress building—proclaiming: ". . . and we will keep fighting!" (*¡¡y seguiremos luchando!!*").

Thanks to the increasing organization of women in civil society as well as the restoration of a national women's agency, women were able to bring about the long-awaited reform of the Civil Code. Even at a time of severe political division, they were able to rise above partisan rivalries using a conjunctural coalition. Ironically, this most successful women's rights campaign was not the result of explicit feminist activism but was an effort to "democratize the family" under the leadership of a minister with no experience in promoting women's issues. Nonetheless, her strategy made possible the skirting of partisan rivalries as well as the antifeminist prejudices of a *machista* society. The reform garnered supporters from all the parties and several major interest groups. Moreover, the reform campaign continued to foster autonomous organizing among women, albeit using state and party re-

35. Dáger compared his belief in the necessity of a patriarchal family structure to the light that shines even after a star's death, and he continued: "Today, with pride, I want to make amends and to say in front of you that I see and understand that Venezuelan society has changed, that the reform of the Civil Code is just and necessary. . . . I recognize—as a Christian Democrat—my error" (*Diario de Debates* Tomo XII, 1:604–5).

Fig. 4.5   "And the family? Much better, thanks." Cover of
popular education brochure describing the reformed Civil
Code.

sources, uniting women's groups that spanned the spectrum of classes and
ideologies.

Women's efforts to regender structures and debate gender interests in the first
period of democratic consolidation were wide-ranging and had important results. Under a somewhat more propitious set of political opportunities than
that of the transition period, women demanded an entry into the state itself
and challenged gender-biased institutions in political and civil society. The
more radical revisions of gender relations formulated within these new structures were badly received by a still largely *machista* society. But women's advancement in organizational capacity challenged the hegemony of
party-driven politics. Influenced by their foremothers and reinvigorated by a
changing international climate, women developed a loose-knit coalition
based on women's autonomous or semiautonomous activism that stretched
across partisan lines.

Strategically, this coalition avoided reliance on the parties, which had
proved even in their most alternative forms to be gender-biased in both membership and leadership. Instead, coordination took place through the regen-

dered state and nongovernmental structures. Party resources were not completely rejected, however; key coalition members included highly placed or well-connected party activists. In addition, the coalition effort was based on rhetorical strategies that did not openly threaten gender difference. Using such approaches, women reformed one of the most discriminatory Civil Codes in Latin America and developed tactics that they would rely on in future mobilizations.

Needless to say, legal reform was not the answer to all women's problems. In interviews, many reform advocates noted that its new protections were not well publicized and that many husbands simply had their wives sign over their power to make family decisions. But the reform had its positive effects. For example, a comparative analysis of the situation of women workers in two state-sponsored development projects showed that following the reform, women's relative power over household decision making vis-à-vis their partners increased, with positive impacts on their economic status (Rakowski 1995).

The reform movement also inspired other forms of women's activism across classes. The effort to reach out to women from the *barrios* resulted in some becoming political actors in crucial and visible parts of the reform campaign. But in addition, through taking part in the CFP workshops on the reform, participants began to question what exactly it meant to be women, to develop themselves as human beings, to be rights-holders. Thus they asked for another set of workshops to continue to explore these questions. The CFP responded by initiating the "Valuing our Lives as Women" (*Valorizando nuestra vida de mujer*) program to help women evaluate their roles in and outside of the home. They emphasized self-esteem and individual development (Inocencia Orellana interview). This offshoot of the reform process, which still continues today, provides striking evidence of the sort of identity transformation that often follows participation in a social movement.

Feminists also benefited from their participation in the reform. The feminist Eighth of March Street Theater Group (Grupo de Teatro en la Calle 8 de Marzo) was founded in 1983 to publicize the results of the reform. The troupe began its work in Caracas but went on national and then international tour with its play explaining the reform issues. The group continued to be active long after this effort, not only performing feminist street theater but also founding one of the two feminist women's centers in the country (see Chapter 6).

But most crucially for women's organizing as a whole, despite the failure to create a mass-based women's movement, the loose-knit coalition of women in politics, professional women, feminists, and other activists brought together for the reform would continue to press for equality and justice for women in new contexts. In doing so, they would continue to provide an example of successful nonpartisan activism with few parallels in male-dominated Venezuelan political history. As journalist Rosita Caldera said in an interview:

> The political women of this country demonstrated a more mature and rational manner of taking action than that of the men, [because] there was a consensus among women of the different political factions, above all, of extreme positions such as Communist women, and Social Democratic women, and Christian Democratic women, and independent women, and women who aren't part of parties, and women who question political organizations, who were able to conciliate their opinions. . . . This is something that I think from then on, from the reform of the Civil Code, until this moment, continues to function.[36]

36. Another source put this recognition more colloquially: "We are women from different ideological backgrounds, but we are equally screwed" (*somos mujeres de distintas ideologías pero igualmente estamos jodidas*).

INSTITUTIONALIZING SUCCESS:

*Women Unite Within and Outside
of the State for Social and
Political Reform (1984–1990)*

In the context of the relatively stable political opportunity structure of democratic consolidation, women's organizational strength increased through the 1980s. In the second half of the decade, women improved upon the successful model of coalition building that had resulted in the reform of the Civil Code. From inside and outside of the state, women collaborated on three other issues of common concern: educating the public about the plight of poor single mothers, increasing female representation in elective positions, and reforming yet another piece of major legislation, the Labor Law.

The coalitions were the fruit of experiences activist women had acquired in past organizing attempts, particularly their frustrations with party politics. These experiences led them to innovate outside party structures in ways in which those sectors integrated into the party system would not. They did not focus their energies on political society; instead, they institutionalized their previous efforts in state and civil society. As they did so, they continued to regender these channels of representation.

These efforts produced new organizations that were strikingly different from the traditional models of state- and civil society–based representation, which were characterized by hierarchical and usually partisan control over centralized structures. In contrast, the two organizations on which the coalitions of the 1980s depended, the national women's agency and a peak organization of women's nongovernmental organizations (NGOs), were structurally autonomous of parties and relatively decentralized. Their membership was "mixed"—that is, drawn from different parties as well as from people without party affiliation—and included influential political leaders. The organizations were linked together through a set of commissions that assisted in the coordination of women's mobilizations without leading to state-based co-optation. Through their enhanced organizational strategies, women also continued to challenge the gendered discourse of politics in an attempt to advance their changing gender interests.

The advances in women's organizing in this period were predicated on past experience at the national level. But they were further bolstered by changing international and regional opportunities for women. The 1985 Nairobi meeting that concluded the UN Decade on Women encouraged and legitimated national discussion of women's issues. Governments felt pressure to make at least rhetorical gestures in the direction of women's rights, and there were opportunities to prepare both governmental and nongovernmental documents assessing women's status. Regional and international networks blossomed under these auspicious circumstances. Both the national women's agency and the national NGO organization were supported by such developments.

Yet despite the successes women achieved through coalition building, the coalitions were not fully representative of women from all classes. Like earlier efforts, the coalitions continued to be composed principally of, and certainly were led by, professionals, labor leaders, and middle-class political activists. The absence of popular representation led to nonfulfillment of poor women's demands. The dominance of elite women was reflected most strikingly in the reformed Labor Law, which did not extend equal benefits to those women who worked in the home, either their own or someone else's. Some of the reform leaders were not willing to legally acknowledge the work of the women who made it possible for them to have full-time careers by carrying out their families' domestic chores. Because it was felt that compromise was essential to a united women's movement in which these leaders held key positions, the issue was dropped. But the problems of cross-class cooperation would only increase as the economic situation worsened toward the end of the decade.

Because significant shifts in socioeconomic trends came at the end of the 1980s, analysis of the changes in women's status from the early 1980s to the 1990s will be presented in the following chapter, which analyzes their effects. This chapter begins with a discussion of the general and gendered opportunities of the 1980s, then focuses on how women took advantage of these opportunities. It first charts the changes in structures and gender interests of the two organizations responsible for promoting coalition building through the 1980s, the National Women's Office (Oficina Nacional de la Mujer, or ONM) and the Coordinating Committee of Women's NGOs (Coordinadora de Organizaciones No-Gubernamentales de Mujeres, or CONG). It then examines their role in the three successful undertakings of women's coalitions: (1) the campaign to free Inés María Marcano, a young mother accused of child abandonment (1987); (2) the United Women Leaders (Mujeres Dirigentes Unidas) movement to increase women's political representation (1987–88); and (3) the reform of the Labor Law (1985–90). The effects of international-level interest in women's issues are noted where relevant. The chapter concludes with an analysis of the model of coalition building through which Venezuelan women achieved their most significant successes during democratic consolidation.

The Political Opportunities of Further Consolidation

The political opportunity structure of the 1980s continued along much the same lines as in the previous period of democratic consolidation. Politics remained dominated by the centralized state and powerful political parties, which grew increasingly competitive. An independent civil society continued to emerge slowly.

In 1983 Venezuelan voters registered their protest against the first sharp drop in economic prosperity during the democratic period: "Black Friday" (18 February 1983), the day the currency collapsed as a result of a rapid tumble in oil prices. They turned COPEI out of the presidency and elected *adeco* Jaime Lusinchi. In his campaign literature, Lusinchi promised to restore some sort of conciliation process to the political sphere. In place of party-based pacting, he and his advisors came up with a "Social Pact" that sought state mediation of class interests. But the centerpiece of this effort, a national commission to set costs, prices, and salaries that integrated representatives from the peak associations of business and labor, proved ineffective (Navarro 1995a, 16–17).

Civil society–based activities remained largely controlled by those peak associations that parties had had a hand in constructing, most notably the Confederation of Venezuelan Workers (Confederación de Trabajadores Venezolanos, or CTV). They mediated class-based interests through their access to political society and the state. Their centralized and hierarchical structures also continued to reflect traditional forms of representation.

In contrast, new forms of organization were beginning to take hold outside of traditional party politics. Starting from small local groups attentive to the needs of their particular communities, there was a burgeoning of neighborhood and grassroots organizations, human rights and environmental associations, and a cooperative movement. What these groups held in common was a rejection of party-based politics. In explicit reaction against the history of party domination, these organizations did not seek to interact with parties or form their own parties (Salamanca 1995; Levine and Crisp 1995). Nevertheless, as they grew in strength, parties sought to co-opt them, especially the booming neighborhood movement,[1] with mixed results (Ellner 1993–94, 22–28; Hellinger 1991, 170–72).

Gendered Opportunities

Following the success of the Civil Code campaign, unified work on women's issues had subsided as women joined in the general mobilization around the 1983 presidential elections. President Lusinchi had much less interest in promoting women's issues than his predecessor. Both his campaign literature and his National Plan essentially ignored them as a sector.[2] Nevertheless, women improved their capacity for united activism by relying on the network of activists brought together during the 1970s and institutionalizing their various forms of organization, particularly in the state and civil society.

Under the leadership of *adeca* Virginia Olivo de Celli, head of the national agency for women in the Lusinchi administration, women succeeded in creating their own "Social Pact" for the state mediation of interests. The agency remained subordinate to other executive-branch ministries, but its internal reorganization promoted the participation of a wide spectrum of women activists. Mimicking and modifying the influential semicorporatist commission structure established for capital and labor access to the executive branch, the agency included a group of decentralized advisory commissions on different women's issues, ranging from health to political participation.

At the same time, women in civil society created a new type of peak organization of NGOs to represent their interests. Because of women's history of marginalization within the traditional peak organizations, such as the national labor federations and business association, as well as within political parties, the women's NGO umbrella organization differed in important ways from these gender-biased structures. Drawing on the feminist experiments of the 1970s, women created a nonhierarchical, politically autonomous, and widely representative group dependent on volunteer labor.

Continuing in their precedent breaking, women's organizations in state

1. For more extended discussion of the neighborhood movement, see Chapter 7.
2. The word *woman* does not appear in the Sixth National Plan, which admittedly is written in generalities (CORDIPLAN 1984).

and civil society developed a relationship based more on cooperation than co-optation. Women from civil society sat on the state advisory commissions, and members of the state agency threw their weight behind NGO-sponsored campaigns. Because their efforts were focused on social and political change, not on negotiations over the distribution of capital, they avoided more typical clientelistic relationships between the state and civil society.

These national changes were facilitated by new opportunities at international and regional levels. Organizations from the women's sector of the Socialist International to the Inter-American Commission of Women raised their profiles during the UN Decade on Women. With the end of the decade in 1985 came the third UN conference on women's issues at Nairobi and its accompanying NGO forum. Meanwhile, the Latin American Feminist Encounters, started in 1981, continued to be held in 1983, 1985, and 1987. Both the state agency and the civil society–based organization were inspired by, and actively used, these various sources of legitimation and networking to promote women's organizing.

Organizational changes allowed for expression of changing gender interests within the agendas and activities of the state- and civil society–based organizations as well as in the larger campaigns. As with the Civil Code reform, the most successful rhetorical strategies were predicated on improving democratic and familial life, not explicitly challenging gender relations. But there was also explicit advocacy of more egalitarian gender relations as women sought more equality in politics and in the workplace.

Solidifying State Action for Women

After the change of administration in 1984, incoming president Lusinchi closed down the Ministry for the Participation of Women in Development, shutting off the channel of women's access to the state that was so crucial to the Civil Code reform.[3] However, a pivotal member of the new government, Virginia Olivo de Celli, ensured that this key factor for women's mobilization would not be wholly abandoned. In order to justify maintaining a national women's agency, she relied on the legitimation provided by international attention to women's issues. Once she had reestablished the

3. Information for this section comes from interviews as well as from the annual reports of the Youth Ministry and the Family Ministry (1984–88).

women's agency, she improved it. The development of a formalized link between the state and the growing women's NGO community allowed women as a sector increased autonomous political influence at the national level. Moreover, this link, a set of advisory commissions, would make possible a shift in the gendering of public policy on women. Although the office began by focusing on women's inclusion in family-centered or state-centered development, the commissions soon oriented it toward the advancement of women as citizens in their own right.

International influences played a crucial part in Olivo de Celli's efforts. In 1984, as the head of the Family Department of the Youth Ministry, she attended a women's meeting of the Socialist International. There she heard of the need for a state-based source of women's representation. After discussions with collaborators on the Civil Code reform confirmed the key role the now-defunct women's ministry had played, she was determined to maintain some channel for the representation of women within the executive branch. Citing as international justifications the recommendation of the Inter-American Commission of Women that every member state have a women's agency in the executive branch and the need to coordinate a government report for the 1985 Nairobi UN women's conference, Olivo de Celli established the National Women's Office (ONM) in 1984. In line with the traditional subordinate placement of such an agency, it was located in the Family Department, along with offices on economic and social welfare and on children. Its official rationale also reflected its subordinate position by subsuming women's issues to those of national and family development.

Like her predecessor in the women's ministry, Mercedes Pulido de Briceño, Olivo de Celli was well positioned for her activism on women's behalf. She too came from a politically prominent family and did not have a history of activism on women's rights. Her lack of previous involvement in women's struggles had the effect of allowing her, like Pulido, to serve as the nonthreatening screen for women's transformative actions within the state. However, it simultaneously made it essential for her to encourage collaborative work. To facilitate collaboration, she chose as head of the ONM Rosa Paredes, a founder of the Popular Women's Circles, who was well known to women's rights activists.

Olivo de Celli's desire to benefit from a diversity of views, as well as the obvious success of collaborative efforts around reforming the Civil Code, led to a significant difference in organization between the ONM and the previous women's ministry. The ONM went one step beyond the ministry's frequent nongovernmental consultations to explicitly incorporate women from outside the government within its very structure. Responding to the current context of women's activism, mainly channeled through small groups, the ONM prioritized relations with them from its inception. The first description of the function of the ONM issued by the Youth Ministry included interaction with several organizations mentioned by name: the "feminist groups of Venezuela," AVESA, CFP, FEVA, and journalists—not coincidentally, several of the key players in the Civil Code reform (Ministerio de la Juventud 1984, 50). Members of these and other groups were to be incorporated into the work of the office through the mechanism of *comisiones asesoras,* or advisory commissions. There were commissions on several subjects: education, employment, health, media, political participation, and legislation; and although these were not given de jure status until 1986, they began operating de facto from the inception of the ONM two years earlier.

In keeping with past collaborative efforts, commission membership ranged across parties and philosophies. The official swearing-in ceremony brought together some of the most radical feminists with women from the different parties to serve as colleagues (Gioconda Espina interview). But Olivo de Celli noted that the "different and even antagonistic ideologies" of the members did not interfere with "cooperative work inside the commissions, because the cause of women *(la causa de la mujer)* does not have a political color."[4] Notwithstanding ideological orientation, she explained, "the prejudices against women are very substantial, women's problems are general, and all women suffer from them." To address these general problems, she made the ONM into a meeting place where nongovernmental women "knew that there was a space in the government where we could come to agreement to do things together" (Olivo de Celli interview).

As Olivo de Celli was promoted through the executive branch, she took the women's office with her. "It ascended as I ascended," she said in an interview. In 1986 when she became vice-minister of youth, the ONM became attached to her office and widened its mandate, sponsoring women's offices in individual states. In 1987 Olivo de Celli was made head of the newly created Ministry of the Family, and she converted the ONM into its own department, the Directorate for Women's Advancement (Dirección General Sectorial de Promoción a la Mujer). By this time, 170 women were partici-

4. To simplify political participation for illiterates in the democratic period, each party had a color associated with it that would appear on every ballot next to the appropriate electoral list. AD was white, COPEI green, and MAS orange.

pating in the commissions, and 17 state women's offices were operating (Ministerio de la Familia 1987, 60).

Policy design, not execution, was still the limited prerogative of the women's agency. However, its increase in status was also accompanied by a notable transformation in the gender interests expressed through its policy making. This transformation was spurred on by the input of the commissions. From focusing on women within development priorities and as family members, policies gradually shifted to ending gender discrimination and promoting women's economic and social status. In 1985, besides coordinating the government report for Nairobi, the ONM promoted new reforms of the Penal Code and Labor Law to eradicate their many discriminatory articles, developed credit and nontraditional income-generating projects for low-income women, and analyzed the socioeconomic status of young women. Literacy, sex education, and family education remained persistent concerns, as did ending stereotyping in the media and in school textbooks (Ministerio de la Juventud 1985, 64–65). In 1986 combating violence against women appeared on the agenda for the first time (Ministerio de la Juventud 1986, 27). In 1987 providing legal services was added, as was training for local police around family violence issues (Ministerio de la Familia 1987, 61). The main push in 1988 was to support the movement to increase women's representation in political parties and elected offices (Ministerio de la Familia 1988, 53).

The institutionalization of women's representation through the ONM/Directorate resulted in a gendered modification of state-based interest mediation through the semicorporatist network of commissions. Instead of incorporating the major players of interest-group politics, the women's advisory commissions formed a decentralized network with a fair amount of autonomy in its decision making and represented a wide range of women. While other national agencies and societal sectors were privately conciliating class interests through the state by striking bargains over economic resources, the ONM/Directorate and its commissions became the motors for public campaigns on women's issues carried out through the three conjunctural coalitions of the period.

The collaborative model of the ONM/Directorate proved so successful that at the UNICEF-sponsored regional meeting "State and Civil Society Joining Forces to Support Women" (Caracas, 15–17 August 1988), the Venezuelan experience was presented as a model of successful cooperation (Rocha Sanchez 1991). But the model was also dependent on its other half: the increasingly organized women in NGOs. Their input was essential to developing more explicitly women-focused policies.

Fig. 5.1
Cover of advisory commission report to the state Directorate for Women's Advancement.

Inclusive Autonomy in Civil Society:
The Coordinating Committee of Women's NGOs

The Coordinating Committee of Women's NGOs (CONG), formed in 1985, was yet another alternative to traditional organizing.[5] Developed in reaction to women's experience of political marginalization, the CONG brought together feminists, professional women, popular women, and women from left-wing parties under a new kind of peak organization that was both an umbrella and a network NGO. The innovative structure of the CONG made possible the diversity of the organization. Instead of building a peak organization highly dependent on party resources and access, CONG member groups maintained their autonomy from parties and from one another. They entirely rejected the hierarchical, centralized model of political organization. Although it proved problematic in the long run, initially their decentralization made possible their heterogeneity as well as making feasible several campaigns on behalf of women that crossed the wide class divide and challenged traditional gender relations. The CONG also promoted state-civil so-

---

5. Descriptions of the CONG were provided by members Ofelia Alvarez, Fernando Aranguren, Nora Castañeda, and Benita Finol.

ciety interaction: many of its members sat on the ONM/Directorate commissions.

The Civil Code reform provided an opportunity for women from different NGOs to work together, but further cooperative efforts were delayed by national politics—and then relaunched by international politics. The presidential campaign of 1983 took up the energies of the many women still involved with political parties. Quite a few nonpartisan feminists also stepped back into formal politics, tempted by the promise held out by MAS of the first platform focused on women's rights in a presidential campaign. But partisan rivalries diminished in intensity following the election of President Lusinchi and the evidence that MAS had only paid lip service to women's issues. At this point, international forces came into well-timed play. The Nairobi meeting was to include not only the official UN conference of governmental delegates but also a parallel gathering of NGOs in an international meeting of their own, the NGO Forum. Thus a call was put out to women's organizations across the world to start assembling NGO reports on the status of women in their respective nations to bring to Nairobi.

It is widely recognized that this call for action was the spark that led to the creation of the CONG (CONG 1988b; García and Rosillo 1992). *Masista* (MAS member) Ofelia Alvarez heard about the conference through the communist women's network, the International Democratic Women's Federation, and brought it to the attention of her fellow professors at the Central University.[6] Five NGOs that had interacted during the Civil Code reform—FEVA, the women's department of the Communist union confederation (Central Unitaria de Trabajadores de Venezuela), the feminist journalist group "Women and Communication," the women's studies program at the Central University, and the feminist publication *La Mala Vida*—sponsored a meeting on 22 March 1985 for women's NGOs to discuss plans for Nairobi. However, the twenty groups that came to this historic meeting decided to go beyond efforts directed at Nairobi. They established the Coordinating Committee of Women's NGOs (CONG), the fulfillment of a long-felt need for a nonpartisan association to promote women's rights.

The CONG was the first organization to bring together feminist and

6. In her interview, Ofelia Alvarez described a gratifying moment of unsolicited gender solidarity. A check for a few U.S. dollars was needed in order to send for the NGO applications for the Nairobi conference. Because at this time there were stringent exchange controls on U.S. currency in Venezuela (following the first devaluation of Venezuelan currency and in anticipation of massive capital flight), it was quite difficult to get foreign exchange. Proof of need was required, in this case a signed letter of invitation from conference sponsors. However, when Alvarez approached two women tellers at a bank and explained the reason for the check, they waived the necessary paperwork for this "women's thing" *(cosa de mujeres)*.

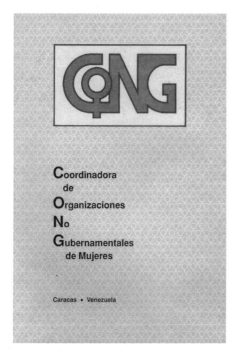

Fig. 5.2
Cover of the CONG's
self-descriptive pamphlet.

nonfeminist women's groups on an ongoing basis. Its official statutes instituted its "unity within diversity," a phrase that would frequently be used to describe it. Its stated purpose was to bring together groups working against legal, economic, social, political, and cultural discrimination against women and to promote women's full participation in the national life. All types of groups were welcomed: social, political, economic, labor, religious, professional, cultural, and neighborhood.[7] This diversity led to—and was dependent on—the development of the group's alternative structure.

The Structure of the CONG

The ability not only to create but also to maintain the heterogeneity of the CONG was made possible through its structural innovations. These were developed in direct response to the way in which Venezuelan parties had coopted almost every sector of civil society—while marginalizing and separat-

7. The first NGOs organizing the CONG were feminist, professional, popular, labor, and political solidarity groups. When it was officially constituted, party-linked, religious, and health groups also joined (CONG 1988a).

ing women. Nora Castañeda, a CONG member, gave as an example the way AD and the PCV essentially created their own unions, which were then bound to the parties through their labor bureaus. But the parties had done very little for women, because the women's bureaus did not function as well as the others. "There was a discussion over how the parties had taken over the forms of organization through which the people expressed themselves . . . [and] how the women's bureaus within the parties had limitations in their work" (Castañeda interview). Therefore CONG founders wanted to construct an organization that would focus on women's concerns without imposing a "party line."

Because of the influence of the dominant models of representation, however, a new structure had to be carefully negotiated between those who rejected the traditional forms altogether and those still working within them. When the CONG statutes were being discussed, many of the member groups proposed highly centralized structures modeled on the party-based or party-influenced organizations in which they had learned their social activism. But feminist members took matters in hand, "launching into the antipatriarchal discourse" to show how the organizations that men had developed fostered centralized control over membership, not room for a variety of perspectives such as were assembled in the CONG. After considerable debate, the feminists managed to convince the other members that a very different structure would be more conducive to their goal: to bring together women's organizations to exchange information and work on common projects without interference in the specific workings of any member group (Fernando Aranguren interview).

As a result of feminist influence, the CONG statutes called for decentralization and nonhierarchical decision making. Each member group was autonomous: "The member organizations will have autonomy and independence from the CONG, which can neither restrict nor interfere with the objectives, goals, and ends of each affiliated organization" (CONG 1988a). Direct representation of these autonomous groups, overseen by a weak governing body, insured a nonhierarchical structure. All decisions were to be based on the consensus of the group representatives who attended bimonthly meetings. The activities of the CONG were to be coordinated by the *trio*, a three-person council whose membership rotated among the groups every six months and was chosen by direct and open election. Initially the *trio* was strictly limited to coordinating general activities and could not make public pronouncements on behalf of the CONG (a restriction that was later relaxed).

The difference between this innovative structure and the dominant model of organizing was illustrated in a self-descriptive pamphlet issued by the CONG. The very first paragraph discussed the problems that verticality, presidentialism, and authoritarianism presented to the development of participatory social relations. These traditional organizational elements were then contrasted with the horizontal, coordinated, and consultative interactions that the CONG promoted. The new dynamics of a more egalitarian model of organization could teach people to take control of social decision making rather than leaving them to be its mere objects. "Such a free conception of an organization allows each person to feel like a representative of the organization" (CONG 1988b).

The rejection of traditional organizing had an impact not only on the structure of the CONG, but also on its membership. The inclusion of women representing political parties was initially quite a contentious issue. AD and COPEI were excluded; the CONG saw itself as in opposition to mainstream politics. But party activists on the left, many of whom had worked for years on women's issues, were interested in representing their parties. Some CONG members feared that, as had happened so often in the past, partisan women would try to colonize the group on behalf of their party. At first some felt strongly that members should only be included on the basis of their affiliation with an NGO. The extent to which partisan loyalties were embedded in Venezuelan society could not be ignored, however. It was soon recognized that many of the NGO affiliates were also active in parties. Moreover, those women who were party activists made no attempts to take over the CONG. Finally it was decided that women could represent left-wing parties.

To ensure that no party would exert undue influence, the *trios* never included more than one party representative at a time. They generally represented the three different types of activists who made up the CONG: feminists or professionals, party activists, and grassroots organizers. Thus the CONG was able to include women from different sectors, including not only party activists but also representatives from the major peak associations (principally unions).

A factor contributing to early unity in the group was, paradoxically, a lack of funding. This was yet another factor that differentiated the CONG from traditional interest-group organizing, often predicated on support from party organizations. The resources of the CONG were always strained. Dues came in sporadically, and there was hardly any outside support. However, the lack of funding was not seen as an obstacle, at least at first. The CONG met in a space donated by the Ateneo, Caracas' principal cultural center and long a source of support for women's organized activities.[8] Members voluntarily

---

8. Members of the Ateneo had been active in the suffrage movement (see Chapter 2).

shared the infrastructural duties. Several members were able to attend the Nairobi meeting because Fidel Castro chartered a plane from Cuba to Kenya to ferry one hundred Latin American activists.

Meanwhile, not having resources to distribute precluded some potential schisms. One member noted how surprised a few of the CONG women were to find out at the regional feminist meeting in Argentina (1990) that conflicts had arisen between professional feminists running NGOs and the women in whose name they supposedly raised funds. In contrast, they saw that their organization's lack of outside funding actually protected them from such infighting (Nora Castañeda interview).

The decision of the CONG member groups to focus on women specifically, across ideological and programmatic differences, stood in sharp contrast to the parties' rejection of gender as a principal focus of organizing. In fact, gender became increasingly salient to members' other work as a result of their interaction within the CONG. The head of one leftist party's women's bureau described how prior to her participation in the CONG, she considered it acceptable that her group undertook the infrastructural tasks and supported the male candidates. But as a result of her interactions especially with the feminists of the CONG, she learned "about the effects of gender, to defend women's rights." She realized that her women's bureau should not exist only to serve men. As a result, she reoriented the work of the bureau to serve women's needs, introducing leadership workshops and talks on women's social position (Benita Finol interview).

Reflecting its unity within diversity, the CONG reproduced, in a somewhat altered form, the multi-issue women's conferences of 1940 and 1975 in the event Women Take Over the Cultural Center! (¡Las Mujeres Toman el Ateneo!). In March 1986, with the support of the Ateneo, the CONG coordinated three weeks of meetings, movies, and lectures on a variety of women's issues. The wide range of presentations reflected the advances in the analysis of gender oppression and gender difference. Speakers addressed such subjects as feminism, abortion, sex education, violence against women, women and culture, women and power, women and media, women and peace, women's centers, and the ONM; and they provided updates on the former object of the united women's movement, the Civil Code, as well as the next one, the Labor Law.

The CONG also used its diversity in unified efforts on women's behalf. Gender solidarity was evident in its campaign for the restoration of a "women's page" in the national newspaper, El Nacional. Written for years by established journalist, feminist, and founding CONG member Rosita Caldera, the column had been crucial in publicizing the Civil Code campaign and continued to be a key source for information on women's activism. However, the column was suddenly dropped in mid-1987 to the general dismay of those who relied on it for networking and publicity. Over nine months, the CONG's efforts to have the page restored included a letter-writing campaign and pickets in front of *El Nacional*'s main office building. The column was reinstated in mid-1988.

CONG-State Relations

In view of the dominance of the Venezuelan state and the key channel of access the state agency for women had become, members of the CONG understood that interaction between women inside and outside of the government was a sine qua non of successful women's activism. This interaction was facilitated by the network of activists fostered through decades of past experience: "We rely on something which is essential: the friendship among women of the different parties which has developed over time. So at certain moments the separation between the nongovernmental and the governmental [women] is like an almost invisible thread," said Fernando Aranguren in an interview. These friendships were reinforced by the family ties often underpinning Venezuelan politics. For example, the mothers of then-Minister of the Family Virginia Olivo de Celli and CONG member and congressional deputy Argelia Laya had worked together in the relational feminist group of the 1930s, the Women's Cultural Association.

As described in previous sections, the mechanism put in place to solidify NGO-state cooperation was that of the advisory commissions. Many women from the CONG sat on these commissions and took an active part in much of the ONM/Directorate's work. To illustrate the close collaboration with the women's agency, consider the commissions' first task: to help collect the information needed for the governmental report to the Nairobi Conference in 1985. One CONG member remembered an incident at the conference that illustrated the importance of their participation. She and a fellow CONG and commission member ran into a woman from a Mexican NGO rushing off to a meeting of governmental delegates. The Mexican woman asked them if they were going to attend the official meeting. No, they replied, they were quite tired, and anyway, wasn't it all the same, what was said in the governmental and nongovernmental meetings? The Mexican woman reacted with shock—certainly not! Didn't they want to know what lies their government might be telling about the status of women in their country? "Well, my government had better be careful," one CONG member answered, "to not mess up our work, because we wrote its document too!" (Ofelia Alvarez interview).

Despite its close relationship with the state, the CONG membership did not consider that it was putting its autonomy in jeopardy. At the 1988 UNICEF meeting where organizers presented the relationship between the Venezuelan state and women's NGOs as a model for women's rights advocacy, CONG members explained that they had no explicit methodology for their work with the state agency. Much as in their own campaigns, members of the CONG cooperated with the agency around conjunctural issues. This method was the only one possible, given the heterogeneity of political outlooks represented in the CONG and the state administration. "The link between the NGOs and the State ought to be tactical and not strategic. Because the link was established to advance work on women (gender struggle) but not [to promote] certain social classes or a conception of society. Those who do not share the same political project cannot offer common strategies" (Rocha Sanchez 1991, 42–43). Moreover, the lack of financial support for the CONG from the state agency helped prevent a more traditional clientelistic relationship from developing.

In summary, the politically autonomous and decentralized structure of the CONG allowed for a fruitful interaction among partisan and independent women as well as making possible a link to the state:

> Perhaps the principal achievement that has come about in Venezuela in terms of women's organizations is the Coordinating Committee of Women's NGOs. It has been a meeting space of very diverse organizations and had a very democratic organization which allowed for dialogue between "pure" feminists and political feminists and nonfeminists, and religious groups and cultural groups, and groups which were focused on other things. . . . Moreover, it has been an important interlocutor with the government. (Magdalena Valdevieso interview)

The cooperation between organizations undergirded the three campaigns of the period.

Conjunctural Coalition Building

All three of the successful conjunctural coalitions of this period were similar in their heavy reliance on the organizational innovations of the CONG and the ONM/Directorate. However, they also differed in significant ways, depending on their particular configurations of gender interests, actors, and discursive strategies. The campaign to free Inés María Marcano, a young single mother unjustly imprisoned for child abandonment, was largely an effort of the CONG membership in conjunction with women from the *barrios*. Beyond winning Inés María's freedom, the feminist-oriented CONG members also sought to challenge the gendered discourse that regarded poor women themselves, instead of class and gender hierarchies, as solely responsible for their plight. The United Women Leaders movement to improve women's positions on party electoral lists was coordinated by the Directorate with the help of CONG members and elite party women. In trying to improve women's representation in democratic politics, its rhetorical strategy was to play down, rather than to emphasize, gender differences. Finally, the campaign to reform discriminatory aspects of the Labor Law drew on the entire spectrum of women activists, from union members to politicians to feminists. It also challenged the gendered discourse around work, making a clear distinction between working women and working mothers. But the significant involvement of elite women resulted in a reform that excluded the interests of many popular women.

The Campaign to Free Inés María Marcano: Una en Un Millón (1987)

In 1987 the CONG coordinated a campaign to seek the release of Inés María Marcano, a young single mother who had been imprisoned on the charge of child abandonment after her daughter was raped and killed by two delinquents.[9] Beyond resulting in Inés María's release, the campaign also raised the consciousness of the nation around the plight of women in her situation. This success was based on a concerted combination of the different strengths of the CONG member groups and their sympathetic allies in government. Moreover, middle-class feminists and professional women were able to use their skills on behalf of, and in direct communication with, poor women from the *barrios*.

Inés María was a twenty-year-old single mother of two children who lived in a *barrio* outside of Caracas called *El Infiernito* (Little Hell). Living up to its name, the area was crime-ridden and lacked basic municipal services; most of the houses were zinc-roofed shacks perched precariously on a sloping dirt hillside.[10] One night, in order to go to a party and with no options for

9. The story of Inés María is taken from the CONG publication (and accompanying video) about the case (CONG 1988c).
10. Unlike the poor areas of many Latin American metropolises, which are often found below

childcare, Inés María left her children locked in but with the radio and lights on to deceive potential thieves. Tragically, her ruse did not work. Two drunken young men broke in through the flimsy roof, kidnapped the two-year-old girl, raped her, and threw her down a nearby canyon to her death. The criminals were found shortly afterward, convicted, and imprisoned. But a distraught Inés María was also taken into custody on the charge of child abandonment, and her young son was put into foster care.

Upon becoming aware of the incident, one member group of the CONG, the feminist health organization AVESA, held a press conference on the day when Inés María's case came up in court. AVESA argued what would become the wider campaign's position: rather than an unfit mother, Inés María was a victim of her circumstances—a poor, abandoned, working woman who had no one with whom to leave her children, living in a dangerous area with no police protection, bad housing, and inadequate state services. The group's outspokenness brought it to the attention of Inés María's neighbors. These women had organized previously through their fight to improve the dangerous conditions of the *barrio* by such means as replacing the type of flimsy zinc-covered shelter through which the daughter's murderers had had no trouble entering. The neighborhood organization approached AVESA about developing a campaign for the release of Inés María.

Meanwhile others, including ONM lawyers, had become aware of the case. Along with members of FEVA, they offered Inés María's lawyer legal assistance—an offer he ignored. The lawyers then joined their efforts with those of the CONG. By this time AVESA had called a general meeting of the group at which the following strategy was developed: to work not only on getting the arrest charges dropped but also on changing public opinion about the case. To begin the campaign, the two CONG organizations most closely associated with popular women's struggles—All (Women) Together (Todas Juntas)[11] and the Popular Women's Circles—issued press releases. These were followed by a CONG-sponsored press conference at which deputy and CONG member Argelia Laya presented the organization's objections to Inés María's imprisonment.

Other members of the group gained audiences with the attorney general and the president of Congress, both of whom offered their support. The attorney general stated that in Inés María's case "the classification of 'abandonment' has been an exaggeration." He went on to ask, "What would we do

---

the wealthy areas on the hills, most of Caracas' *barrios* creep up the hillsides above the crowded valley of the capital.

11. A network of popular women's organizations.

if we had to imprison all of the men who abandon their children for a night, a month, or all of their lives?" To which one of his visitors responded, "We'd have to lock up the country!" (CONG 1988c, 16).

On 25 November 1987, the CONG marked the first Venezuelan observance of the regionally inspired International Day Against Violence Against Women,[12] and used the occasion to advance their campaign on Inés María's behalf. Members referred to her plight in speeches throughout the day. In order to increase pressure on the attorney general, the CONG also sought signatures to a letter supporting her release from prison. Meanwhile Vice-Minister of Justice Sonia Sgambatti, who happened to be a longtime activist against gender-based discrimination in the law, issued a public statement in favor of Inés María's release. The CONG then amplified press coverage. It had been going forward with the help of one member group, the feminist journalist organization "Women and Communication" But now several prominent male social critics also wrote columns about the case, and a few popular TV talk shows took it up. They broadcast interviews with Inés María's neighbors attesting to her devotion as a mother. In a final coup, members of the CONG were able gain admittance to Inés María's prison and interview her on her birthday. When aired on TV, the interview had a significant effect on public opinion. Minister of the Family Olivo de Celli and her legal commission weighed in with their support, and finally the multifaceted public campaign succeeded: a Superior Court judge released Inés María shortly before Christmas.

The document that the CONG published about the campaign, entitled *A Woman and the Common Struggle: In the Case of Inés María Marcano, One in a million* (La Mujer y la Lucha Solidaria: En el caso de Inés María Marcano, Una en un millón), reflected the cooperative effort of the CONG members to rescue one particular woman while making her the symbol of discrimination against women in her position: poor single mothers. It was jointly written by Gioconda Espina of the Wednesday Feminist Group, Marta Yadira Rodríguez of AVESA, and Inocencia Orellana and Diana Vegas of the women's program of the community activism group CESAP, with photographs by Franca Donda, another member of the Wednesday Feminist Group. Deputy Argelia Laya wrote the introduction, in which she stated: "I cannot hide the pride that I feel in being able to share the birth of a new

12. November 25th was declared the International Day Against Violence Against Women by the first Feminist Encounter for Latin America and the Caribbean in Bogotá, Colombia, in 1981. It was chosen to commemorate the brutal murder of the activist Miraval sisters by the Trujillo dictatorship in the Dominican Republic on this date in 1960. For a fictionalized account of their lives, see J. Alvarez 1994.

Fig. 5.3   Inside cover of CONG pamphlet covering the story
of Inés Maria Marcano.

women's leadership in Venezuela." The document carefully records the
names of the many different groups and individuals who participated in the
campaign, highlighting one of the explicit purposes of the publication: to
show that a heterogeneous coalition united around one issue could change
misguided public opinion.

The CONG sought to make public opinion more receptive to the gender interests of women in Inés María's circumstances. Through its multifaceted efforts, the coalition hoped to show that poor single mothers were not
irresponsible, even dangerous parents. Instead, women like Inés María were
shown to be victims of a classist and sexist society that did not provide decent
living conditions, affordable child care, or nonsexist education (to teach men
to be responsible fathers). While the CONG campaign did not solve the
larger problems besetting Inés María, it did raise the public's awareness of the
plight of women in the *barrios* and set a useful precedent. When a similar case
came up in 1988, it was dismissed by a newly educated judiciary (CONG
1988c, 25–26).

Women Take on Political Society:
The United Women Leaders Movement (1987–1988)

While the CONG-driven campaign on behalf of Inés María focused on the issues of poor women, another coalition effort of the period championed the cause of female party leaders. However, in a complete departure from normal politics, it reached across partisan lines. The elections of 1988 were preceded by the most widespread and explicit multiparty women's organizing yet to be seen in Venezuela by women from almost every party who were seeking to increase their share of elected and decision-making party positions. The United Women Leaders (Mujeres Dirigentes Unidas) movement was made possible thanks to coordination efforts by the state-based Directorate for Women's Advancement and the CONG. The coalition that they and other actors brought together was based on the autonomous, decentralized, and pluralist organizational model. It also employed a gendered discourse that, while implicitly subverting gender hierarchy as well as challenging gender difference, did not explicitly reference gender relations. Like most of the activities undertaken in this period, the movement was legitimated by reference to international and regional pronouncements. The result was a challenge to men's dominance of political life.

The movement was begun in response to the low levels of women's representation in parties and electoral positions despite their high levels of party membership. By 1987 women formed 50 percent of party membership, reflecting the high degree of partisan affiliation in the country. But very few ascended to leadership positions. AD had three women on its National Executive Committee (Comite Executivo Nacional or CEN), COPEI had three, and MAS had two.[13] Between 1958 and 1983, women's representation in the lower house of Congress had increased from three to twelve (6 percent). During the same period there were never more than two women in the Senate, and more often than not, none at all. In state legislatures women had increased their representation (albeit unevenly) from 1.6 percent in 1958 to 7.8 percent in 1983, still a poor showing (see Table 1).

Women active in the Directorate and the CONG decided to take advantage of the opportunity presented by the elections. They built upon a numerical advantage: the "gender gap" of the 1988 elections, in which women would make up over half of the electorate. In July 1987, the CONG planned its election strategy. In keeping with its nonpartisan outlook, a CONG working paper stated that the group as a whole would not support a specific

---

13. These would represent around 2.5 percent of the entire CEN of each party.

Table 5.1:   Number and percent of women in national congress and state legislative assemblies (1958–1983)

Congress:

Year	Deputies			Senators		
	Total	# Women	% Women	Total	# Women	% Women
1958	133	3	2.3	51	0	0
1963	178	5	2.8	47	0	0
1968	214	6	2.8	52	2	3.8
1973	200	6	3	47	0	0
1978	199	9	4.5	44	2	4.5
1983	200	12	6	44	0	0

Legislative Assemblies:

Year	Total	# Women	% Women
1958	312	5	1.6
1963	314	18	5.7
1968	329	13	4
1973	277	11	4
1978	281	15	5.3
1983	308	24	7.8

(SOURCE: CSE 1984, 1988, 1989, 1993)

candidate in the following year's election. But as the CONG sought women's equality in all areas, including politics, it would make gender-specific demands on candidates and parties. Several members were drawing up a list of qualified women candidates for elected office who had worked for women's rights in the past, as well as a minimum program of women's demands to be presented to all the candidates (CONG 1987).

Through the Directorate's Political Participation Commission, which included several members of the CONG as well as other members of "social and political groups," some of these demands made their way onto its "Common Minimum Program of Venezuelan Women Leaders to Political Parties." The Minimum Program claimed that international support existed for the proposals that followed, citing the conclusions of the 1985 Nairobi conference as well the UN Convention for the Elimination of All Forms of Discrimination Against Women, which Venezuela had ratified in 1982. The Minimum Program then outlined the unequal representation of women in political life. Although they constituted 50 percent of party membership and many had high qualifications, women held few decision-making positions in parties, elected positions, and cabinet posts (Dirección n.d.).

In response to the low levels of women's representation, the Minimum

Program proposed a series of steps to be taken by both parties and government to ensure women's equal inclusion. These ranged from copying the model of the commission structure itself in other ministries (to insure consultation with NGOs on all policy concerning women), to insisting on a 30 percent quota of women in party decision-making positions and in winning positions on party electoral lists.[14] With the help of the Directorate, the Minimum Program was publicized across the country in early 1988. Women from different parties participated in state assemblies, conducting discussions on the need to increase women's representation in leadership. In an ironic contrast, as the campaign by the women cooperating through the Directorate went forward, the women's bureaus of the parties used the occasion of International Women's Day to promote their parties' male presidential candidates (*El Nacional*, 7 March 1988).

As elections neared, the multiparty United Women Leaders movement took off, still relying on the coordination provided by the Directorate and the CONG. On 22 July Olivo de Celli, minister of the family, and the Directorate sponsored a meeting for women from all parties as well as activists from the CONG. Because none of the parties was willing to offer its headquarters for a gathering to which women from rival parties were invited, the meeting took place in a hotel (Fernando Aranguren interview). Drawing support from regional organizing, Olivo de Celli presented the latest program of the Inter-American Commission of Women, which called for the "full and equal participation of women in politics." Representatives from the various parties made presentations exhorting those in attendance to unite to achieve this goal. In the end, those present agreed to draw up a list of common demands and participate in a public march (*El Nacional*, 22 July 1988).

The upsurge in organizing was strategically timed to coincide with the political opportunity provided by the drawing up of party lists for the 1988 elections. On the day after the women's meeting, journalists sought out party leaders for their reactions to the women's challenge. Rosita Caldera summed them up as "astonishment for the unitary capacity that the women were demonstrating in allying themselves, independently of their respective polit-

---

14. In proportional representation systems such as Venezuela's at this time, candidates for public office do not run individual campaigns; they run as members of political parties, each of which presents a ranked list of candidates to the voters. Voters cast their ballot for an entire party list, and the number of winning candidates from each party is determined according to the percentage of the vote garnered by the party, with the candidate whose name is at the top of the list being the first to be elected, the second next, and so on. Thus placement on the party lists is extremely important. A common gesture toward gender equality among parties was to put women on the lists, but toward the bottom where they would have little chance of election.

ical affiliations, [for] the common goal of demanding leading, and not 'filler' positions." The reactions of the *adecos* testified not only to astonishment. The first deputy approached indignantly claimed that women would not be placed on the lists simply because they were women. At first the president of the party, who would have a great deal of influence over the positioning of candidates' names on the lists, protested that he was not willing to make a statement. But after the journalist insisted on asking whether the president was going to give women winning places, he replied brusquely, "Yes. We are going to put piles of women on. Piles of them" (*El Nacional,* 23 July 1988).

Women leaders publicized their demand for increased representation across the parties in the "Manifesto of the United Women Leaders," published in the national press at the end of July. It opened with a declaration of women's nonpartisan advocacy for their advancement: "We women in a demonstration of true political maturity and a spirit of solidarity have decided to put aside our partisan differences, to build a common front reaching across the nation, around a concrete objective: to gain for the country a relevant presence of women, skilled in quality and just in quantity, in the positions of popular representation." The manifesto made it clear that the movement was autonomous and provisional, "not based on the creation of a new party, nor subject to the manipulation of a particular existing party." All parties were equally put on notice as the women played their ace: over half the voters in 1988 would be women. "The parties and independent groups ought to know that we women are in condition and prepared to defend our right to share political power with men, who have exercised control over it permanently. Today more than ever we are aware that our capacity of decision making is determinative and able to change at any moment the course of the political history of the country, because of the power which is given to us by the possession of a greater electoral force than that of our *compañeros*" (*El Nacional,* 31 July 1988).

The manifesto also illustrated the movement's continuing reliance on rhetorical strategies that advanced women's equality while avoiding a challenge to gender relations. Its authors were careful to associate gender equality with democratization. They made clear that the movement had been deliberately launched just before the elections for president, congress, and state assemblies in order to give it current relevance. But they also claimed transcendence for women's demands. More than an electoral maneuver, women's demands "represent a forward step in the process of Venezuela's historic transformation," and rejection of the promotion of women's leadership would "impede the perfection of democracy." The signatories took credit for the opportunity women already had to assume leadership roles in

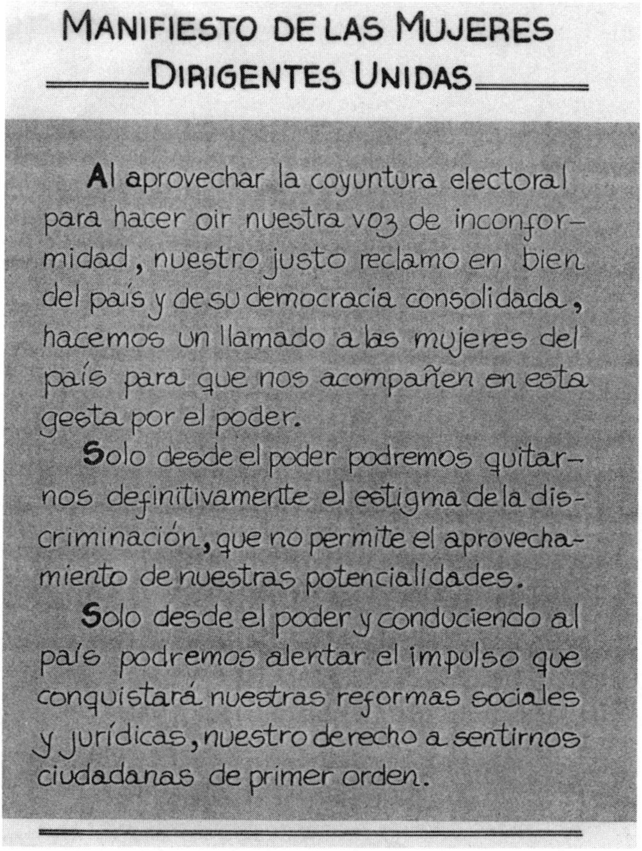

MANIFIESTO DE LAS MUJERES DIRIGENTES UNIDAS

Al aprovechar la coyuntura electoral para hacer oir nuestra voz de inconformidad, nuestro justo reclamo en bien del país y de su democracia consolidada, hacemos un llamado a las mujeres del país para que nos acompañen en esta gesta por el poder.

Solo desde el poder podremos quitarnos definitivamente el estigma de la discriminación, que no permite el aprovechamiento de nuestras potencialidades.

Solo desde el poder y conduciendo al país podremos alentar el impulso que conquistará nuestras reformas sociales y jurídicas, nuestro derecho a sentirnos ciudadanas de primer orden.

Fig. 5.4   Flier distributed during a United Women Leaders rally.

[By taking advantage of the occasion of the elections to make heard our nonconformist voice, our just demand for the good of the country and its consolidated democracy, we call to women of the country to accompany us in this heroic claim for a position of power.

Only from a position of power will we be able to definitively rid ourselves of the stigma of discrimination, which does not permit us to take advantage of our potential.

Only from a position of power and running the country will we be able to encourage the momentum that will win our social and juridical reforms, our right to consider ourselves first-class citizens.]

parties and political institutions. But they explicitly rejected the charge that their current demand for increased representation was based only on the fact of their being women. On the contrary, they deserved leadership because of their active citizenship: "An objective examination of the authentic revolution that we Venezuelan women have led in this century and the decisive role that we have played in the establishment and consolidation of the democracy, confers upon us the full right to run the country."

The most concrete demand of the manifesto was that political parties give a "noticeably greater expansion of the representation of women in the Congress, [state] Legislative Assemblies and Municipal Councils of the country." The 30 percent quota specified in the Minimum Program of 1987 was not included because of the objection of the COPEI members to "reverse discrimination." This omission illustrates the compromises that movement participants had to make in order to continue presenting a united front. However, the quota issue would be more successfully resolved a decade later.

To reinforce its demands, the movement sponsored a public demonstration on August 3. Hundreds of women marched through the center of Caracas carrying banners, signs, and the national flag. National and state party leaders were joined by former collaborators on the Civil Code reform: workers and union leaders, teachers, journalists, professionals, and women activists from the *barrios*, many of whom were CONG members. Olivo de Celli herself had been forbidden from taking part in this multiparty event by *adeco* President Lusinchi, but the Directorate was also represented. The manifesto, signed by women from all but two small parties,[15] was delivered to the National Election Commission and to Congress.

The result of the multiparty organizing was to overcome party leaders' initially hostile reception of the women's demands. The percentages of women elected in 1988 increased noticeably. Whereas there had been no women serving in the Senate, there were now three (6.5 percent); from twelve deputies they increased to nineteen (from 6 to 9.5 percent); and they gained an additional seventeen seats in state legislatures (for a total of 11.2 percent) (CSE 1988; see Table 1).

The United Women Leaders movement illustrated how the two pivotal organizations of the period were able to work together to promote women's political leadership, while relying on past solidarity and international legitimation. CONG members took their ideas to the state through the mecha-

---

15. The representatives of the MEP (Movimiento Electoral del Pueblo or People's Electoral Movement) and the PCV did not sign the manifesto because of pressure from party leadership, which insisted that their already meager congressional representation would be diminished if they put women higher on their lists.

nism of the advisory commissions. The Directorate then coordinated the initial meeting of women from different parties. United, women leaders made a highly public demand for increased representation, drawing support from international norms and the coalition of activists from the Civil Code reform. The leaders used a rhetorical strategy that promoted gender equality as further democratization, couching a de facto challenge of gender difference in politically acceptable terms. The result was impressive: using an alternative model of organization built around the parties that had excluded them and fragmented their organizing, women inserted themselves within the male-dominated hierarchy of the parties.

The Reform of the Labor Law: Working Women and the Social Function of Maternity (1985–1990)

The movement to reform the Labor Law had many similarities to that of the United Women Leaders. Reforming this legislation to end unwarranted discrimination against women while enhancing maternity and parental benefits was the result of another coalition of women organized by the CONG and ONM/Directorate. Again women used the different resources at their disposal to mount a successful challenge to legal discrimination, taking advantage of a moment of national attention to labor issues as well as of international attention to women's issues. Like the previous effort, this reform was oriented to the needs of middle- and upper-class women.

The reformers continued to rely on and update older rhetorical strategies, both accepting and challenging gender difference. Like their predecessors of the 1940s, activists of the 1980s also relied on the state to resolve the conflict between women's equality at work and inequality at home. But reflecting the changes in women's status since the last time the law was reformed (1936), the discourse of the reformers now focused on the social function of maternity as the underlying justification for gender-sensitive workplace policies. They clearly separated this social function from the equally important need to guarantee working women's equal rights.

Issues of women and work had been on the agenda of women's groups since 1936. But demands for the reform of the Labor Law were only put forward in earnest at the 1975 First Venezuelan Congress of Women, stimulated by the participation of women leaders from the union confederations. The need for reform was reiterated at the Meeting on Women's Participation in the Workforce held by the Ministry for the Participation of Women in Development in 1982 (Hernandez 1985). Thus there was a history of demands in place when the ONM was established in 1984.

The ONM began work on the reform early in its tenure. In the evaluations undertaken for the Nairobi conference, the need for reforms in the Labor Law, as well as the Penal Code, surfaced with renewed vigor. In one of the first uses of the advisory commissions, in February 1985 Olivo de Celli called together women from political and civil society to discuss the proposals for reforms. Work on the Penal Code went forward in the Legislation Commission, and the ONM submitted a reform proposal to Congress in late 1985. Among the reforms proposed were articles that aimed at the liberalization of abortion restrictions: decriminalizing abortion in the cases not only of risk to the mother's life but also if the pregnancy were the result of rape or incest or if the fetus were badly malformed (Sgambatti 1992, 81, 85). As before, the abortion proposals provoked severe dissension among legislators, and reform of the Penal Code was quickly put aside.

The tabling of the Penal Code reform illustrates the problem women continued to face in altering discriminatory legislation. Anything that could seen as a radical departure from traditional gender relations, such as increasing women's control over reproduction, was highly suspect. Historically, women's successful reform efforts had relied on gender difference rather than substantially challenging it. Proposals that could be viewed as favoring and encouraging maternity appealed to a broader public than proposals seen as likely to limit it. Therefore, it is not surprising that when they turned to the Labor Law, the reform advocates emphasized the importance of protecting the mothers of future generations of Venezuelans. As will be explained, however, this protection was justified in a way that recognized that not all working women were working mothers.

The ONM found highly placed allies in its quest to reform the Labor Law. Ex-president Rafael Caldera, coauthor of the original 1936 legislation, headed a bicameral congressional commission already preparing a comprehensive reform. The preparations for Nairobi helped extend this effort in the legislative branch in the form of the Commission to Evaluate the Decade on Women. Under the guidance of *adeca* deputy Paulina Gamus, the commission took up the reform of the Labor Law as a priority for women. These efforts were united in a commission workshop in early May attended by those already working on the reform: the ONM, CONG members, the women and children's section and legal consultants of the Labor Ministry, and the business peak organization Venezuelan Federation of Chambers of Commerce and Production (FEDECAMARAS).

At this workshop those present agreed that there were two types of discrimination to be addressed in the Labor Law. Working women were still subject to antiquated protections (such as limitations on night work), but working mothers needed increased workplace rights (such as the provision of on-site nurseries for the infants of nursing women). This differentiation challenged the automatic association of women with motherhood. The protections rejected were refused on the grounds that working women should work under the same conditions as men. The increased rights were sought on the basis of the central importance of healthy maternity to family and social life. In promoting these demands, supporters cited their existence in international agreements such as the UN Convention to End All Forms of Discrimination Against Women (Comisión Especial n.d., 5-1.).

But in the general agreement over changes to be made in the Labor Law, one point of contention stood out: which classes of women would be covered. Domestic workers' rights were fiercely debated at the workshop. Gamus and a few of the FEVA lawyers spoke against their inclusion, while the ONM and CONG members Argelia Laya and Eumelia Hernandez fought for it (*Ultimas Noticias,* 5 May 1985). Shortly after the workshop, the CONG sent a letter to Olivo de Celli making clear that as an organization, it supported the equality of home- with workplace-based workers. The ONM was in agreement; as a result of her experience organizing women in the *barrios,* Rosa Paredes, its director, understood the need to protect domestic workers' rights.

The debate pointed up the clashing gender interests among women. Those opposed to extending the Labor Law to cover domestic workers were not willing to acknowledge their class privilege and to recognize that their ability to lead professional lives was based on the potential exploitation of other women. Those *for* inclusion insisted that all women deserved equal rights at the workplace, no matter the impact on particular classes. The issue was left unresolved among the advocates.

To ensure representation of nongovernmental women's perspectives in the reform, the CONG began its own reform deliberations. In October the CONG held a three-day meeting to analyze the proposals coming out of the ONM and the two congressional commissions. Members had few disagreements with the proposals from the ONM and the Decade Commission. But as explained by CONG member organization All (Women) Together, Caldera's version, which had been introduced into Congress in August 1985, was problematic. It left in place too many outdated protections, did not strengthen the requirement for the provision of workplace nurseries for workers' children, and paid little attention to the situation of home-based workers (*Revista SIC* 49:484:159–60).

The final proposals that CONG agreed to support were written by lawyer and judge Yolanda Poleo de Baez, who had also drafted the Civil

Code reform. This new reform was as comprehensive in its amendment of a discriminatory law as her earlier effort. To end discrimination against working women, she proposed eliminating sex-specific employment advertising, banning pregnancy exams for female applicants, and prohibiting any other sex-specific limitations on employment. In apparently neutral but gender-freighted provisions, she sought flexible and shorter workdays (which would make women's balancing of home and work duties easier), an end to the policy whereby one spouse (almost always the husband) could request the termination of the other's work (almost always the wife's) on the grounds of its being "prejudicial to the family," and the limitation on workers' early liquidation of their severance benefits to 50 percent without the consent of their spouses, to guard against the loss of married women's community property.

In order to clarify that she sought these reforms for the purpose of supporting maternity (or parenthood) and not women per se, Poleo de Baez proposed changing the title of the section "Women and Minors" to "Protection of Maternity and the Family." In it she argued for an expansion of pre- and postnatal leave from twelve to eighteen weeks and for the adoption of a *fuero maternal* or maternity exemption protecting pregnant women and new mothers from being fired. The demand for a *fuero maternal* was modeled on the policy of *fuero syndical,* which protected union organizers from being fired during union drives and while serving in union positions. If firing procedures were started for some severe violation of the rules governing workplace conduct, they had to be carefully monitored by a state labor inspector. Applying these conditions to pregnant women was, in a sense, to protect the "union" being formed between mother and child.

To help new mothers, Poleo de Baez proposed a six-hour work day for nursing mothers, the expansion of workplace nurseries into child-care centers for the children of male and female workers,[16] and fines, forced closing, or imprisonment for owners who did not protect pregnant women and provide on-site child care. She also proposed obligatory social security for housewives and, finally, equal protection for domestic workers, including set hours, vacation time, and social security, the latter also to be provided to home-based workers and pieceworkers (*La Mala Vida,* March 1986, 3).

Shortly after the CONG meetings, a tragic incident gave the reform movement a powerful case around which to mobilize support for their cause. Cípriana Velásquez was a pregnant office worker in, of all places, the Labor

16. According to the original 1936 Labor Law, all businesses with more than thirty employees were supposed to provide nurseries where nursing mothers could breastfeed during the workday. The reform sought to have all businesses with more than twenty employees provide day care for both female and male employees' children up to the age of six.

Ministry. She had been working as close as possible to the end of her term in order to save her six-week prenatal leave to add to her six-week postnatal leave, a strategy used by many women who wanted more than a month and half to spend with their newborns. However, upon receiving a notice in late October stating that the procedure for firing her had been initiated because of several unexplained absences, Velásquez went home, became hysterical, and despite a recent medical examination that had found her to be in good health, went into shock. She died shortly after.

No sooner than her death made a banner headline in *El Nacional* on October 31, than the CONG started organizing. As in the case of Inés María Marcano, member groups combined efforts to bring the individual tragedy and its social meaning to the public's attention. The following day, Deputy Laya demanded a full investigation of the case in Congress. The matter was taken up by the Committee on Social Affairs within the week. Meanwhile, the current president of FEVA issued a press release declaring the case one more consequence of a faulty Labor Law. CONG members from the Central University quickly established the Cípriana Velásquez Committee, bringing together professors, staff, and students in a public demand for the firing of Cípriana's boss, who under the current law ought to have given at least three verbal warnings to her employee before initiating firing procedures. Women from the major labor confederation, the CTV, used the case to highlight the need for *fuero maternal:* it would have granted Cípriana, as a pregnant worker, an exemption from job termination. On November 6, women from the CTV, the Cípriana Velasquez Committee, and the feminist organizations La Mala Vida and the Wednesday Feminist Group held a protest outside the Labor Ministry and Congress to demand the immediate reform of the Labor Law, especially the protection of pregnant women, longer maternity leave, and on-site day care. This protest set off others in cities in the interior (*El Nacional*, 31 October–6 November 1987).

At the Caracas-based protest, the CONG resurrected a tried-and-true method of political pressure. In honor of Cípriana, the organization began a petition drive to have their version of the reformed Labor Law introduced in Congress. This petition drive, like the ones for women's suffrage and the Civil Code reform, raised awareness of the issues throughout the country. But reflecting the higher degree of organization among women, this petition was completed in record time. Rather than taking three years, as did the petition drive for the Civil Code reform, a mere six months later, on 8 April 1986, twenty thousand signatures were delivered to Congress. Outside, the Eighth of March Street Theater Group, launched in 1983 to spread news of the Civil Code reform, performed a new piece publicizing issues in the Labor Law reform: a parody of the Cinderella story entitled "The Shoe Fits Everyone." CONG members passed out leaflets claiming that "the Venezuelan State should recognize maternity not as a particular and private problem of a woman and her family, but as a social and public problem which requires State policies."

As a result of the petition drive, the CONG-sponsored reforms joined those already under discussion in Congress. While the drawn-out process of revising articles continued for the next two years, governmental and non-governmental women remained active. Supportive congresswomen sat on the bicameral commission overseeing the reform. Caldera gallantly allowed members of FEVA and women representing each of the four labor confederations to sit in on the commission's discussions and even to speak during debates on certain articles. For example, when members of FEDECAMARAS, also in attendance, started to attack the section on "Protection of Maternity and the Family" as the weak point by which to break up the entire reform effort, Caldera opened the discussion to anyone with a coherent proposal. The author of that section, FEVA member Poleo de Baez, had one ready. Caldera then turned to the representatives of business for their proposal. Because they did not have one, he claimed he simply had to give full consideration to Poleo de Baez's suggestions (Interview with Haydee Deutch, former secretary general of CODESA, the COPEI-linked labor confederation).

Work slowed during the electoral season as the parties turned their energies elsewhere, and the women had other concerns as well: it was the moment of the United Women Leaders. When Caldera introduced the reform for congressional consideration in August 1988, he straddled the fence on supporting women's demands, acknowledging that "women have been the sector most interested" in the reform but also warning that the "overprotection" of women might make employers prefer to hire men (*El Nacional*, 4 August 1988). In June 1989 the debate started to heat up again, and the coalition of women was ready. The CONG and labor confederations declared the establishment of a united front to fight for their reforms, helped by two state-based organizations for women's issues: the latest version of the executive-branch women's agency, and a new commission in Congress.

By this time the national agency for women had taken on yet another form with the change in administration in 1989 (see Chapter 6). Under pressure from *adeca* women, the reelected *adeco* president, Carlos Andrés Pérez, reestablished his presidential advisory commission COFEAPRE. Although linked with a new administration, COFEAPRE continued the reform campaign of the Directorate and made public its support for the reform. In its press releases, COFEAPRE affirmed the separation of the goal of guarantee-

ing women equal work conditions from that of protecting the "social function" of maternity and cited international norms in support of it:

> We support the proposal of the Labor Law in all its parts, because
> it constitutes a significant advance in Venezuelan labor legislation
> and incorporates in it the modern humanistic conception which
> contemplates work as a social act and not as a mere economic re-
> lation which is that which has been held heretofore. Chapter
> Seven [on maternity and family protection] deserves special at-
> tention because it considers maternity as a social function, con-
> tains dispositions which protect it and achieves the objective of
> the principles contained in our Magna Carta and the UN Con-
> vention on the Elimination of All Forms of Discrimination
> Against Women, so that women might exercise their right to em-
> ployment in conditions of equality, might have access to all the
> economic activities and enjoy the social benefits for their condi-
> tion of female worker, such as *fuero maternal.* (*El Nacional,* 7 Au-
> gust 1989)

During the course of the debates, Congress also instituted a new mechanism for women's representation in the legislature, which congresswomen
put at the service of the reform effort. The idea for the Bicameral Commission for Women's Rights (Comisión Bicameral de Derechos de la Mujer)
originated in the wake of the furor over the death of Cípriana Velásquez,
when congresswomen proposed a specific commission to oversee women's
rights issues (Senator Ixora Rojas interview). Officially convened in June
1989, the commission was taking an active role in the reform by mid-1990. It
was guided by none other than the former head of the women's ministry,
Mercedes Pulido de Briceño, now a senator. As had been done during the
campaign to reform the Civil Code, the Bicameral Commission sponsored a
series of forums to keep discussion of the Labor Law reform alive in state legislatures and city halls across the country.

Meanwhile, women outside the government teamed up with a congressional representative to insure the continued effectiveness of the women's
coalition. Amarylis Valor, a member of the CTV and recently elected congressional deputy, brought together female party leaders and CONG members in regular meetings on the reform. She would report on the
congressional commission's discussions of the issue, and everyone would
help to plan what she would say on the floor of Congress (Valor interview).
One of Valor's interventions in particular underscored both this con-

certed consultation and the lessons women had learned from prior mobilization: speak of the family, but make sure everyone knows that united women
are behind the effort. Valor's speech began: "Notice, citizens, that we are not
talking about women. We are speaking without bias about the Law which
protects families." Yet despite her universalistic rhetoric, throughout the rest
of her speech Valor continually mentioned the range of women consulted on
this bill and their refusal to let it be tabled, as had happened to the first proposals to reform the Civil Code (*Diario de Debates*, 4 July 1989, 33). To make
sure the message got through, every time Valor was scheduled to speak on the
floor of Congress, CONG activists picketed outside on behalf of the reform.
Occasionally they took their protest inside, unfurling a big banner in the balcony declaring "We women want the reform of the Labor Law NOW" *(las
mujeres queremos la reforma de la Ley del Trabajo YA)* when debate was particularly intense (Benita Finol interview).

　　As had happened in the reform of the Civil Code, the opposition to the
Labor Law grew fiercest toward the end of the deliberations. The main opponent was FEDECAMARAS, despite its earlier support of reform efforts.
It was generally against the proposal by reformers to increase worker benefits and protections in a time of changing economic conditions,[17] but the section protecting maternity also came under intense attack. According to
FEDECAMARAS, *fuero maternal* would only result in employer reluctance
to hire women. Moreover, small businesses would go under if they had to
provide the level of child care specified in the law. Providing that sort of social service, business argued, was the responsibility of the state.

　　To make the threat of such displacement tangible, during the last stages
of deliberation on the reform, several businesses fired all of their female
workers and hired men to replace them. However, in one supermarket where
the cashiers were replaced, the owners found that over the weekend the men
had gotten so drunk that they did not come to work on Monday. So the owners rehired the women and gave them the pay they had lost. A cosmetics and
a stocking factory made the same about-face when their owners also found
the men unreliable or too clumsy to do the work that women had done (Valor
interview).

　　In response to the opposition, women turned again to appeals based on
the family-oriented nature of maternity protection. In the closing congres-

---

17. Accusing the reformers of "populism," business leaders claimed that the reform would
drive up business costs on the order of 30 percent, increase inflation and consumer costs, discourage foreign investment, hurt efforts at privatization, and generally derail new economic efforts (*El Nacional*, October–November 1990). For further discussion about the economic
situation of the early 1990s, see Chapter 6.

Las mujeres irán al Congreso a defender el fuero maternal

Fig. 5.5 Headline from *El Nacional:* "The Women Will Go to Congress to Defend Maternity Exemption."

sional debates on the reform, congresswomen took the floor to defend the different provisions of the section on "Maternity and the Family." A *copeyana* defended *fuero maternal* by citing the need to insure the well-being of children: "We are protecting future Venezuelan society, the children who have to count on an income. And who can tell me now which family is not in need of the income of a man and a woman to guarantee a better quality of life for the children who are being raised and for the future Venezuela?" (*Diario de Debates,* 27 November 1990, 3). An *adeca* continued along these lines: "It is not women we are protecting in a special manner by considering them inferior to men, they are equal to men, they have the same rights and duties in that which does not have to do with the function of maternity; when women are mothers, it is their children whom we ought to protect, and that has been the intention of this Chapter which refers to maternity and to the family" (8).

Because the Labor Law reform was not only concerned with women, they were far from alone in their advocacy for it. But they took advantage of the political opportunity afforded by reform debates to advance women's interests. Being on the side of the workers was a claim all parties in Venezuela had made at some point in their history, and this claim now generated a great deal of political support for the reform. Party objections to the accusations by FEDECAMARAS of political interference in the economy culminated in a Senate resolution stating that it had been offended by the way in which the business community had publicly disrespected

Congress (*El Nacional,* 16 November 1990). The reform passed on 27 November 1990.

The new Labor Law included many of the original proposals generated by the ONM and the CONG. From the removal of discriminatory articles to the adoption of the newly entitled chapter "Of the Labor Protection of Maternity and the Family," the reform made clear that no provisions were to be permitted that disadvantaged working women, only those that allowed them to combine work and motherhood. Thus discrimination on the basis of sex—in employment, advertising, and work conditions (e.g., mandatory pregnancy testing)—was banned, and neither spouse could now demand that the other's work to be terminated on the basis of family needs. At the same time, the special maternity dispensations were explicitly labeled as nondiscriminatory. Pregnant women were exempted without penalty from work that might endanger their pregnancies and granted eighteen weeks of maternity leave. The *fuero maternal,* protecting women's employment while they were pregnant and for one year following birth (or adoption), was included. Nursing women were given the right to two half-hour breaks to nurse their children at on-site nurseries, or two one-hour breaks if their children were at home. Finally, employers of more than twenty workers had to supply a child-care center or make provisions for child care for all of their employees (male and female) with children under six years old.

But because the predominantly upper-class women who had led the reform campaign could not agree to protect popular women's rights, class-based discrimination remained in the final document. Although domestic workers continued to be legally entitled to one day off a week, ten hours of rest a day, fifteen days of paid vacation a year, and yearly bonuses, they were not given healthcare benefits or social security coverage. Pieceworkers and home-based workers were also excluded from these benefits.

Two years after the law's passage, business continued to object to it—and the coalition of women continued to maintain their victory. In November 1992 a business lawyer brought a case to the Supreme Court to nullify the child-care provisions in the Labor Law and its enabling legislation. He argued that the extension of these provisions went against the original spirit of the law, which was only to provide a place for women to nurse infants, not to supply day care for the young children of workers of both sexes. The coalition partners reunited to oppose his claim, filing a brief that explained that the intent of the reform was not to violate its spirit, but to bring the law up to date by protecting *all* workers' children. They defended the extension of parenting rights to men by calling up the familiar bogey of the female-headed household. How were fathers going to learn to take responsibility if the laws themselves left them off the hook? The point behind the reform was to change the "patriarchal legislation which yields as a consequence in our society irresponsible paternity and a matricentric organization" (García Prince et al., 1993).

As had happened with the Civil Code, the implementation of the Labor Law left much to be desired. Following the Supreme Court suit, a few of the enabling provisions were nullified, making it easier for businesses to pay parents directly to provide for their own child care, the preferred solution of those businesses that complied with the law.[18] Moreover, the sanctions put in place against the many businesses that violated the provisions were not as stringent as the activists had asked for. Finally, the growing informal labor sector—where many of the poorest worked—could not be obliged to comply with any legislation.

As much of a problem as implementation would turn out to be, the movement to reform the Labor Law was yet another success of women's coalition building. Women continued to work outside the normal channels of politics, uniting through the CONG and through the executive and the new legislative branch women's institutions to achieve a substantial revision of many of the discriminatory articles of this piece of national legislation. In doing so, they managed to use familial rhetoric while for the first time distinguishing women's social roles as workers from those as mothers. The coalition proved a successful mechanism for reform, albeit one that excluded many women who were without formal political power.

The model of coalition building that came to full flower in the United Women Leaders movement and the effort to reform the Labor Law was largely dependent on the innovations of two interlinked coordinating organizations. The ONM/Directorate provided a forum for the expression of women's demands by a range of political and independent activists and helped advance these demands through the mechanism of its advisory commissions. Meanwhile the decentralized, nonhierarchical CONG significantly altered the traditional model of peak organizations; it united women in civil society around issues of common concern and maintained access to the state. Both organizations took advantage of the development of international processes directed at women. One activist described their influence as decisive: "They have acted like a motor for the most organized women to meet

---

18. Despite the failure of the demand for nullification of the child-care provision as a whole, on-site child care continues to be scantily provided. Its implementation, though regularly called for by women's and children's advocates, has largely taken a back seat to the home-based daycare program, which President Carlos Andrés Pérez revived when taking office again in 1989.

and discuss issues. And in this collective process of reflection, we have all advanced" (Nora Castañeda interview). Part of their advancement was an ability to redefine gender interests, albeit within a limited political discourse and a dispute over which classes of women were to be represented.

Created by women who as a group shared a common experience of marginalization or exclusion from traditional politics, the model of organizing responsible for the successful movements of the 1980s had little in common with the dominant model of representation through highly centralized, hierarchical party structures. The result was hardly the "mass organization" envisaged by Isabel Carmona at the 1975 First Women's Congress. But in the context of Venezuelan politics, such an organization would have inevitably fallen victim to the same clash of partisan rivalries that for so long had separated women.

In contrast, organizing in loose-knit coalitions around specific issues allowed women to work together despite their many differences—the very differences that would most likely have destroyed a highly structured women's organization. Reflecting on the major successes of women's organizing, from suffrage to the reform of the Labor Law, longtime activist Esperanza Vera, in an interview, described the "intermediary form" of organization Venezuelan women had developed through long experience:

> We have not achieved a permanent organization . . . on the model of the parties. But there [exists] something which is not de jure but de facto. When an interesting proposal is made, and a call is put out, we all go . . . because the necessity for unity exists. . . . It is as though reality is showing us that women, through this method of not being organized in the traditional manner but being unified around something which interests us, are creating something like a different form of collective action. It exists, only those of us who continue to insist that we ought to build an organization probably are insisting on acting traditionally. Maybe what has happened to us is that we have created some intermediary form that allows the conversion of this climate of coincidences into something a little more organic. Even if it might not be exactly the same as the organizations that we know. . . . It's like a way to avoid the frictions. And to also avoid the differences, because the differences exist. And if we are all together in an organization that has requirements like the traditional ones, these differences will come into conflict every day. Meanwhile, as we are, we only unite when there are coincidences. . . . It's a good

strategy, but [rather than coming from theory] it has arisen from the activism itself.

One product of such a contingent form of organizing was compromise, leaving out the more radical demands that presented too strong a challenge to the gender or class status quo. But considering the nature of Venezuelan political society, the coalition model was remarkable. Through it, one of the most politically excluded groups demanded and achieved political inclusion and legislative reform in their own interest. But the delicate balance of cooperation, which avoided the pitfalls of co-optation on one hand and debilitating friction on the other, proved unstable in the face of the new set of political opportunities that emerged with the political and economic crises of the 1990s.

THE DECLINE OF COALITION BUILDING DURING DEMOCRATIC CRISIS (1989–1995)

The political opportunities of the 1990s confronted women with a new set of challenges. The country reaped the consequences of chronic economic mismanagement as debt piled up and oil prices plummeted. Simultaneously, it faced the most severe political upheaval in its democratic history, beginning with riots in 1989, two military coup attempts in 1992, and the impeachment of the president for corruption in 1993. To address these interrelated crises, the government made a turn toward a neoliberal, market-oriented economy and continued to take steps in the direction of a more decentralized polity.

Women organized on their own behalf within civil society, political society, and the state to address these changing national opportunities. But the changes also exacerbated tensions and divisions among women that impeded the development of further conjunctural coalition building. Moreover, in contrast with the positive effects of the 1985 UN Women's Conference, the international influences stemming from the 1995 UN Fourth World Conference on Women contributed to the diminution of women's effective national organizing.

The economic crisis and first steps toward its resolution underscored the class cleavage within the women's movement. As living conditions for the majority of Venezuelan women deteriorated sharply, the gender interests of poor women became even more focused on basic needs such as feeding their families. Although activists from other classes were attentive to the changes in poor women's status, they had little experience to draw on in order to go beyond individual responses. As a result, multiclass, gender-focused responses to the economic crisis were few.

The move toward decentralization in both state and party structures strengthened women's institutional position to a certain extent. The national women's agency gained in autonomy and resources, and developed links with decentralized women's agencies in the different states. The cooperation between women in NGOs and the state agency became more formalized. Some gender-focused activism also continued in the women's bureaus of the parties. More sophisticated analyses of women's situation undergirded these advances.

However, the further institutionalization of women's activism also brought with it some of the negative aspects of traditional politics. In the face of changing opportunities, certain traditional patterns emerged in women's organizing style. Paradoxically, or perhaps predictably, as women's organizations gained in importance and resources, they also became sites of hierarchical leadership and clientelistic relations. The worst manifestations of the change could be called "instrumental feminism": the use of feminist rhetoric and institutional resources dedicated to the advancement of women as a group for the personal advancement of individual female leaders or of other goals. Although these practices did not preclude all work on behalf of women, they did compromise the long-sought cooperation that had been forged among activists from different walks of life.

Ironically, at a time of restricted resources, the "Midas touch" that had corrupted Venezuelan politics as a whole reached into women's organizations.[1] After many years of neglect, international funding organizations now saw debt-ridden Venezuela as a country deserving of some aid; and women's organizations benefited from some of this kind of investment, which included, for example, financial support for organizing efforts directed toward the Fourth World Conference on Women. But such funding underwrote the emergence of traditional participation patterns, which contributed to difficulties with coalition building during the period of democratic crisis. Increasingly, instead of providing alternatives to "normal" Venezuelan politics, women's organizing reflected them.

This chapter begins by discussing the changes in women's status and political opportunities that accompanied the crises of the period. It then examines the transformation of women's organizing in civil and political society and in the state in the face of shifting national and international opportunities. It assesses the advances as well as analyzing the problems that occurred, paying particular attention to how conjunctural coalition building receded in the face of growing class tension and the rise of "politics as usual," strikingly illustrated by the appearance of instrumental feminism.

1. Karl (1997) uses the legend of King Midas—whose ability to turn all he touched to gold brought him more pain than profit—as a metaphor for Venezuelan politics.

Women's Status in a Time of Crisis (1990s)

Responding to economic necessity, women took on even more responsibilities in the area of production—but in ways that continued to reflect the subordinate status of their gender. By 1990 they formed 30 percent of the labor force. They were entering it at a higher rate than men because of their historically lower numbers. Between 1970 and 1990 the number of female workers increased by 205 percent, while their male counterparts increased at half that rate. In 1990 twice as many women as men were looking for work for the first time (Huggins Castañeda and Dominguez Nelson 1993, 38, 46).

Women's work was still limited in gender-specific ways. The new female workers typically found jobs in highly feminized occupations that, not coincidentally, were low-paying. Women's salaries as a percentage of men's grew by 10 percent but still remained lower, around 87 percent (Huggins Castañeda and Dominguez Nelson 1993, 49). Sixty-five percent of all women working in the officially reported formal sector were either office workers, saleswomen, or service providers (who formed a quarter of the whole). New statistics estimating employment in the informal sector found that women formed at least 30 percent of this sector (OCEI 1990). Women continued to make up over half of the "professional and technical" sector (OCEI 1993). However, their employment in this sector was threatened by the reductions in state-based employment, which were an integral part of economic restructuring. In 1990, 37 percent of all women with college or professional degrees were employed in the public sector, constituting 40 percent of all state employees (OCEI 1990).

While women's fertility rates declined to an average of three children per woman by 1990 (Huggins Castañeda and Dominguez Nelson 1993, 26), women were often solely responsible for their families' support, and in decidedly difficult circumstances. Although the national rate for households headed by women nationwide was high at 25 percent, among the poor it reached 50 percent (JUVECABE 1995, 14).

Thus there were plenty of objective factors that might have indicated the need for women to organize on their own behalf. How were they mediated by the opportunities of the period?

The Political Opportunities of Democratic Crisis

From 1989 on, the political opportunity structure changed markedly as actors and institutions tried to mitigate the consequences of the, by now, unavoidable economic crisis and ossifying political institutions. By 1988 debt was 41 percent of gross national product, and oil prices had declined to a third of their all-time high, severely reducing the resources on which the polity was dependent (Karl 1995, 42; Kelly 1995, 289). As a result, not only economic policy but also political life was altered. With his reelection in 1988, President Carlos Andrés Pérez was determined to see the country through "the Great Turnabout" (*el Gran Viraje*)—his national plan to liberalize the economy and decentralize the polity. Although the great turn did not lead into a complete dead end, neither was it very successful.

The economic policies President Pérez tried to implement were similar to those recommended for the entire region: stabilizing and liberalizing the economy in order to engage global markets. They were integrally based on "shrinking the state," reducing state involvement not only in economic development but also in the provision of social services and subsidies for transportation and food. The rapidity with which the administration tried to implement these policies proved misguided. It did not take into account public expectations, nurtured since the inception of democracy, in ongoing state support. Increasingly distanced from his own party, Pérez relied on well-educated but politically remote technocrats for policy development and failed to educate the public on the need for reforms (McCoy and Smith 1995, 252). As a result, these new policies were soundly rejected by the majority of Venezuelans.

In February 1989 the largest riots of the democratic period erupted, sparked by a sudden increase in bus fares. Conservative estimates put casualties at three hundred dead and over one thousand injured (Martz 1995, 31). Increasing discontent with the economic situation and the corruption in, and extensive control of, political parties was the key factor in the two military coup attempts of 1992 (Agüero 1995). Eventually, Pérez himself was indicted by the Venezuelan Supreme Court for the embezzlement of $17 million in government monies and was held under house arrest in 1994.

The economy was not the only arena undergoing change. Political reform was high on the agenda in the early 1990s, manifest in the attempts to create a new "pact" to promote political decentralization as well as in the internal democratization of political parties (Navarro 1995a). These measures included shifting some responsibility for social programs and economic development from the central government to state and local governments as well as giving more power to state and local assemblies and political party branches.[2] Certain electoral reforms were put in place, such as the direct elec-

---

2. For further discussion of the political changes Venezuela has experienced since 1989, see Ellner 1993–94; Goodman et al. 1995; McCoy et al. 1995.

tion of mayors and governors (1989) and expanded uninominal (single-member constituency) voting on the municipal (1989) and then national levels (1992/3). Both reforms were promoted as democratizing measures since they gave voters more direct power over the selection of their political representatives. Moves toward decentralization progressed unevenly through the states.

These efforts probably helped to head off complete collapse of the government following the military coup attempts. The 1992 gubernatorial elections allowed voters to express their ire through democratic channels, and they turned over the majority of governorships from AD to COPEI. Thanks in part to the electoral reforms, other parties attracted more voters disillusioned with the two major parties' worn-out model of consensus building and their clientelism.

Party leaders did not act quickly on the policies aimed at reducing their power and that of parties themselves, however. They continued to exert control over local elections and to broker deals with the major peak organizations in civil society. But citizens' support for the parties, which were now seen as ossified and ineffective, declined markedly (Templeton 1995, 100).

Although the near-daily demonstrations by different sectors revealed a civil society anxious for systemic change, the weakness of these efforts, often hardly more than noisy street protests, showed how little an autonomous associational sphere had been fostered by years of party-led democracy. The one sector that seemed to have made the most headway was the neighborhood organizations, estimated to have numbered ten thousand by 1995 (Salamanca 1995, 210). They sought to take advantage of the processes of decentralization but were still wary of the parties' penchant for political co-optation.

Gendered Opportunities

During the period of crisis, women continued to organize through the various mechanisms developed during democratic consolidation. Spurred by increasing poverty, popular women expanded their national group, the Popular Women's Circles, which left its parent organization. It continued to raise a national voice on behalf of its members' gender interests. In the face of new electoral laws that had a negative impact on the election of women, even the women's branches of the major parties turned toward promoting women's leadership.

The two major organizing centers that undergirded the successful coalition building of the past, the national women's agency and the nongovernmental organization umbrella group, the CONG, also continued to function. The national women's agency, although still dependent on the good will of sitting presidents, grew in status and size. It established its own local branches through which it could implement (and not just develop) policy on women's issues. Members of the CONG were incorporated more directly into the agency's work, and member groups received some international financial support through its auspices. This cooperation resulted in advances in the extent and depth of gender analysis promoted (at least at the level of discourse) through the state agency.

But these advances also brought with them new obstacles for women's organizing. Some of the decentralized branches of the agency, intended as another alternative arena for women's participation, were used instead by the newly elected mayors to furnish social services no longer adequately provided by the national state—and to reward their clientele. The links between the state agency and the CONG empowered certain leaders to the detriment of democratic process within the NGO group. Moreover, female political elites seeking to augment their own or their party's power misused the institutions and resources established to advance women's interests.

These trends were brought into sharp relief by the UN Fourth World Conference on Women (Beijing 1995). Newly available international funds for organizing around the conference proved to be a mixed blessing. Their distribution further empowered certain leaders within the CONG, leading to the growth of central control—and the defection of those who objected to it—within the decentralized organization. These leaders did oversee the construction of a national dialogue on women's issues. But on the whole, they lacked contact with the majority of Venezuelan women, even as they claimed to represent them on a global stage.

Divergences in Civil Society:
The Popular Women's Circles and the CONG

Two groups exemplified the types of changes taking place in women's organizing in civil society. The Popular Women's Circles (CFP) continued to develop, drawing poor women into a framework of organizing oriented to their needs and increasingly attuned to their own gender interests. The group became strong enough to leave its parent organization, CESAP, and the discrimination it faced therein. However, the CFP's growing success did not translate into coalition building through the NGO umbrella organization, the CONG, on any issues of national importance. The CONG became less able to serve as the focal point for women's campaigns. Its decentralized structure proved a weakness in the face of growing political tensions and the emergence of unofficial leaders. Moreover, the delicate balance it had struck between cooperating with the national women's agency and maintaining its autonomy became skewed toward a more clientelistic relationship.

Popular Women Organize

Coping with the effects of the economic crisis was the main preoccupation for poor women at the end of the 1980s and into the 1990s. But even under these difficult conditions, the Popular Women's Circles expanded. It not only became the largest nonpartisan women's group in Venezuelan history, but it also took on a more active role in representing the gender interests of poor women to the nation. Despite the help that certain middle-class activists offered the CFP, there was little organized cross-class response to the crisis on the part of women.

Although Pérez's policies were unpopular among many sectors, they had a particularly harsh impact on the poor. To cushion the impact of economic restructuring on the poorest of the poor, President Pérez put into place the Plan to Confront Poverty (Plan de Enfrentamiento a la Pobreza), including direct subsidies for food[3] and education and a massive increase in day care. But these measures did not forestall a sharp decline in the economic well-being of the poor. One source noted a dramatic increase between 1988 and 1989 in the number of households living in poverty, which rose from 46 percent to 62 percent of the total; those in critical poverty jumped from 14 to 30 percent. These figures remained high over the next few years (JUVE-CABE 1995, 12).

Poor women's individual strategies to confront the crisis generally involved working longer hours themselves and, frequently, putting their children to work. The exhausting workday of these women, which included household chores, child care, informal work in their homes or domestic service in someone else's, or other paid work, had deleterious effects on the health and welfare of the women and their families. Most female heads of households struggled simply to provide the bare necessities and had scant time or energy for community participation, much of which continued to be domi-

3. The largest of these programs was the Program for Maternal-Infant Assistance (Programa de Asistencia Materno-Infantíl, or PAMI), established on 11 November 1989. Directed at low-income nursing mothers and children under six, the program distributed free milk, corn flour, and nutritional supplements through local clinics.

nated by parties attempting to enlarge their support in the face of increasing competition (Bethencourt G. 1988; Tur 1990).

Under these trying circumstances, the CFP continued to expand its local membership and make its presence felt on the national level. By 1989 there were 230 circles operating in urban[4] and rural settings throughout the country, with a combined membership of over two thousand (Orellana 1991). The national organization had acquired its own headquarters from which it coordinated national actions to address the harsh impact of the economic crisis on the poor.

The CFP particularly focused on issues salient to poor women. During the 1988 presidential elections the CFP published an open letter to presidential candidates, stating that "you yourselves will be the destabilizers of the democracy if you do not permit reform to be executed, if there is no redistribution of income, if there is no response for the petitions and propositions of the people." The letter went on to demand the application of constitutional principles protecting the family and maternity, and to remind the candidates of the need to improve education, employment opportunities, health care, rural housing, and social security provision (*Ultimas Noticias*, 6 November 1988). In the following year, alarmed at the steady rise of prices, the CFP sent the Supreme Court an appeal for protection of access to food by the poor. This was followed in 1990 by the organization's successful lobbying to have the "right to eat" incorporated in a proposal for constitutional reform (CFP 1994, 27).[5]

As membership grew, the CFP continued to challenge traditional models of organization, aided by individual feminist activists.[6] In 1992 it split from its parent organization, CESAP. While this move was a logical one for a group as large as the CFP had become, it was also motivated by a desire to escape from the male dominance of the parent institution. The directors of CESAP, like the male leaders of other organizations, had been wary of the emphasis on gender in the programming of the CFP, an emphasis that only increased as a result of members' exposure to feminist ideas in the CONG:

> The leadership of . . . CESAP is predominantly male and does not welcome the division of the poor or "popular" population by gender. As was the case in leftist political parties and the environ-

---

4. Juana Delgado, the national coordinator of the CFP at the time of her interview, noted the effect of the crisis on the Caracas-based circles in her 1995 interview. At that time only eight were operating in the capital; many women feared to leave their houses at night because of the soaring rates of crime in the city (more than thirty deaths, most of which took place in situations of violence or drug use in the *barrios*, were reported over many weekends in 1994–95).

5. This reform effort was derailed in the early 1990s following the political upheaval around the coup attempts (Kornblith 1995).

6. The following information was provided by members and advisors of the CFP.

mental groups, the male leaders of CESAP believe that the incorporation of specific female, or gender, demands could disturb the general purposes of the organization. For this reason, women from [the CFP] have been afraid of being labeled "feminists" since the beginning of their participation in the CONG. However, in the course of working together with feminist groups in CONG, they have developed a solidarity with women's problems and agendas and have implicitly started to question male leadership, the gender division of labour, and practices existing in CESAP. (García Guadilla 1993, 76–77)

The implicit questioning became more explicit as the expanding CFP experienced direct discrimination at the hands of the male CESAP leadership. One CFP leader claimed that the parent organization was receiving outside funding targeted for the women's program and diverting it for other uses. Moreover, the director of CESAP sought to reassert his control over the organization as the female leadership grew in strength, accusing them of programming that was "too feminist." So the CFP broke away from CESAP by institutionalizing its autonomous status.

The 1994 National Congress of the CFP, celebrating its 20th anniversary, illustrated how far popular women had advanced in organizing around their own interests. In sharp contrast to other national women's conferences held from the 1940s on, this one did not focus on poor women as the object of middle-class women's social activism, but it allowed them to be subjects in their own right. The event, entitled "20 years traveling the paths of solidarity and justice" (*20 años recorriendo los caminos de la solidaridad y la justicia*), brought seven hundred delegates—nearly one-third of the membership—together in Caracas (CFP 1995, 7). The organization's national visibility was affirmed by the speakers' roster, which included the minister of the family. The congress proceedings attested both to popular women's collective work and to their powers of critique regarding the current socioeconomic and political context.

The thirty essays published in the congress booklet for discussion at the two-day meeting covered a multitude of issues: economic (informal work and unemployment, alternative forms of employment, current national situation); educational (neoliberalism and educational crisis, popular education, rural education); health (effects of the economic crisis, women's health); legal (women's rights, peasant women's rights); spiritual (personal growth, self-esteem of peasant women, church attitudes); and political (the history of women's political participation, women's leadership). The range of the essays was not their only remarkable feature. They had been composed by members of the CFP themselves, many of whom had never written an essay before, let alone done research in a library. Congress coordinator and CFP advisor Inocencia Orellana explained that the process of producing the essays was deliberately planned as yet another way in which members could develop their capacities, here as researchers into issues affecting their own situations.

Another advance exemplified by the essays was the CFP participants' critical discourse on their class- and gender-based subordination both inside and outside of their communities. Household duties, the *machismo* of their partners, and their structural subordination in unions and political parties were all seen to present obstacles to popular women's participation. But the authors of these essays also made it clear that the women themselves had to accept some responsibility for their condition: low self-esteem and lack of awareness of their subordination, distrust of politics, lack of solidarity, and adoption of traditional models of leadership impeded their advancement.

Despite their critical perspectives on political participation, CFP members were aware that it was of vital importance if they wanted to be involved in formulating the governmental policies that determined much about their lives. Thus essayists presented critiques of the current context. One essay described how the involvement of the CFP in government-sponsored day care, the Daily Care Homes (Hogares de Cuidado Diario, or HCD),[7] had only maintained women's traditional subordination within an insufficiently funded and badly managed program.[8] Another essay addressed the impact that national economic policies had had on the population's diet and suggested the promotion of local agriculture to make staple foods more affordable, and farmers' markets to distribute produce. This remark from yet another essay summarizes the participants' perspective: "Enough already with the pretty and theoretical discourse on hunger and misery, because it isn't the same thing to live misery and to feel the pain of an empty stomach. It is necessary to formulate concrete proposals and act upon them, so that we can hope for a better tomorrow" (CFP 1994, 30).

Certain middle-class advisors were central to the development of the

---

7. See Chapter 4. In 1988 the program served 7,172 children. This figure jumped to 21,876 in 1989, and by 1993 it was up to an impressive 252,439 (Fundación del Niño 1988; Ministerio de la Familia 1989–93).

8. The special edition of the CFP bulletin *Mujeres en Lucha* (Women in Struggle) dedicated to the congress described in detail the problems encountered by the local circles that participated in the HCD program: community blame directed at the CFP for matters that were the responsibility of the government; the lack of involvement of men in the program; the contradictory information given out by the central administrator of the HCD, the Family Ministry, and its regional branches; and a lack of respect for the women running the centers (*Mujeres en Lucha* 12:23:5).

Fig. 6.1 Cover of essay collection distributed at CFP's twentieth-anniversary conference.

CFP, including in the organization of the congress. But overall, the increased mobilization of poor women took place at a time of decreasing contact with middle-class CONG member groups. Although the economic crisis created many issues around which to construct coalitions, the class divide precluded such conjunctures. This was illustrated by the way in which the CFP organized around the Beijing conference, a potential though largely missed conjuncture for national coalition building. While CFP members took part in the national organizing effort run by the CONG, their main efforts were directed through a regional network of popular educators. This outcome was due to the inability of the CONG to focus on the priorities of the majority of Venezuelan women.

The Compromising of the CONG

The CONG had had episodes of important cross-class collaboration, including the campaigns to indemnify Inés María Marcano in 1987 and to include recognition of domestic workers' rights in the Labor Law reform. But as the economic crisis deepened, the group became less able to unite women across class lines. Following the CONG sponsorship of a large demonstration protesting the rising cost of living in 1989, it did little more in the following years to respond to the economic crisis than issue an occasional declaration criticizing the government's economic policy. The struggle for individual economic survival left even middle-class women little time for organized response to the crisis.

However, even the effort the CONG did focus on in this period—putting together the national NGO report for the 1995 UN Fourth World Conference on Women—earned it accusations of skewed priorities at a time of national suffering. The loss of this opportunity for coalition building was due to the weakness of the CONG structure and the concurrent emergence of traditional political patterns.

The most visible CONG actions around the economic crisis came early in its development, in April 1989. The group joined an organization of Central University staff to sponsor a public protest against the neoliberal structural adjustment "package" *(el paquete)* of the Pérez administration and against the influence of the International Monetary Fund over Venezuelan policies.[9] Drawn by the message that women, as the mothers, housewives, and single heads-of-households responsible for putting food on the table, were the sector most adversely affected by the new economic policies, over two thousand women participated in the protest held on April 28. Protesters banged on empty skillets and milk cans to make their message ring loud and clear. Three leaders of the CONG spoke at the rally following the march (*Ultimas Notícias*, 28 April 1989). But the rally would prove to be a flash in the pan.

While the defined population and clear goals of the CFP made its autonomous, decentralized structure an asset, the same characteristics did not serve the CONG as well. The extreme decentralization of the group combined with the very different goals and political ideologies of its member organizations inclined it toward weakness. This was especially visible when political differences emerged. For example, the organization came close to complete breakdown over which side to support during the first military coup attempt against the Pérez government in February 1992 (*Fempress*, February/March 1993, 8). Some of the member groups associated with radical leftist parties wanted the CONG to publicly support the coup attempt and its leader Lieutenant Colonel Hugo Chávez Frías. But many other members opposed the coup attempt as a subversion of democracy, however imperfectly it was being carried out at the moment. As a result of this conflict, the CONG bulletin published in 1992 in support of democracy was the only one ever issued without editorial consensus.

9. In order to qualify for continuing loans from the IMF, Venezuela was subject to conditional terms that helped to dictate macroeconomic policy.

Although the CONG survived the political upheaval following the coup attempt, it continued to experience many of the problems typical of nonhierarchical groups.[10] As one member explained, "The horizontality got in the way of action." Official leadership (the *trio*) changed so frequently (twice a year) that infrastructural tasks were largely ignored. In the mid-1990s there was no regular calendar of meetings published, dues were rarely collected, and the mail was not even picked up from the post office on a regular basis. Attendance at meetings rose and fell sporadically (rising highest during elections for the *trio*). CONG meetings often lost out to the other demands on members as life became more complicated.

At the same time, this decentralization allowed the formation of an unofficial hierarchy by a few longtime activists, most of whom had leftist party backgrounds, who effectively controlled CONG activities. Group dynamics illustrated this phenomenon: decisions made at CONG meetings would not be considered valid without the attendance of certain de facto leaders, and activities would be quickly reoriented to their priorities when they participated. Many of these activities were directed at worthy causes, from supporting health care campaigns to organizing seminars. But they did not result in sustained coalition building nor did they encourage the development of new leadership.

The unofficial leadership did not seek to "colonize" the CONG directly for use by a particular party. They did try to exert control over the supposedly decentralized group, however. One way in which this was done was by the creation of "ghost" organizations that existed essentially in name only but gave their "founders" further claims to representation. In a July 1994 count of CONG member groups, six women were listed as the primary contacts for two such groups each, and one woman for four. Another effect of this unofficial CONG hierarchy was that the same people appeared as speakers at various forums for discussion of women's issues. They certainly spoke as feminists, forcefully addressing topics of great significance to women: the feminization of poverty, the lack of women's representation in decision-making positions, domestic violence, inadequate social services, and single motherhood. But in their style and rhetoric, it often seemed as though the speakers were forging ahead as the vanguard of the new revolution, simply replacing the word *workers* with the word *women* in their speeches.

In a sense, the CONG was reaping what party-based activism had

10. For more general discussion of this issue, see Siriani 1993; Razavi and Miller 1995. The analysis of the activities of the CONG during this period is based on the author's participant observation of its meetings, as well as on formal and informal interviews with past and current members.

sown. Although the feminist groups of the early 1980s had been faulted for too much "cooking together in the same sauce" *(cocinéndose en la misma salsa)*—spending too much time contemplating the internal dynamics of their groups and the nature of women's oppression instead of doing outreach—the relative lack of consciousness-raising among CONG members proved equally detrimental. CONG members did hold periodic meetings to discuss feminist principles and try to iron out differences. But these remedies could not completely counteract the influences of party-based activism.

Many members' actions reflected their political socialization, which taught appropriation of, or obedience to, leadership. One critique leveled at such actions was that women leaders were occupying the autonomous space for women's activism and subordinating other women as surely as men had done by monopolizing the power of parties. Several members commented on this pattern, ironically echoing an old phrase from the early days of AD organizing, "We are all *Adecos*" *(Todos somos Adecos).*

The emergence of hierarchical leadership was also catalyzed by changes in the relationship with the national women's agency. Tensions arose when several of the most active CONG members were appointed to the board of COFEAPRE. Although NGO members did not vote on final decisions, their presence on the directing board was a clear indication of power-holding. Such an appointment was an advance for the few women involved, but it detracted from the democratic nature of women's representation in the state. The conflict that relations between NGOs and the state produced within the CONG was reflected in the conclusions from a CONG workshop held in February 1989, which stressed its need for independence from the government. Collaboration with government entities was declared to be acceptable only on a case-by-case basis, and only when the CONG would participate in an executive capacity. Moreover, the "risks of such collaboration" were to be kept in mind (CONG 1989).

Another sign of its adoption of traditional politics was its increasing reliance on state funding. As early as January 1989, members of the CONG met with congresswomen to ask for funding from Congress and/or the Ministry of the Family, and a congressional subsidy was approved in 1992. In 1990 the CONG signed a pact with the National Culture Commission to support the publication of its bulletin, *De las mujeres* (From [or About] Women). Individual CONG groups also initiated projects funded by the national women's agency. The proposal that the CONG itself should be housed within the Ministry of the Family (circulated at CONG meetings in 1994–95) would only tie the organization more firmly to the state.

The assurance of financial support appeared highly advantageous to a

Fig. 6.2 Cover of the CONG publication "Of the Women."

group run entirely by volunteers, but the danger of state support was its potential to direct the CONG into the longstanding pattern of civil society dependence on the state. One founder of the CONG said as much in reflecting on "the paralysis that is at the point of erasing us from the map of the alternatives to traditional governmental clientelism." The innovative group was losing its autonomy on account of its search for funding, now to be granted only at the favor of the government agency for women. The funding priorities made women think first of their individual projects and tailor these to the priorities of the government agency, abandoning any radical elements in the process (Espina 1995).

The rise of hierarchy and near-clientelism within the organization resulted in the alienation of many CONG members. Women from the popular sectors, in whose name the leadership spoke but considered insufficiently "prepared" to speak for themselves, sought other avenues of expression. Feminists activists withdrew to other work. Solidarity was compromised in many directions. As a striking example, when the "women's page" in *El Nacional* was dropped again—this time following columnist Rosita Caldera's faithful and critical reporting on the debate over Venezuelan participation at the 1994 UN Conference on Population and Development in Cairo[11]—it disappeared with barely a murmur of protest from the CONG.

The Beijing Preparations of the CONG

Because of the rise of traditional political patterns within the CONG, the effect of the international organizing opportunity of the 1990s was quite different from the one of the 1980s. The prospect of the 1985 UN Women's Conference in Nairobi galvanized women activists into organizing the CONG. From its inception, the membership pledged not only to gather information on the status of women for the international meeting but also to focus its efforts on the reform of the Labor Law. In contrast, the linkage by the CONG of national preparations for the 1995 UN Fourth World Conference on Women in Beijing to women's struggles within the country stayed mainly at the level of discourse. The preparations also seemed to be yet another process by which hierarchy was reinforced, underwritten here by international funding.

Beijing preparations spread out over a year and a half and involved a series of meetings whose purpose was to compile information on the situation of women in Venezuela. Under the initial leadership of CONG members, who later formed the committee United for Venezuela en Route to Beijing (Juntas por Venezuela Camino a Beijing or JUVECABE), six assemblies were held in different cities in early 1994 to gather local information about women's status in political, economic, and social life. This information was

11. A scandal erupted among women's NGOs involved in conference planning. According to Caldera's reports in *El Nacional*, the Christian Democratic minister of the family collaborated only with a few high-profile Catholic activists who strongly opposed birth control and abortion, instead of including a representative sample of NGO positions, for the Cairo report. In response, Virginia Olivo de Celli, the former minister, who now headed her own NGO focused on women's issues (Center for Social Research, Training, and Women's Studies, CISFEM), coordinated an alternative report with several other population and/or family planning groups, which she circulated at Cairo. During the conference, one of the Catholic activists took such an uncompromising stand in support of making the Vatican position on birth control that of Venezuela that even the minister came out publicly against it. But after the conference, this activist's connections allowed her to pressure *El Nacional* to punish Caldera for airing the controversy by eliminating her column.

then compiled at the national level during a two-day conference in March 1994. Over the next months the national results were taken to a subregional meeting in La Paz, Bolivia. The subregional results were in turn presented at the regional preparatory meeting in Mar de Plata, Argentina. National-level organizing around the conference continued throughout the next year until it convened in Beijing in September 1995.

The Beijing preparatory process was not without its productive aspects. It rekindled organizing suspended during a period of divisiveness and reinvigorated activists nationwide who compiled hitherto unavailable information on women's status. Furthermore, instead of relying on a few experts to collect data on women across the country, as suggested by United Nations Development Fund for Women (UNIFEM), the six assemblies solicited testimony from women who reported on their local contexts. Press coverage of women's issues increased as the regional and international meetings grew near.

During the conference preparations the CONG also received an infusion of external funding: $8,000 of direct support as well as indirect support through the regional coordination for Beijing. This came from funders such as the Canadian International Development Agency (CIDA), the United Nations Development Fund for Women (UNIFEM), and USAID. Such support was crucial in allowing the CONG to carry out its Beijing preparations.

But those "United for Venezuela" were clearly "en Route to Beijing." The new resources had the result of focusing the attention of the CONG almost entirely in that direction as well as empowering the few women who were in contact with the external funders. Not surprisingly, they were several of the same leaders who served as national representatives to the various regional and international meetings. As a result of these developments, few activities over the course of the preparatory process addressed the impact of the national economic crisis on women.

The CONG general assembly in January 1995 made apparent the organization's external orientation, its growing attachment to the state, and its declining ability to represent Venezuelan women. Thirty people attended, representing some fifteen different groups, many of which had no more than two or three members. The most high-profile NGOs, including FEVA, CFP, and CISFEM (see note 11), did not send representatives. The low turnout reflected the diminished status of the CONG and its chronic lack of organization: some invitees found out only three days before the national assembly that it was going to take place.

The group's orientation toward Beijing activities, as well as its relationship with the government, was debated in the plenary session. Two women, a feminist activist and the director of a local women's center, challenged the emphasis on Beijing as out of step with the real needs of Venezuelan women. Those who were most involved in the process defended it as an effective mechanism for developing crucial networks both inside and outside the country. The one example of government/CONG collaboration discussed at the assembly, a literacy project, was applauded by some but also criticized by others for the lack of gender analysis informing the "technical solutions" of the Education Ministry.

Contrary to the expressed goals of the CONG itself, which were in their majority nationally focused, an examination of the group's activities for 1994 shows that its major preoccupation was with Beijing. Among the goals in the summary of the year's goals and activities distributed at the assembly were listed the promotion of women's groups throughout the country, national-level organizing against discrimination, and the promotion of state policy sensitive to the needs of women of all classes and ideologies. However, one other goal was the one that came close to justifying the bulk of that year's activities, which centered on maintaining good relations with the national women's agency and participating in international events: the exchange of experiences with other women's groups both "nationally and internationally."

In the order presented, the activities of the CONG in 1994 were: (1) maintenance of a close relationship with the national women's agency, especially through the presence of a representative of the CONG on the board of directors; (2) involvement in the Beijing coordinating committee, JUVE-CABE; (3) participation in governmental and nongovernmental research and meetings to draw up reports for Beijing; (4) attendance at the subregional and regional meetings for Beijing; (5) work on the implementation of a new law against discrimination; (6) sponsorship of one gender workshop; (7) cooperation on the literacy project at the Ministry of Education; (8) preparation for the UN Social Summit in Copenhagen (1994); and (9) organization of events for International Women's Day and the International Day Against Violence Against Women.

As this list of activities demonstrates, the CONG was not prioritizing the needs of the majority of Venezuelan women.[12] Women's organizing in Venezuela had never been adequately focused on these needs. But the deepening economic and political crises, coupled with the gearing of resources

---

12. A survey of the participants at the general assembly revealed that the attendees were not very representative of Venezuelan women: their average age was 46; 82 percent had had some form of higher education; and 50 percent belonged to a leftist party. Interestingly enough, they were similar to the majority of Venezuelan women in two other aspects: 70 percent were unmarried (either single, divorced, or widowed), and 70 percent had children (and 50 percent, great-grandchildren).

and energies toward an international conference that few women would be able to attend or benefit from directly, brought the disjuncture into high relief. In her written critique of the January 1995 CONG general assembly, founding member and outspoken feminist Gioconda Espina commented on the focus of the group and the potentially region-wide problem of misdirected international efforts:

> Counting all of the participants, we did not reach thirty. Nevertheless, the most delirious of the delirious who do not want to confront reality . . . insisted on declaring in the installation of the "national assembly" that "here we are representatives of fifty-eight[13] organizations of the country." It shames me to know that this lie was said in Mar de Plata[14] and will be repeated in Peking [Beijing]. I'm concerned that a similar situation is happening in other countries in Latin America and the Caribbean and that, thus, we are lying one to another, from network to network, while the [vast majority] of women, those whom we ought to be assisting and awakening to justify so many trips and so many preparatory pamphlets for Peking, do not know us and, when they get to know us, will scorn us for misappropriating funds in their name. "Just the same as what the men have done in the name of the people," they could say of us with complete reason. (Espina 1995)

Thus the CONG seemed to be reproducing aspects of the very politics it was set up to counteract: top-down leadership that misdirected resources and alienated supporters.

One final illustration of this lack of attention to, and simultaneous appropriation of, the representation of Venezuelan women is the video the group produced to take to Beijing. Not unaware of the controversy surrounding the focus on Beijing, the speakers following the first showing of the video justified their concentration on the international event as generating resources for, and promoting communication about, women's issues both inside and outside of the country. But the video is an almost poignant, if rather deceptive portrayal of their failings. A few of the unofficial leaders of the CONG appear frequently to promote the success of national organizing. While they are speaking about the "Venezuelan women's movement," the

13. The number of member groups of the CONG.
14. The site of the 1994 Latin American Regional Preparatory Conference for the Beijing conference, in Argentina.

footage shown is of crowds of protesters who happen to be mainly women. However, they are precisely the women with whom the CONG had little organized contact: the hungry mothers, angry neighbors, and disillusioned professionals reeling from the economic crisis.

The ability of the CONG to unite women during a time of crisis was impeded by its decentralized structure and the history of class divisions. But other developments exacerbated these problems. Close and ongoing cooperation with the government and international funding institutions threw the group's autonomy into question and lent support to hierarchical leaderships within the NGO community. While continuing to work to end women's oppression, these leaders repeated the lesson learned from years of party-based activism: centralized personal control. Referring to the reproduction of a hierarchical leadership style among supposedly feminist women, one former CONG member quoted an adage: "Witches don't exist, but those that fly, fly" (Las brujas no existen, pero las que vuelan, vuelan). The organizing around the UN Women's Conference in Beijing illustrated how far the CONG had drifted from national priorities. It directed its resources and energies toward an international goal that meant little to the majority of Venezuelan women.

Gendered Opportunities of Political Society

While civil society groups struggled with the effects of changing economic and political opportunities, female party activists, ironically, found themselves the victims of efforts to further democratize Venezuelan politics. Because they did not take gender into account, some of the very political reforms that were focused on ameliorating the highly centralized and elitist Venezuelan polity seemed to work against the promotion of women's electoral success. The most dramatic result of the electoral reforms that expanded uninominal voting was the decline of women's political representation for the first time in democratic history.

When uninominal voting was first introduced on the local level in 1989, the percentage of women fell from 21.5 to 16.4 percent of city councils. After its partial introduction on the national level in 1993, the percentage of women elected to Congress declined from 9.3 to 6.5 percent. Because congressional voting was still "mixed," that is, with some votes cast for party lists and some for individuals, the new rule's gender bias was clear: 63 percent of the women elected were those whose names appeared on the lists (see Table 2).

Table 6.1   Number and percent of women in national congress (1988–1993) and city councils (1984–1989)

Congress:

Year	Deputies			Senators		
	Total	# Women	% Women	Total	# Women	% Women
1988	201	19	9.5	46	3	6.5
1993	199	13	6.6	48	3	6.3

City Councils:

Year	Total	# Women	% Women
1984	1,592	343	21.5
1989	1,963	321	16.4

(SOURCE: CSE 1984, 1988, 1989, 1993)

As their representation declined, women continued to press for more positions of responsibility within their parties. Having introduced the idea through the 1988 United Women Leaders movement, women succeeded in having quotas established in AD and MAS, both of which adopted 20 percent quotas in all levels of decision making in 1989 and 1990, respectively. The quotas were more effectively implemented on the local than on the national level; in 1991 women made up 13 (AD) and 16 (MAS) percent of party national executive committees. Only at the most local of elected positions, the parish level, were AD and MAS women "overrepresented" (in terms of their quotas) at 26 and 24 percent respectively (Lara 1991).

But with the spread of uninominal voting, the quota system was not easily implemented. It was one thing to agree to put women up for 20 or 30 percent of the positions on party lists, however sporadically the quotas were implemented. But putting women up as candidates for uninominal election was much riskier, since the outcome was wholly dependent on their individual success. The parties assumed that voters "tend to elect those who coincide better with the dominant cultural norms or models" of politicians—that is, men—and that changes in statutes could not overcome this bias (CISFEM 1992, 191).

However, women continued to work from within parties to change both male and female attitudes. Ever vigilant, *masista* women continued to press for attention to women's issues in their party's policy making. They also tried yet another structural innovation with the establishment in 1989 of the Parliamentary Office on Women's Issues (Oficina Parlamentaria de Asuntos de la Mujer, or OPAM). OPAM was to be a place within Congress where women could raise gender-specific issues. The head of OPAM was given an office within the MAS congressional suite and the right to attend the meetings of the *masista* delegation. While the presence of OPAM was a positive step toward the inclusion of a gender perspective within the MAS legislative representation, the new bureau suffered from the familiar neglect of women's issues. Its director had to struggle to have her input taken seriously by MAS congressmembers.[15] However, with the election of historic feminist and CONG member Argelia Laya as MAS president in 1990, women continued to have an important ally within the party structure.

The women's bureaus of the centrist parties, AD and COPEI, also showed signs of reorientation toward the promotion of women's leadership, if not their other interests. Unlike the CONG, which was an inappropriate place for emergence of leadership, even an unofficial one, because it was founded to coordinate activities on issues of common concern to different women's groups, the parties' women's bureaus *were* an appropriate avenue for leadership development. The AD women's department, although compromised by its use as a personal fiefdom (see below), offered leadership training to female party members. In December 1994 a young woman who was interested in promoting women's advancement in politics and in the party was elected head of the *copeyano* women's bureau. At its national conference in March 1995, leadership training began. Workshops were held on pressing social and economic issues as well as women's participation in local politics.

Despite these moves toward restructuring party politics to give more prominence to women and their issues, they still faced significant exclusion. Recent history suggested that renewed coordination among female politicians as well as among those active in civil society could have been helped by the intervention of the national women's agency as it had been during the successful United Women Leaders movement. But the infiltration of traditional politics into this pivotal center of women's organizing contributed to the decline of women's effective coalition building.

Institutionalization Brings Instrumental Feminism to the State

From 1989 on, the national women's agency gained in importance. It grew from a presidential advisory commission into a full-fledged autonomous institute with its own local agencies and budget. But as its funding and reach

15. This struggle began when OPAM was first organized. The day it was to move into the congressional suite, the MAS office manager tried to lock out the women who had come to help set it up. However, anticipating such a reaction, a contingent of CONG sympathizers came with the head of OPAM and helped her occupy the space (Ofelia Alvarez interview).

extended, so did its mirroring of traditional politics. Some of its decentralized agencies were used by local politicians to promote clientelism, while the state agency itself became the site of hierarchical leadership. As a result, even those events that could have resulted in coalition building were turned to another end: instrumental feminism, the promotion of individual women leaders and/or their parties through events and mechanisms designed for women's advancement as a whole.

The New Women's Agency: COFEAPRE and CONAMU

As was to be expected by now, the new administration in 1989 changed the structure of the state women's agency. As in 1974, President Pérez found himself under pressure from women in his party, AD. They were not about to give up their strategic structural resource. Before the 1988 elections they had published a "women's plan" that focused on policy concerning women's issues and included the demand for an executive-branch agency to oversee its implementation. Therefore, the president added another agency to the extant women's office in the Family Ministry, reestablishing the Presidential Women's Advisory Commission (Comisión Femenina Asesora a la Presidencia, or COFEAPRE) in March 1989.

COFEAPRE "2" had more status than the original COFEAPRE of 1975: its director was called the State Minister for Women (Ministro de Estado para la Promoción de la Mujer) and was entitled to sit in on cabinet meetings. However, having been established by presidential decree, not through a statute, the national agency was still subject to the disposition of the current administration.

The mission of the second COFEAPRE was to assess women's legal, economic, and social conditions; monitor those in which women experienced discrimination; and advise state and private agencies how to address such conditions (COFEAPRE 1991). It continued to develop the decentralized offices of the former Directorate, now gearing them toward limited policy implementation. COFEAPRE sponsored workshops, participated in intersectoral government meetings, and formulated gender-sensitive public policy. The most visible of its achievements was the sponsorship of the Second Venezuelan Congress of Women (II Congreso Venezolano de la Mujer) in March 1992. Over three thousand women participated in seventeen preparatory meetings all over the country, and two thousand attended the congress itself in Caracas.

Pérez appointed *adeca* Evangelina García Prince as the state minister for women in 1991. Illustrating the growing acceptability of state action on behalf of women, García Prince, unlike the previous directors of state women's agencies, was a known activist for women's issues both inside and outside of AD. She presided over a tripling of the COFEAPRE budget, the expansion of its decentralized agencies, and an advancement in its gender perspective *(perspectiva de género)*.[16] By 1991 COFEAPRE claimed that it was interested in both "practical and strategic" gender interests, that is, those that both accepted and challenged the gendered division of labor (COFEAPRE 1992).[17] Its major focuses included reducing domestic violence, teenage pregnancy, and breast and uterine cancer, and revising the discriminatory articles of the Penal Code.

However, in his effort to "shrink the state" and further decentralize executive power, Pérez eliminated state ministers in mid-1992. Women from various sectors manifested their displeasure at the elimination of the cabinet position for women. The CONG published a paid advertisement that emphasized the importance of the state ministry in advancing women's rights and its foundation in international laws to which Venezuela was a signatory.[18] The ad demanded a replacement for the eliminated ministry in the form of a national women's commission that would not be subject to the whims of the particular administration in power but would be instituted by statute (*El Nacional*, 30 July 1992). Although such a statute was not proposed, under advice from *adecas* such as García Prince, Pérez did change the nature of the agency in December 1992, establishing the National Women's Council (Consejo Nacional de la Mujer, or CONAMU).

Reflecting the continued efforts to decentralize the executive branch, CONAMU was established as an autonomous institute under the aegis of the Presidential Secretariat. It was directed by a president and a four-person advisory committee. In a significant advance from previous agencies, it was assigned officially designated advisors from other ministries (labor, education, family, health, and justice). It also kept the commission structure of the previous women's agencies (ONM/Directorate). However, now these commissions were to design policy that would be carried out by a set of direct executors: the various regional and local-level agencies attached to CONAMU.

16. This term is the one currently and broadly used in Spanish to indicate a focus on women's and gender issues and the use of gender analysis.

17. This claim reflected the increasing influence of feminist discourse within the agency; the dualism, while questionable in its formulation, holds great currency among analysts of Latin American women's organizing. See Chapter 1 for further discussion of the separation between strategic and practical interests.

18. Most prominently, the Convention to End All Forms of Discrimination Against Women (CEDAW), which Venezuela had signed in 1982.

The decentralized reach of CONAMU extended through several different types of local women's agencies. These included a few state-level women's commissions, Comprehensive Service Centers for Women (Centros de Atención Integral a la Mujer), and the most widespread agency, the Municipal Women's Centers (Casas Municipales de la Mujer). Another significant organizational element of CONAMU was the sponsorship of national networks of NGOs. Seven networks existed by 1993, organized around the following topics: women and the environment; sexual and domestic violence support services; rural and indigenous women; women leaders of unions and professional organizations; municipal women's centers, offices, and centers for women's comprehensive services; women's studies centers; and the movement of the United Women Leaders.

The Women's Agency Adapts to Traditional Politics

Despite the improvement in the status of COFEAPRE and then CONAMU—or perhaps in part because of it—traditional political practices surfaced within the national agency. Some of its decentralized agencies, although originally founded to achieve feminist goals, were turned to clientelistic uses by local mayors. Moreover, the increased prestige of the agency's leadership began to affect its interaction with NGOs.

The reflection of traditional politics was manifest in new structures linked to COFEAPRE and CONAMU for decentralized outreach to women, despite their promising beginnings. The original aim of the Municipal Women's Centers was to provide an alternative space for feminist action and discussion. The Feminist League of Maracaibo (Liga Feminista de Maracaibo, in Zulia state) opened the first such center in 1984 to promote feminist ideas on a broad, cross-class basis, paying particular attention to the needs of poor women (CONG 1988b, 19). The center provided a place where women could hold discussions and hear talks on gender-based issues, and it offered psychological, legal, health, and employment advice to women who could not receive it elsewhere. When the Feminist League was unable to procure outside financing, it turned to the city government. With the help of MAS leader Argelia Laya, the league got in contact with a *masista* city council member who agreed to sponsor the center. League members, well aware of the nature of partisan politics, then also convinced an *adeca* and a *copeyana* council member to support the project so that it would not be seen as a *masista* program. The funding from the city (and later, state) government was always sporadic because the center insisted on maintaining its autonomy in all decision making (Interview with founder Gloria Comesaña).

The Maracaibo Center was an inspiration for a second feminist center in Maracay, Aragua state, started by the Eighth of March Street Theater Group. After traveling with their various shows promoting women's rights, members of the troupe decided that their next undertaking should be to establish a women's center. They visited Maracaibo and took the league's center as a model for their own, the Juana Ramirez[19] Women's Center (Interview with founder Laly Armengol). This center also sought to reach out to poor women through work that did not reproduce the "old vices of sectarianism, verticality, dogmatism" (CONG 1988b, 17).

Once the two feminist groups had developed the women's center model, Argelia Laya promoted it throughout the country using MAS-led city council initiatives. One of the most active centers was founded in Caracas in 1985 with the help of the Manuelita Sáenz[20] Women's Studies Program (Cátedra Libre de la Mujer) at the Central University. Others were established in municipalities in other states. Although the *copeyanas* had to be convinced that the centers should remain women's centers, and not centers for the family or the family and women, and although *masista* men wondered why they should not also found "Men's Centers" (Casas del Hombre), the women's centers took root and numbered thirty-two in eighteen states and the Federal District (Caracas) by 1993.

But as political decentralization proceeded, so did the co-optation of many of the local centers. This change resulted from efforts on the part of local politicians to increase their control during the devolution of political power. The two independent feminist centers in Maracaibo and Maracay maintained autonomy in their programming and personnel decisions, as did the Caracas center, which benefited from its link to feminist professionals at the university.[21] Starting in 1989, however, the first directly elected mayors began to use the centers set up by the municipalities to fill gaps in social service provision as well as to fulfill more direct clientelistic goals.

As a result, most municipal centers have become "one more appendage of the mayoralty," and they "change together with the policies of the mayor and reflect partisan commitments" (Interview with Luisa Melo, staff member

19. Juana Ramirez was the daughter of a freed slave who fought in the Venezuelan wars of independence.
20. Manuela Sáenz was the mistress of Simón Bolívar, the great "liberator" of the Andean region during the independence period, and is widely believed to have helped him plan his military strategies. She is known as *"la libertadora del libertador"* (the liberator [fem.] of the liberator [masc.]).
21. This center, besides providing services and workshops for women, also functions as a site for ongoing research on women's issues by faculty and students at the Central University (Rodríguez 1992).

of the Juana Ramirez Center). Typically, they are run by mayor's wives in ways that benefit their husbands' political careers.[22] Appointments to the center staff are often made to pay off political debts, and this practice has resulted in personnel "who are not always committed to the project" and who change with each new municipal administration (Rodríguez 1992, 9). Not only the continuity but also the focus of the programming through the center has been affected. Many of the centers have turned to more direct assistance services, such as day care, and at least one has held a local beauty pageant.

The use of the centers as a vehicle for clientelism has subverted the original purpose of local women's centers: cross-class feminist consciousness-raising and empowerment. As Juana Ramirez Center staff member Luisa Melo explained, "We are looking for the woman herself to begin to generate her own alternatives for change, respecting her decisions. That her life really goes through a process of change [as a result of her contact with center services and staff]." But this feminist perspective was lost by those centers attached to municipal governments. Their personnel rarely had any tie to women's organizing efforts or a dedication to women's issues. For example, when municipal centers took up an issue like domestic violence, many staff members would not discuss the broader context of gender power relations. They would not be likely to encourage a battered wife to consider divorce as an option because their priority was to maintain the family unit (Melo interview).

A 1995 visit to what was then the newest center, in Tucupita, capital of Delta Amacuro state, illustrated how the original purpose of the centers has changed.[23] The wife of the mayor was indeed the president of the center, which was more oriented toward providing day care and preschool child care than services for women's legal, psychological, and physical well-being. While child care is a priority issue for many women in the area, its provision was not the original purpose of the centers, which are increasingly assuming the burden of providing services that used to be provided by the state. Of the four separate rooms of the building, two were sex-segregated playrooms, and one served simultaneously as the center's office and as a consulting room for women. There was no provision made for in-house gynecological exams.

Thus the process of political decentralization resulted in the co-optation of the most widespread alternative structure for women's empowerment. But

22. Most of the mayors are men: in the first direct election (1989) 8.6 percent of all mayors were women; in the second (1992), this number declined to only 6.4 percent.
23. Author's visit, 8 March 1995. The comparison between the feminist and clientelistic centers is also made in Rodríguez (1992) and Montenegro, et al. (1994).

the mayors have not been the only ones to promote traditional practices. Hierarchical leadership emerged in the state agency as it had in the civil society–based groups like the CONG, especially around their interaction.

The increased control of women's organizing by COFEAPRE was well intentioned. For example, the establishment of NGO networks *(redes)* by COFEAPRE was a strategy intended to create attractive sites for heretofore scarce international funding. However, the networks were created in a top-down process by the head of COFEAPRE, Minister García Prince. As she explained in an interview, "I promoted them. It was my idea, and I called people to participate. I wrote the first founding documents of the network." As a consequence of the minister's establishment of the networks and her control over the funds they generated, the collected groups "have not participated at all in the direct administration of those resources [generated by the networks], whose sum is a mystery for the 'networked' *(en-red-adas)* organizations" (Espina 1994, 171).

Because the networks were not organic—that is, they did not grow from the inclinations and reasons to collaborate of the NGO themselves—they did not continue to operate much beyond their founding meetings. For example, the organic movement that came together as the United Women Leaders movement in 1988 and had led to an increase in women's representation in government was formally convoked as a network by the CONAMU on International Women's Day, 8 March 1993. One hundred and fifty-four participants signed on to the founding document. But the network did little afterwards.[24] Most networks are not actively operating today.

Instrumental Feminists Undermine Coalition Building

Beyond the compromising of women's organizing structures, effective conjunctural coalition building declined during this period. Little legislation of particular consequence to women was passed after the reform of the Labor Law in 1990. Attempts at enforcing the workplace day-care provisions of the reformed Labor Law went no further than the periodic denunciation of its absence by various groups. Finally, no coherent message about, or set of solutions to, the gendered effects of the economic crisis was brought to the public's attention. Instead, the most visible manifestations of women's united activity in the 1990s were permeated by instrumental feminism.

---

24. As JUVECABE described this network in the book about Venezuelan women's organizing prepared for Beijing, *Mujeres: Una Fuerza Social en Movimiento* (Women: A Social Force in Movement), "Unfortunately, a series of factors, not yet sufficiently studied, prevented it from becoming a positive success" (Delgado Arrias 1995, 26).

The COFEAPRE-sponsored Second Women's Congress, entitled "Women and Power" (Mujer y Poder) took up many matters that had not been discussed in previous conferences. It covered included a wide range of topics that affect women: gendered relationships of power, politics, civil society, economics, union and professional organizing, quality of life (including health and poverty), violence, education, international relations, and communication.

The congress not only focused on issues of women and power but also exemplified women's use of power politics. Feminist commentator Espina called it the "millionaire congress about poor women" (*El Nacional,* 26 March 1991), yet another example of female leaders' inability to connect with the majority of Venezuelan women. She attributed this failure to the worst vices of "machista activism" that women had developed the habit of duplicating: "disorganization, authoritarianism, scorn of base-level activists, misappropriation of public moneys, competition, sabotage of the presentations by women of the 'other' party, including of the 'other' tendency of the same party" (Espina 1994, 171). Was this not the very same sort of conduct fostered in male-dominated parties, she argued, that had led women to feel the need to organize separately? (*El Nacional,* 28 February 1991).[25]

In another of the more detrimental misuses of the hard-won attention to women's issues, an important law benefiting women was derailed by the actions of one instrumental feminist. She forced through Congress a largely unnecessary and ill-prepared piece of legislation, the Equal Opportunities Law (Ley de Igualdades de Oportunidades). Unlike proposals genuinely aimed at improving women's economic or social situations, this effort was transparently a power grab on the part of an *adeca* senator, who, according to various sources, had already "captured" the women's bureau of her party for her power base. In 1990 she decided to introduce her proposal around the time when COFEAPRE—which happened to be headed by a political rival—introduced its own carefully researched proposal to have the state women's agency finally established by national law and no longer subject to presidential decree. Congress would not consider both proposals, so over the next two years the congressional Bicameral Commission for Women's Rights negotiated a merger.

25. In columns published soon after the congress, Espina responded to the objection that she should not be airing the women's movement's dirty laundry in public. Conference organizers entreated women to "act like the men" and close ranks, keeping their differences to themselves. Espina argued that such behavior also replicated the "machista" activism that had gotten women nowhere (*El Nacional,* 26 March 1991). Her February 28 column was pointedly entitled "Igual a *Ellos*" (Equal to Them [*ellos* = masc. third person plural]).

The result was an unwieldy law that repeated much of the antidiscrimination legislation already contained in the constitution, the Civil Code, the Labor Law, and CEDAW. It also established a Women's Defense Office that would overlap with the extant Women's Unit in the attorney general's office. Finally, the law did legally establish the national women's agency, calling for the founding of the National Women's Institute (Instituto Nacional de la Mujer, or INAMU). This would put an end to its uncertain status and design, dependent on the whims of passing presidents. Although the law was widely recognized to be full of flaws, its sponsor cashed in political chips to get it passed in a flurry of end-of-the-year bills in 1992.

Because the law had not been generated through the same coalition-building effort underlying past campaigns, it lacked supporters who would fight for its implementation. As a result, President Rafael Caldera, re-elected in 1994, chose to decree the continuation of CONAMU instead of complying with the law to permanently establish INAMU. Thus the one real advance in the badly flawed law, the founding of the permanent national agency for women's rights, proved useless. Meanwhile Bicameral Commission meetings were taken up with discussion of how to implement the new law, with its sponsor's loyal political allies declaring that it should remain unchanged and a few dissenters suggesting its revision.[26]

Assembling the official delegation to Beijing proved to be another occasion for exploiting opportunities for women's advancement for personal gain. Every member of the Bicameral Commission on Women's Rights and two of their "consultants" asked for congressional funding to participate in the delegation. The many requests for several-thousand-dollar trips to China in the midst of Venezuela's worst financial crisis caused such a scandal in Congress that only three deputies were subsidized, and then *all* paid congressional travel outside of the country was suspended for the rest of the year (*El Nacional,* 9 July 1995). The official representatives to Beijing included four members of CONAMU (including one who also was active in the CONG), the Venezuelan representative to the Organization of American States, and a staff member from the foreign affairs ministry. They were accompanied by fifteen "consultants," including the three deputies and the two CONG members who worked most closely with CONAMU.

Instrumental feminists also showed their colors in the struggle over political control of the Caracas municipality, a struggle that was evident in its celebration of International Women's Day (8 March 1995). The speakers roster was carefully balanced between women from the two main parties com-

26. Author's observations during 1994–95.

peting for control of the municipal government: AD and Radical Cause (Causa R).[27] Little schooled in the arts of instrumental feminism, the Causa R women did not take full advantage of the opportunity; one even questioned the need for a women's day because she herself had never felt discriminated against. The *adeca* speakers, on the other hand, noted that the *causa errista* (Causa R member) mayor, Aristóbulo Izturiz, had not deigned to participate in the assembly and questioned his party's commitment to women's issues. But their own motives were questionable. The *adeca* senator who had sponsored the problematic Equal Opportunities Law ended her speech by shouting, "All women are *adecas!*" (*¡Todas las mujeres somos adecas!*). She received loud applause and cheers from a balcony packed with supporters from AD's women's bureau, bussed in for the occasion. Thus, even the celebration of the traditional day for promoting women's causes was turned to the advancement of particular political positions.

As a result of the rise of traditional politics and instrumental feminism, the model of coalition building that women had built up through much effort had been rendered largely useless by the mid-1990s. The prominent events of the period between 1990 and 1995 were exploited to promote certain highly placed women leaders or their parties, and opportunities were lost to make significant improvements benefiting all Venezuelan women.

The 1990s saw a decline in women's conjunctural coalition building. Faced with the concurrent transitions in economic and political models, women's organizing also changed, but not toward increasing collaboration. Poor women, never fully included as subjects of previous women's mobilizations, continued to organize nationally through their own group, the Popular Women's Circles. They confronted the devastating effects of the economic crisis by increasing their activism around basic needs, while continuing to develop a gender-based awareness of their position in the home, community, and nation. Although they were helped in their efforts by individual middle-class activists, there was little significant cross-class organizing in response to the new conditions.

Women's efforts to reach across the class divide and to build coalitions, while never fully effective, were complicated by the crisis. But they were also compromised by the introduction within women's organizations of certain patterns of behavior reminiscent of traditional politics. Although many of

27. Causa R (the "R," for Radical, is usually written backwards, invoking a vaguely Soviet link) is a workers' party that rose to national prominence in the late 1980s, effectively challenging MAS as the "third force" in Venezuelan politics.

the problems the CONG, the national NGO network, had in organizing women stemmed from its weak structure, they were exacerbated by the emergence of an unofficial leadership. While they played an essential role in founding the alternative space for women's organizing, they continued to act in part according the party model of political interaction, relying on centralized and hierarchical command and hand-in-glove cooperation with the national women's agency. This tendency toward centralization was compounded by the new financial linkage of the two organizations and by the receipt of other sources of financing from abroad. Such linking jeopardized the delicate balancing act between autonomy and co-optation through the "Midas touch" that had corrupted other aspects of Venezuelan political life.

The state agency for women also reflected these traditional patterns, allowing for its decentralized agencies to succumb to clientelistic treatment on the part of local politicians and asserting control over NGO operation. Instrumental feminists also began to use the resources available to promote themselves or their parties. As a result, the few potential opportunities for coalition building, including the Beijing conference, were severely compromised by the predominance of traditional political behavior.

VENEZUELAN ALTERNATIVES,
GENDERED OPPORTUNITIES, AND
WOMEN'S ORGANIZING IN LATIN
AMERICAN DEMOCRATIZATION

Few who study Latin American politics have thought about the growing impact of women's political participation, and few who study women's movements have cared about political parties or the state. Democracy, and women, deserve better.

—Jane S. Jaquette, The Women's Movement in Latin America

By examining the development of Venezuelan women's organizing during the process of democratization, this book has aimed at giving the study of both women and democracy in Latin America what they "deserve": a focused analysis of the interaction between women's movements and formal political institutions. The specific cases at hand illuminate general problems women face in taking part in democratic politics. The changing political opportunities conditioning social mobilization in the transition to democracy, though paradoxically freeing some sectors to act politically under authoritarian rule, can also freeze their actions with the return of democracy. But women have to contend with particular, gendered obstacles to their participation. In facing such obstacles, women often turn to regendering their opportunities.

Before presenting a summary of the obstacles to women's participation and the responses women have devised, this chapter briefly analyzes another innovative political movement in Venezuela: the neighborhood movement. As mentioned in previous chapters, this movement has presented itself as an alternative to traditional politics, particularly in its attempts to act independently of political parties. Comparing the development of this autonomous movement with that of women's organizing reveals some of the more general (as opposed to gendered) challenges that women have confronted and what lessons can be learned for civil society as a whole from the two movements.

Venezuelan Neighborhood Organizing

Women have not constituted the only group marginalized by the dynamics of Venezuelan democratization. Party- and state-based representation has historically privileged class-based interests to the exclusion of other claims. As discussed in Chapter 2, labor in particular benefited from its effective structural incorporation into political parties. In their study of the semicorporatist network of interest groups linked to the executive branch, Brian Crisp, Daniel Levine and Juan Carlos Rey (1995, 154–55) found that economically defined groups participated five times more frequently than other types, confirming this link as a channel for the more traditional of interest groups.[1]

Among some observers of contemporary Venezuelan politics, the neighborhood movement and its organizational base in the Neighborhood Associations (Asociaciones de Vecinos, or AVs) has appeared as one of the best hopes for the transformation of citizen politics.[2] Active for three decades, this movement has as its primary goal the representation of the territorial-based interests of local communities—or of neighbor-citizens. However, its frustrations with politics as usual has led it beyond seeking local benefits to demanding reform of the entire political system in order to give individual citizens greater say in the politics that govern their lives. Not coincidentally, it also attempts to limit the power of the historically monopolistic parties.

---

1. As a result, they call for a restructuring of the mechanism by moving commissions from the executive to the legislative branches and expanding representation: "Entirely new sectors must also be given a voice. After all, civil society is comprised of more than economically defined groups. Traditionally important sectors like the Church, military, or students have long had a reduced role, and new groups such as feminists, human rights advocates, environmentalists, *vecinos* (neighbors), and the like have yet to be granted access at all" (Crisp, Levine, and Rey 1995, 158). As Chapters 4, 5, and 6 show, feminists in fact did have a channel of access to the state in the national women's agency, albeit one that varied in importance and effectiveness.

2. As Edgardo Lander claims: "Of all the social movements that have arisen in the last decades, the neighborhood movements, especially the Neighborhood Associations, are the most important new social actors in the Venezuelan democratic political system. Other movements . . . have not had the continuity, nor the levels of theoretical/political elaboration which have resulted in the neighborhood movements achieving a symbolic efficacy that has permitted them to have an intercession in the political system that is greater than their organizational force" (1995, 131, n. 8). For more on the neighborhood movement, see Santana 1983; García Guadilla 1994; Levine 1998.

In Latin America, neighborhood-based organizing is typically associated with the popular classes. During the Venezuelan transition to democracy, *barrio*-based organizations called Communal or Pro-Development Councils (*Juntas Comunales* or *Juntas Pro-desarrollo*) were established. But unlike similar organizations in the region, often assembled by the neighbors themselves to demand services and organize around other neighborhood-related issues, these early councils were primarily created by the national government to distribute unemployment benefits to a restive population (Lander 1995, 38; García Guadilla 1994, 61). In this capacity they functioned more as clientelistic vehicles than as autonomous organizations for the defense of the urban poor.

In contrast, by the late 1960s middle-class urban residents in Venezuela, concerned about the abuse of municipal political power and the encroachment of urban development on their neighborhoods, were beginning their own AVs (neighborhood associations). To coordinate their efforts, fourteen AVs joined together to form the Federation of Urban Community Associations (Federación de Asociacíones de Comunidades Urbanas, or FACUR) in 1971. With the 1978 reform in municipal law giving city governments the responsibility for fostering the growth of AVs, such organizing spread across the country (Ellner 1993–94, 22). FACUR became a model: by 1990 similar associations had spread to every state, reaching all classes. The Neighbors' School (Escuela de Vecinos, or EV) has helped spread the movement through leadership training, publications, weekly radio shows, and a television show (Hellinger 1991, 170–71; Lander 1995, 38; Levine 1998, 25–27).[3] Currently, between ten and fifteen thousand AVs exist. In order to form a Neighborhood Association, fifty family representatives have to agree to participate and register with local government (Hillman 1994, 82; *El Universal*, 28 March 1998).

The activities of the movement extend from the local to the national level. Local events include cultural activities, workshops on neighborhood issues, environmental activism, historical preservation, and contact with other civil society–based groups (Hellinger 1991, 171; Lander 1995, 40). With another reform of municipal laws in 1985, AVs also became empowered to represent neighborhoods before their city councils. This step into municipal governance has led to increased activism at the national level, directed at ensuring citizen participation in democratic politics. At this level, they have focused on such issues as decentralization and electoral reform.

3. Elías Santana (current president of the Neighbors' School and historic leader of the movement) broadcasts the program *Buenas Noticias* (Good News) to highlight the work of neighborhood leaders, as well as to publicize community events and useful publications for neighborhood organizations (*El Universal*, 20 March 1998).

Supported by a petition signed by 140,000 people, the neighborhood movement spearheaded the successful reform of electoral laws in 1991. This effort, under the guidance of the EV spin-off group We Want to Choose (Queremos Elegir), resulted in the direct election for the first time of governors, mayors, and parish councils, and the possibility of recalling government officials (Navarro 1995b; Levine 1998, 25). We Want to Choose continues to promote electoral reform, from backing the 1998 reform of the Suffrage and Political Participation Law to surveying citizens' attitudes toward politics (*El Universal*, 7 October 1998). One neighborhood movement-based group, Citizen Decision (Decisión Ciudadana), has even won in a municipal election (Salamanca 1995, 206–7).

Through its legal reform efforts, the neighborhood movement has positioned itself in favor of a democracy of citizens rather than a democracy of parties (Lander 1995, 133). Municipal law forbids AV leaders, when acting in official capacity, from identifying their partisan affiliations (Ellner 1993–94, 26). Many AVs have viewed political parties as primarily interested in co-optation. Indeed, all major parties have tried to capture neighborhood organizations by channeling state and party patronage their way in exchange for partisan support and control (Hellinger 1991, 171; Levine 1998, 27). In the 1980s AD and COPEI started "neighborhood" bureaus and secretariats to further "partisan penetration and co-optation" (García Guadilla 1994, 62). Such efforts increased with the growing power of AVs in municipal matters.

As a result of the parties' behavior, the rhetoric of the movement is strongly antiparty. It recognizes parties as having had a role in consolidating democracy but now sees them as "the principal obstacles in deepening it" (Lander 1995, 132, n. 13). Thus the movement promotes reforms such as uninominal elections in order to ensure more direct, less partisan representation of citizens in matters concerning them. In theory, uninominal or single-candidacy elections give individual voters, instead of political parties, the choice over their representatives. Parties have more control when lists, particularly closed lists, are used in a proportional representative system. In practice, however, the reforms have reinforced the representation of traditional parties, whose candidates have the resources and experience through which to mount the most successful campaigns (Lander 1995, 134, n. 18).

In a party-permeated context complete political autonomy has not been possible. Even FACUR, as it became stronger and more effective—that is, more institutionalized—fell prey to charges of partisanship and clientelistic behavior. As a result, several leaders left the organization to start other nonpartisan groups (Gómez Calcaño 1997). Fear of party penetration has impeded extensive national coordination of the movement (Ellner 1993–94, 27).

But at least in middle-class associations, and to a great extent at the national level, avoiding politicization continues to be a principal goal.

Perhaps unavoidably, especially when the focus is on local issues rather than the promotion of democracy, the neighborhood movement has split along class lines (García Guadilla 1994, 67). Because they lack resources, the more numerous *barrio*-based AVs are more inclined to enter into clientelistic relationships with parties (Ellner 1993–94, 25). Moreover, in a situation of scarcity, the promotion of neighborhood-based claims, such as the attempt by middle-class AVs to contain the spread of neighboring *barrios,* often brings poor and well-off neighborhoods into direct conflict (Hellinger 1991, 171). One analyst has gone as far as to identify the model of citizenship promoted by the movement as more "the defense of that which exists" (private property) as opposed to "the securing of that which isn't possessed" (state welfare) (Lander 1995, 140). Such a model reflects the desires of the middle-class founders.

Whatever its ultimate success in either bridging the class divide or democratizing the state, the neighborhood movement has clearly presented an alternative to party-based representation. Its organizing style tends to be decentralized and network based rather than hierarchical and leader driven. Moreover, instead of focusing on gaining power, the movement has sought to change the "rules of the game" (Levine 1998, 30, 35). The continuing insistence on autonomous action has meant that AVs often draw together during what are perceived as party-created economic and political crises (Hellinger 1991, 171). In presenting such alternatives, the movement can be fairly said to be having an impact on the political culture of Venezuela (Lander 1995, 38).

Comparing the neighborhood movement to women's organizing reveals several differences. Clearly, the neighborhood movement is much larger than the women's movement, garnering a significant following all over the country. The aims of the movements differ as well, the AV's tending to be either specific to a particular area or concerned with reforming the political institutions of democracy.

But comparison also reveals that the two movements have faced similar challenges and have responded with some parallel strategies. Throughout their organizing, both have experienced partisan manipulation and the threat of co-optation, including parties' attempts to channel the movements' demands and energies through party bureaus. In response, both have developed alternatives to the parties' representational monopolization. Started by middle-class activists, both neighborhood and women's organizations have sought to democratize Venezuela by changing the rules of the game through legal reform. To do so, they have developed alternative, network-based structures allowing for autonomy among member groups. Both have experienced conflict over class differences.

In general, thus, the representation of those social categories that are not strictly class-based experience similar structural discrimination. They cannot be easily represented by institutions constructed to represent class or occupational interests. As a result, they are more likely to seek alternative avenues of expression. Such innovation may or may not have a direct effect on the political system, but it clearly augments the capacity of civil society to expand citizen representation. However, because interests that are not class-based—the so-called identity-based interests—cannot be as easily defined or expressed as those based on class, institutionalization remains problematic.[4]

One potential solution to the problem of institutionalizing the representation of nonclass-based identities is to build a political party specifically for the representation of given identities. For example, Green parties have been established to represent the "postmaterial" demands of voters, including, but not limited to, preservation of the environment (Kitschelt 1993, 94).[5] These parties seem to be most electorally viable when promoting issues that are both salient to significant sectors of the electorate and not explicitly addressed by more "catch-all" parties. Moreover, they tend to be less hierarchically organized and more participatory than traditional parties.

Green parties have succeeded in the formal political representation of nonclass-based identities as well as in serving as a bridge between formal political institutions and informal social movements. However, their radically democratic structures have resulted in some of the familiar problems of such organizations, including a lack of formalized accountability mechanisms and high demands on activists' time, as well as a firmly middle-class basis of active membership. Moreover, environmental movement participants are wary of only forming alliances with one, admittedly less powerful, party (Kitschelt 1993, 101). And finally, the success of party-based solutions to identity representation will vary depending on the characteristics of a given identity. For example, because women as a gender do not share all the same interests, building a women's party around a single set of issues would prove quite difficult.

---

4. Philip Oxhorn (1995, 29–34) makes similar points with respect to the difference between party/labor and party/popular organization relationships.

5. The material/postmaterial dichotomy is widely held to indicate relative focus on physical security and material prosperity versus more lifestyle-oriented issues of those who have "resolved" their immediate material needs (See Inglehart 1991; Kitschelt 1993, 94). The so-called new social movements of environmentalism and feminism are often seen as prime examples of postmaterial politics. However, as this study (among others) shows, such a clear division between material and postmaterial concerns does not hold up particularly well, at least in the developing world.

Several important questions regarding women's struggles for democratic representation remain. How have the political opportunities of democratization marginalized women? How have they responded? What additional challenges do they face as democracy becomes consolidated? To answer these questions, Venezuelan women's experiences are compared below with findings from the rest of Latin America and, occasionally, the world. Such comparisons reveal that even in different contexts women have confronted similar structural and ideological impediments to their participation and often have adopted similar strategies to contend with them. The chapter concludes with an additional reflection on the study of women and democratization: Can women be treated as an interest group, the sine qua non of civic participation in democratic regimes?

Gendered Political Opportunities

The primary exclusionary institution examined in this study is the political party. Even before the inception of democracy, the democratic centralist parties that provided the model of Venezuelan political participation, through both their own organizations and those they heavily influenced (such as the major peak organizations), institutionalized gender discrimination within their very structures. Because of parties' strength and entrenchment in society, this has had a seriously detrimental impact on women's participation. But similar discrimination can be found in other countries in the region, both historically and in current contexts.

Party Leadership

In terms of decision making, participation in the leadership ranks of the most powerful organizations in civil and political society was based on requirements not easily fulfilled by women. These requirements formed a constellation that revolved around the central obligation: a leader's full-time devotion to party life. Most women had (or were assumed to have) the traditionally female responsibilities of the private sphere that kept them from exercising this role.

Such de facto exclusion from party leadership has of course not been unique to Venezuela. And even when, elsewhere in the region, women have ascended to leadership positions, they have found themselves marginalized. For example, although women's rights activist Magda Portal was the first secretary-general of Peru's historically powerful APRA party, she could not prevent the party leadership from setting aside women's agenda of seeking equality in civil, economic, and political rights. When she protested, she was demoted and sent abroad. As described in her novel *La Trampa* (The Trick), the party leadership barred her from policy meetings and ignored her suggestions. Yet it kept her on as the only woman on the executive board so that "no one [could] accuse the party of excluding women" (Chaney 1971, 300; see also S. Alvarez 1986, 122).

In more recent times, a vice president of the Christian Democratic party in Chile explained why few women could compete with men for leadership positions in parties: "The good leader in our traditional style is he who visits with the members, goes out in the evenings, holds meetings at night, goes to all the neighborhood organizations. In the case of a provincial leader, he ought to have time to visit all the provincial organizations, and a woman has objective limitations" (as quoted in Muñoz Dálbora 1987, 158–59). Yet even those women who have managed to overcome their "objective limitations" and hold leadership positions in the now democratic country are not completely accepted by their male peers. Those who are may have gained acceptance because of their association with (and presumed obedience to) male leaders:

> Even though women have gained some leadership positions within the parties, they are still viewed with unease and distrust by their male peers, who are bothered by the women's "otherness" and try to avoid or push them aside. Women are subject not only to discrimination but also to the political control of their male peers in government and within political parties. Often this political control is practiced, implicitly or explicitly, by a family member or spouse. Thus, quite a few women who have been nominated to decisionmaking posts are directly related to a male political leader. Even though these women certainly have credentials of their own to make them eligible, their family links seem to make them more trustworthy in the eyes of the political establishment. (Frohmann and Valdés 1995, 290)

Globally, the proportion of women in leadership positions in parties is quite low. In one survey of 871 parties, 67 percent had no women in their governing body, with the remaining parties having "at least one" woman (IPU 1997, 15). Few studies reveal political parties to be unforced promoters of women's leadership or issues. Where discrimination has been particularly pervasive, women have chosen to organize outside of parties, as described below.

However, where women have united from inside and outside of parties, they have succeeded in improving their numbers in leadership positions. Those parties that have responded often have initiated some form of "positive discrimination," such as quotas for internal and external elections and appointments. Not surprisingly, quotas are becoming more popular as a mechanism to increase women's leadership in Latin American parties: according to one study, at least one party in Argentina, Bolivia, Brazil, Costa Rica, Ecuador, Mexico, Uruguay, and Venezuela has established such quotas, and in some of these countries more than one (IPU 1997, 67). Recent research on the implementation of such quotas in Argentina and Nicaragua has shown that beyond fixing a proportion of candidates for office, a strategy such as the *trienza* ("braid")—which requires the insertion of the names of female candidates regularly throughout party lists to give them a proportion of winning positions—is needed to ensure that the quotas are more than window dressing (Jones 1996; Luciak 1997).

As described in Chapter 1, national laws requiring that all parties implement some level of quota have been passed in several Latin American countries. Recent developments in Venezuela reflect regional trends. Responding to the low levels of female representation in elective positions, the National Women's Council and congresswomen active in the Bicameral Commission for Women's Rights promoted an article within the 1998 Suffrage and Political Participation Law to ensure that all parties' electoral lists, whatever the election, would have at least 30 percent female candidates.

This reform has the potential to ensure the election of a certain number of women. But there are problems to be anticipated that may keep women's electoral successes low. First, the reform does not include a provision for ensuring women's representation throughout the electoral list, such as the Argentine *trienza* that gives women and men the same chance at electable positions. Without such a provision, women may find themselves at the bottom third of the lists, far from the winning positions. Second, with the increasing use of uninominal elections, in which list-specific quotas cannot be implemented (and are in any case specifically prohibited by the new quota legislation), this particular solution is unavailable.

In general, while quotas have been heralded—and adopted—as the best solution to women's underrepresentation in political participation, they are not without their pitfalls. Without question, they can improve the numbers of women in leadership positions. It is unclear, however, whether an increase in women's numbers will automatically lead to the representation of their other interests. Particularly in countries where party loyalty is strong, women elected from party slates may feel more pressure to represent party interests than those of women. Moreover, in countries such as those in the Latin American region where the executive branch is stronger than the legislative branch—or where power resides outside of elective channels—ensuring women's presence in the legislature may not ensure legislation promoting the substance of women's interests.

Party Membership

The vast majority of female party members will always remain within the membership ranks. But the manner in which they are often incorporated into the parties has made a marked difference in the influence they wield in comparison to other sectors. In Venezuela, the mechanism designed to bring women into parties, the women's bureau, has not functioned for women the way it has for sectors such as labor and the peasantry. Whereas those originally male sectors were organized in such a way as to successfully represent their interests and even include some of their leadership in high party positions, women were mainly mobilized to take on infrastructural tasks. The founders of parties incorporated the traditional gendered division of labor into membership structures. The result was that the women's sectoral organizations took on the reproductive tasks of the political sphere, becoming the "housewives" of the parties.

This type of inclusion was justified by the fact that when the parties were originally founded, in the 1930s and 1940s, a great majority of women did focus on reproductive tasks in the home. Thus, extending those responsibilities into the public sphere was an effective way to give women a niche. But even at that time such incorporation ignored that women were already busily working to improve their subordinate position in society, law, and the economy. As the activists of the time discovered, their incorporation into party politics did not help them much in their efforts. Instead, it made them responsible for doing the party's dishes.

Women's marginalization within party politics and its detrimental impact on their organizing efforts is a common theme in Latin American history. One chronicler of this history, Francesca Miller, writes: "The usual strategy was to create a 'women's section' of a party, a tactic that at once mobilized women on its behalf and marginalized them from leadership and policymaking power, which remained in the hands of the male political hierarchy" (1991, 112). Such an effect was evident in the first period of

Chilean democracy. By the mid-1930s women from leftist parties, women's organizations, and workers' associations had founded a national group, the Movement for the Emancipation of Chilean Women (Movimiento pro Emancipación de Mujeres de Chile, or MEMCH), to promote women's economic, social, and legal rights. It also supported the Popular Front (Frente Popular), the multiparty, left-leaning coalition of disaffected elites, the middle class, and organized workers. However, MEMCH went into decline when parties within the Popular Front started to recruit women into their own organizations through women's bureaus (Gaviola Artigas et al. 1986; Muñoz Dálbora 1987, 60–61).

Recent democratization attests to continuing problems with incorporation through women's bureaus. Argentine women's activism during the "Dirty War" (1976–82) led to "the inescapable need to incorporate women into the process of democratization," and in the transition to democracy every party started a women's bureau. However, following the first democratic elections in 1983, political leaders did not follow through on women's demands (Feijoó and Nari 1994, 116–17). Similar results occurred in the democratization process in Chile (Chuchryk 1991, 173–74).

Indeed, there is now worldwide evidence that women's bureaus, while remaining the most common mechanism to facilitate the entry of women into party life, are not usually employed for the advancement of women or their issues through the party. One study of sixty-eight countries reveals that women's bureaus exist in three out of four of them and in over half of all political parties; in some countries all parties have such bureaus. It is often the only means for incorporating women into political life. However, there is no evidence of direct correlation between the existence of a women's bureau and increased legislative representation for women, increased preparation of female candidates, or improved party policies to encourage women's participation (such as providing day care or holding meetings in the evenings) (IPU 1997, 137–38).

As with women's advancement in party leadership, the rare instances in which a women's bureau has contributed to women's advancement have been those in which three conditions prevail: parties have at least a nominal commitment to women's inclusion; women's organizations within the parties have some organizational flexibility; and women are positioned outside of parties to take advantage of a mechanism for representation. For example, the Salvadoran guerrilla-force-turned-political-party, the FMLN, is over one-third women. Its women's bureau proved to be a key factor in the increase of women's representation in national decision-making bodies to 33 percent and the adoption of a women's rights agenda in the party platform. It also ensured that female candidates had autonomy in conducting their 1997 election campaigns so as not to suffer from gender discrimination in the distribution of resources (Luciak 1997, 2). AMNLAE, the women's organization of the FMLN's Nicaraguan counterpart, the FSLN, also fought successfully for increased female representation within the party. Both organizations have instituted gender-awareness training within the decision-making ranks of their respective parties and have joined with other groups in civil society to promote women's platforms during recent electoral periods (Luciak 1997).

Similarly, as this study has shown, Socialist Women, a social movement organization linked to the socialist party MAS, was able to have some influence on party platforms and help its members develop a socialist-feminist perspective on society. Its members went on to participate in every gender-based campaign in civil society and continue to remain active in promoting women's issues within MAS.

The State

The other gendered institution examined in this study is the state bureaucracy. From the inception of democracy in Venezuela, the semicorporatist network of the decentralized administration and advisory commissions attached to the executive branch facilitated the state-based representation of class-based interest groups, primarily labor and capital. This mechanism was a crucial channel of communication for these sectors' demands because it provided a source of direct access to the powerful executive branch. But, as was the case with political parties, the incorporation of sectors in this manner was based on the representation of predominantly economically defined groups, usually composed mainly of, and led by, men. State-based representation excluded women as a group.

Women strategized to regender this political opportunity by demanding the establishment of a national women's agency. But once established, the agency did not guarantee women's access to the state. Since its inception in 1974, the mechanism for women's representation within the executive branch has been placed in a subordinate position vis-à-vis other state bureaus. It has had a history of insufficient resources, and its very existence has been subject to the whims of passing administrations. Even after a law was passed institutionalizing the agency as a permanent part of the executive branch, the next president refused to take the necessary steps for the implementation of the National Women's Institute, preferring to reestablish the National Women's Council by decree. The structural inscription of women's subordinate status in the state hierarchy was compounded by the choice of subjects assigned to the women's agency, such as social affairs instead of economic planning. A study of national women's agencies in the region shows that they are often accorded a similar secondary status (Htun 1998, 18–23).

Legislative branches are also arenas for structural gender discrimination. Here again, even where women have succeeded in gaining a commission on women's rights, the overwhelming majority of legislators are usually men who are not interested in according such a commission much influence. Perhaps the best-known example of a gendered element of a legislature is the "authoritarian enclave" within the democratic Chilean senate. Because of the presence of nine senators appointed by former dictator Augusto Pinochet, the senate has a distinctly patriarchal and rightist bias that translates into opposition to progressive gender policies. The national women's agency, the National Women's Service (Servicio Nacional de la Mujer, or SERNAM), has suffered in both its institutional capacity and its ability to implement policy because of the opposition of such senators and their supporters (Morgan 1996, 77; Waylen 1996a, 109).

International Opportunities

International opportunities oriented toward improving women's status also formed a crucial part of the context in which Venezuelan women's organizing developed. The women's suffrage campaign of 1940–47 drew support from regional networking on the issue. The more contemporary feminist movement was influenced by the spread of "second-wave" feminism throughout the Western world. Women drew on the legitimation of women's issues fostered by the UN's International Women's Year (IWY) in 1975 to demand the establishment of the national women's agency. It was also the occasion of a state-sponsored national women's meeting, the first in the sixteen years since the transition to democracy began. The second incarnation of the national women's agency, the Ministry for the Participation of Women in Development, was established partly in response to the theme of the UN Decade on Women (1976–85) that women should be integrated into development. Proponents of the 1982 Civil Code reform cited international documents in support of women's equality in the family. The 1985 meeting in Nairobi that closed the UN Decade on Women proved to be a watershed for activists in Venezuela: it inspired the creation of a national NGO umbrella network, the maintenance of some form of state women's agency, the cooperation of these two entities, and the justification and legislative support required for the reform of the Labor Law.

These international influences are hardly unique to Venezuela. Studies of the development of women's movements in Latin America and elsewhere invariably note the important role that IWY and the Decade on Women have had on stimulating both state action on women's issues and women's movement formation (Jaquette 1994a; Basu 1995a). For example, because the UN conference to mark IWY in 1975 was held in Mexico, it also served as a catalyst for the development of the Mexican feminist movement. Mexican women held an alternative "counter congress" to voice the demands of nongovernmental activists and increased cross-class linkages between middle-class and poor women (Lamas et al. 1995, 332, 325). In Ecuador, the initiation of the Decade on Women sparked the growth of both an autonomous women's movement and state attention to women's issues (Lind 1992, 140). Even the authoritarian Brazilian regime allowed women to organize commemorations of International Women's Day during IWY, which spurred the expansion of the women's movement in that country (S. Alvarez 1990, 82; Soares et al. 1995, 307).

But international opportunities have not produced wholly positive developments for women's organizing. Analysis of the effect of transnational organizing opportunities on national contexts reveals that domestic conditions combine with global opportunities in ways that may be detrimental as well as productive for national women's movements. The process of preparing for the 1995 UN Fourth World Conference on Women in Beijing, like the preparatory process for Nairobi, had its salutary consequences in Venezuela. It provided another opportunity for studying the status of women, including the collection of data on many subjects by NGOs around the country. However, the influx of international funding around Beijing encouraged the emergence of traditional patterns of centralized leadership within the NGO network. Moreover, the focus on an international event at a time of intertwined social, economic, and political crises within the country alienated some supporters and failed to generate much of a national response from women. Congresswomen's requests for funding to attend the conference were greeted by a national outcry of disapproval.

Regionally, the impact of Beijing has been mixed. As a whole, the international conference process again served to legitimize local, national, and regional demands for greater attention to gender-related issues. Governments set up commissions and workshops to assemble national reports on women's status. In the NGO community, the influx of funding allowed for the convocation of meetings, many of which served to mobilize or reenergize women's movements and promote dialogue on women's issues inside and outside of activist communities. New regional and national networks set up to facilitate organizing around the conference provided strategic links among advocates of gender justice.

But the process also illustrated and at times increased ongoing tensions in national women's organizing. The funding of NGOs to take on the work of preparing for Beijing widened the gap between these organizations and the diffuse movements they are often taken to represent. The new networks were faulted for their lack of democratic process and attention to local issues. And much of the dialogue generated at meetings was about women's differences, as opposed to their similarities, surfacing conflicts around race, ethnicity, sexuality, and class (S. Alvarez 1998).

Political Discourse

The final gendered opportunity considered in this study is political discourse. During periods of repression under the Venezuelan dictatorships of Gómez (1908–35) and Pérez Jiménez (1952–58), the assumption of women's nonpolitical identity actually afforded women some protection when they joined the opposition. This presumption was also strategically exploited by the clandestine parties fighting Pérez Jiménez, which recruited women to act as *enlaces* or liaisons and form women-only resistance groups.

Similar, if not more dramatic examples of the power of gendered discourse have been noted in democratizations throughout Latin America. The Chilean dictatorship justified its persecution of internal subversion as the protection of Chilean womanhood. But the traditional model of the family that the dictatorship claimed to be promoting and protecting was in fact subverted by the regime's political and economic actions: kidnappings and killings tore families apart, and many women were driven out of their homes into factories, the informal sector, or soup kitchens to make ends meet and feed their families (Valenzuela 1987). These consequences led women from different classes to join the opposition, with feminists making the connection between authoritarianism in the polity and in the home. The gendered policies of the authoritarian Brazilian regime were undertaken using a parallel discourse with like effects: poor women organized against their declining standard of living, and middle-class women objected to the lack of opportunity for professional advancement. Other members of the Brazilian opposition, in particular the progressive church and the Left, promoted gendered discourses of liberation that justified women's activism and demanded their adherence to the general goals of social transformation while avoiding transformation in gender relations (S. Alvarez 1990, chaps. 2, 3).

With the transition to democracy, the justification of women's activism on the basis of either opposition to dictatorship or their traditional roles could not be sustained. Like other sectors of the opposition, women had lost their principal target. But unlike other sectors, women faced obstacles stemming from the previous use of the paradoxically liberating traditional gendered discourse. As this study has shown, the incorporation of traditionalist discourses within the very structures of democratic institutions has resulted in women's structural exclusion or marginalization. Male elites have exacerbated this tendency through their own co-optation of maternalist rhetoric to garner women's support without follow-through on women's demands. For example, Raúl Alfonsín, the first democratically elected president following Argentina's "Dirty War," adopted the slogan of the women's human rights group the Mothers of the Plaza de Mayo for his campaign. But he did not ultimately support the group's demands for full accountability for human rights abuses (Feijoó and Nari 1994, 116). Their demands remain in dispute today.

Moreover, women's reliance on traditionalist discourse in the democratic context has narrowed their sphere of action. Entering into the negotiations and compromises of democratic politics cannot be done easily by actors who have defined themselves (or have been defined) as above politics and have defined their issues as nonpolitical. This has been the case with the mothers who organized to oppose the human rights abuses perpetrated under dictatorship. Political action based on women's private role, especially their association with motherhood, has proved to be inadequate in the long term in a democracy. It stresses the very attributes for which women have been excluded from political participation: "nonpolitical" actors addressing "private" issues from a moral, not a political, standpoint.

But the rejection of traditional gendered discourse does not leave women much room to assert themselves in the political sphere. Demanding gender equality without upholding gender difference, as illustrated periodically over the history of Venezuelan women's organizing, has been badly received by society at large. From the earliest women's movement in the 1930s to the reform of the Civil Code in 1982, women often took great pains to deny that they were feminists, a classification clearly associated with a challenge to traditional gender relations. They have not been alone in this denial. Brazilian, Chilean, and Cuban suffragists also sought to distance themselves from "English-style" suffrage, that is, one based on equality with men (Hahner 1990, 153; Gaviola Artigas et al. 1986, 27; Stoner 1991).

Feminism as a concept and an identity is in considerably greater use today, as women throughout the region define it to suit local conditions. As cross-fertilization has advanced among middle-class feminists and grassroots activists, so-called "popular" or "grassroots" feminism has emerged. Combining an awareness of class and gender oppression, this type of feminism takes the daily experience of women of the urban poor as its basis (Stephen 1997, 141–42). It has been nurtured by the increasingly representative regional feminist meetings in which women have the opportunity to engage in dialogue across differences in developing feminist consciousness.[6]

Women's Organizing

Venezuelan women responded to the gendered political opportunities of democratization by regendering institutions in political and civil society and the state. However, their most successful strategies steered fairly clear of the most powerful and most discriminatory institution, party politics. Unified, if sporadic organizing around particular issues, coordinated through civil society and state structures, worked for a limited time to promote women's leadership and certain gender interests. Women also innovated in their political discourse. But it was not possible for them to wholly escape either the imprint of the dominant institutional culture or the divisions among themselves.

The Lessons of the Foremothers

The first women's movements provided an early example of how women's organizing through their own groups could lead to at least partial success. Prior to the monopolization of interest representation through parties and the state, the relational feminists of the mid-1930s and 1940s debated their interests and took united demands for suffrage and legal reform to the state. With the repression of democratic institutions following the three-year experiment with democracy (the *trienio*, 1945–48), women were incorporated as individuals into the clandestine opposition to the Pérez Jiménez dictatorship. They took on important roles as *enlaces*, performing crucial infrastructural tasks on which the movement depended. However, individual efforts were not rewarded with the advancement of women as a whole within the

6. In perhaps the most vivid illustration of the growth in feminist identity, at the final plenary of the 1987 regional feminist meeting in Taxco, Mexico, the assembled participants from every walk of life chanted, We are all feminists! (*"Todas somos feministas!"*) in response to the suggestion by more "historical" activists that feminist and other concerns should not be combined (Saporta Sternbach et al. 1992, 226).

clandestine or soon-to-be legal party structures. In contrast, those women who had the opportunity during this time to collaborate in women's groups, albeit party-linked ones, learned to question their subordinate position in party hierarchies and developed leadership skills. This development, in turn, provided the underpinning for the unification of women's efforts across lines of party affiliation. To support women's opposition at the end of the dictatorship, several leaders founded the Women's Committee of the Patriotic Council, the coordinating body of the entire opposition.

When the Women's Committee fell victim to the dynamics of the pacted transition to democracy, women either joined different parties or left political activism. But their inability to achieve equality within the new structures of representation led women to continue their organizational innovations. Thus began women's efforts to regender those institutions that excluded them.

Regendering Opportunities in Political Society, the State, and Civil Society

As the arena with the most firmly entrenched sources of structural discrimination and—not coincidentally—political power, political society proved the most difficult for women to alter. Because of its innovative history, the socialist party MAS offered women on the left the widest opportunity for the development of gender-sensitive policies and practices within a major party. The women of MAS made valiant attempts to take advantage of such an opportunity through their re-creation of the women's bureau, first as a semiautonomous women's movement organization (Socialist Women), and then as an incorporated but feminist sector of the party (the Feminist Front). Their long-term impact on the party was disappointing, particularly once the party adopted the more traditional structure in the late 1970s. But feminist party members went on to provide many of the activists for the women's rights campaigns of the last few decades. In the major parties, AD and COPEI, women first contested the need for a women's bureau and later tried to use it to support the development of women leaders within the party, if not other women's issues. Most recently, they fought successfully for the passage of legislation mandating quotas for women on all party lists.

In the state, women saw how other sectors achieved representation directly through the executive branch and demanded their own channel of access. Although its form was subject to the whims of successive administrations, some type of national women's agency existed from 1974 onward. Here too, women regendered this mechanism for representation by gradually improving the overall standing of the agency, objecting to its provisional status until they were successful in having it instituted by law in the early 1990s. Moreover, the advisory commissions attached to the agency gave women outside of the government the opportunity to have some influence on policy making.[7]

Very little would have been achieved from this channel of access alone had it not been for the ways in which women experimented with organizational forms in civil society. Not every experiment turned out to be a solution to the problems of women's underrepresentation as a sector, but important steps were taken in different directions. In the 1970s both middle-class feminists and poor women rejected the party politics that had done so little to promote their interests. They formed wholly autonomous organizations that were deliberately constructed in opposition to the hierarchical and centralized structures the parties promoted. This worked quite well for poor women. Through the Popular Women's Circles they managed to build the largest nonpartisan women's group in the country, with active branches that responded to the needs of local women and a national body that represented them to the nation. Feminists did not fare as well in terms of expanding their reach. Their emphasis on gender equality was seen as too threatening, and their rejection of party politics too radical, to gain them a large following.

What did prove most effective, at least for a time, was the coordination of women's groups through the Coordinating Committee of Women's NGOs (CONG). In trying to provide a voice for women's interests, the CONG continued to differ from traditional peak organizations, which had taken the lead from party organizing in their high degree of centralization and reliance on partisan support. In contrast, the member groups of the CONG remained autonomous in their functioning, its leadership rotated often, and party activists had no more clout within the organization than other members.

Conjunctural Coalition Building

The relationship between the CONG and the national women's agency also contrasted with traditional interest group–state interaction, at least initially.

7. Venezuelan women continue to innovate organizationally in their channels of access to the state. At a follow-up meeting to the Fourth World Conference of Women, participants established the Alternative Forum (Foro Alternativo), a meeting place for women's rights activists working inside and outside of the state to discuss strategies for improving gender-based policy. Their major issues in 1997 included the establishment of the National Women's Institute and the passage of the quota amendment.

Instead of basing their interaction on the distribution of resources, which often resulted in the effective co-optation by the state of civil society groups, they worked together toward common goals. In doing so, they developed a model of "conjunctural coalition building" that allowed them to work in concert at particular times around particular issues without demanding organizational or ideological coherence. Such coherence would have been impossible to achieve, given the diversity of women's gender interests and partisan loyalties. This model of coalition building can be found as far back as the first campaigns for legal reform in the 1930s and 1940s. But it came into full flower in the highly successful second campaign to reform the Civil Code, the alliances formed to free the unjustly imprisoned mother Inés María Marcano, the United Women Leaders movement to increase the number of women in elected office, and the reform of the Labor Law.

This use of coalitions was an early manifestation of a strategy that has spread throughout Latin America: the use of networks to draw women together at the national level to articulate their demands. In Chile the National Coalition of Women for Democracy (Concertación Nacional de Mujeres por la Democracia, or CNMD) was created in 1989 as an autonomous women's coalition in support of the center-left Coalition of Parties for Democracy (Concertación de Partidos por la Democracia), which won the first democratic elections in Chile following the Pinochet dictatorship. Drawing together party members, women from NGOs, and feminists, the CNMD sought to raise gender issues in the transition to democracy. It clearly influenced governmental policy making, proposing most of the gender-specific policies implemented by the first democratic government. Moreover, as a response to the CNMD, all political parties, even those outside the coalition, included gender-specific proposals in their platforms and paid at least lip service to promoting female leadership (Frohmann and Valdéz 1995, 289).

Women in El Salvador, after finding themselves largely excluded in the peace process that initiated the transition to democracy, formed the "Women '94" (Mujeres '94) coalition. Its purpose was to use the opportunity of the 1994 elections as a means of raising gender consciousness in the new democracy. Women '94 had three plans of action: (1) to develop a women's political platform and publicly credit any parties that responded to their demands; (2) to support female candidates who promoted the platform; and (3) to help register the many thousands of unregistered voters, estimated to be 75 percent female. Their efforts added large numbers of women to voting lists, although turnout among all voters was disappointing. On the municipal and national levels, the number of women elected stayed the same or declined.

However, the government and opposition coalition had signed a document on International Women's Day promising to fulfill a minimum set of women's demands regardless of the outcome of the election (Saint-Germain 1996). The coalition was active in 1997, when members again worked during the election campaign to promote a women's initiative for equality in political participation (Luciak 1997, 4). In a similar development, Nicaraguan women from the entire political spectrum participated in the National Women's Coalition to develop a minimum agenda promoting women's political, social, and economic rights. All parties but the one that won the presidency signed on to it during the 1996 election campaign (Luciak 1997, 6).

In Brazil, the Beijing preparation process sparked the formation of the Articulation of Brazilian Women for Beijing '95, which assembled nearly one hundred representatives of women's groups to "bring Beijing home to Brazil." It organized a series of preparatory conferences throughout the country, seeking to capitalize on the international attention to gender inequality by raising awareness at the national level. Hundreds of organizations participated in this process through meetings held in twenty-five of Brazil's twenty-six states. Although the process was faulted for its lack of inclusiveness, it did attempt to engage women at the local level around their own issues as well as to influence the governmental efforts around Beijing (S. Alvarez 1998).

Regendering Discourse

To strengthen their organizational efforts, Venezuelan activists also innovated in the rhetorical resources they employed. Sometimes they relied on an appeal to gender difference, sometimes to gender equality, adapting to changing contexts with mixed results. It seemed clear in their earliest campaigns for women's rights in the 1930s that presenting their demands as somehow linked to their roles in the private sphere would be more socially acceptable and therefore more successful. Women's association with motherhood and the family was used to justify their demands for equal rights for over forty years. Another strategy employed in the 1980s was to deny the gendered character of their demands as much as possible and to appeal to the principles of democracy. These were to be extended to the most fundamental building block of society, the family, and to empower all of democracy's supporters, including women. However, more recent campaigns have also challenged the traditional idea of women's roles. For example, in the campaign to reform the Labor Law, a clear distinction was drawn between the rights of women workers and those of working mothers.

Challenges to Women's Organizing

As has become evident in this study, one of the principal challenges to women's organizing is the institutional context in which it takes place. Gendered elements of the political opportunity structures of democratization have been discussed throughout this study. But it is also essential to consider how political culture permeates all forms of organizing, even those that seek to challenge traditional patterns. In Venezuela, both the national women's agency and the NGO umbrella group suffered from an increase in centralism and clientelistic behavior as they became institutionalized, and partisan rivalries were never wholly absent from the different forms of organizing.

Other challenges stem from the divisions among women. One of the strongest is class. At every stage of its development, the women's movement in Venezuela struggled with class differences. As a result, those issues most salient to women from the popular classes were often excluded from consideration. Once organized nationally, they were able to voice their own demands; but as noted in Chapter 6, little sustained cross-class attention to the current economic crisis has developed among women as a whole. Class differences, as well as those of race and ethnicity, have proved similarly difficult to manage in the movements of other countries[8] and have led to the emergence of groups focused on particular crosscutting issues. For example, in Brazil black women who have found feminist organizations insufficiently attentive to issues of race, and Afro-Brazilian groups inattentive to issues of gender, have formed their own organizations (S. Alvarez 1998, 301).

Another unsolved dilemma of women's organizing is determining when and how far to engage in state–civil society cooperation. Cross-arena collaboration has been effective. As noted above, Venezuelan women found a way to forge alliances between state and civil society organizations that allowed them to go around the exclusionary political society without compromising the autonomy of the NGOs involved. But such a relationship has inherent tensions: state representatives are not only responsible to their civil society–based constituents but are also responsive to bureaucratic pressures and/or the political agendas of particular administrations. The continuing connection between the CONG and the state women's agency grew less effective overall as their ties strengthened. NGO leaders alienated their followers by simultaneously operating as members of the agency. And the

---

8. For example, Dandavati (1996, 139–40) discusses issues of class difference with regard to the contemporary Chilean women's movement.

top-down creation of NGO issue-based networks by a state minister for women drew little support from the NGO community. Moreover, a formerly feminist organizational structure linked to the agency, the municipal Women's Center, was taken over by local administrations to provide social services or jobs for loyal supporters.

The problematic nature of the relationship between state- and civil society–based organizations for women is apparent throughout the region. Latin American women have come to see the potential benefits of entry into dominating executive branches. The state women's agencies in both Chile and Brazil were established at the behest of organized women's movements. SERNAM in Chile, however, has not developed as an effective institutional interlocutor for its movement. Some analysts find that in effect the movement has been "beheaded" by the incorporation of its leaders into the state. Also, a clientelistic relationship has developed between NGOs and SERNAM, because NGOs must now apply to SERNAM for access to much international funding. Generally, middle-class groups are privileged in this interaction because of their familiarity with application procedures. Finally, on particular issues the women's agency's hands are tied by a government that tends to follow the dictates of the Catholic Church when it comes to gender relations. As a result, its programs for employment and poverty alleviation have been more successful than its limited attempts to open dialogues on abortion and divorce legislation (Waylen 1996a, 113–14; Chuchryk 1994, 93; Dandavati 1996, 110–13; Schild 1998, 101–2). After its initial term, positions on the Brazilian National Council on Women's Rights (Conselho Nacional dos Direitos da Mulher) were filled with the supporters of a particular administration, not the feminists responsible for its creation, thus compromising its ability to dialogue with women's movements (S. Alvarez 1990, 245). Furthermore, it is questionable how effective reliance on state-based solutions to gender struggles can be in a time of overall reduction in state resources and efforts to shrink state bureaucracies.

Funding sources pose yet another challenge to women's organizing. Whether from the state or international funders, the provision of extra-NGO or -movement support can skew relationships within activist communities, privileging certain leaders or issues, creating rifts over territory, or bringing in leaders who are not dedicated to activism. As noted in an analysis of the Peruvian women's movement, in the case of feminist centers that are dependent on external sources of support, "it is difficult to determine whether the centers are operating on the basis of militancy, that is, as groups of people committed to a set of beliefs and to voluntary action, or on the basis of em-

288 UNFINISHED TRANSITIONS

ployment, because the centers provide paid professional work" (Barrig 1994, 162).

In Venezuela these problems were particularly evident during the Beijing process; in fact, the influx of international funding that came with the Beijing-related regional efforts had a significant impact on national women's movements throughout Latin America. In particular, it exacerbated a deep fissure in regional organizing between the autonomous feminists and those who accept government or external funding to support their NGOs. This fissure was evident in the polarization during the 1996 regional feminist meeting (S. Alvarez 1998, 311–12; *El Nacional,* 20 January 1997). It is an open question what will happen with the drying up of that particularly deep well of support.

Both state/civil society cooperation and funding issues revolve around a central point: the debate over degrees of autonomy. Others besides state actors and funders—political party militants, grassroots organizers, and church representatives—have all sought to intercede in women's organizing at various times; and women's organizations and movements have sought their support. Perhaps the ideal of complete autonomy is unrealizable (or even undesirable), given the very real need for financial and political support. But how far these relationships should progress is an ever-present question, especially in view of the potential for co-optation. Gioconda Espina offers the opinion that it is "ethics and not financing that defines autonomy"; accepting outside help is reasonable as long as it is used to promote feminist goals (*El Nacional,* 20 January 1997).

The final quandary is how to organize representation. Over the past decade the proliferation in Latin America of women's studies centers, feminist NGOs, popular women's groups, and national and regional networks on issues from domestic violence to ecofeminism shows that women continue to innovate organizationally to advance their issues. But increasing institutionalization brings with it not only the risk of a return to traditional patterns but also the question of how best to organize women to represent their interests. As noted above, there is regional debate over the "NGOization" of women's movements. On the one hand, the professionalization of movements seems the most viable strategy now that they have the opportunity—and the need—to interact with state agencies and funding organizations in a democratic context. On the other hand, NGOs can alienate grassroots women's rights activists, whether historical feminist or urban popular. The groups are far from democratic; and, in contrast to more movement-oriented organizations, they rarely have a membership to be accountable to (Edwards and Hulme 1996, 6). Even if they do not claim representation for whole movements, they are often treated by outside actors as if they had such claims, provoking ire within women's rights communities.[9] And finally, there is the concern that the rapid transformation of women's movements into professional organizations has not allowed for sufficient *concienciación* (consciousness-raising) among women to ensure their commitment to gender-based activism.[10]

Beyond their individual relevance, as a whole the issues outlined in this section can be seen as the challenges that face women as they seek to enter into democratic politics as an interest group. But stepping back from the empirical struggles, the next and final section reflects on whether women, who have often been united during the early phases of democratization, can or should be assumed to form a coherent interest group in consolidated democracies.

Are Women an Interest Group?

With the transition to democracy and its consolidation, those sectors that participated in the opposition to authoritarian rule have to make the difficult shift from organizing to defeat a common enemy to representing their particular interests through mechanisms of democratic participation. For class-based or "functional" groups, such as workers, professionals, or capitalists, the challenge of aggregating interests is often alleviated by a previous history of unionization or other forms of association, as well as by a new set of institutions built (or rebuilt) on the basis of their inclusion. Moreover, their common goals in a democratic setting may be relatively clear-cut, centering on their positions within the workplace (or in the relations of production).

Other groups, generally those based on "identity" rather than "function," such as those organized around human rights, neighborhood-based demands, and gender issues, face a more daunting prospect. They are not likely to have as enduring a history of organizing, and are likely to find a new institutional context that has not been constructed with their needs in mind. Moreover, the challenge of aggregating their common demands may be considerably more complex than for functional groups because of the deep cleavages cutting across identity-based interest groups.

9. Sonia E. Alvarez (1998, 313) makes this point with regard to the involvement of NGOs in the Beijing process.
10. I am indebted to Gioconda Espina, Magally Huggins, and Luis Salamanca for insight into this feature of Venezuelan women's organization; it is also mentioned as a concern in S. Alvarez (1998, 315–16).

Here the examination of women's experience can help to shed light on more general mechanisms of exclusion. Analysis of the marginalization of women by parties and state-based networks, the major channels of political participation, reveals that in Venezuela, interest representation was established on the basis of economic function, through the linkage of peak associations to parties and the state. This analysis implies that any group associated by other criteria will be structurally excluded from politics. And indeed, evidence to support such a conclusion is provided by the decimation of the independent student movement in the 1930s, as well as by the more current uphill battles groups organized around location (neighborhood organizations) and issue (environmental groups and human rights groups) face in gaining recognition in the Venezuelan polity (García 1992; Crisp, Levine, and Rey 1995; Salamanca 1995). The near absence of national organizing around racism or for the advancement of Afro-Venezuelans, despite the existence of racial discrimination, may be due at least in part to the absence of race as an expressed interest within the traditional structures of representation.[11]

The problems women encounter in entering gender-biased institutions have been described amply in this study. But what about the basis for the aggregation of their interests? Many of the studies of women's organizing reveal an implicit assumption about the nature of women's common interests; they are taken to be those that women share by virtue of their differences from men. Thus, their interests involve somehow resolving women's subordinate status in the gendered division of labor, which accords women primary responsibility for the tasks of the private sphere or mirrors this association of women with domestic life in all else that they do. Globally, women carry out (or must find someone else to carry out) the greater share of child rearing, elder care, food preparation, clothing maintenance, and household chores (UN 1995, 105–9). These tasks, despite their importance in the development of society's future generations and the daily maintenance of the current ones, are rarely reported in national statistics, valued by governments, or acknowledged by the majority of citizens.[12] Similarly, the work that women do outside the private sphere is often seen as less important than men's work or in other ways reflecting the subordinate status of women's gendered duties.

As argued in Chapter 1, there are two fundamental ways to go about re-

11. Interestingly enough, one group actively organizing on race issues is the Union of Black Women (Unión de Mujeres Negras), which has been supported in its development by the CONG and a regional network of women of African heritage.

12. However, there is a move afoot within UN circles to improve global measurement and valuation of unpaid domestic work (UNDP 1995, chap. 4).

solving the problem of the low status of women's private duties and women's association with them in the public sphere. Challenging gender hierarchy involves revaluing the activities that women do inside and outside of the home without seeking to share these activities with men or necessarily include within them those activities considered part of men's domain. Challenging gender difference, on the other hand, implies sharing private and public activities more evenly between the genders with the expectation that new, gender-neutral ways of judging the value of all work will arise. Because arguments can be and are made for both strategies, choosing between them forms one potential line of division among women, as has been evident in the conflict over whether to demand special protections for women or to seek equal rights with men in the workplace.

Other divisions that make it difficult to draw a clear map of women's interests are created by those crosscutting interests that women may hold by virtue of their "social positioning"—as members of a particular class, race, ethnicity, sexuality, or political party. These cleavages mean that policies that somehow address the imbalance in the gendered division of labor, either by revaluing women's work or by sharing it between men and women, may not be in the interest of all women if they do not simultaneously address their other interests. Some conflicts are resolvable; others, such as the struggle over improving the conditions of female domestic workers at their female employers' expense, pose more of a problem.

However, there is one area in which all women clearly have a common interest: augmenting their presence at all levels of decision making. Although all women may not agree on the substance of specific policy outcomes, they do have a common interest in being present when policy is being made. Not surprisingly, it is when women have formed a united pressure group to achieve parity in presence, that they have often been most successful.

What does the foregoing imply in terms of women's participation in interest-group politics? If women were able to unite as a bloc around a common set of interests, including not only presence but also other matters of substance, then gender-segregated mechanisms such as women's bureaus of political parties, national agencies for women, and civil society-based women's movements would be both the necessary and sufficient venues for action, and the demand for increased representation through quotas would be the ultimate solution to the representation of women's interests.

But barring this clear aggregation of interests, it seems as though the best strategies for women's organizing on their own behalf are (1) to fight for the right to representation in all decision-making arenas by joining together from inside and outside of political institutions, and (2) to rely on periodic cooperation around conjunctural issues. To repeat the words of Venezuelan activist Esperanza Vera, "It is as though reality is showing us that women, through this method of not being organized in the traditional manner but being unified around something which interests us, are creating something like a different form of collective action."

Of course, even if there were institutional remedies to be found, they could not be the entire solution to the long history of gender discrimination women have endured both inside and outside of politics. Although the focus of this work has been on women's experience with the formal institutions of democratic politics, there are other arenas to consider. Purely political reforms are helpful in ameliorating gender discrimination, but in the words of one of the first political scientists of the modern era to engage in the study of women and politics, "It is probably still more important to fight against the deeply-rooted belief in the natural inferiority of women" (Duverger 1955, 130).

APPENDIX

Chronology of Events

YEAR	MAJOR POLITICAL EVENTS	WOMEN'S ORGANIZING EFFORTS
1908–1935	**Dictatorship:** Rule of General Juan Vincente Gómez PCV (1932)	Participation in opposition ACF (1935)
1936–1940	**Liberalized Authoritarianism:** Rule of General Eleazar López Contreras Opposition through April Bloc (1936) National Democratic Party (1936–38)	AVM, other women's groups (1936–40) Preparatory Conference of First Venezuelan Congress of Women (1940)
1941–1945	**Liberalized Authoritarianism:** Rule of General Isais Medina Angarita AD (1941)	Movement for Civil Code Reform (1940–42) Civil Code reformed (1942) Suffrage Movement (1941–45/7) Municipal suffrage granted (1945)
1945–1948	**Democratic Transition:** *Trienio,* AD in power COPEI (1946)	National suffrage granted (1946)
1948–1958	**Dictatorship:** Rule by Junta (1948–52) Rule of Major Marcos Pérez Jiménez (1952–58) Opposition through clandestine parties (AD, PCV); Patriotic Council (1957)	*Enlace* participation in opposition Young Women's Union (1951) Young Women's Association (1951) National Women's Union (1952) Women's Committee of the Patriotic Council (1957) FEVA (1957)
1958–1968	**Democratic Transition:** Punto Fijo Pact (1958) Presidency of Rómulo Betancourt (1959–63) Presidency of Raul Leoni (1964–68) Guerrilla movement (1960–68)	International Women's Day Rally (1958) National Women's Union (1960) First Seminar for the Evaluation of Women in Venezuela (1968)

1969–1973	**Democratic Consolidation:** Presidency of Rafael Caldera MAS (1971)	Women's Legion (1970) Socialist Women (1972) Women's League (1972)
1974–1978	Presidency of Carlos Andrés Pérez	COFEAPRE (1974) First Venezuelan Congress of Women (1974) Popular Women's Circles (1974) Movement for Civil Code Reform (1976–82) The Spell, Person Wednesday Feminist Group (1978)
1979–1983	Presidency of Luis Herrera Campins	Ministry for the Participation of Women in Development (1979) Feminist Front of MAS (1981) Reform of the Civil Code (1982)
1984–1988	Presidency of Jaime Lusinchi	ONM (1984) CONG (1985) Directorate for Women's Advancement (1987) Campaign for Inés María Marcano (1987) United Women Leaders Movement (1987–88) Movement for Labor Law Reform (1985–90)
1989–1993	**Democratic Crisis:** Presidency of Carlos Andrés Pérez Coups attempts (1992) Pérez's trial and arrest (1993–94)	COFEAPRE "2" (1989) Reform of the Labor Law (1990) CONAMU (1992) Equal Opportunity Law (1992)
1994–1998	Presidency of Rafael Caldera	Beijing preparations (1994–95)

BIBLIOGRAPHY

4 Presidentes: 40 años de acción democrática. Vol. 2, *Raúl Leoni, Carlos Andrés Pérez.* 1981. Caracas: Ediciones de la Presidencia de la República.

Acker, Joan. 1990. "Hierarchies, Jobs, Bodies: A Theory of Gendered Organizations." *Gender and Society* 4 (2): 139–58.

Ackerly, Brooke. 1997. "What's in a Design? The Effects of NGO Choices on Women's Empowerment and on Family and Social Institutions in Bangladesh." In *Getting Institutions Right for Women in Development,* ed. A. M. Goetz, 140–58. London: Zed Books.

Acosta, Mayita, and Gioconda Espina. 1982. "Programa de gobierno y plan de acción del MAS hacia la mujer." Paper prepared for the IV Jornada Nacional de Mujeres Socialistas, Caracas.

Action Survey of IWY. 1976. New York: Unifo Publishers.

ACF (Agrupación Cultural Femenina). n.d. "Estatutos." Caracas: ACF.

Agüero, Felipe. 1995. "Debilitating Democracy: Political Elites and Military Rebels." In *Lessons of the Venezuelan Experience,* ed. L. W. Goodman et al., 136–62. Washington, D.C.: Woodrow Wilson Center Press and Baltimore: Johns Hopkins University Press.

Agüero, Felipe, Charlie Gillespie, and Timothy Scully. 1986. "The Role of Political Parties in the Return to Democracy in the Southern Cone: Rapporteurs' Reports." Paper presented at conference on The Role of Political Parties in the Return to Democracy in the Southern Cone, 9–12 September, at the Woodrow Wilson International Center for Scholars, Washington, D.C.

Alexander, Robert J. 1969. *The Communist Party of Venezuela.* Stanford, Calif.: Hoover Institution Press.

Ali, Kecia. 1995. "The Historiography of Women in Modern Latin America." Raleigh: Duke-University of North Carolina Program in Latin American Studies. Working Paper #18.

Alvarez, Julia. 1994. *In the Time of the Butterflies.* New York: Penguin Books.

Alvarez, Ofelia. 1987. "Comisión Asesora de Políticas hacia la Mujer." Caracas. Photocopy.

Alvarez, Sonia E. 1986. "The Politics of Gender in Latin America: Comparative Perspectives on Women in the Brazilian Transition to Democracy." Ph.D. diss., Yale University.

———. 1990. *Engendering Democracy in Brazil.* Princeton: Princeton University Press.

———. 1997. "Reweaving the Fabric of Collective Action: Social Movements and Challenges to 'Actually Existing Democracy' in Brazil." In *Between*

Resistance and Revolution: Cultural Politics and Social Protest, ed. R. Fox and O. Starn. New Brunswick: Rutgers University Press.

———. 1998. "Latin American Feminisms 'Go Global': Trends of the 1990s and Challenges for the New Millennium." In *Cultures of Politics/Politics of Cultures,* ed. S. E. Alvarez, E. Dagnino, and A. Escobar, 293–324. Boulder, Colo.: Westview Press.

Alvarez, Sonia E., Evelina Dagnino, and Arturo Escobar. 1998. "Introduction: The Cultural and the Political in Latin American Social Movements." In *Cultures of Politics/Politics of Cultures: Latin American Social Movements Revisited,* ed. S. E. Alvarez, E. Dagnino, and A. Escobar, 1–29. Boulder, Colo.: Westview Press.

Alvarez T., María José. 1989. *Magnitud del aborto provocado.* Caracas.

Andreas, Carol. 1985. *When Women Rebel: The Rise of Popular Feminism in Peru.* Westport, Conn.: Lawrence Hill and Co.

Appleton, Andrew, and Amy G. Mazur. 1993. "Transformation or Modernization: The Rhetoric and Reality of Gender and Party Politics in France." In *Gender and Party Politics,* ed. J. Lovenduski and P. Norris, 86–112. London: Sage Publishers.

AVM (Asociación Venezolana de Mujeres). 1942. *La Mujer ante la ley.* Caracas: Coop. de Artes Gráficas.

Avendaño Lugo, José Ramón. 1982. *El militarismo en Venezuela: la dictadura de Pérez Jiménez.* Caracas: Ediciones Centauro.

Baldwin, Margaret A. 1997. "Public Women and the Feminist State." *Harvard Women's Law Journal* 20:47–162.

Barrig, Maruja. 1994. "The Difficult Equilibrium Between Bread and Roses: Women's Organizations and Democracy in Peru." In *The Women's Movement in Latin America,* ed. J. Jaquette, 151–75. Boulder, Colo.: Westview Press.

Basu, Amrita, ed. 1995a. *The Challenge of Local Feminisms: Women's Movements in Global Perspective.* Boulder, Colo.: Westview Press.

———. 1995b. "Introduction." In *The Challenge of Local Feminisms,* ed. A. Basu, 1–21. Boulder, Colo.: Westview Press.

Bergquist, Charles. 1986. *Labor in Latin America: Comparative Essays on Chile, Argentina, Venezuela, and Colombia.* Stanford: Stanford University Press.

Betancourt, Rómulo. 1979. *Venezuela: Oil and Politics.* Translated by Everett Bauman. Boston: Houghton Mifflin.

———. Archives. Fundación Rómulo Betancourt, Caracas.

Bethencourt G., Luisa M. 1988. "La organización doméstica y la condición de la mujer en los sectores populares." *Cuadernos del CENDES* 9:31–45.

Blachman, Morris J. 1980. "Selective Omission and Theoretical Distortion in Studying the Political Activity of Women in Brazil." In *Sex and Class in Latin America,* ed. J. Nash and H. I. Safa, 245–64. New York: J. F. Bergin Publishers.

Borchorst, A. 1994. "Welfare State Regimes, Women's Interests, and the EC." In *Engendering Welfare States: Combining Insights of Feminist and Mainstream Research,* ed. D. Sainsbury, 26–44. London: Sage Publishers.

Brewer-Carías, Allan R. 1988. *Problemas del estado de partidos*. Caracas: Editorial Juridica Venezolana.

Briceño Caldera, Maria, Cira Carmen Brito Salazar, and Silvia Guadalupe Mirabal Faria. 1977. "Participación política de la mujer en los partidos políticos y en las organizaciones femeninas. B.A. thesis, Universidad Central de Venezuela.

Brockett, Charles D. 1991. "The Structure of Political Opportunities and Peasant Mobilization in Central America." *Comparative Politics* 23:253–74.

Caldera, Rafael. 1968. *Programa de gobierno de COPEI 1969–1974*. Reprinted in *El Nacional*.

Calderón, Fernando, Alejandro Piscitelli, and José Luis Reyna. 1992. "Social Movements: Actors, Theories, Expectations." In *The Making of Social Movements in Latin America*, ed. A. Escobar and S. E. Alvarez, 19–36. Boulder, Colo.: Westview Press.

Canel, Eduardo. 1992. "Democratization and the Decline of Urban Social Movements in Uruguay: A Political-Institutional Account." In *The Making of Social Movements in Latin America*, ed. A. Escobar and S. E. Alvarez, 276–90. Boulder, Colo.: Westview Press.

Cardoso, Ruth Correa Leite. 1992. "Popular Movements in the Context of the Consolidation of Democracy in Brazil." In *The Making of Social Movements in Latin America*, ed. Escobar and Alvarez, 291–302. Boulder, Colo.: Westview Press.

Carrillo, Teresa. 1990. "Women and Independent Unionism in the Garment Industry." In *Popular Movements and Political Change in Mexico*, ed. J. Foweraker and A. Craig, 213–33. Boulder, Colo.: Lynne Rienner Publishers.

CFP (Círculos Femeninos Populares). 1994. *Primero Congreso Nacional: 20 años recorriendo los caminos de la solidaridad y la justicia, Resumen de Ponencias*. Caracas: CFP.

———. 1995. "¿Que son los Círculos Femeninos Populares?" Caracas: Editorial Tinta, Papel y Vida.

Chaney, Elsa. 1971. "Women in Latin American Politics: The Case of Peru and Chile." Ph.D. diss., University of Wisconsin.

———. 1979. *Supermadre: Women in Politics in Latin America*. Austin: University of Texas Press.

Chaney, Elsa M., and Mary García Castro. 1989. *Muchachas No More: Household Workers in Latin America and the Caribbean*. Philadelphia: Temple University Press.

Chodorow, Nancy. 1974. "Family Structure and Feminine Personality." In *Women, Culture, and Society*, ed. M. Zimbalist Rosaldo and L. Lamphere, 43–66. Stanford: Stanford University Press.

Chuchryk, Patricia M. 1991. "Feminist Anti-Authoritarian Politics: The Role of Women's Organizations in the Chilean Transition to Democracy." In *The Women's Movement in Latin America*, ed. J. Jaquette, 149–84. Boulder, Colo.: Westview Press.

———. 1994. "Feminist Anti-Authoritarian Politics: The Role of Women's Organizations in the Chilean Transition to Democracy." In *The Women's*

Movement in Latin America, ed. J. Jaquette, 65–108. Boulder, Colo.: Westview Press.

CISFEM (Centro de Investigacion Social, Formacion y Estudios de la Mujer). 1992. *Situación de la mujer en Venezuela.* Caracas: CISFEM/United Nations Children's Fund (UNICEF).

Clemente Travieso, Carmen. 1961. *Las Luchas de la mujer venezolana.* Caracas: Agrupación Cultural Femenina.

COFEAPRE (Comisión Femenina Asesora de la Presidencia de la República). 1991. *Las mujeres son nuestra prioridad.* Caracas.

———. 1992. *Memoria y Cuenta.* Caracas.

Cohen, Jean L. 1985. "Strategy or Identity: New Theoretical Paradigms and Contemporary Social Movements." *Social Research* 52 (4): 663–716.

Comisión Especial de la Camara de Diputados del Congreso de la República de Venezuela para Evaluar el Decenio de la Mujer. n.d. "Informe." Caracas. Photocopy.

Conferencia preparatoria del Primer Congreso Venezolano de Mujeres. 1941. Caracas: Editorial Bolivar.

Connell, R.W. 1994. "The State, Gender, and Sexual Politics: Theory and Appraisal." In *Power/Gender: Social Relations in Theory and Practice,* ed. H. L. Radtke and H. J. Stam, 136–73. London: Sage Publishers.

———. 1995. *Masculinities.* Berkeley: University of California Press.

CONG (Coordinadora de Organizaciones No-Gubernamentales de Mujeres). 1987. "La Coordinadora de Organizaciones No Gubernamentales de Mujeres (CONG) Ante el proceso electoral que se avencina." Caracas. Photocopy.

———. 1988a. "Estatutos." Caracas. Photocopy.

———. 1988b. *CONG.* Caracas: CONG.

———. 1988c. *La Mujer y la lucha solidaria: En el caso de Inés María Marcano, una en un millón.* Caracas: CONG.

———. 1989. "Taller de la CONG: Conclusiones y propuestas." Caracas. Photocopy.

Coordinadora de Mujeres de Izquierda. 1981. "De la mitad de la revolución a la otra mitad." Caracas. Photocopy.

Coppedge, Michael. 1994. *Strong Parties and Lame Ducks: Presidential Partyarchy and Factionalism in Venezuela.* Stanford: Stanford University Press.

CORDIPLAN (Oficina Central de Coordinación y Planificación). 1960. *Plan de la Nacion 1960–64.* Caracas.

———. 1964. *Plan de la Nación 1963–66.* Caracas.

———. 1966. *Plan de la Nación 1965–68.* Caracas.

———. 1971. *Plan de la Nación 1970–74.* Caracas.

———. 1981. *IV Plan de la Nación 1981–1985.* Caracas.

———. 1984. *VII Plan de la Nación 1984–1988.* Caracas.

Costain, Anne N. 1992. *Inviting Women's Rebellion: A Process Interpretation of the Women's Movement.* Baltimore: Johns Hopkins University Press.

Craske, Nikki. 1993. "Women's Political Participation in *Colonias Populares* in Guadalaraja, Mexico." In *Viva: Women and Popular Protest in Latin America,* ed. S. Radcliffe and S. Westwood, 112–35. New York: Routledge Press.

———. 1999. *Women and Politics in Latin America*. New Brunswick: Rutgers University Press.

Crisp, Brian F., Daniel H. Levine, and Juan Carlos Rey. 1995. "The Legitimacy Problem." In *Venezuelan Democracy Under Stress*, ed. J. McCoy et al., 139–70. New Brunswick: Transaction Publishers.

CSE (Consejo Supremo Electoral), División de Estadística. 1984. *Los Partidos políticos y sus estadísticas electorales 1946–84*. Vol. 1. Caracas.

———. 1988. *Elecciones 1988*. Caracas.

———. 1989. *Elecciones 1989*. Caracas.

———. 1993. *Elecciones 1993*. Caracas.

Dalla Costa, Giovanna Franca. 1995. "Development and Economic Crisis: Women's Labour and Social Policies in Venezuela in the Context of International Indebtedness." In *Paying the Price: Women and the Politics of International Economic Strategy*, ed. M. Dalla Costa and G. F. Dalla Costa, 91–120. London: Zed Press.

Dalton, Russell J., and Manfred Kuechler, eds. 1990. *Challenging the Political Order: New Social and Political Movements in Western Democracies*. New York: Oxford University Press.

Dandavati, Annie G. 1996. *The Women's Movement and the Transition to Democracy in Chile*. New York: Peter Lang Publishing.

Davis, Diane E. 1994. "Failed Democratic Reform in Contemporary Mexico: From Social Movements to the State and Back Again." *Journal of Latin American Studies* 26 (2): 375–408.

de Leonardi, Maria Teresa R. 1983. "El Movimiento Femenino, 1932–1983." In Ministro de Estado, *Venezuela: Biografia inacabada evolucion social 1936–1983*, 593–636. Caracas: Banco Central de Venezuela.

Delgado Arrias, Carol, ed. 1995. *Mujeres: Una fuerza social en movimiento*. Caracas: JUVECABE.

Despacho de la Ministro de Estado para la Participacion de la Mujer en el Desarrollo. 1984. *Ley de reforma parcial del Código Civil*. Caracas.

Diamond, Larry. 1994. "Toward Democratic Consolidation." *Journal of Democracy* 5 (3): 4–17.

Diamond, Larry, Juan J. Linz, and Seymour Martin Lipset, eds. 1989. *Democracy in Developing Countries: Latin America*. Boulder, Colo.: Lynne Rienner Publishers.

Dirección General Sectorial de Promoción a la Mujer, Ministerio de la Familia. N.d. "Programa Mínimo Comun de las Mujeres Dirigentes Venezolanas a los Partidos Políticos." Caracas. Photocopy.

Domínguez, Jorge I., and Abraham F. Lowenthal, eds. 1996. *Constructing Democratic Governance* (3 volumes). Baltimore: Johns Hopkins University Press.

Duverger, Maurice. 1955. *The Political Role of Women*. Paris: UNESCO.

Eckstein, Harry. 1975. "Case Study and Theory in Political Science." In *Handbook of Political Science*. Vol. 7, *Strategies of Inquiry*, ed. F. Greenstein and N. Polsby, 79–137. Reading, Mass.: Addison-Wesley.

Edwards, Michael, and David Hulme, eds. 1996. *Beyond the Magic Bullet: NGO Performance and Accountability in the Post-Cold War World*. West Hartford, Conn.: Kumarian Press.

Ehlers, Tracy Bachrach. 1991. "Debunking Marianism: Economic Vulnerability and Survival Strategies Among Guatemalan Wives." *Ethnology* 30 (1): 1–16.

Eisinger, Peter K. 1973. "The Conditions of Protest Behavior in American Cities." *American Political Science Review* 67:11–28.

Ellner, Steve. 1988. *Venezuela's Movimiento al Socialismo: From Guerrilla Defeat to Innovative Politics*. Durham: Duke University Press.

————. 1993–94. "The Deepening of Democracy in a Crisis Setting: Political Reform and the Electoral Process in Venezuela." *Journal of Interamerican Studies and World Affairs* 35 (4): 1–42.

Emberley, Julia V. 1993. *Thresholds of Difference: Feminist Critique, Native Women's Writings, Postcolonial Theory*. Toronto: University of Toronto Press.

Erickson, Lynda. 1993. "Making Her Way In: Women, Parties and Candidacies in Canada." In *Gender and Party Politics*, ed. J. Lovenduski and P. Norris, 60–85. London: Sage Publishers.

Escobar, Arturo. 1992. "Culture, Economics, and Politics in Latin American Social Movements Theory and Research." In *The Making of Social Movements in Latin America*, ed. A. Escobar and S. E. Alvarez, 62–85. Boulder, Colo.: Westview Press.

Escobar, Arturo, and Sonia E. Alvarez, eds. 1992. *The Making of Social Movements in Latin America*. Boulder, Colo.: Westview Press.

Espina, Gioconda. 1994. "Entre sacudones, golpes y amenazas. Las Venezolanas organizadas y las otras." In *Mujeres y participación política*, ed. M. León, 167–80. Bogotá: Tercer Mundo Editores.

————. 1995. "La CONGA diez años despues." Caracas. Photocopy.

Evans, Peter, Dietrich Rueschemeyer, and Theda Skocpol, eds. 1985. *Bringing the State Back In*. Cambridge: Cambridge University Press.

Ewell, Judith. 1984a. *Venezuela: A Century of Change*. London: C. Hurst.

————. 1984b. "Venezuela since 1930." In *The Cambridge History of Latin America*, Vol. 8, ed. L. Bethell, 727–90. Cambridge: Cambridge University Press.

Farías Toussain, Julia, María de la Cruz Mejías, and Miriam Rodríguez Sánchez. 1985. "Participación política de la mujer en el proceso historico que culmino el 23 de enero 1958." B.A. thesis, Universidad Central de Venezuela.

Feijoó, Maria del Carmen, and Marcela María Alejandra Nari. 1994. "The Challenge of Constructing Civilian Peace: Women and Democracy in Argentina." In *The Women's Movement in Latin America*, ed. J. Jaquette, 109–30. Boulder, Colo.: Westview Press.

Feldblum, Miriam, and Kay Lawson. 1994. "The Impact of the French Electoral System on Women and Minorities." In *Electoral Systems in Comparative Perspective*, ed. Rule and Zimmerman, 79–88. Westport, Conn.: Greenwood Press.

Ferguson, Kathy E. 1984. *The Feminist Case Against Bureaucracy*. Philadelphia: Temple University Press.

Fergusson, Erna. 1939. *Venezuela*. New York: Alfred A. Knopf.

FEVA (Federación Venezolana de Abogadas). 1987. "La Ciencia del derecho al servicio de la comunidad." Caracas: FEVA.

Fisher, Jo. 1993. *Out of the Shadows: Women, Resistance, and Politics in South America*. New York: Monthly Review Press/Latin America Bureau.

Fitzsimmons, Tracy. 1995. "Paradoxes of Participation: Organizations and Democratization in Latin America." Ph.D. diss., Stanford University.

Foweraker, Joe. 1995. *Theorizing Social Movements*. London: Pluto Press.

Foweraker, Joe, and Ann Craig. 1990. *Popular Movements and Political Change in Mexico*. Boulder, Colo.: Lynne Rienner Publishers.

Franzway, Suzanne, Dianne Court, and R. W. Connell. 1989. *Staking a Claim: Feminism, Bureaucracy, and the State*. Oxford: Polity Press.

Freedman, Estelle. 1979. "Separatism as Strategy: Female Institution Building and American Feminism, 1870–1930." *Feminist Studies* 5 (3): 512–29.

Frente Feminista del MAS. 1983. "Política hacia la mujer." Caracas. Photocopy.

Frohmann, Alicia, and Teresa Valdés. 1995. "Democracy in the Country and in the Home: The Women's Movement in Chile." In *The Challenge of Local Feminisms*, ed. A. Basu, 276–301. Boulder, Colo.: Westview Press.

Fundación del Niño. 1979. *Informe Quinquenal* (April 1974–March 1979). Caracas.

———. 1988. *Memoria y Cuenta*. Caracas.

García, Carmen Teresa, and Carmen Rosillo. 1992. "Conquistando nuevos espacios: La investigación y las organizaciones de mujeres." *FEMENTUM: Revista Venezolana de Sociologia y Antropologia* 2 (4): 3–17.

García, María Pilar. 1992. "The Venezuelan Ecology Movement: Symbolic Effectiveness, Social Practices, and Political Strategies." In *The Making of Social Movements in Latin America*, ed. A. Escobar and S. E. Alvarez, 150–69. Boulder, Colo.: Westview Press.

García Guadilla, María-Pilar. 1993. "*Ecologia:* Women, Environment, and Politics in Venezuela." In *Viva: Women and Popular Protest in Latin America*, ed. S. Radcliffe and S. Westwood, 65–87. New York: Routledge Press.

———. 1994. "Configuración espacial y movimientos ciudadanos: Caracas en cuatro tiempos." In *Las Ciudades hablan: Identidades y movimientos sociales en seis metrópolis latinoamericanas*, ed. T. R. Villasante, 51–69. Caracas: Nueva Sociedad.

García Ponce, Guillermo, and Francisco Camacho Barrios. 1982. *Diario de la resistencia y la dictadura 1948–1958*. Caracas: Ediciones Centauro.

García Prince, Evangelina. 1993. *La Mujer Venezolana en el Proceso de Toma de Decisiones*. Caracas: COFEAPRE.

García Prince, Evangelina, et al. 1993. Amicus brief to Supreme Court. Caracas. Photocopy.

Gaviola Artigas, Edda, Ximena Jiles Moreno, Lorella Lopresti Martínez, and Claudia Rojas Mira. 1986. "*Queremos votar en las proximas elecciones*": *Historia del movimiento femenino chileno 1913–1952*. Santiago: Centro de Análisis y Difusión de la Condición de la Mujer.

Goetz, Anne Marie. 1995. *The Politics of Integrating Gender to State Development Processes*. Geneva: UNRISD Occasional Paper.

Gómez Calcaño, Luis. 1997. "Nuevos actores y viejas prácticas: Asociaciones de vecinos y partidos políticos en Caracas." Paper delivered at the 30th Meeting of the Latin American Studies Association, Guadalajara, Mexico.

Goodman, Louis W., Johanna Mendelson Forman, Moisés Naím, Joseph S. Tulchin, and Gary Bland, eds. 1995. *Lessons of the Venezuelan Experience*.

Washington, D.C.: Woodrow Wilson Center Press and Baltimore: Johns Hopkins University Press.

Gordon, Linda, ed. 1990. *Women, the State, and Welfare.* Madison: University of Wisconsin Press.

———. 1994. *Pitied But Not Entitled: Single Mothers and the History of Welfare.* Cambridge: Harvard University Press.

Grupo Feminista Miercoles. 1979. "Grupo Feminista Miercoles." Caracas. Photocopy.

Guadagnini, Marila. 1993. "A 'Partitocrazia' Without Women: The Case of the Italian Party System." In *Gender and Party Politics,* ed. J. Lovenduski and P. Norris, 168–204. London: Sage Publishers.

Haggard, Stephan. 1993. "Import-Substitution Industrialization." In *The Oxford Companion to Politics of the World,* ed. J. Krieger, 414–16. New York: Oxford University Press.

Hagopian, Frances. 1990. "'Democracy by Undemocratic Means'? Elites, Political Pacts, and Regime Transition in Brazil." *Comparative Political Studies* 23 (2): 147–70.

Hahner, June. 1980. "Feminism, Women's Rights, and the Suffrage Movement in Brazil, 1850–1932." *Latin American Research Review* 15 (1): 65–111.

———. 1990. *Emancipating the Female Sex.* Durham: Duke University Press.

Hays-Mitchell, Maureen. 1995. "Voices and Visions from the Streets: Gender Interests and Political Participation Among Women Informal Traders in Latin America." *Environment and Planning D: Society and Space* 13 (4): 445–69.

Hellinger, Daniel C. 1991. *Venezuela: Tarnished Democracy.* Boulder, Colo.: Westview Press.

Hellman, Judith Adler. 1992. "The Study of New Social Movements in Latin America and the Question of Autonomy." In *The Making of Social Movements in Latin America,* ed. A. Escobar and S. E. Alvarez, 52–61. Boulder, Colo.: Westview Press.

Henriquez, Monica. "Crónicas Gineológicas." 1989. Videotape. Caracas: Lagoven.

Hernandez, Eumelia. 1985. *Una Vida una lucha.* Caracas: Fundación Para el Desarrollo Social de la Region Capital.

Herrera Campins, Luis. 1978. *Mi compromiso con Venezuela: Programa de gobierno para el periodo 1979–84.* Vols. 1 and 2. Caracas: COPEI.

Herrera, Clara E. 1991. "La economia venezolana y la particpación de la mujer en la vida política del país (1980–1989)." B.A. thesis, Universidad Central de Venezuela.

Higley, John, and Richard Gunther, eds. 1992. *Elites and Democratic Consolidation in Latin America and Southern Europe.* Cambridge: Cambridge University Press.

Hillman, Richard S. 1994. *Democracy for the Privileged: Crisis and Transition in Venezuela.* Boulder, Colo.: Lynne Rienner Press.

Hipsher, Patricia L. 1996. "Democratization and the Decline of Urban Social Movements in Chile and Spain." *Comparative Politics* 28 (3): 273–97.

Historia Gráfica de Venezuela. 1958. Caracas: *El Nacional.*

Hoecker, Beate. 1994. "The German Electoral System: A Barrier to Women?" In

Electoral Systems in Comparative Perspective, ed. W. Rule and J. F. Zimmerman, 65–78. Westport, Conn.: Greenwood Press.

Hollander, Nancy Caro. 1977. "Women Workers and the Class Struggle: The Case of Argentina." *Latin American Perspectives* 4 (1–2): 180–93.

Htun, Mala. 1998. "Women's Political Participation, Representation, and Leadership in Latin America." Issue Brief. Washington, D.C.: Women's Leadership Conference of the Americas.

Huggins Castañeda, Magally. 1992. "Mujer, maternidad, y genero en America Latina: Redefiniendo la acción política." Universidad Central de Venezuela. Unpublished.

Huggins Castañeda, Magally, and Diana Dominguez Nelson. 1993. *Mujeres latinoamericanas en cifras: Venezuela*. Santiago: FLACSO.

Huntington, Samuel P. 1968. *Political Order in Changing Societies*. New Haven: Yale University Press.

———. 1993. *The Third Wave: Democratization in the Late Twentieth Century*. Norman: University of Oklahoma Press.

Inglehart, Ronald. 1991. *Culture Shift in Advanced Industrial Society*. Princeton: Princeton University Press.

IPU (Inter-Parliamentary Union). 1997. *Men and Women in Politics: Democracy Still in the Making. A World Comparative Study*. Reports and Documents Series, no. 28. Geneva: IPU.

———. 1998. "Women in National Parliaments." Online at http://www.ipu.org/wmn-e/classif.htm.

Instituto Venezolano de Seguros Sociales. 1957. *Los Seguros sociales en Venezuela bajo El Nuevo Ideal Nacional, 2/12/52–2/12/57*. Caracas: IVSS.

Jaquette, Jane S. 1991. *The Women's Movement in Latin America: Feminism and the Transition to Democracy*. Boulder, Colo.: Westview Press.

———. 1994a. *The Women's Movement in Latin America: Participation and Democracy*, 2nd ed. Boulder, Colo.: Westview Press.

———. 1994b. "Women's Movements and the Challenge of Democratic Politics in Latin America." *Social Politics* 1 (3): 335–40.

Jaquette, Jane S., and Sharon L. Wolchik, eds. 1998. *Women and Democracy: Latin America and Eastern Europe*. Baltimore: Johns Hopkins University Press.

Jelin, Elizabeth, ed. 1990. *Women and Social Change in Latin America*. London: Zed Books.

Jenson, Jane. 1987. "Changing Discourse, Changing Agendas: Political Rights and Reproductive Policies in France." In *The Women's Movements of the United States and Estern Europe*, ed. M. F. Katzenstein and C. M. Mueller, 64–88. Philadelphia: Temple University Press.

Jones, Mark. 1996. "Increasing Women's Representation via Gender Quotas: The Argentine Ley de Cupos." *Women & Politics* 16 (4): 75–99.

JUVECABE (Juntos Para Venezuela en Camino a Beijing). 1995. *Venezuela: The Status of Women*. Caracas: JUVECABE.

Kanter, Rosabeth Moss. 1977. *Men and Women of the Corporation*. New York: Doubleday Books.

Karl, Terry Lynn. 1987. "Petroleum and Political Pacts: The Transition to Democracy in Venezuela." *Latin American Research Review* 22 (1): 63–94.

———. 1990. "Dilemmas of Democratization in Latin America." *Comparative Politics* 23 (1): 1–21.

———. 1995. "The Venezuelan Petro-State and the Crisis of 'Its' Democracy." In *Venezuelan Democracy Under Stress*, ed. McCoy et al., 33–55. New Brunswick, N.J.: Transaction Publishers.

———. 1997. *The Paradox of Plenty: Oil Booms and Petro-States*. Berkeley: University of California Press.

Katzenstein, Mary Fainsod, and Carol McClurg Mueller, eds. 1987. *The Women's Movements of the United States and Western Europe*. Philadelphia: Temple University Press.

Kelly, Janet. 1995. "The Question of Inefficiency and Inequality: Social Policy in Venezuela." In *Lessons of the Venezuelan Experience*, ed. L. W. Goodman et al., 283–310. Washington, D.C.: Woodrow Wilson Center Press and Baltimore: Johns Hopkins University Press.

Kenney, Sally J. 1996. "New Research on Gendered Political Institutions." *Political Research Quarterly* 49 (2): 445–66.

Kirkwood, Julieta. 1986. *Ser política en Chile: Las Feministas y los partidos*. Santiago: FLACSO.

Kitschelt, Herbert. 1993. "The Green Phenomenon in Western Party Systems." In *Environmental Politics in the International Arena: Movements, Parties, Organizations, and Policy*, ed. S. Kamieniecki, 93–112. Albany: State University of New York Press.

Klein, Ethel. 1984. *Gender Politics: From Consciousness to Mass Politics*. Cambridge: Harvard University Press.

Kolinsky, Eva. 1993. "Party Change and Women's Representation in Unified Germany." In *Gender and Party Politics*, ed. J. Lovenduski and P. Norris, 113–46. London: Sage Publishers.

Kornblith, Miriam. 1995. "Public Sector and Private Sector: New Rules of the Game." In *Venezuelan Democracy Under Stress*, ed. McCoy et al., 77–103. New Brunswick, N.J.: Transaction Publishers.

Kornblith, Miriam, and Daniel H. Levine. 1995. "Venezuela: The Life and Times of the Party System." In *Building Democratic Institutions*, ed. S. Mainwaring and T. Scully, 37–71. Stanford: Stanford University Press.

Koven, Seth, and Sonya Michel. 1993. *Mothers of a New World: Maternalist Politics and the Origins of Welfare States*. New York: Routledge Press.

La Mala Vida. 1985. *La Mala Vida 1985*. Caracas: La Mala Vida.

Laclau, Ernesto. 1985. "New Social Movements and the Plurality of the Social." In *New Social Movements and the State in Latin America*, ed. D. Slater, 27–42. Amsterdam: CEDLA.

Lamas, Marta, Alicia Martínez, María Luisa Tarrés, and Esperanza Tuñon. 1995. "Building Bridges: The Growth of Popular Feminism in Mexico." In *The Challenge of Local Feminisms*, ed. A. Basu, 324–47. Boulder, Colo.: Westview Press.

Lander, Edgardo. 1995. *Neoliberalismo, sociedad civil, y democracia: Ensayos sobre América Latina y Venezuela*. Caracas: UCV, Consejo de Desarrollo Científico y Humanístico.

Lara, Arelis. 1991. "La Participación femenina en los partidos políticos venezolanos:

Casos Acción Democratica y Movimiento al Socialismo." B.A. thesis, Universidad Central de Venezuela.

Lavrin, Asunción. 1995. *Women, Feminism, and Social Change in Argentina, Chile, and Uruguay, 1890–1940*. Lincoln: University of Nebraska Press.

León, Magdalena, ed. 1994. *Mujeres y participación política*. Bogotá: Tercer Mundo Editores.

Lerner, Elisa. 1984. *Crónicas Ginecólogicas*. Caracas: Linea Editores.

Leitinger, Ilse Abshagen, ed. 1997. *The Costa Rican Women's Movement: A Reader*. Pittsburgh: Pittsburgh University Press.

Levine, Daniel H. 1973. *Conflict and Political Change in Venezuela*. Princeton: Princeton University Press.

———. 1978. "Venezuela Since 1958: The Consolidation of Democratic Politics." In *The Breakdown of Democratic Regimes: Latin America*, ed. J. J. Linz and A. Stepan, 82–109. Baltimore: Johns Hopkins University Press.

———. 1989. "Venezuela: The Nature, Sources, and Prospects of Democracy." In *Democracy in Developing Countries*, L. Diamond, J. J. Linz, and S. M. Lipset, 247–90. Boulder, Colo.: Lynne Rienner Publishers.

———. 1998. "Beyond the Exhaustion of the Model: Survival and Transformation of Democracy in Venezuela." In *Reinventing Legitimacy: Democracy and Political Change in Venezuela*, ed. D. Canache and M. Kulishek. Westport, Conn.: Greenwood Publishers.

Levine, Daniel H., and Brian F. Crisp. 1995. "Legitimacy, Governability, and Reform in Venezuela." In *Lessons of the Venezuelan Experience*, ed. L. W. Goodman et al., 223–51. Washington, D.C.: Woodrow Wilson Center Press and Baltimore: Johns Hopkins University Press.

Lewis, Jane, and Gertrude Astrom. 1992. "Equality, Difference and State Welfare: Labor Market and Family Policies in Sweden." *Feminist Studies* 18:59–87.

Libro Negro 1952: Venezuela bajo el signo del terror. 1983. Edición Facsimil. Caracas: Ediciones Centauro.

Lijphart, Arend. 1971. "Comparative Politics and the Comparative Method." *American Political Science Review* 65:682–93.

Lind, Amy. 1992. "Power, Gender, and Development: Popular Women's Organizations and the Politics of Needs in Ecuador." In *The Making of Social Movements in Latin America*, ed. A. Escobar and S. E. Alvarez, 134–49. Boulder, Colo.: Westview Press.

Linz, Juan J. 1992. "Types of Political Regimes and Respect for Human Rights: Historical and Cross-national Perspectives." In *Human Rights in Perspective. A Global Assessment*, ed. A. Eide and B. Hagtvet, 177–222. Cambridge, Mass.: Blackwell.

Linz, Juan J., and Alfred Stepan. 1996. *Problems of Democratic Transition and Consolidation: Southern Europe, South America, and Post-Communist Europe*. Baltimore: Johns Hopkins University Press.

López Maya, Margarita, Luis Gómez Calcaño, and Thaís Maingón. 1989. *De Punto Fijo al pacto social: Desarrollo y hegemonía en Venezuela (1958–1985)*. Caracas: Fondo Editorial Acta Científica Venezolana.

Lovenduski, Joni. 1993. "Introduction: The Dynamics of Gender and Party." In

Gender and Party Politics, ed. Lovenduski and Norris, 1–15. London: Sage Publishers.

Lovenduski, Joni and Pippa Norris, eds. 1993. *Gender and Party Politics.* London: Sage Publishers.

Luciak, Ilja A. 1997. "Women and Electoral Politics on the Left: A Comparison of El Salvador and Nicaragua." Paper delivered at the 30th Meeting of the Latin American Studies Association, Guadalajara, Mexico.

Luna, Lola G., and Norma Villarreal. 1994. *Movimientos de mujeres y participación política en Colombia, 1930–1991.* Barcelona: Universitat de Barcelona Seminario Interdisciplinario Mujeres y Sociedad/CICYT.

Macías, Anna. 1982. *Against All Odds: The Feminist Movement in Mexico to 1940.* Westport, Conn.: Greenwood Press.

MacKinnon, Catharine A. 1989. *Toward a Feminist Theory of the State.* Cambridge: Harvard University Press.

Magallanes, Manuel Vicente. 1973. *Los Partidos políticos en la evolución historica venezolana.* Madrid: Editorial Mediterraneo.

Mainwaring, Scott. 1987. "Urban Popular Movements, Identity, and Democratization in Brazil." *Comparative Political Studies* 20 (2): 131–59.

Mainwaring, Scott, Guillermo O'Donnell, and J. Samuel Valenzuela. 1992. *Issues in Democratic Consolidation: The New South American Democracies in Comparative Perspectives.* Notre Dame: University of Notre Dame Press.

Mainwaring, Scott, and Timothy R. Scully, eds. 1995. *Building Democratic Institutions: Party Systems in Latin America.* Stanford: Stanford University Press.

Martz, John D. 1966. *Acción Democrática: Evolution of a Modern Political Party in Venezuela.* Princeton: Princeton University Press.

———. 1995. "Political Parties and the Democratic Crisis." In *Lessons of the Venezuelan Experience,* ed. L. W. Goodman et al., 31–53. Washington, D.C.: Woodrow Wilson Center Press and Baltimore: Johns Hopkins University Press.

Martz, John D., and David J. Myers, eds. 1986. *Venezuela: The Democratic Experience.* New York: Praeger Publishers.

Matland, Richard E., and Michelle M. Taylor. 1997. "Electoral System Effects on Women's Representation: Theoretical Arguments and Evidence from Costa Rica." *Comparative Political Studies* 30 (2): 186–210.

McAdam, Doug. 1982. *Political Process and the Development of Black Insurgency.* Chicago: Chicago University Press.

McAdam, Doug, John D. McCarthy, and Mayer N. Zald. 1988. "Social Movements." In *Handbook of Sociology,* ed. N. Smelser, 695–737. Newbury Park, Calif.: Sage.

McCoy, Jennifer. 1989. "Labor and the State in a Party-Mediated Democracy." *Latin American Research Review* 24 (2): 35–67.

McCoy, Jennifer, Andrés Serbin, William C. Smith, and Andrés Stambouli, eds. 1995. *Venezuelan Democracy Under Stress.* New Brunswick, N.J.: Transaction Publishers.

McCoy, Jennifer, and William C. Smith. 1995. "From Deconsolidation to Reequilibration? Prospects for Democratic Renewal in Venezuela." In

Venezuelan Democracy Under Stress, ed. J. McCoy et al., 237–83. New Brunswick, N.J.: Transaction Publishers.

McDonald, Ronald H., and J. Mark Ruhl. 1989. *Party Politics and Elections in Latin America.* Boulder, Colo.: Westview Press.

McIntosh, Mary. 1978. "The State and the Oppression of Women." In *Feminism and Materialism: Women and the Modes of Production,* ed. A. Kuhn and A. Wolpe, 254–89. London: Routledge and Kegan Paul.

Melucci, Alberto. 1985. "The Symbolic Challenge of Contemporary Movements." *Social Research* 52 (4): 789–816.

———. 1988. "Social Movements and the Democratization of Everyday Life." In *Civil Society and the State,* ed. J. Keane, 245–60. London: Verso Press.

Mijares, Silvia. 1980. *Organizaciones Políticas de 1936: Su Importancia en la Socialización Política del Venezolano.* Caracas, Venezuela: Academia Nacional de la Historia.

Miller, Francesca. 1991. *Latin American Women and the Search for Social Justice.* Hanover, N.H.: University Press of New England.

Ministerio de Educación. Various. *Memoria y Cuenta.* Caracas.

Ministerio de Fomento. 1968. *Memoria y Cuenta.* Caracas.

Ministerio de la Familia. Various. *Memoria y Cuenta.* Caracas.

Ministerio de la Juventud. Various. *Memoria y Cuenta.* Caracas.

Ministerio de la Secretaria de la Presidencia. 1980. *Memoria y Cuenta: Participación de la mujer en el desarrollo.* Caracas.

Ministerio Público. 1990. *La Mujer en la ley venezolana, 1830–1990.* Caracas: Ediciones Biblioteca "Rafael Arvelo Torrealba."

Ministro de Estado para la Participación de la Mujer en el Desarrollo. 1983. *Venezuela: Biografia inacabada evolucion social 1936–1983.* Caracas: Banco Central de Venezuela.

Mink, Gwendolyn. 1990. "The Lady and the Tramp: Gender, Race and the Origins of the American Welfare State." In *Women, the State, and Welfare,* ed. L. Gordon, 92–122. Madison: University of Wisconsin Press.

Mohanty, Chandra Talpade, Ann Russo, and Lourdes Torres, eds. 1991. *Third World Women and the Politics of Feminism.* Bloomington: Indiana University Press.

Molyneux, Maxine. 1985. "Mobilisation Without Emancipation? Women's Interests, State and Revolution in Nicaragua." In *New Social Movements and the State in Latin America,* ed. D. Slater, 233–59. Amsterdam: CEDLA.

———. 1998. "Analysing Women's Movements." *Development and Change* 29 (2): 219–45.

Montenegro N., Ana Yadira, Zorymar Nottaro A., and Mercedes Sanches S. 1994. "Evaluación de los programas de asistencia a la mujer victima de violencia llevados a cabo por las organizaciones gubernamentales y no gubernmentales." B.A. thesis, Universidad Central de Venezuela.

Montero, Maritza. 1987. "La psicología política en América Latina: Una Revisión bibliográfica, 1956–1986." In *Psicología política latinoamericana,* ed. M. Montero, 15–65. Caracas: Panapo.

Morgan, Amanda Lynn. 1996. "The State Institutionalization of Women's Issues: A Case Study of Chile's SERNAM." B.A. thesis, Stanford University.

Morris, Aldon D., and Carol McClurg Mueller, eds. 1992. *Frontiers in Social Movement Theory*. New Haven: Yale University Press.

Moser, Caroline O. N. 1993. *Gender, Planning, and Development: Theory, Practice, and Training*. New York: Routledge Press.

Mujeres Socialistas. 1973. *Plataforma de las Mujeres Socialistas*. Caracas: Mujeres Socialistas.

———. 1974. *Las Mujeres Socialistas ante la asamblea del MAS*. Caracas: Mujeres Socialistas.

Munck, Gerardo. 1991. "Social Movements and Democracy in Latin America: Theoretical Debates and Comparative Perspectives." Paper presented at the 16th Meeting of the Latin American Studies Association, Washington, D.C.

———. 1995. "Political Regime, Transition, and Consolidation: Conceptual Issues in Regime Analysis." Paper presented at the 18th Meeting of the Latin American Studies Association, Washington, D.C.

Munck, Ronaldo. 1989. *Latin America: The Transition to Democracy*. London: Zed Press.

Muñoz Dálbora, Adriana. 1987. *Fuerza feminista y democracia: Utopía a realizar*. Santiago: Ediciones Documentas.

Navarro, Juan Carlos. 1995a. "In Search of the Lost Pact: Consensus Lost in the 1980s and 1990s." In *Venezuela Under Stress*, ed. J. McCoy et al., 13–32. New Brunswick, N.J.: Transaction Publishers.

———. 1995b. "Venezuela's New Political Actors." In *Lessons of the Venezuelan Experience*, ed. L. W. Goodman et al., 118–19. Washington, D.C.: Woodrow Wilson Center Press and Baltimore: Johns Hopkins University Press.

Navarro, Marysa. 1989. "The Personal Is Political: Las Madres de Plaza de Mayo." In *Power and Popular Protest: Latin American Social Movements*, ed. S. Eckstein, 241–58. Berkeley: University of California Press.

Nelson, Barbara J., and Najma Chowdhury, eds. 1994. *Women and Politics Worldwide*. New Haven: Yale University Press.

Norris, Pippa. 1993. "Conclusions: Comparing Legislative Recruitment." In *Gender and Party Politics*, ed. J. Lovenduski and P. Norris, 309–30. London: Sage Publishers.

Norris, Pippa and Joni Lovenduski. 1993. "Gender and Party Politics in Britain." In *Gender and Party Politics*, ed. J. Lovenduski and P. Norris, 35–59. London: Sage Publishers.

O'Donnell, Guillermo, and Philippe Schmitter. 1986. *Transitions from Authoritarian Rule: Tentative Conclusions About Uncertain Democracies*. Baltimore: Johns Hopkins University Press.

OCEI (Oficina Central de Estadística e Informática). 1961. *Censo General*. Caracas.

———. 1971. *Encuesta de Hogares Por Muestra*. Caracas.

———. 1981. *Encuesta de Hogares Por Muestra*. Caracas.

———. 1990. *Censo General*. Caracas.

———. 1993. *Indicadores de Fuerza de Trabajo*. Caracas.

Offen, Karen. 1988. "Defining Feminism: A Comparative Approach." *Signs* 14 (1):119–57.

Okin, Susan. 1979. *Women in Western Political Thought*. Princeton: Princeton University Press.

———. 1989a. *Justice, Gender, and the Family.* New York: Basic Books.

———. 1989b. "Reason and Feeling in Thinking about Justice." *Ethics* 99 (2): 229–49.

Orellana, Inocencia. 1991. *El Liderazgo de las coodinadoras de los Círculos Femeninos Populares.* Caracas: CEPAP.

Orellana, Inocencia, and Delvina Ortiz. n.d. "¿Que son los Círculos Femeninos Populares?" Caracas: Publicaciones El Pueblo.

Oropezo, Ambrosio. 1986. *La Nueva Constitución Venezolana 1961.* Caracas: Biblioteca de la Academia de Ciencias Políticas y Sociales.

Oxhorn, Philip D. 1995. *Organizing Civil Society: The Popular Sectors and the Struggle for Democracy in Chile.* University Park: Pennsylvania State University Press.

Palumbo, Giovana. 1988. "Reforma legislativa y liderazgo político: Código civil venezolano 1982." Caracas: IESA.

Paredes, Rosa, and Gonzalo Tapia. 1989. "Los Círculos Femeninos Populares—Un Modelo de organización de mujeres de base." Caracas. Photocopy.

Pateman, Carol. 1988. *The Sexual Contract.* Stanford: Stanford University Press.

———. 1989. *The Disorder of Women: Democracy, Feminism and Political Theory.* Stanford: Stanford University Press.

———. 1994. "The Rights of Man and Early Feminism." In *Frauen und Politik/Femmes et Politiques,* ed. H. Kriesi, 19–31. Geneva: Publications de l'Association Suisse de Science Politique.

Peeler, John. 1992. *Latin American Democracies: Colombia, Costa Rica, Venezuela.* Chapel Hill: University of North Carolina Press.

Petras, James. 1990. "The Redemocratization Process." In *Democracy in Latin America: Visions and Realities,* ed. S. Jonas and N. Stein, 85–100. New York: Bergin and Garvey.

Petzoldt, Fania, and Jacinta Bevilacqua. 1979. *Nosotras tambien nos jugamos la vida: Testimonios de la mujer venezolana en la lucha clandestina, 1948–1958.* Caracas: Editorial Ateneo de Caracas.

Phillips, Anne. 1991. *Engendering Democracy.* University Park: Pennsylvania State University Press.

———. 1994. "Must Feminists Give Up on Liberal Democracy?" *Political Studies* 40 (5): 93–111.

Powell, John Duncan. 1971. *Political Mobilization of the Venezuelan Peasant.* Cambridge: Harvard University Press.

Pridham, Geoffrey. 1991. "Southern European Democracies on the Road to Consolidation: A Comparative Assessment of the Role of Political Parties." In *Encouraging Democracy: The International Context of Regime Transition in Southern Europe,* ed. G. Pridham. New York: St. Martin's Press.

Primer Congreso Venezolano de Mujeres. 1975. *Acta Final.* Caracas: COFEAPRE.

Primer seminario de evaluación de la condición de la mujer en Venezuela. 1968. Caracas: Primer Seminario.

Prince de Kew, Carmen. 1990. *Reforma parcial del Código Civil: Análisis de una política pública.* Caracas: Congreso de la República.

Pringle, Rosemary, and Sophie Watson. 1992. "'Women's Interests and the Post-Structuralist State." In *Destabilizing Theory: Contemporary Feminist*

Debates, ed. M. Barrett and A. Phillips, 53–73. Stanford: Stanford University Press.

Pulido de Briceño, Mercedes. 1982. "Igualdad de opciones y condiciones para la igualdad de posibilidades: Política y líneas de acción." In *Informe Final: Primera Jornada Nacional sobre el Trabajo y la Productividad de la Mano de Obra Femenina,* 90–145. Caracas: Despacho de la Ministro de Estado para la Participación de la Mujer en el Desarrollo.

Radcliffe, Sarah A., and Sallie Westwood, eds. 1993. *Viva: Women and Popular Protest in Latin America.* New York: Routledge Press.

Rakowski, Cathy A. 1995. "Planned Development and Women's Relative Power: Steel and Forestry in Venezuela." *Latin American Perspectives* 22 (2): 51–75.

Randall, Margaret. 1994. *Sandino's Daughters Revisited: Feminism in Nicaragua.* New Brunswick: Rutgers University Press.

Randall, Vicky. 1998. "Gender and Power: Women Engage the State." In *Gender, Politics, and the State,* ed. V. Randall and G. Waylen, 198–205. New York: Routledge Press.

Rawls, John. 1971. *A Theory of Justice.* Cambridge, Mass.: Belknap Press.

Razavi, Sharhashoub, and Carol Miller. 1995. *From WID to GAD: Conceptual Shifts in the Women and Development Discourse.* Fourth World Conference on Women Occasional Paper. Geneva: UNRISD/UNDP.

Reif, Linda L. 1986. "Women in Latin American Guerrilla Movements: A Comparative Perspective." *Comparative Politics* 18 (2): 147–69.

Rey, Juan Carlos. 1989. *El futuro de la democracia en Venezuela.* Caracas: Colección IDEA.

Rhode, Deborah. L. 1994. "Feminism and the State." *Harvard Law Review* 107 (6): 1181–208.

Rocha Sanchez, Lola. 1991. *Estado y sociedad civil conjugando esfuerzos en apoyo a la mujer.* Bogotá: UNICEF.

Rochon, Thomas R. 1990. "Political Movements and State Authority in Liberal Democracies." *World Politics* 42 (2): 299–313.

Rodríguez, Beatriz. 1992. "Casa, Otro Espacio Ganado." *Ultimas Noticias,* 8 March 1992, 9–10.

Rugeles, Aura. 1981. "El MAS y la participación de la mujer." Paper Prepared for the Jornadas Preparatorias del Encuentro Nacional de Mujeres Socialistas, Caracas.

———. 1982. "Papel de trabajo" Paper Prepared for the IV Jornada Nacional de Mujeres Socialistas, Caracas.

Ruiz Piñeda Papers. Hemeroteca Nacional, Caracas.

Rule, Wilma. 1994a. "Women's Underrepresentation and Electoral Systems." *PS: Political Science and Politics.* 27 (4): 689–92.

———. 1994b. "Parliaments of, by, and for the People: Except for Women?" In *Electoral Systems in Comparative Perspective,* ed. W. Rule and J. F. Zimmerman, 15–30. Westport, Conn.: Greenwood Press.

Rule, Wilma, and Joseph F. Zimmerman, eds. 1994. *Electoral Systems in Comparative Perspective: Their Impact on Women and Minorities.* Westport, Conn.: Greenwood Press.

Sainsbury, Diane. 1993. "The Politics of Increased Women's Representation: The

Swedish Case." In *Gender and Party Politics*, ed. J. Lovenduski and P. Norris, 263–90. London: Sage Publishers.

Saint-Germain, Michelle A. 1996. "*Mujeres '94:* Democratic Transition and the Women's Movement in El Salvador." Paper Presented at the 1996 Western Political Science Association Meeting, San Francisco, California.

Salamanca, Luis. 1995. "The Venezuelan Political System: A View from Civil Society." In *Venezuelan Democracy Under Stress*, ed. J. McCoy et al., 197–241. New Brunswick, N.J.: Transaction Publishers.

Santana, Elias. 1983. *El Poder de los vecinos*. Caracas: Ediciones Ecotopia.

Saporta Sternbach, Nancy, Marysa Navarro-Aranguren, Patricia Chuchryk, and Sonia E. Alvarez. 1992. "Feminisms in Latin America: From Bogotá to San Bernardo." In *The Making of Social Movements in Latin America*, ed. A. Escobar and S. E. Alvarez, 207–39. Boulder, Colo.: Westview Press.

Sarvasy, Wendy, and Birte Siim. 1994. "Gender, Transitions to Democracy, and Citizenship." *Social Politics:* 1 (3): 249–55.

Schild, Verónica. 1998. "New Subjects of Rights? Women's Movements and the Construction of Citizenship in the 'New Democracies.'" In *Cultures of Politics/Politics of Cultures*, ed. A. Alvarez, E. Dagnino, and S. E. Escobar, 93–117. Boulder, Colo.: Westview Press.

Schmitter, Philippe C. 1992. "Interest Systems and the Consolidation of Democracies." In *Reexamining Democracy*, ed. G. Marks and L. Diamond, 156–81. London: Sage Publishers.

———. 1993. "Corporatism." In *The Oxford Companion to Politics of the World*, ed. J. Krieger, 195–98. New York: Oxford University Press.

———. 1998. "Contemporary Democratization: The Prospects for Women." In *Women and Democracy*, ed. J. Jaquette and S. Wolchik, 222–37. Baltimore: Johns Hopkins University Press.

Schneider, Cathy. 1992. "Radical Opposition Parties and Squatters Movements in Pinochet's Chile." In *The Making of Social Movements in Latin America*, ed. A. Escobar and S. E. Alvarez, 260–75. Boulder, Colo.: Westview Press.

———. 1995. *Shantytown Protest in Pinochet's Chile*. Philadelphia: Temple University Press.

Scott, Joan W. 1988. *Gender and the Politics of History*. New York: Columbia University Press.

Sgambatti, Sonia. 1992. "Legislación Penal." In *II Congreso Venezolano de la Mujer* (Tomo I), ed. COFEAPRE, 81–85. Caracas: COFEAPRE.

Shanley, Mary Lyndon. 1991. "Marital Slavery and Friendship: John Stuart Mill's *The Subjection of Women*." In *Feminist Interpretations and Political Theory*, ed. M. L. Shanley and C. Pateman, 169–80. University Park: Pennsylvania State University Press.

Silva Donoso, María de la Luz. 1987. *La participación política de la mujer en Chile: las organizaciones de mujeres*. Buenos Aires: Fundación Friedrich Naumann.

Silverberg, Helene. 1990. "What Happened to the Feminist Revolution in Political Science?" *Western Political Quarterly* 43 (4): 887–903.

Simms, Marian. 1993. "Two Steps Forward, One Step Back: Women and the

Australian Party System." In *Gender and Party Politics,* ed. J. Lovenduski and P. Norris, 16–34. London: Sage Publishers.

Siriani, Carmen. 1993. "Learning Pluralism: Democracy and Diversity in Feminist Organizations." In *Democratic Community: NOMOS XXXV,* ed. J. W. Chapman and I. Shapiro, 283–312. New York: New York University Press.

Skocpol, Theda. 1992. *Protecting Soldiers and Mothers: The Political Origins of Social Policy in the United States.* Cambridge, Mass.: Belknap Press.

Slater, David, ed. 1985. *New Social Movements and the State in Latin America.* Amsterdam: CEDLA.

Smith, Lois M., and Alfred Padula. 1996. *Sex and Revolution: Women in Socialist Cuba.* New York: Oxford University Press.

Soares, Vera, Ana Alice Alcantara Costa, Cristina Maria Buarque, Denise Dourado Dora, and Wania Sant'Anna. 1995. "Brazilian Feminism and Women's Movements: A Two-Way Street." In *The Challenge of Local Feminisms,* ed. A. Basu, 302–23. Boulder, Colo.: Westview Press.

Stambouli, Andrés. 1980. *Crisis política: Venezuela 1945–58.* Caracas: Editorial Ateneo de Caracas.

Starn, Orin. 1992. "'I Dreamed of Foxes and Hawks': Reflections on Peasant Protest, New Social Movements, and the *Rondas Campesinas* of Northern Peru." In *The Making of Social Movements in Latin America,* ed. A. Escobar and S. E. Alvarez, 89–111. Boulder, Colo.: Westview Press.

Stetson, Dorothy McBride, and Amy G. Mazur, eds. 1995. *Comparative State Feminism.* Thousand Oaks, Calif.: Sage.

Stephen, Lynn. 1997. *Women and Social Movements in Latin America: Power From Below.* Austin: University of Texas Press.

Stevens, Evelyn. 1973. "*Marianismo:* The Other Face of *Machismo* in Latin America." In *Female and Male in Latin America,* ed. A. Pescatello, 89–102. Pittsburgh: University of Pittsburgh Press.

Stoner, K. Lynn. 1991. *From the House to the Streets: The Cuban Woman's Movement for Legal Reform, 1898–1940.* Durham: Duke University Press.

Suarez Figueroa, Naudy. 1983. *Programas Políticos Venezolanos de la Primer Mitad del Siglo XX.* Vol. 1 and 2. Caracas: Colegio Universitario Francisco de Miranda.

Tarnoi, Ladislao T. 1954. *El Nuevo Ideal Nacional de Venezuela: Vida y Obra de Marcos Pérez Jiménez.* Madrid: Ediciones Verdad.

Tarrow, Sidney. 1991a. "'Aiming at a Moving Target': Social Science and the Recent Rebellions in Eastern Europe." *Political Science and Politics* 26 (1): 12–20.

———. 1991b. *Struggle, Politics, and Reform: Collective Action, Social Movements, and Cycles of Protest.* Western Societies Program Occasional Paper No. 21 (2nd ed.), Center for International Studies, Cornell University.

———. 1994. *Power in Movement.* Cambridge: Cambridge University Press

Templeton, Andrew. 1995. "The Evolution of Popular Opinion." In *Lessons of the Venezuelan Experience,* ed. L. W. Goodman et al., 79–114. Washington, D.C.: Woodrow Wilson Center Press and Baltimore: Johns Hopkins University Press.

Todaro, Michael P. 1994. *Economic Development,* 5th ed. New York: Longman.

Tur, Flor Isabel. 1990. "Poca luz en el túnel: Mujeres jefas de hogar." *Revista SIC* 53 (528): 365–67.

Umaña Bernal, José. 1958. *Testimonio de la revolución en Venezuela.* Caracas: Tipografico Vargas, SA.

UN (United Nations). 1992. *Integración de lo femenino en la cultura latinoamericana: En busca de un nuevo modelo de sociedad.* Serie Mujer y Desarrollo. Chile: UN.

———. 1995. *The World's Women 1995: Trends and Statistics.* Social Statistics and Indicators Series K, no. 12. New York: United Nations.

UNDP (United Nations Development Programme). 1995. *Human Development Report 1995.* New York: Oxford University Press.

———. 1996. *Human Development Report 1996.* New York: Oxford University Press.

Valdevieso, Magdalena. 1982. "El MAS y la mujer, proposiciones organizativas." Paper prepared for the IV Jornada Nacional de Mujeres Socialistas, Caracas.

Valdevieso, Magdalena, and Ivo Castejon. 1981. "Algunas reflexiones sobre la participación de la mujer en el MAS." Paper prepared for the Jornadas Preparatorias del Encuentro Nacional de Mujeres Socialistas, Caracas.

Valdéz, Teresa, and Enrique Gomáriz. 1995. *Latin American Women: Compared Figures.* Santiago: FLACSO.

Valenzuela, María Elena. 1987. *La Mujer en el Chile militar: Todas ibamos a ser reinas.* Santiago: CESOC/ACHIP.

Waylen, Georgina. 1994. "Women and Democratization: Conceptualizing Gender Relations in Transition Politics." *World Politics* 46 (3): 327–54.

———. 1996a. "Democratization, Feminism, and the State in Chile: The Establishment of SERNAM." In *Women and the State: International Perspectives,* ed. S. M. Rai and G. Lievesley, 103–17. London: Taylor and Francis, Ltd.

———. 1996b. *Gender in Third World Politics.* Boulder, Colo.: Lynne Rienner Publishers.

———. 1998. "Gender, Feminism, and the State: An Overview." In *Gender, Politics, and the State,* ed. V. Randall and G. Waylen, 1–17. New York: Routledge Press.

Wickham-Crowley, Timothy P. 1992. *Guerrillas and Revolution in Latin America: A Comparative Study of Insurgents and Regimes Since 1956.* Princeton: Princeton University Press.

Wieringa, Saskia. 1994. "Women's Interests and Empowerment: Gender Planning Reconsidered." *Development and Change* 25:829–48.

Yashar, Deborah J. 1995. "Civil War and Social Welfare: The Origins of Costa Rica's Competitive Party System." In *Building Democratic Institutions,* ed. S. Mainwaring and T. Scully, 72–99. Stanford: Stanford University Press.

Young, Iris Marion. 1990. *Justice and the Politics of Difference.* Princeton: Princeton University Press.

Zago, Angela. 1990. *Aquí no ha pasado nada.* Caracas: Editorial Planeta Venezolana.

Newspapers, Newsletters, Bulletins, Serials

A Pesar de Todo
Al Margen
Ahora
Correo Cívico Femenino
De Las Mujeres
Diario de Debates (Caracas: Congreso Nacional de la República)
El Nacional
El Nuevo Venezolano
El Universal
Fempress
La Esfera
La Mala Vida
La Religion
Mujeres en Lucha
New York Times
Revista SIC
Ultimas Noticias
Veneconomy

Interviews

(All interviews conducted by the author in Caracas, unless otherwise specified.)

Alvarez, María del Mar. 7/12/94.
Alvarez, Ofelia. 11/30/94.
Andrés Pérez, Carlos. 3/16/95.
Aranguren, Fernando. 4/23/94.
Armengol, Laly. 4/29/94. Maracay.
Bello de Guzmán, María. 8/17/92; 5/13/94.
Betancourt, Luisa. 5/12/94.
Betancourt, Virginia. 3/5/95.
Borges de Tapia, Elia. 8/15/94.
Boulton de Bottome, Margot. 4/27/94.
Caldera, Rosita. 8/31/92.
Carmona, Isabel. 5/27/94.
Castañeda, Nora. 8/30/94.
Castillo, Adecia. 8/2/94.
Colmenares, Alcira. 5/17/94.
Comesaña, Gloria. 7/15/94. Maracaibo.
Cova, Antonio. 9/11/92.
Dáger, Douglas. 9/2/92.
de Astorga, Amarilis G. 9/1/92.
de Guevara, Lisbeth. 8/13/92.
Delgado, Juana. 2/20/95.
Donda, Franka. 1995.
Deutch, Haydee. 1995.

Espina, Gioconda. 8/23/92.
Fermín, Mercedes. 8/2/94.
Fernandez, Marisabel. 5/13/94.
Ferrara, Vicki. 4/1/95.
Finol, Benita. 7/26/94.
Gamus Gallegos, Paulina. 5/23/94.
García, María Pilar. 3/28/95.
García Maldonado, Ana Lucina. 8/16/92.
García Ponce, Guillermo. 12/19/94.
García Prince, Evangelina. 6/13/94.
Herrera Campins, Luis. 9/11/92.
Hilabert, Eulalia. 4/29/94. Maracay.
Huggins Castañeda, Magally. 6/10/94.
Laya, Argelia. 8/29/92; 6/16/94; 2/8/95.
Lopez Maya, Margarita. 5/31/94.
Melo, Luisa. 4/29/94. Maracay.
Olivo de Celli, Virginia. 9/10/92; 6/6/94.
Orellana, Inocencia. 8/24/92; 1995.
Palumbo, Giovana. 9/1/92.
Paredes, Rosa. 2/13/95.
Parentelli, Gladys. 1994.
Pérez Marcano, Marelys. 3/10/94.
Piñuela, Mari. 3/29/95.
Poleo de Baez, Yolanda. 8/25/92.
Prince de Kew, Carmen. 8/4/92.
Pulido de Briceño, Mercedes. 8/12/92.
Rojas, Ixora Paz. 9/9/94.
Romero, Cira. 6/6/94.
Salvatierra, Isolda. 5/30/94.
Salamanca, Luis. 5/18/94.
Sanabria, Morella. 4/6/95.
Sandoval Maracano, Mercedes. 5/17/94.
Sanoja, Clarisa. 5/29/94.
Senior, Ana. 7/25/94; 8/9/94.
Trujillo, Evelyn. 6/3/94.
Valdevieso, Magdalena. 12/20/94.
Valor, Amarilis. 8/1/94.
Vegas, Diana. 8/20/92.
Vethencourt, Jose Luis. 8/25/92.
Vera, Esperanza. 7/13/94.
Villasmil, Humberto. 4/24/94.

INDEX

Velasquez, Luisa, 110
Venezuelan Association for an Alternative
  Sex Education (Asociación
  Venezolana para una Educación
  Sexual Alternativa, or AVESA), 168,
  199, 210–21
Venezuelan Association of Women
  (Asociación Venezolana de Mujeres,
  or AVM), 70–72, 75–76, 80–83, 135
Venezuelan democratization
  in comparison with region, 2–4
  as model, 8–9
Venezuelan Federation of Chambers of
  Commerce and Production
  (FEDECAMARAS), 220, 224,
  226–27
Venezuelan Federation of Teachers
  (Federación Venezolana de Maestros,
  or FVM), 72, 107 n. 10
Venezuelan Federation of Women Lawyers
  (Federación Venezolana de
  Abogaddas, or FEVA), 134 n. 54,
  141, 174–81, 186, 188, 199, 202, 210,
  221, 223–24, 249
Venezuelan Organization (Organización
  Venezolano, or ORVE), 58–60,
  65–66, 72, 74, 130
Venezuelan Women's Union (Unión
  Femenina Venezolana), 98
Vera, Esperanza, 112, 116, 128, 152, 230, 292
Villalba, Jovito, 127–28
Villaparedes, Yolanda, 118, 127 n. 40

Waylen, Georgina, 35 n. 29
We Want to Choose (Queremos Elegir), 268
Wednesday Feminist Group (Grupo
  Feminista Miércoles), 164–65, 211, 223
Women and Communication, 202, 211
women as interest group, 289–92
Women's Action (Acción Femenina), 87
Women's Association for Civic Education
  (Asociación Femenina de Educación
  Cívica), 88–89
women's bureau, 38–39, 60, 72, 95–97,
  130–31, 140, 147, 151–53, 160–62,
  170, 204, 274–75
Women's Committee of the Patriotic
  Council (see Patriotic Council)

Women's Cultural Association (Agrupación
  Cultural Femenina, or ACF), 61 n. 3,
  65–88, 98, 117, 189, 207
Women's Culture (Cultura de la Mujer), 67,
  75, 78, 82–83, 85
Women's League (Liga de Mujeres), 164
Women's Legion (Legión de Mujeres), 135
Women '94 (Mujeres '94, El Salvador), 284
women's organizations, 50–51
women's organizing
  against Pérez Jiménez: as individuals,
    108–14; in groups, 114–20
  Catholic Church's impact on, 7
  challenges to, 286–89
  in civil society, 163–74
  class divisions in, 63, 163
  coalition strategy of, 190–92, 229–31,
    283–85
  compared to neighborhood movement,
    269–70
  Coordinating Committee of Women's
    NGOs, 201–8
  decline with democratization, 97–98,
    125–28
  feminist, 47–49, 163–69
  history in Latin America, 45–50
  in Latin American democratization, 5–8
  and motherhood, 46–47, 49, 148
  and partisan divisions, 22, 97–98, 135,
    125–8, 152–53
  party influence on, 168–72, 204, 243–48
  in political parties, 146–47, 153–62, 253
  strategies debated, 150–52
  versus authoritarianism, 48–49
women's socioeconomic status
  before 1936, 56–58
  1950–1970, 103–4
  1974–1984, 141–44
  1990s, 235

Yashar, Deborah J., 38 n. 33
Young Women's Association (Asociación
  Juvenil Femenina), 115, 118
Young Women's Union (Unión de
  Muchachas), 114–17

Zago, Angela, 129
Zetkin, Clara, 127 n. 42